THE SUB-PREFECT SHOULD HAVE HELD HIS TONGUE

AND OTHER ESSAYS

HUBERT BUTLER

Edited and with an Introduction by
R. F. FOSTER

ALLEN LANE
THE PENGUIN PRESS
In association with
The Lilliput Press

ALLEN LANE
THE PENGUIN PRESS
Published by the Penguin Group
Penguin Books, 27 Wrights Lane, London W8 5TZ, England
Viking Penguin, a division of Penguin Books USA Inc.,
375 Hudson Street, New York, New York 10014, USA
Penguin Books Australia Ltd, Ringwood, Victoria, Australia
Penguin Books Canada Ltd, 2801 John Street, Markham, Ontario, Canada L3R 1B4
Penguin Books (NZ) Ltd, 182–190 Wairau Road, Auckland 10, New Zealand

Penguin Books Ltd, Registered Offices: Harmondsworth, Middlesex, England

Escape from the Anthill first published by The Lilliput Press 1985;
The Children of Drancy first published by The Lilliput Press 1988;
Grandmother and Wolfe Tone first published by The Lilliput Press 1990

This selection first published in Great Britain by Allen Lane The Penguin Press 1990
1 3 5 7 9 10 8 6 4 2

Printed in England by Butler & Tanner Ltd.,
Frome and London

A CIP catalogue record for this book is available from the British Library

ISBN 0–713–99042–2

CONTENTS

=====

CONTENTS

EDITORIAL ACKNOWLEDGMENT

All these essays were originally included in three volumes of Hubert Butler's collected writings published by The Lilliput Press. Numbers 3, 4, 6, 10, 11, 12, 13, 15, 19, 22, 26, 28, 29, 30, and part of number 5, appeared in *Escape from the Anthill* (1985); numbers 2, 7, 14, 16, 18, 20, 21, 23, 24, 25, 27, 32 and 33 in *The Children of Drancy* (1988); and numbers 1, 8, 9, 17, 31, and part of number 5, in *Grandmother and Wolfe Tone* (1990). The original provenance of many of the essays is detailed in these collections. Notes that appeared in this standard three-volume edition of Butler's essays, published by The Lilliput Press, are indicated by an asterisk and appear at the foot of the page; my editorial notes are indicated by a superior figure and appear at the end of the essay.

For help in compiling and editing this selection I am indebted to Antony Farrell, Paul Keegan, Richard Evans, Michael Wheeler and Hubert and Peggy Butler.

R. F. Foster
London, February 1990

INTRODUCTION

═══

'When I was a boy of fourteen I decided I was going to live in the place where I was born and where my father, grandfather and great-grandfather had lived before me.' In Hubert Butler's deceptively modest ambition, decided the year the First World War broke out, that place stood in general for Ireland. But in specific terms it meant his family's house, Maidenhall: a pervading presence, though only obliquely described, in many of the essays that follow. It is a small Georgian house strategically placed in the cleft of a hill above the River Nore, on a back-road leading out of the village of Bennettsbridge, County Kilkenny. (Its eighteenth-century owners were the Griffiths, failed flaxmillers and successful authors, who figure in 'Henry and Frances', below.) It can be glimpsed only sideways from the road; the avenue describes a charac-teristic hairpin shape up the hill, allowing the opportunity to go through a second gateway and to slow down as you approach the house.

From outside, there is a strict but friendly proportion; a sort of loggia runs along the front, where chairs can be drawn out after long lunches, or to catch the fugitive sun. The view takes in water-meadows, the river, and in the distance a ruined Norman castle and a much more ancient Celtic church. Inside it is cool, creaky-floored, haphazardly but pleasantly arranged, with vivid small pictures (and the icon, mentioned in 'Peter's Window', angrily relegated to the laundry-basket by Butler's Leningrad landlady in 1931). The atmosphere of the house is distinctive: Irish, slightly eccentric, cultured and somehow Russian – not only because of that icon, or the fact that some of the books and papers lying around are in Cyrillic characters. One thinks of Chekhov, so often instanced by Butler himself; and also, recalling Butler's return to the house from Oxford in the early 1920s, inflamed with ideas, one remembers Tur-genev's *Fathers and Sons*.

In the first number of *The Bell* in 1940, a journal with which Butler was closely connected, his friend and family connection Elizabeth Bowen published an essay on the Big House in Ireland. Many of them, as she pointed out, were not 'Big' at all, but all the same their isolation made them like ships out at sea; and she exhorted their owners to rediscover the original function of these houses, that of sociable intercourse. '"Can we not", big, half-empty rooms seem to ask, "be, as never before, sociable? Cannot we scrap the past, with its bitterness and barriers, and all meet, throwing in what we have?"' The year after she wrote this, Hubert Butler's father died and he returned with his artist wife Peggy to live in Maidenhall, which has been his base ever since. His foster-son, Joseph Hone, has written about childhood at Maidenhall in the 1940s: local self-sufficiency, travel by pony and trap, light by Aladdin oil-lamps, entertainment that was 'almost entirely self-starting, familial and non-mechanical'; and a belief that an integrated life must stress not only the continuity of family, but also the importance of local inter-connections and vitalities, threatened by centrifugal cosmopolitanism in Ireland as everywhere else.

The work that has come out of the house recalls Elizabeth Bowen's dictum; it has been dedicated to breaking down barriers and affirming the need for sociability in the widest sense, but never to 'scrapping the past'. The essays in the following pages – the earliest written in 1930, the most recent in 1988 – bear witness to Butler's affirmation that he belonged in Kilkenny, and that a resolute identification with local ident-ities need not rule out national commitments and European contro-versies. His research, whether into Irish saintly origins or Yugoslav war atrocities, has stirred whirlpools whose backwash has rocked national correspondence columns as well as local affairs in Kilkenny; for all his agreement with Lord Charlemont's dictum that 'our social duties as they expand grow fainter, and lose in efficacy what they gain in extent', the world is never far from his door. Maidenhall has not only welcomed a steady stream of literary visitors, but has been home to those displaced and orphaned by the European holocaust fifty years ago. Butler has written of houses like Edgeworthstown, Moore Hall, Coole Park and Bowen's Court which, unlike most of their kind, sheltered an attempt to blend two traditions, and represented a devotion to creating a common culture in Ireland. Maidenhall can join that company. And unlike the others, it is still standing unchanged.

Hubert Butler was born in 1900, with the century. His background and tradition is indicated often enough in these essays: small gentry, long rooted in Kilkenny, with once-grand connections and firm local attachments, if not much land. But Gaelic Leaguers as well as Christian Scientists cropped up among his redoubtable relations, and there were heterodox opinions about nationalism from his cousin Theobald Butler and his friend Eric Dodds. (Dodds's *Missing Persons* is as necessary a text as Elizabeth Bowen's *Bowen's Court* in exploring this tradition.) 'You got all that off Theo and Dodds,' Mrs Butler scoffed: but what her son made of it is all his own work. His sense of family and tradition is powerfully expressed in the necessarily controversial essay that closes this selection, 'Little K'. 'The true nature of family love ... develops out of ties of blood, out of shared memories and associations, responsibilities ... the sense of continuity plays a huge part in the love we bear for our children and their children.' Elsewhere he writes of less intimate but still fundamental associations: 'it is as neighbours, full of ineradicable prejudices, that we must love each other, not as fortuitously "separated brethren".' Both beliefs carry a particularly Irish resonance.

That Irish identification survived the English schooling hilariously described in 'A Fragment of Autobiography'. After Oxford, Butler worked for the County Libraries movement in Ireland from 1922 to 1923, under the guidance of George Russell (AE) and Horace Plunkett, veterans of the effort to blend Irish traditions in an inclusive nationalism. Lennox Robinson, Frank O'Connor, Helen Roe, Thomas McGreevey and Geoffry Taylor were among his companions. But a characteristic imbroglio over a supposedly blasphemous short story by Lennox Robinson ran the movement into the ground, as far as Ireland was concerned, and possibly helped develop Butler's readiness to combat *ex cathedra* interference in intellectual and artistic matters, from whatever source. It may also have helped encourage the probing approach towards Irish beliefs, and social mores in rural Ireland, devastatingly delineated in 'The Eggman and the Fairies'.

But his horizons were also widened by the peripatetic life he embarked upon in the mid-twenties: teaching in Egypt in 1927, turning up in Latvia in 1930, moving on to teach again in Leningrad for the winter of 1931, arriving in Zagreb in 1934 for a three-year stint on a scholarship from the School of Slavonic Studies in London. (This formed the base for visits like that to Podgorac which he describes in 'Nazor, Oroschatz and the von Berks', printed in this volume.) Though he was back in Ireland by 1938, during 1938–9 he worked with a Quaker organization in Vienna, helping arrange exits for Viennese Jews. This, he tells us in 'The Kagran Gruppe', was one of the happiest times of his life. For once, a positive if tiny effort could be cast in the scale against 'the immense unhappiness that all humanity has to suffer'. Two years later, he returned to Maidenhall to live. There were sorties to Russia, China, America and the Balkans, and the reader of this book profits by them. But he remained in Kilkenny, broadcasting, writing and setting up organizations like the revived Kilkenny Archaeological Society and the annual Kilkenny

Debates between teams from Northern Ireland and the Republic.

The resonance of his writing, and the immense success of his trilogy of essay collections, *Escape from the Anthill* (1985), *The Children of Drancy* (1988) and *Grandmother and Wolfe Tone* (1990), reflect the idiosyncratic but assured angle from which he has viewed the universe on his hillside above the Nore. The idea of 'tilt' recurs in his work. On the first page of *Escape from the Anthill*, he recalls how 'not only was all my education slanted away from Ireland, but the whole island was tilted eastwards. It was very hard to stand upright unsupported on this precipitous slope, for as many people were pushing me from the west as were pulling me to the east.' Of the island as a whole he wrote in 1957:

Living in social harmony is a most difficult art, the most absolute concentration is required, and perfect equilibrium. Our island is dangerously tilted towards England and towards Rome, good places in themselves, but best seen on the level. Everybody is rolling off it and those that remain, struggling hard for a foothold, drag each other down.

Thirty-odd years later, it is easier to be slightly more optimistic. But Butler is committed to celebrating the work of those (often, as it happens, nineteenth-century scholars from Big Houses) who 'managed to prove they were Irish by being indispensable to Ireland'. His work for the Jews of Vienna was in part galvanized by the kind of chauvinism represented by anti-Semitic ravings from a Dail TD. 'I was as Irish as Oliver Flanagan and I was determined that Jewish refugees should come to Ireland.'

Butler has been described, in Maurice Craig's perceptive introduction to *Escape from the Anthill*, as a 'Protestant republican'. This seems not quite right. 'Ascendancy nationalist' or even 'Anglo-Irish nationalist' might be nearer the mark, if Anglo-Irish is understood as a tradition rather than as a tribal identification. Butler himself has chosen the term 'Anglo-Irish nationalist' to describe Otway Cuffe; in a 1950 broadcast he remarked that the idea of a reconciliatory future when such people can drop the hyphen would probably have to await reconciliation in the north of Ireland as well. Even more presciently, he speculated whether such reconciliations of historical antipathy might develop by stressing regional rather than national loyalties – an idea now being floated once more. He provided for the Kilkenny Archaeological Society a motto from Camden which carries a particular and personal resonance. 'If any there be which are desirous to be strangers in their own soile and forrainers in their own citie they may so continue and therein flatter themselves. For such like I have not written these lines nor taken these panes.'

Butler's own roots are Norman and Old English, going back far enough
to need no apologies or hyphens; literally interpreted, the 'Anglo-Irish'
tag rightly irritates him. Again like Elizabeth Bowen, he articulates a
distinct but carefully angled claim on Irishness; and like her, his punc-
turing of English middle-brow pretensions is deadly, especially in the
realm of genteel cultural imperialism. Arthur Bryant has long been a
favourite target: 'He mixes sentimental smugness and common sense in
a frothy drink that is nourishing enough and only healthily intoxicating.
If we could drink it down without retching it would do us no harm,
but can we?' And the gifts bestowed by the British Council and UNO
to Yugoslavian universities in the mid-1940s, in the form of works by
Charlotte Yonge and Sir Henry Newbolt, are mordantly noted: 'The
patient is in a nervous state: give bromides!'

For nervous complaints, Hubert Butler does not resort to bromides.
Boils are lanced, and fevers are ruthlessly inflamed to their crisis. Often
this has the curative effect of the homoeopathic principle, but soft answers
and easy panaceas are invariably rejected. In the selection that follows,
this is demonstrated when he trails the Croatian mass-murderer Artukovitch through Franciscan networks in postwar Ireland, or inexorably
explores the unbearable fate of 'The Children of Drancy': the documented and witnessed deportation of more than 4,000 Jewish children
from Paris to Auschwitz in 1942. The facts are there, but the details have
become blurred. 'I believe we are bored because the scale is so large that
the children seem to belong to sociology and statistics. We cannot
visualize them reading Babar books, having their teeth straightened,
arranging dolls' tea parties. Their sufferings are too great and protracted
to be imagined, and the range of human sympathy is narrowly restricted.'

The work in this book moves like a searchlight from that narrowly
restricted range, to take in and illuminate the largest questions imagin-
able. The subjects chosen may be travel, literature, philosophy, autobiography or (characteristically) move easily through all four inside a
dozen pages. They are handled with wit, passion, humour and an almost
offhand virtuosity of style: also a power of narrative and a facility for
economic but unforgettable delineation of character. The saga of the
Cuffe family of Desart and the 'gentry wars' provoked by Standish
O'Grady's newspaper campaigns in turn-of-the-century Kilkenny
('Anglo-Irish Twilight') would be at home in the world of George
Birmingham's novels. But the same creative power is evident in historical
reconstructions like 'The Eggman and the Fairies', or the recollections
of people once known and treasured, now disappeared, in 'Peter's
Window'. The Chekhovian theme recurs; Butler, in fact, translated and

adapted *The Cherry Orchard* for his brother-in-law Tyrone Guthrie's Old
Vic production in 1933–4. (It provided Charles Laughton with his debut
performance as Lopahin.) The inspiration of this translation (published
in 1934) is its lightness of tone, a notably original emphasis for the time.
The same note is sounded in the Russian portraits here, like the Mexican
lady communist enduring a Russian winter by filling her room with
scents of jasmine and lily, producing 'an appalling primeval smell that
was neither Slav nor Latin: Lihachev said it was Aztec'. Or the tale of
the *ci-devant* rich doctor who after the Revolution made his house a
commune for all his friends and relations, but found it lacked the sport
of the old days, when they had to travel long distances to quarrel with
each other. The Irish echo of this Russian lament is unmistakable, and
recalls the incident when two local Republicans arrived at Maidenhall
during the Civil War and demanded money for the cause. Though it
will be found later in this book, it is too suggestive and characteristic
not to be quoted here:

My mother and I were in the porch and she danced about with fury. 'I know
who you are,' she said to one of them. 'You're Jim Connell. Take your cigarette
out of your mouth when you're talking to me.' He took it out and I began to scold
my mother for interrupting what might have been a revealing conversation. It
was only the second time I had seen a Republican, and when I went back to
Oxford I wanted at least to say what they were like and what their plans were.
My mother answered me sharply and we started an angry argument. The two
men looked at each other in embarrassment and slunk politely away.

With another, cosier, writer this would be followed by a discussion of
the easy, necessary collusion between the Big House and tenantry, in the
Somerville and Ross style; but Butler's tone is bleaker and more realistic,
as the rest of this essay, 'Divided Loyalties', will show.

Butler's literary criticism also deserves close attention, and reflects his
experience as review editor of *The Bell* in that journal's great days,
recalled in *Escape from the Anthill*. The exactly timed detonation of self-
importance and self-delusion in 'Graham Greene and Stephen Spender'
still carries a charge; so, from a later date, does his careful evaluation of
Pasternak, as well as many other commentaries which were excluded
from this selection for reasons of space. But it seemed important to
include some episodes of controversy, because their echoes resound
through Butler's career and through his writing.

It may be difficult at this remove to recapture the kind of sensibilities
inflamed by open discussion of issues like clerical authority and censorship, implicit as well as explicit, in Ireland during the 1950s – though
essays like 'Boycott Village' help to recall them. Like his mentor Horace

Plunkett (whose *Ireland in the Twentieth Century* in 1902 unwittingly
provoked a storm that brought much of his life's work crashing down
on his head) or his own contemporary Sean O'Faolain, Butler himself
hardly anticipated the results of his determined campaign to publicize
the forced conversion and eventual massacre of thousands of Orthodox
Serbs by the collaborationist regime of 'Independent Croatia' in 1941.
He tells the story himself in 'The Sub-Prefect Should Have Held His
Tongue', and it echoes in many other essays, so it need not be repeated
here. It is important to realize that when Butler raised the matter at a
Dublin meeting in 1952 which happened to be attended by the Papal
Nuncio, most Irish – and Western – opinion saw little beyond Catholic
martyrs and Communist tyranny; it is also relevant that Butler's knowledge of Yugoslavia is compounded by a preoccupation with what
happens to historical truth under collaborationist regimes (see 'The
Invader Wore Slippers'). But the sad and salient point is that the scandal
of 'the Papal Insult' erupted into local life, splitting the Kilkenny Archaeological Society and forcing Butler, like a latter-day Standish O'Grady,
out of the localist, intellectual, historically minded, non-sectarian
meeting of hearts to which so many of these essays are dedicated. Unlike
Sean O'Casey (who refers sympathetically to the Papal Nuncio incident
in his own autobiography), or Plunkett and AE, who ran similar gaunt-
lets, Butler did not withdraw to England; his belief remained in a national
but pluralist dispensation, of the kind which was apparently offered for
a brief moment towards the end of the Irish eighteenth century. Though
it is eloquently defended in writings like *Wolfe Tone and the Common
Name of Irishman*, Butler may rather idealize this mirage of the road not
taken; the folk-memory of the missed chance for reconciliation is a
necessary condition of the Anglo-Irish mind. At any rate, while regret-
ting the outcome, he would not have kept quiet. And his enforced
withdrawal to the life of a country scholar produced his book on the
origins of early Irish hagiographical tradition, *Ten Thousand Saints*
(1972). Its arguments are encapsulated in 'Influenza in Aran', and they
landed him in controversy – albeit academic rather than headline-
grabbing – once more.

It was apposite that the enterprising publisher who decided to issue a
collected edition of Butler's essays, Antony Farrell, was himself a 'localist'
running a small press on a shoestring from a farm in County Westmeath.
When *Escape from the Anthill* appeared from The Lilliput Press in 1985,
the resonance of its reception was surprising: large-scale and ecstatic
reviews in a wide variety of journals, followed by literary prizes, critiques
and interviews. The next volume, *The Children of Drancy*, appeared in
1988 with a lead review in the *Times Literary Supplement*, programmes

on Irish television, further prizes. Even the controversial arguments of 'Little K', dealing with the rights of parents with brain-damaged children, aroused scant objection. By the time of the third collection, *Grandmother and Wolfe Tone*, Butler had – in his ninetieth year – become widely accepted in Ireland as an inspirational figure: almost an institution. The irony was not lost on him. His own scepticism, irony and integrity, like those of Ernest Renan, had held proof against various arrows and slings in a long life spent pursuing the truth – but a Truth 'friendly, not hostile, to the imagination'. 'I think', he writes, 'that Renan differed from other great sceptics like Voltaire and Lucretius by his sensitive, unscornful handling of the ideas that he had rejected. He was neither a revolutionary nor a self-sufficient scholar. He was a Celt whose emotions were swayed by memories and personal loyalties.' And he was grounded as firmly in Brittany as Butler himself has adhered to Kilkenny.

Butler's life as well as his work has similarly been dedicated to a resolute suspicion of established authority stepping in to dictate decisions which should be personal. And as the third volume went to press, the 1989 revolutions of Eastern Europe made many of his reflections and preoccupations about the Balkans, Mitteleuropa, the historical effects of communism and the enduring potency of regional identity seem more prescient than ever. For at the end, the kernel of Butler's work lies around 'the small community' which inspires the reflections at the close of 'Little K'; or 'the real world, small, personal and concrete, into which we are born', where he locates Wolfe Tone's lasting influence. In this small world, Butler has quoted Chekhov on the enduring importance of the solitary individual: 'No man is a prophet in his own country and these solitary individuals, of which I speak, play an imperceptible role in society; they do not dominate it but their work is visible.' Butler has done this, for his own small community; but in becoming at last a prophet in his own country, he has acted for wider interests too. He once likened his observation of Irish history over his long lifetime to being on a scenic railway in a funfair: all is circular and delusive. 'We pass through towering cardboard mountains and over raging torrents and come to rest in the same well-trodden field from which we got on board.' It does not seem too pretentious to see the distilled experience of these essays as an odyssey, from Ireland to East, West, and back again: stemming from and returning to an intellectual tradition which takes in Montaigne and Turgenev as well as Swift and Shaw; beginning and ending in a family house in County Kilkenny.

R. F. Foster

THE AUCTION

—

I am not quite sure how soon after Otway Cuffe's death, in 1912, Mrs Cuffe gave up Sheestown and went to live in Kerry, but I was already a public schoolboy, a Carthusian, and ripe to be embarrassed when my relations made scenes publicly, and there had been just such a scene at the Sheestown auction to which I had gone with my mother in the pony-trap. Mr McCreery, the auctioneer, had offered for sale a large wooden hut and my mother, who needed a new hen-house, rather tremulously bid it up to £17. It was knocked down to her, and she was walking away, appalled at her own audacity, when someone remarked how kind the Cuffes had always been to the poor of Kilkenny. Not one tuberculous slum-child but several had passed successive summers in that hut in a leafy glade by the Nore. Tuberculosis! My mother for a couple of seconds was frozen with horror, and then she was gesticulating frantically across the crowd to Mr McCreery and to Aunt Harriet, who stood within reach of him. 'Tell him! Stop him!' I felt a *frisson* of sympathy and dismay. Tuberculosis! Tuberculous poultry! Tuberculous eggs! A quiver like an electric current ran through all the better-dressed bosoms in front of me, because Lady Aberdeen, the Lord Lieutenant's wife, had started a crusade against tuberculosis – it was a word that was on everybody's lips, particularly unionist lips. I must here permit myself a digression about tuberculosis.

It was one of those rare and blessed battle-cries, like co-operative creameries and village halls, which appeared to have no political or religious implications. Indeed it was better than either, for often a priest wanted to consecrate a village hall or put a crucifix instead of a clock above the rostrum, and there were rumours that the creameries were used for political agitation when the farmers' boys for miles around, having taken their milk-churns from their donkey-carts, had leisure for exchanging views. But nobody could say anything of the kind about

1

tuberculosis. When my mother had started a branch of the Women's National Health Association in Bennettsbridge, Lady Aberdeen had come down and talked to the Association and driven round the neighbourhood. My sister had sat on one side of her and Miss Foley, the priest's sister, on the other, and Mrs Cuffe beside the chauffeur. It was an immensely amiable, non-political, non-religious occasion. Tuberculosis acted like a love-potion, and at the end of it we children had distinctly heard Miss Foley say, 'A thousand thanks, Countess, for my most delightful drive.' With the savage snobbery of children, learning for the first time the exciting art of speaking in inverted commas, we had pestered each other for months and months with poor Miss Foley's over-unctuous gratitude. So now tuberculosis, which had once seemed a sordid, almost shameful secret between the doctors and the dying, was invested with dignity and importance. Now that it was made everybody's business, it attracted to itself not only the tender and the charitable but also the ambitious and the interfering and the timid, who saw that sympathy for the sick might be interposed as a fluffy bolster between themselves and Home Rule which they saw irrevocably approaching. But because I found it all a bore when I was in my teens, I am likely to underestimate the self-denial and unrewarded service of those who like my mother spent endless hours with ledgers, petty-cash books, subscription lists, committees. My mother, unlike the Cuffes, had never been sustained by any golden dream of a new era in Ireland, but simply by a Victorian sense of duty to the poor and her own humorous curiosity about other people's lives.

For a moment or two I felt rather proud of the effect that my mother had caused in the large crowd with the magical word 'tuberculosis'. All the expected responses could be seen and even Aunt Harriet, who as a Christian Scientist considered tuberculosis 'a form of false thinking', had leant over loyally and, seizing Mr McCreery by the sleeve, had whispered some agitated remarks into his ear. But quickly the mystical moment passed, the auctioneer and the public began to get impatient, and at my elbow I heard the curate of St John's, Kilkenny, say sourly to his neighbour: 'I don't wonder she wants to get out of it. £17! Ridiculous! Why, I could knock it up myself for £7. As for tuberculosis, all that's needed is a little disinfectant.' I was greatly mortified on my mother's behalf and scarcely noticed how the episode ended. (I think she decided to write herself to Mrs Cuffe.)

I wriggled unhappily out of the crowd in the yard and walked down past Cuffe's Model Dairy to the river, which for a mile or two upstream above Sheestown weir flows under park trees through the small demesnes

of Sheestown and Kilfera on its western banks. It is full of trout and
salmon, and all the way from Durrow in Co. Laois to New Ross in
Co. Wexford there are meadows of rich grass on each bank, the Scotch
firs and larches grow straight and thick, and every now and then, south
of Kilkenny town, beeches spread themselves out extravagantly over
bluebells and wood sorrel. Through them you can see the hindquarters
of a fat pony, the sparkle of a tomato-house, the corner of a tennis net
and, less frequently, a real exotic like a contented Jersey cow or a
disconsolate but still defiant cricket pavilion. Surely this valley had
everything in the world that anyone could wish for, the raw material
for every variety of happiness? Why is the manufactured article so rare?
Why, at sixteen, were my parents convinced that I would never be able
to live here? Has any river in the world carried so many cargoes of
nostalgia and bitter-sweet memories to the sea, for one could cover an
acre with faded newsprint about the Nore, sad simple verse composed
in Tasmania or Bangkok or Pittsburgh, and sent home to Kilkenny? If
the Nore ends one line you will know infallibly that a succeeding line
will end with 'days of yore', 'distant shore', 'never more', 'long years
before', 'memory's door', 'parting sore'. The answer to my last question
is no doubt that all the rivers of Ireland are the same.

In fact, though, I don't want an answer, because the answer is obvious.
I want an admission. Living in social harmony is a most difficult art; the
most absolute concentration is required, and perfect equilibrium. Our
island is dangerously tilted towards England and towards Rome, good
places in themselves but best seen on the level. Everybody is rolling off
it and those that remain, struggling hard for a foothold, drag each other
down. But it is not necessary to argue, it is only necessary to look.

Sheestown is divided from Kilfera by a small rocky glen in which St
Fiachra's Well is situated, and beyond it across smooth lawns, a tennis
court and a high embankment built above the rapids of the Nore, you
can see the Norman castle of the Forrestals now incorporated into Kilfera
House. There is also the ruined church of Sheestown in which the
Forrestals and Shees are buried, and the small cemetery of Kilfera where
the roots of the beech trees have tilted or flattened half the tombs. A
headless statue of a medieval ecclesiastic is propped against the railings
of the Victorian table-tomb of Mr Kenny Purcell, 'One-time Clerk of
the Peace Kilkenny' and a former owner of Kilfera. It is said locally to
be St Fiachra himself, that much-travelled saint, who in Kilkenny gave
his name to Kilfera, and in Paris gave it to the 'fiacre', because there was
a cabstand beneath his church; but the statue is a thousand years later
than Fiachra's time and is probably an abbot from some dissolved

medieval monastery, Jerpoint perhaps, or Kells. A small stone building, said to be his hermit cell, had to be removed when Mr Kenny Purcell went to his rest in 1869, but he too has been disrespectfully treated because the marble walls of his sepulchre are gaping apart. My toes were just small enough to get a foothold between the iron bars and I could see a couple of stones and a tin can, but no trace of the Clerk of the Peace.

You get all the confusion of Irish history in a few acres. First St Fiachra, then the Norman Forrestals, then, overshadowing them, the Shees, English you would suppose. But no, they are Irish Uí Seaghdha from Kerry, who anglicized their name and their habits with immense rapidity and success in Tudor times. Robert Shee had allied himself with Piers Butler, eighth Earl of Ormond, and had been killed in 1493 in Tipperary fighting against the O'Briens of Munster at the head of a hundred Kilkennymen. The Shees were one of the ten great merchant families of Kilkenny, the other nine all being English. Robert Shee's son, Richard, had become Sovereign of Kilkenny; his grandson, Sir Richard, had been educated at Gray's Inn, became legal adviser to Queen Elizabeth's friend Black Tom Butler, the tenth Earl of Ormond, and when Ormond became Lord Treasurer of Ireland, was made Deputy Treasurer. He and his family acquired great wealth and many houses in Kilkenny town and county and had built the Alms House in which Standish O'Grady had established his knitting industry and permanent craft exhibition.[1] Sir Richard's son, Lucas, married the daughter of Lord Mountgarret, whose other daughter married the eleventh Earl of Ormond. Lucas's son, Robert, when the Civil War broke out, persuaded his uncle Mountgarret to accept the presidency of the Confederation. The royalist parliament was held in the Shee mansion in Parliament Street which till 1865 stood where the gates of the Market now are.

The Shees were an urbane and cultivated family who wrote for each other long epitaphs in elegiacs and hexameters, which are more pagan than Christian. '*Homo bulla* ... (Man is a bubble) ...':

> *Nec genus antiquum nec honesta opulentia rerum*
> *Nec necis imperium lingua diserta fugit*
> *Nec fidei fervor nec religionis avitae*
> *Cultus ab extremo liberat ense nihil.*

> (Neither ancient lineage, nor honourably
> amassed wealth nor eloquence can evade the
> stern summons of death, nor can fervent faith
> and the practice of the religion of our fathers
> reprieve us from the sword of doom.)

Then a prayer is asked for a speedy passage to Heaven, supposing, that is to say, heaven exists:

Si tamen haec mors est transitus ad superos...

Elias Shee, from whose tomb in St Mary's, Kilkenny, I have taken these five lines, is described by Richard Stanyhurst as 'born in Kilkenny, sometime scholar of Oxford, a gentleman of passing good wit, a pleasing conceited companion, full of mirth without gall. He wrote in English divers sonnets.' I do not think the Shees or the nine other Kilkenny merchant families, all Catholics, all dispossessed by Cromwell, could be considered 'priest-ridden'. Had fate treated them more kindly, would they, like the wealthy Flemish burghers, have become patrons of the arts and sciences; would they have produced their own Erasmus and formed eventually the nucleus of a proud and independent Anglo-Irish civilization? Elias Shee was described by his sorrowing relatives as '*orbi Britannico lumen*', a light to the British world, because of his wit, his learning, his breeding, but his family remained conscious of their Irish descent, calling themselves after Cromwellian times O'Shee, when more prudent families were dropping their Os and Macs.

Yet I cannot feel very confident of any such Anglo-Irish development in the seventeenth century. Is there, perhaps, as AE (George Russell) suggested, 'some sorcery in the Irish mind' rebelling against any peaceful and prosperous fusion, some intense pride of race?

When I got back to Sheestown I found that my mother had bought me a bookcase full of Otway Cuffe's books. She was looking at them apprehensively, wondering whether she was not infecting me with something more virulent than tuberculosis, and, when we were driving home, she tried to counteract any possible bad effects by telling me how Cuffe's heart had been broken by ingratitude and that, when a couple of years before he had invited the Cave Hill Players from Belfast to act in a play of O'Grady's about Red Hugh O'Donnell at Sheestown, a couple of thousand spectators had streamed out from Kilkenny. They had trampled down some rare shrubs, and stolen and broken teacups. She also said that O'Grady's play was very bad, and that she had had to laugh at Otway Cuffe in a saffron kilt reciting a roistering rebel Irish ballad in a refined English voice. Manager after manager had cheated Cuffe at the woollen mills and woodworks. And she said that all the intelligent people had emigrated. Her own brothers, Etonians, Harrovians, Carthusians, had all gone, except Uncle Charlie at Graiguenoe, and were British officers or Indian civilians. Ireland was an exhausted country. 'Look how stupid X is!' and she mentioned one of my father's oldest friends.

Everything she said was true, yet I knew that she herself would never grudge her teacups or her shrubs where her own ideals and affections were involved, and that she was trying to inoculate me against the terrible virus of nationalism. My responses cannot have satisfied her, for a few days later I found that she had torn out from some of the books the blank page on which Cuffe had written his name, and had used upon the title-page the little machine for stamping notepaper with our address, Maidenhall, Bennettsbridge, Co. Kilkenny. I diverted some of the annoyance I felt with my mother to the little machine, which I ever afterwards regarded with abhorrence. I could remember our excitement when it had arrived ten years before and we had won countless pennies for the League of Pity by stamping notepaper for my mother and father with it.

My mother bought a large red book called *Careers for Our Boys* and tried vainly to engage me in conversation about the British consular and diplomatic services. She suspected rightly that I was not merely indifferent but hostile: she trembled for me because the 1914–18 War was on and all the heresies which had seemed so venial a couple of years earlier now carried on them the mark of Cain. Our bishop, Dr d'Arcy, the successor of Dr Crozier, a mild and scholarly commentator on the Pauline Epistles, had himself a few years before, as Bishop of Down, consecrated Unionist machine-guns to be used against Home Rulers, and sometimes Kipling's poem on Ulster was quoted. I remember only one verse:

> We know the war declared
> On every peaceful home,
> We know the Hell prepared
> For those who serve not Rome.

It would have been social suicide to question that God and the Empire were indissolubly allied. My mother was not herself given to adamantine loyalties, there were few of them which she could not have adjusted in our interests. She was not a Roman matron like my grandmother, who would have sacrificed us all upon the altar of God or Empire, but she saw that we, unlike the Cuffes and Lady Desart, were not in the income group which could afford to be unorthodox. My father belonged to the minor Anglo-Irish gentry and, except for remote kinship of blood, had no link with the two or three noble Butler dynasties which still reigned nearby, and which we were to survive in Kilkenny. And if ever I made some heretical remark about the Easter Rebellion, she would look at me not with indignation but with loving anxiety, as though I had coughed up a spot of blood onto my handkerchief. There was no precedent for it in my upbringing or my heredity. Nothing like it had been seen in her own family; in my father's there had been Aunt Harriet, but when the Gaelic League had become 'political' Aunt Harriet had shut her Dinneen[2] forever and become a disciple of Mrs Eddy. It could not, therefore, be a congenital disorder, it must have been acquired by contagion, and looking round in a wide sweep for possible 'carriers' she fixed on my distant cousin Theobald Fitzwalter Butler, who had been head boy at Charterhouse a term or two before I had gone there and who had visited us several times and had made contentious remarks at mealtimes. 'He's got it off Theo,' I often heard her murmur dismally, desperately to my father, after some evening of unprofitable disagreements.

Theo and his friend, Eric Dodds, had done relief work in Serbia before conscription had come and then, dissociating themselves from the war, had returned to their own country. Theo had taught at a school in Co. Down, Dodds at Kilkenny College. One day Dodds, a stocky independent fellow, walked out to tea from Kilkenny and inflamed my grandmother by his pacifism and his defence of Irish sedition. Theo told us that Dodds had won 'The Craven Scholarship'. Ritual Irish jokes, one part mirth, three parts gall, were later made about the Craven, though not by my grandmother, who was too deeply shocked and too fastidious, in the well-bred English way, for puns. Dodds did not come again. But nonetheless, almost as much as Theo (who was thought more insidious because he was more ingratiating), he was supposed to have corrupted me and perhaps, indeed, he did leave behind a stimulating breeze of heterodoxy for which I should be grateful, though it would have needed a hurricane to do more than ruffle our settled Anglo-Irish loyalties.

I wish I had seen more of them, since they could have helped me to a less inhibited introverted patriotism, with facts and external contacts; had I had more confidence and been less dependent on my family, I could have been pleasanter to them. I could have acknowledged, I think, that my mother's powerful intuitions were often right, even when they were irrelevant. Of Dodds and Theo she said: 'They're great Irish patriots now, but when the war is over they'll take jobs in England.' And so indeed it happened. They are both of them now, like Elias Shee, '*orbi Britannico lumina*', since Dodds is Regius Professor of Greek at Oxford and Theo a legal luminary at the Inner Temple. Yet I cannot regard

either of them as backsliders. Though it seems to me to be man's duty
to work in and for the community which he acknowledges to be his
own, we also have a duty to develop our faculties to their fullest extent.
Often these two duties cannot be reconciled and we have to choose
between spiritual and intellectual frustration. So long as we do not
accept our mutilated destiny with levity or resignation, we cannot be
condemned as dodgers.

My mother's intuition about Cuffe's books was also sound. Among
those from which she removed Cuffe's name was Edward Martyn's *The
Heather Field*. This now almost unreadable play, which George Moore
declared to be 'the first play written in English inspired by the example
of Ibsen', has not yet lost its magic for me, but forty years ago I found
it overwhelming. Is it sentimental, morbid, is the dialogue forced and
preposterous, are the characters overdrawn? I am still blind to all its
defects; it seems to me the most poetic expression I know of the terrifying
intellectual isolation of Ireland, its power to breed ideas, ideals and
emotions in rich abundance, its incapacity to nourish them or defend
them from the venomous dislike of the 'niddys' (I got that word from
Standish O'Grady) and the professionally virtuous. It shows how
isolation, in time, breeds isolationism, driving poetry into suicidal
extravagance and generating in sane and sober people every variety of
arrogance and eccentricity. Carden Tyrell, who tried to reclaim a heather
field with grants from the Board of Works, is a tragic figure, a symbol
of the incompatibility of poetry and practical life. The drainage of the
heather field swamps the land below it and that necessitates more loans
from the Board of Works and 'a vast ramification of drains' to carry the
water away to the sea. Carden is hypnotized by the magnitude of the
enterprise, the huge tract of luxuriant pasture which will take the place
of swamp and heather. But it is the vast expenditure that appals his wife
and her worldly friends, and she tries to get Carden certified as insane.
Carden becomes more and more the slave of his dreams, till one day his
little son comes in joyously with a posy of purple flowers. Then Carden
does, in fact, enter the dream-world of the insane, a world of happy
hallucination, in which reality is a passing nightmare and the rainbow
fantasies of his boyhood alone are permanent. Everyone is bewildered
with the wild and witless poetry of his remarks, till his friend Barry
Ussher solves the mystery with the curtain-line: 'The wild heath has
broken out again in the heather field.'

That line could almost act also as an epitaph on O'Grady's work in
Kilkenny, on Cuffe's, on Lady Desart's, on the work of the scores of
poetical social reformers who flourished in Ireland in the first quarter of

the century. In every case the wild heath has broken out again in the heather field, and the memory of those who tried to eradicate it by 'modern' methods has failed. Yet the urbane nihilism of the Shees belongs to a more prosperous age. 'HOMO BULLA. *Vita quid est hominis gracilis nisi spuma, quid ipse? Nil nisi bulla.*'

I don't suppose anyone, for example, will write about old Albinia Broderick, the sister of Lord Midleton, the leader of the southern unionists, who conceived it her mission to atone for the sins of her ancestors, exacting landlords of the south-west; she dressed as an old Irish countrywoman and ran a village shop, while behind her on a stony Dunkerron promontory rose the shell of a large hospital which she had built for the sick poor of Kerry, but which, because of its unsuitable though romantic site, had remained empty and unused.[3] There is a labyrinthine story of idealism, obstinacy, perversity, social conscience, medicine, family, behind this empty structure. The man who could unravel it would be diagnosing the spiritual sickness of Ireland, and diagnosis is the first step to a cure. It might be a more worthwhile task than the hospital, had it come into being, could ever have performed. But that task belongs to Kerry, not Kilkenny.

Here, I want to find out what happened to Otway Cuffe. This implies a rejection of that mystical interpretation of Irish dreaming which Shaw has expressed so memorably through the mouth of Larry Doyle:

Here [in England], if the life is dull, you can be dull too, and no great harm done. But your wits can't thicken in that soft moist air, on those white springy roads, in those misty rushes and brown bogs, on those hillsides of granite rocks and magenta heather. You've no such colours in the sky, no such lure in the distances, no such sadness in the evenings. Oh, the dreaming! the dreaming! the torturing, heart-scalding, never satisfying dreaming, dreaming, dreaming, dreaming! No debauchery that ever coarsened and brutalized an Englishman can take the worth and usefulness out of him like that dreaming.

Shaw, the great realist, had nothing but a fatalistic philosophy of abdication to offer the Irish, 'Leave Ireland.' It was the same philosophy which my parents, rejecting it for themselves, offered to their children, and, rejecting it for myself, I have not yet anything better to offer mine. Yet malaria has not always existed in marshes and can now be expelled from them, and frustration and melancholy are not ineradicable in any corner of the world.

Looking at my own family history, I was unable to trace a single one of my paternal ancestors who had lived out of Ireland since the thirteenth century, when they came here: why should our island in my generation suddenly become uninhabitable for us? I could not and I cannot accept that there is anything inevitable about this, or that misty rushes and magenta heather inevitably debauch the intelligence.

Seen against the backcloth of a lunatic world, Irish lunacy is an ephemeral and contingent disorder. Sometimes cosmic lunacy dwarfs and counteracts the regional kind. Hitler's war stopped the importation of foreign timber and building materials to Ireland. They became costly rarities and Miss Broderick's chimerical hospital turned under demolition into a profitable business investment, I have been told. In a less crude way projects doomed to failure, like Carden Tyrell's, are not unprofitable if the apparent waste of energy and enthusiasm can be scrupulously recorded. Perhaps Cuffe would have been more of a Carden Tyrell than he was if O'Grady had not published two of Edward Martyn's other plays that were in the Nore Library in Kilkenny, and if *The Heather Field* had not been in that bookcase at Sheestown.

[1957]

1. For Standish O'Grady see 'The Deserted Sun Palace', pp. 39–55.
2. Rev. Patrick Dinneen (1860–1934), Gaelic Revivalist and Jesuit scholar, compiled the standard Irish–English dictionary. It was first published in 1904 as *Foclóir Gaedhilge agus Béarla*, and rewritten in 1927.
3. She has been briefly written about in M. Ward, *Unmanageable Revolutionaries: Women and Irish Nationalism* (London, 1983). Under her Gaelicized name of Gobnait ní Bruadair she remained a strong Republican presence on Kerry County Council and in Sinn Feín whose newspaper, *Irish Freedom*, she owned. In 1933 she seceded from the women's organization, Cumann na mBan, and formed Mna na Poblachta, dedicated to preserving the pure Republican conscience.

A FRAGMENT OF AUTOBIOGRAPHY

My father farmed about six hundred acres, half of them at Burnchurch farm near Bennettsbridge and half at Drumherin, some six miles north-east of Kilkenny City. From the time I was eight I used to bicycle with him to Drumherin where the two Phelan brothers, Johnnie, who was enormously fat, and Paddy, who was thin, were stewards. It is, I believe, the wild country where John Banim placed his story, 'Crohoore of the Billhook'. For a long way the road to Ballyfoyle was lined with tall beech trees soaring above the banks on which moss, eight inches deep, half smothered the primroses and ferns within it. There was a big lake on the farm, the Kilkenny reservoir, which my father had sold to the Corporation. He and Paddy and Johnnie went round the fields prodding the bullocks. Paddy had a stick which he dipped in cow dung and slapped on the back of those which were to go to the fair. My father must have hoped I would make some interested comment, but I was always thinking of something else and never did.

Burnchurch farm, where a third brother, Joe Phelan, was the steward, is only half a mile away from Maidenhall and is beside Burnchurch rectory which my great-grandfather had built for himself five miles from Burnchurch church. He was a portly pre-Disestablishment rector and a friend of the Bishop, who pressed on him a second parish, that of Trim in Co. Meath. He persuaded his son, Richard, who was at Balliol, to come home and be rector of Trim. Richard, whose memory I revere, was a distinguished archaeologist who lived out the rest of his life in Trim and published with the local printer a still valuable history of the town, republished in 1978 by the Meath Archaeological Society. He was married to Harriet, the liveliest of Maria Edgeworth's many half-sisters.

To his eldest son, James, my great-grandfather gave Priestown, the small family home near Dunboyne in Meath which had been Butler property since the time of Edward II. After his father's death, when the

11

remarkable twelfth Baron Dunboyne had died, my great-uncle James was one of several distant cousins who claimed to succeed him. He failed. The twelfth Baron was the Roman Catholic Bishop of Cork and, sooner than be succeeded by remote Protestant relations, he had defied the Pope and married, hoping to rear a son whom he would bring up in the Catholic faith. But he had no son, and he got an appalling denunciation in Latin from Pius VI for 'living in foul concubinage with a heretic woman'.

Though we live in Kilkenny we are only distantly related to the Butlers of Ormonde who had lived in Kilkenny Castle since 1391. Since they are gone and their memory is fading, in 1967 I formed the Butler Society with the present Lord Dunboyne so that a large and once powerful family should not lose its place in history. I only rarely met my Priestown cousins but I had very many English cousins through my English grandmother. Till I went to school my father taught us maths, my grandmother taught us history and my mother taught us French and English and at the same time managed to run the dairy and keep ducks and hens. She used to send them, wrapped up in butter-paper, to relations in England, in particular to my cousin Alice Graves, who in return sent me the suits that her two sons, Cecil and Adrian, had out-grown. They were at school in Berkshire and I was appalled one day to learn that I was to follow them to Bigshotte Rayles. It was in the prep-school belt of the Home Counties, a land of pine trees and heather and chalk and golf courses.

It was so extraordinary to be dumped in this strange place that I thought my parents had given me away. My first few weeks I wandered round in a swoon and when anyone asked a question I gaped at them. When one day Miss Reeve, the headmaster's sister, took my temperature (two boys had measles and lived behind a flapping carbolic sheet) I bit the thermometer in half; she tried again and I bit the second one.

I have forgotten the names of thousands of former acquaintances but I remember the names and faces of all the boys at Bigshotte. I remember all the shrubs between the pavvy and the swimming-bath. Hundreds of episodes present themselves in heavy type. Everything else since is in italics. It is said of prep schools 'that they rub the corners off'. This agonizing process was applied to me, and it could not have been more painful and irreversible were it done with a pincers and a file. I was well fed and never beaten or much bullied. Indeed, I was the favourite pupil of Mr Reeve, the headmaster, and he cast a blight over one Easter holiday by coming to stay. He was an excellent teacher and, thanks to him, I got the top mathematical scholarship to Charterhouse.

My enthusiasm for mathematics started when I got to trigonometry and discovered there was an abstract world which ran parallel to the treacherous concrete one and could not be reached from it. I had stopped believing in Heaven and everything I had been told about it soon after I got to Bigshotte. (How could Mr Reeve or anyone else possibly know?) I was proud that, when the prayer-bell rang, I began my second prayer, the one my mother taught me, 'Lord God, if thou existest...'. Here in trigonometry was an escape route I could believe in.

Ronnie Huggard and I were to sit for scholarships to Charterhouse and when the other boys had drunk their cocoa and gone to bed Mr Reeve set us problems (he called them 'riders') to do in the empty classroom. It was wonderfully peaceful. We could hear Mr Reeve reading aloud to Miss Reeve on the Private Side, the flames flickering in the dying fire, Rex, the school dog, snoring, and upstairs Matron saying 'Lights out!' It was a magical hour. At half-term Ronnie and I went up to Charterhouse and some weeks later the news came that I had got my scholarship. There was a whole holiday to celebrate my victory and it was spent playing cricket, though I would much rather have spent it indoors doing riders with Ronnie. But Ronnie was weeping bitterly. He had yearned to go to Charterhouse but without a scholarship his father could not afford to send him.

Mr Reeve made me Head Boy early on. Since all I wanted was to get away this did not mean much to me. It was announced at Evening Prayers and this time I heard the sound of Bernie Cooper snuffling piteously behind me as we knelt. He had thought he was going to be Head Boy.

Years later an unpleasant idea occurred to me. Perhaps Mr Reeve favoured me not because he thought me interesting and clever but because Cousin Alice Graves was Sir Edward Grey's sister and he was English Foreign Secretary at the time. Their mother and my English grandmother were sisters. I only knew of him because Granny used to write him disapproving letters about his commitment to Home Rule.

About Charterhouse there is no need to say much as Robert Graves, who was a nephew of Cousin Alice, has said it all in *Goodbye To All That*. He reports a conversation he had with Nevill Barbour, who became a friend of mine at Oxford. It wouldn't be enough, they agreed, to dismiss the whole school and staff and start all over again. No. 'The school buildings were so impregnated with what was called the public school spirit, but what we felt as fundamental badness, that they would have to be demolished and the school rebuilt elsewhere and its name changed.'

At Charterhouse, except in class, there was no mixing between the houses and the scholars sat together at a small table in Upper Long. There were two other scholars at Verites but I found them both uncongenial and there was no escape from them. As for the masters, all the younger ones were at war and old ones were rescued from retirement to replace them. A. H. Tod, my dreadful one-eyed housemaster, must have been one of these.

My love affair with trigonometry ended during my first term, when in broad daylight Mr Tuckey, a Cambridge Wrangler, told us all about Functions in a crowded classroom in the Science Building. It was no longer numinous and mystical and I scarcely minded not understanding. Next term the headmaster Frank Fletcher (he was called Fifi and his wife Mimi) shifted me over to Greek. I caught up on it fairly quickly. Mr Dames Longworth, the fifth form master, was a tweedy Irish gentleman from Co. Westmeath. He swaggered about the room twirling his moustache and swaying his shoulders dramatically as he recited Greek iambics in a booming voice. 'And old crocks for Studio?' he used to exclaim when the drawing master poked his head round the door to collect two pupils who were excused OTC (Officers' Training Corps) once a week. He was wealthy and had made himself irremovable by presenting the school with a racquets court. He and A. H. Tod had together compiled a famous book, *Tod and Longworth's Unseen Passages of Greek and Latin Translation*, which circulated round all the public schools of Britain. Tod's other distinction was that years before, drilling the OTC in Founder's Court, he had stepped back into the fountain. In the New Bugs exam at Verites every examinee was expected to know this.

As a housemaster Tod was a disaster. He was becoming senile and he never knew my name. Once he stopped me and said: 'Heh, Butler, send Butler to me!' My happiest day at Verites was when it caught fire and we had to toss all Tod's furniture and his collection of brass horse ornaments out of the window. I was the school swot and I sat in my study poring over Virgil and Homer but without real enjoyment, because Tod and Longworth seemed to lie between. I climbed very quickly to the top of the sixth and my mother was worried that I was not Head Boy or even a School Monitor. It was their privilege to stroll round Founder's Court, hands in pockets and coat swept behind them, in a special manner. I did not mind. As at Bigshotte, all I wanted was to be away.

At the end of the summer term in 1918 my moment came. I got all the five scholarships and prizes that were available in the classical sixth. Since my academic career ended disastrously and since they may still exist, I do not think it is boastful to give their names. I got the Talbot Scholarship and Medal for Greek, the Thackeray Prize for English Literature (Thackeray had been at Charterhouse), the Petilleau Prize for French and the top leaving scholarship. For many terms I had got the Form Prize, but as the war was on all prize money was given to the Red Cross and we got slips to stick into the books we already had and I think most of the money for the Petilleau Prize went to the Red Cross, too, because I was given *Princess Mary's Book of France*, which I had no use for, and there was no money for a second prize. When M. Petilleau, who lived in Godalming, heard this, he was very much distressed and went to his bookshelves and took down the complete works of Molière, bound in calf, and gave it as second prize. I was very good at Latin verse, which seems to me now the most futile of accomplishments and, on the strength of a translation of part of Shelley's *Adonais* into Lucretian hexameters, Fifi decided to send me up for the scholarship at Balliol, where he had been himself.

I failed but got the top scholarship at St John's. Fifi called me into his study to tell me. I was too old to cry like Ronnie Huggard but I had been humiliated and wanted to leave in a blaze of glory, so I did cry. Fifi patted me on the shoulder and said something about the Southern Irish temperament and that I wanted to be 'aut Caesar aut nullus'. There were still two terms to put in before Oxford but I told my parents I was leaving. It was an unheard of thing as the war was over, but I got them to agree.

My mother had wanted me to go into the Foreign Office as she thought Edward Grey might take an interest in me but my father still hoped I might be a farmer, so it was agreed I should take an agricultural course at Reading University where William de Burgh, an Irishman, a cousin through the Greys, was Professor of Philosophy, and he and his family became life-long friends. Eric Dodds was lecturing there, too, a stage in his progress from teaching at Kilkenny College to being Regius Professor of Greek at Oxford. In his book *Missing Persons* he has written a charming account of de Burgh. I was happy and free for the first time. I learned no agriculture and I do not believe that the demobilized officers for whom the course was planned learnt any either. It had been hastily put together by experts on soil and pasture, book-keeping and the building of pig-sties and cow sheds (for this we started at the beginning with slides of Doric and Ionic columns), but the farm was some distance away and we only rarely cast a glance at cows and crops. Yet there was something conclusive about it. I had a younger brother, and nature clearly did not want me to be a farmer.

When I was fifteen I had passed through Dublin, still smoking after the Easter Rebellion, and I had decided I was an Irish Nationalist. This led to constant quarrelling with my family, which became worse when I found an ancient copy of *Robert Elsmere* by Mrs Humphry Ward at home and became a 'Free Thinker'. This was an exciting new phrase for me and I felt proud that unknown to myself I had been one at Bigshotte three years before and had never felt, like Elsmere, 'a castaway on a shoreless sea'. On the contrary, it had opened up to me the new abstract world of trigonometry and helped me to get my scholarship to Charterhouse. Elsmere's friend, Henry Grey, said to him consolingly: 'The parting with the Christian mythology is the rending asunder of bones and marrow. It means parting with half the confidence and joy of life. But have trust! Reason is God's like all the rest. Trust it. I trust Him. The leading strings of the past are dropping away from you; they are dropping from all the world.' I found this intoxicating, but who could I talk to about it? I had to go to Mr Tod with the two other scholars to be prepared for confirmation. But how could I tell that dreadful old man in the armchair that the leading strings of the past had dropped away from me and that I did not wish to be confirmed? No I couldn't, not possibly, and so the Bishop of Winchester laid his hands on me and asked God that I should daily increase in the Holy Spirit more and more.

I consoled myself with the thought that when I got to Oxford all would be well again, but I found when I got there that Mrs Humphry Ward had become a sort of joke and nobody agonized about their doubts as Elsmere had done. Religion had become a subject, like Philosophy or Physics. You either took it or you didn't.

Yet in the lovely relaxed atmosphere I was no longer bored and I ceased to be a compulsive swot. Instead I was distracted by all that was new to hear and read and see.

There was still Plato and Thucydides and all the others, and Caesar and Virgil the third time round, but I could no longer concentrate. I never replaced my large Liddell & Scott's *Greek Lexicon*, which had got burnt in the Verites fire. For me only Lucretius survived the lecture-room and I still sometimes read him in an unscholarly way. It seems to me that if the atomic physicists who succeeded him two thousand years later had written in verse as he did, they would have seen that knowledge is only the beginning of wisdom. It is not safe in the hands of those who are not sensitive, as he was, to the beauty of the earth and the fragility of all we value.

I saw *John Bull's Other Island* and read *The Irish Statesman* and learnt about my own country, which I had previously only known from ground level. In the long vac. I met Sir Horace Plunkett and visited him at Kilteragh, the house he built for himself at Foxrock, which he had made a meeting place for all those who were interested in their country and, aided by his secretary, Gerald Heard, for all the leading writers of the day. It would be pointless to mention all the eminent people I met there as I was too inexperienced and shy to talk to them. Lennox Robinson took me to one of Yeats's evening parties and I went to AE's also, and a world unknown in Bennettsbridge opened up for me.

All my thoughts and hopes were about Ireland and I only got a second in Mods. But all the same two of the dons at St John's, Last and Costin, told me I was being considered for a Fellowship. I listened politely, with my mind elsewhere. I knew that I would disappoint them in Greats.

Two years later I was back in Ireland with a bad degree, a third, or to be more precise no degree, because from what I took to be principle, but must have looked like pique, I refused to go through the ceremony. I cannot defend myself, as I gave offence to many who had nothing but good-will towards me.

My brother-in-law Tyrone Guthrie, who was at St John's with me, got a fourth but he had already found his vocation in the theatre and quickly recovered.

Cannot some alternative be found to exams in which ten people are bruised for every one who is exalted? One is not consulted when one's feet are put on the bottom rung of a ladder, and the higher you go the more painful the fall.

At home I found that the new world I had discovered was closing in again. The civil war had started, soon Kilteragh was to be burnt because Sir Horace was a senator, and AE was to die in England. Yet before this happened Plunkett urged me to join the County Libraries. He had used his influence with the Carnegie Trust to persuade it to start them in Ireland. To AE in the co-operative village the library was to have been the intellectual centre, while the creamery was the economic one. It was he who sent me to learn the trade in Ballymena, the headquarters of the Co. Antrim libraries. The organizing librarian in Dublin was Lennox Robinson, the playwright.

I have written about the libraries in *Irish Writing* of July 1949. They were a cultural bridge between north and south and I believe a great opportunity was lost in Ireland when, owing to an unhappy episode at the Dublin headquarters, their control, while they were still in embryo, was transferred to Dunfermline in Scotland.

This is how it happened. In August 1924 a short-lived periodical

To-morrow published a story by Lennox Robinson called 'The Madonna of Slieve Dun', which the clerical members of the governing body considered blasphemous. They called for Robinson's resignation. The Carnegie Trust was informed and, unwilling to take sides in such a sensitive issue, they abolished the Central Organization in Dublin and resumed control from Dunfermline. From then on each County Library had to work on its own and the happy days, when all the librarians north and south of the border knew each other and visited each other and sought for advice in Dublin, were over. Till then writers had been in charge of all the County Libraries. There was Lennox Robinson and his assistant, Tom MacGreevy, a poet, in Dublin; Robert Wilson, a poet, in Co. Sligo, and Geoffrey Phibbs, a poet, and his wife, the artist Norah McGuinness, in Co. Wicklow; Frank O'Connor in Cork; Helen Roe, an archaeologist, in Co. Leix. Frank O'Connor has written of this period, his apprenticeship, in *My Father's Son*, first in Sligo and then in Wicklow with Geoffrey Phibbs, of whom he has given a delightful account.

I have always blamed Lennox Robinson for the break-up of our little community. His story was unimportant and sooner than take his stand for 'intellectual freedom', which is always at risk in Ireland, he should have resigned and so ensured that the Central Organization survived in Dublin. Soon after this I left the libraries.

Dublin had been in the past, and should be in the future, the cultural if not the political centre of Ireland.

I had a motor bicycle and through my years in the County Libraries I discovered the varied beauties of my country and the rich diversity of its people. Why is it that now we look at the beauty mainly as something we can sell to tourists, and the diversity of its people, their faith and their loyalties, not as an enrichment but a source of bitter antagonism?

I believe it was from AE that I learnt to be an Utopian. He recalled that it was in the small states of Greece, each scarcely bigger than an Irish county, that all our arts and sciences were first developed. What happened once can happen again and he saw the future of Ireland as a union of small co-operative communities. There is no trace of this now, but we have only to wait. The great metropolitan civilization, which has sucked all the vision and enterprise from the provinces, is already under threat. It has armed the ignorant and two embattled mouse-brained dinosaurs, one in the east, one in the west, confront each other. Will they both perish without progeny or will we find some way of liberating ourselves from our machines so that once more as men we can handle man-sized problems?

When my father died in 1941 I came home with my wife Peggy to live in Bennettsbridge. I brought home with me some refugees from Vienna, where after the Anschluss I had been working with the Quakers at the Freundeszentrum in Singerstrasse, and I soon found friends in Kilkenny. There was James Delehanty, who ran *The Kilkenny Magazine* to which many later well-known writers contributed. There was the Kilkenny Archaeological Society, which with friends I revived in Kilkenny after a coma of fifty years. It is still thriving. There was also the Kilkenny Arts Society through which in 1952 we started the first Kilkenny Debate. It was on Partition. There were protests in Stormont and fury in Kilkenny and extra guards were drafted into the town. James Douglas, Secretary of the Unionist Council, and Colonel Topping, the Chief Whip, debated Partition with Sean MacBride and Eoin O'Mahony. Myles Dillon was in the Chair. That was the first of nine or ten peacefully contentious occasions. The debate on Neutrality with Basil Liddell Hart, the great military expert, and Brigadier Dorman O'Gowan would still be relevant today. I believe passionately in Irish neutrality, not an ignoble one as in Hitler's war, but one in which each citizen was on a war footing, a war for peace. Three Irishmen have thought in that direction: AE, Paddy Kavanagh and Bernard Shaw, and a plan for civil conscription has been sketched by AE in *The National Being*.

Then there was the Kilkenny Art Gallery Society, which after the death of the founder, George Pennefeather, fell on evil times. It had a new and splendid revival when Lord Ormonde gave Kilkenny Castle to the nation on 12 August 1967 and a spacious, well-planned art gallery was developed from the kitchen premises on the lower ground floor. My wife, Peggy, is its secretary.

I believe that it is in the first twenty-five years of our lives that our characters are shaped and our tastes are formed, and that the rest of our lives are spent either deploying our education, if we are at peace with it, or, if we are at war with it, making some compromise between what is congenital and what is acquired. I was at war with mine on an unremarkable battlefield and I have told in *Escape from the Anthill* whatever seems to have had slightly more interest than if, like satisfied people, I had had a nine-to-five life with a pension at sixty.

Like all my family I have loved growing things. My father was a skilled gardener and strawberries and seakale went in quantities to the Dublin market. He had a gardener and was able to draft extra help as well as manure from the farm, when he needed it. He planted espalier trees round the four quarters of the walled garden. It is over an acre and most of the espaliers are now gone except for a huge and prolific Bramley Seedling that has lost all but three of its eight arms. Till recently we were able to send in fruit and vegetables to the weekly Country Market, which, now that the creameries are gone, seems with its many branches to be the last trace of Plunkett's and AE's co-operative Ireland.

My greenhouses are now tumbling down and I use only a quarter of the garden; with reduced household and elderly appetites it is enough. But gardens, unlike houses, are easily restored and I see nothing final about this.

Can one write in the country far away from publishers and editors? It's difficult but not impossible. I published my first book, *Ten Thousand Saints* (1972), whose argument I still stand over, in Freshford, Co. Kilkenny; my present publisher lives at Gigginstown in Co. West-meath; and I had a long connection with Irish and English journals till they mostly died, and also with Radio Éireann and the BBC Third Programme.

I take comfort from the fact that two centuries ago, Richard and Elizabeth Griffith, who lived here at Maidenhall, ran a flax mill on the river Nore and became well known writers in England in their day.

All culture was not then as now focussed on the capital, yet everything changes with incredible rapidity, and no one can predict what the future holds.

[1987]

HENRY AND FRANCES

One afternoon fourteen or fifteen years ago we were cataloguing the library of our neighbour, Miss Power of Kilfane. It is a long beautiful room with tall windows between the bookcases looking on to a sweep of green lawn and beyond it a classically planted park. The library with its great fire was a delightful place in which to work or shirk work and we found ourselves too often sinking into luxurious arm-chairs and reading the books we were supposed to be cataloguing. Most of them were collected in the eighteenth and early nineteenth century and the family had two ruling passions, Art and Sport. The Kilkenny Theatre and the Kilkenny Hunt were their creations but the first of their two enthusiasms evaporated when the Theatre closed its doors in 1819 and when soon afterwards its founder, Richard Power, died. John Power's hunt still flourishes but the literature of hunting is not large and only a few books appear to have been added to the shelves in Victorian times. In his day, Richard Power filled his bookshelves not only with a unique collection of plays; he had also a fine store of essays, biographies and political pamphlets. I was cataloguing these books when, on one occasion, I took down four small volumes dated 1770. They were called *A Series of Genuine Letters between Henry and Frances*, but they had no author's name and I searched the pages for a clue. Some of the letters were dated from Kilfane and some from Farmley, where Henry Flood, the orator, lived; I exclaimed aloud when I discovered that many of the letters were dated from my own home, six miles away. Maidenhall is a small unpretentious Georgian house and I knew nothing of its history in the eighteenth century for my great-grandfather did not come to the district till 1800 or later, but to the best of my knowledge it was built about 1745. Then I remembered having seen the name Griffith on an old Title Deed. I borrowed the books to compare dates and make what inferences I could from the letters themselves. I was fascinated by the supple and often witty prose and successfully placed the authors, for there were two of them, Richard Griffith (Henry), and his wife, Elizabeth (Frances), who lived here and built this house over two hundred years ago.

The letters are disappointingly meagre about the ordinary social life of Bennettsbridge and Kilkenny; they mainly deal with the complicated, uneasy love affair of Henry and Frances. The Griffiths were a learned and cultivated couple, who for some reason to which they only allude mysteriously, had first to delay then to conceal their marriage for several years. Possibly delays and dissimulations were caused by money difficulties or a disapproving relative but I think it more likely that Frances' pride was the hindrance. Henry did not consider it necessary to be faithful to her and wrote to her about his infidelities in an aloof, philosophical way. For example, he had told her how his maid Nancy had had to be dismissed because she made such a scene about being supplanted in his affections by Sally. Frances tried to reply with equal philosophy but probably her heart was not in it:

As for the affair of Nancy and Sally, it is of no farther consequence to me than if James and the Coachman had been the Disputants. Nor did I mention my Opinion of Sally with any Design; for you may easily conceive that it is a matter of Indifference to me whether your present favourite was called Sarah or Anne; for while I am in possession of the Jewel that is lodged within I care not who holds the Casket.

> O free for ever be his eye,
> Whose heart to me is always true.

Her biographer, Miss Tomkins, has discovered an ingenious sentence in Frances' novel, *The History of Lady Barton*, which suggests a different outlook and may throw light on the postponement of the marriage. 'There is something extremely indelicate in professing a Passion for a virtuous Woman before we have undergone a sufficient Quarantine after the Contagion of an abandoned one, and Man in such a Situation resembles a Centaur, half-human and half-brute.'

Perhaps she was waiting till Henry had been purged by time of all those earlier contagions before she would acknowledge him as her husband.

Henry lived at Maidenhall, farming and building a flaxmill, Frances stayed with her old aunt at Abbey Street, Dublin, and later in lodgings in Chapelizod. Now and again, heavily chaperoned, she paid visits to her husband at Maidenhall. Before they published their letters they must have pruned them drastically, because though they are certainly genuine letters they contain very few of those trivial accounts of everyday life which the originals must certainly have had and which we would today find so enthralling. In the first edition the Irish place-names had been changed to English, so that the polite eye should not be offended by our barbarous nomenclature. Though frank about his morals he is fastidiously evasive about his occupation and finances, and it is only by inference and reference to other works that we find why he paid visits to country houses round Kilkenny and what happened to his flax mills.

He was doing some electioneering work, though for whom he was canvassing I do not know; as for the flax mills, he had got a grant from parliament for starting linen-manufacture on the Nore and in the expectation of a larger one he had built his factory and the house of Maidenhall. Then to set it going he had mortgaged it all. But very soon times changed for the worse, the second grant was withheld and Henry was ruined. It was soon after this that he and his wife decided to publish their letters to see if they could earn by literature what they had lost on linen. They succeeded and she became an immensely popular novelist and the first English translator of Voltaire; he too earned a living by his novels and his philosophical reflections. Most of their original work except the *Letters* is today unreadable but it charmed their contemporaries. Fanny Burney, after she had been reading *The Letters of Henry and Frances*, took up *The Vicar of Wakefield* by a new writer, Oliver Goldsmith, but she tells us she nearly threw it aside after reading a few pages, so disgusted was she with its coarse, indelicate outlook on life and in particular on matrimony; it was a cruel contrast to the 'so elegantly natural, so unassumingly rational' tone of the Griffith *Letters*. In London the Griffiths became well known in the circle of Garrick and Johnson; their little boy, Harry, who in the days of their poverty had to be brought up by his grandmother at Portarlington, became a nabob in India. He returned to Ireland, bought the estate of Millicent in Co. Kildare and played an influential part in Grattan's Parliament. He was the father of Sir Richard John Griffith, the distinguished geologist and civil engineer.

Last year I got a letter from a lady in an American university, enquiring about the Griffiths, on whom she was writing a thesis. Americans are well known for their choice of recondite subjects for theses, but I was ashamed that this learned couple should be the object of careful researches in Alabama, while I, who lived in their house, knew so little about them. I found that an excellent biographical sketch of them had been published in 1938 by the Cambridge University Press by Miss J. M. S. Tompkins, who had collected much new material from English sources. Naturally it was their late London career that interested her most; for me these few troubled years they spent in Bennettsbridge have by far the greatest appeal.

In those days it was possible for country gentlemen to see their lives in terms of classical analogy and imagery. It was easy enough for Irish landlords who left their latifundia to be administered by agents to picture their estates as 'rural retreats' to which they retired like Horace or Cicero from the cares of state to plant trees and study philosophy. They reflected on the vicissitudes of life, its inequalities and injustices, with a freedom that would have seemed to a later generation subversive and disloyal to their class. Henry Flood regarded his substantial estate nearby at Farmley, as 'Tusculum', where he relaxed from toil. He had amateur theatricals and lent his support to the revival of interest in the Celtic past. Griffith, though only an unsuccessful mill-owner with a bare 600 acres, modelled himself naturally on these philosophical grandees, calling his tours around his Bennettsbridge farm his 'Ambarvalia'.

Henry used to attend the Kilkenny assizes and watch with philosophical melancholy the procession of the condemned to the gallows. His contempt for worldly values was of a rather static and literary kind but there are many letters which show him to have been a kindly and original character. He had a peculiar variety of colic, which he treated with opium and horse radish emetic and once or twice with the 'Hygean waves of Scarborough'. When on a journey his agonies used to arouse so much exasperation and compassion in his fellow passengers that he forced himself to fast. Once at an inn he had three ginger-bread nuts and a pint of white wine and the landlord presented him with a bill for the full dinner. Griffith retaliated by going into the street and calling in an old beggar woman, to whom he insisted that the dinner which he had paid for but not eaten, should be served. 'She is my stomach,' he told the furious landlord.

Henry scarcely mentioned his employees or his factory. Before he purchased his machinery he paid a visit of inspection to Smyth's Linen Factory at Waterford and, for Frances' benefit, he tried to assimilate this revolutionary spectacle into his rational philosophy. In the mid-eighteenth century Chartism was still far off and machinery seemed capable of liberating Rational Man, a noble and exalted being, from his dependence on other living creatures. The animal nature, unlike machinery, 'through Caprice is capable of disappointing the Ends of its Creation'. Rational Man, Henry thought, would be made free to contemplate Truth and Beauty and to practise Morality and Religion. 'The Vulgar Herd, who are insensible to these advantages, I take to be more imperfect instruments than a Windmill or a Loom.'

There is no evidence that Henry and Frances were snobbish or insensitive employers. Henry at least was by no means fastidious in his intimacies. But it seemed to them that the higher pleasures were the fruits of the cultivated understanding and those to whom fortune had denied cultivation were of necessity barren and therefore uninteresting. We hear almost nothing about them.

Last autumn, watching a reaper and binder going round one of his fields with a couple of men accompanying it, I remembered how Henry used to sit among the stooks in a barley-field, writing to Frances and reading Pliny's *Letters*. Watching the binders and stackers, he counted forty-seven woman and fourteen men. Yet their lives were more remote from him than the lives of the ancient Romans. When his son was born, he wrote to Frances that if it *had* to be called Pliny he would prefer it to be named after the Younger Pliny than Pliny the Elder, since he would wish it endowed with liveliness rather than learning. Frances too liked to clothe her jokes and reflections in classical dress.

They had great skill in descriptive writing. How could the following account by Henry of a painted ceiling be bettered? 'A Fricassy of Cherubims with here a Head and there a Leg or an Arm, peeping through the Clouds, which look like a good, rich thick Sauce poured about them.'

They were wholly unpolitical people. I doubt whether it ever occurred to them that happiness could be brought about by social legislation. Happiness depended on the right ordering of life, on the enjoyment of rational delights, and the consolations afforded by wisdom and learning. In this system religion had an important function since it gave warmth to life, and Henry and Frances tinker with it experimentally like a pair of amateurs trying to coax heat out of an old-fashioned boiler. The principle on which it worked, they were aware, was Belief in God. This, Henry thought, was accessible to Protestants only. 'The popes of Rome,' he declared, 'by assuming to themselves the powers of Binding and Releasing, have long since superseded their God.' And at the request of a friend of his Henry wrote a strong letter denouncing the Errors of Rome and the Foulness of its Superstitions, its idle Forms and useless Ceremonies.

The occasion for this letter is remarkable. A Roman Catholic neighbour of Henry's had changed his religion in order to receive an estate valued at £700 per annum. He had been crushed by a letter 'all fire and brimstone' from a brother, who was a priest at Bordeaux, and he had asked Henry to compose a reply for him. Henry reproduces his reply of which he was evidently proud. It could only have been written in the Age of Reason, when a Rational Argument was a weapon which could be adapted to every circumstance. It can justify apostasy for £700 per annum and is equally formidable whether it comes from the brain of the apostate or the friend who impersonates him. Henry was too volatile to be called a humbug; he could not deceive himself for long. He was an experimentalist and would quickly have revolted against his own arguments if anyone had imposed them on him as dogma.

'Our Religion,' Henry wrote, 'is deduced from the plain Text of the Scriptures, yours from the sophistical Comments of the Priests. When a Priest once asked a Protestant, where his Religion was before Luther, he answered humorously but not less justly by asking him where was his Face before it was washed?'

He was as satisfied when his speculations led him to an orthodox conclusion as a patience player, when his patience comes out. Riding, once, towards the Castlecomer hills from Maidenhall, he saw the horizon flushed with fire so that he thought the coal seams were ablaze and that the whole earth was burning. He learnt from a passer-by that it was some natural exhalation of the healthy soil but he fell to meditating on the Last Conflagration which is prophesied in the Scriptures. At last it seemed to him that he had found a way of reconciling Religion and the Philosophy of Nature. His explanation is ingenious rather than convincing. It concerns the extra weight of the earth due to God's Creation of Living Things. Bodies attract in proportion to the weight of matter in them. The centripetal by degrees overcomes the centrifugal and the earth rushes into the sun. Hence the conflagration. About this argument Henry said rather smugly: 'As I am not quite orthodox, on some points, I own that I heartily rejoice when I can make amends on others.'

Henry believed in resurrection of the body, but he elaborated this sombre belief with private fancies of his own. He often meditated how his body could best be disposed of so that its elements could be converted into some other animate being or beings with the greatest speed and economy. Mummification he held in horror. 'I could not bear the Thought of lying a moment Idle, alive or dead.' Burning he could tolerate, provided it were not in an 'Asbesto Shroud'. But best of all, he said, 'I would choose to be devoured by Beasts, as by that means, I should more immediately become Part of Living Animals.' He preferred dogs and among dogs he chose a mastiff for its courage, a hound for its sagacity and a spaniel for its fidelity.

Even before his financial crash they were finding life in the countryside lonely and unsatisfying. When Frances was away, he now had no friend to console him for his absence at Maidenhall, save a 'low-spirited cat' called Sultana Puss. 'Her nerves,' he said, 'are so weak (which I attribute to her drinking tea in a morning without Eating), that the least loud Word sets her trembling; so that I dare not chide an awkward Housemaid for fear of putting Madam into her Hysterics.'

On his visits to country houses, Henry was continually affronted by the spectacle of 'bookless, sauntering Youth'. 'Before this century shall be closed,' he wrote, 'it is not impossible that anyone who can commit a Speech or a Sentence to Writing will pass for a Conjurer, who can paint his Thoughts on Paper.' And to Frances he wrote, 'Your Sense, your Principle and your Taste are thrown away upon the Deaf Adder and the very Seeds of them all stifled in the Growth or buried like a bad Ploughman's Grain by Clods of Earth laid over them.' In another letter he compares her writings 'to certain rich Essences which only affect the finest Capillaries'. Their neighbours were sociable enough but without fine capillaries and, thinking of their tedious visits, Henry said, 'Momus very justly found fault with the Construction of a House, because it had no Wheels to be moved by when the Situation became uneasy.'

At last Henry gave up Maidenhall, which he had loved so much. He told Frances how riding home from Dublin, when his decision was made, his impatience to see it grew at every mile. 'The thoughts of quitting it have the more attendered me towards it. If I thought there was a Naiad or a Dryad in the Place who would lament my absence, I should sacrifice my Interests to my Superstition; but my Religion teaches me that wherever we go our Guardian Angel accompanies us. I think I but obey its Call whenever I change my Situation to my Advantage.'

The Griffiths often indulged romantic dreams but they held them under control, submitting themselves constantly to calm and ruthless examination. It is rumoured that their marriage ended in separation, but, even if this were true, I doubt whether either of them would have considered it an ill-advised marriage. Continually at every stage they had tested the flavour of their relationship and found it good. It can only have been the dregs that they jettisoned.

But his marriage was still recent and wholly satisfying when Henry left Maidenhall. He must have felt that a turning-point in his life had been reached and that a rather more solemn self analysis than he had hitherto attempted should be undertaken. On leaving the house he made a will in favour of Frances and her infant son and wrote upon the wrapper the reasons for his marriage and his theological beliefs.

I was not overreached into this Match by Art nor hurried into it by Passion, but, from long experience of her Sense and Worth, I reasoned myself into it... I found that I had so engaged her Affections that no other Man could make her happy and so dallied with her Character, that only myself could repair it... I am in my Religion a Christian; but of the Arian heresy as it is stiled by bigotted Councils. I was for many years a Deist, till Dr. Clayton, Bishop of Clogher, his Essay on Spirit and subsequent Writings on the same Subject had reconciled the doctrine of the Trinity to human reason and metaphysical science.

> Humanum est errare et nescire;
> Ens Entium, misere mei.

Last year the Nore flooded, as it so often does, and flattened out the remaining wall of Griffith's flaxmill, which has been used for some generations as a boundary fence. The mill-stream has long been choked up and it was only quite lately that poking about on the banks of the river I found traces of its stone-built sides. The cottages that housed the mill-hands as well as the sixty-one harvesters have gone without trace, but the elm trees which Henry planted are still standing. As for Maidenhall, it has not changed very much; its successive owners have always been poor and never had the money to make many of those lavish improvements which were admired in Victorian times.

[1950]

BESIDE THE NORE

I have lived for most of my life on the Nore and own three fields upon its banks, some miles before it turns to the south-east and forces its way under Brandon Hill to join the Barrow above New Ross. In sixty years it has changed remarkably little. From a top window, looking across the river towards Blackstairs and Mount Leinster, I can still see the same stretch of cornfields, nut groves and mountain slopes. Beside the woods of Summerhill and Kilfane I can spot the round tower of Tullaherin and Kilbline, the sixteenth-century castle of the Shortalls. There is only one new cottage in sight.

This does not mean that we stagnate. The landscape is domestic and life is mainly prosperous but it has edged away from the rivers. The Nore, which traverses the county of Kilkenny, and passes through the city, and the Barrow, which skirts its eastern border, and all their tributaries gave up work and took to an easy life about a century ago. The mill wheels stopped turning and the roofs fell in on the millworkers' cottages, flags and duck-weed and king-cups choked the mill race and there is so much tranquil beauty around that some hope and many fear that the tourist agencies will soon discover us.

A century ago there were twenty-two flour mills, three large distilleries and four breweries on the Nore between Durrow and Inistioge. But industry had left the rivers long before I was born and as children we were constantly driving donkey carts down little lanes to riverside ruins beside which we bathed and fished and picnicked. And every ruin had its story and the tradition that these stories are worth recording, correcting, analysing has never died out.

Our riverside ruins are mostly not depressing, for many of their founders were original and complex men, whose lives gave evidence that vision and ingenuity can flourish here. Some of their industries did not survive them for long. They subsided gracefully after a generation or two but, like the flowers of summer, were fertile in their decay. Various economic causes can be alleged for their failure but often there is nothing to be said except that men grow old and have bored or stupid sons and that today there are many prosperous industries which would be more admirable as ruins covered with valerian and wild wall flowers.

One of our favourite picnic places was Annamult Woollen Factory, a very stylish and spacious ruin on the King's river just before it joins the Nore. Before the king-cups and the bullocks took over, it was in 1814 one of the most progressive factories in the British Isles. Its owners, Messrs Shaw and Nowlan, rivalled Robert Owen, the Utopian industrialist, in their concern for their 400 work people. The children all had free schooling and lesson books, their fathers and mothers had health insurance cards, and every Sunday they danced to the fiddle in the large courtyard. George Shaw and Timothy Nowlan were stern but just, and rather quizzical. (Shaw was, I believe, a great great uncle to George Bernard.) Employees who misbehaved were punished but not sacked. Sometimes the offender, dressed in a yellow jacket, was obliged to roll a stone round the courtyard in full view of the Sunday merrymakers. The factory, while it lasted, was hugely successful. The Prince Regent and all the employees of the Royal Dublin Society dressed themselves in its woollens and the fields around Annamult were white with a flock of 600 Merino sheep, vast bundles of wool with tiny faces, which the Prims, a famous Kilkenny family with Spanish relations, had imported from Spain.

The Marble Works at Maddoxtown, below Kilkenny, is another beautiful spot with proud memories. Children still hunt about among the loose strife and the willow herb for polished slabs, green Connemara, pink Midleton, and Kilkenny which is black with white flecks. William Colles, who invented special machinery for cutting and polishing by water power, was so clever that his neighbours thought him a necromancer. He almost succeeded in making dogs weave linen by turning wheels, and he invented an instrument, like an Aeolian harp, which played tunes as it floated down the Nore. His house and his manager's house, which face each other across the Bennettsbridge road, are still among the pleasantest of the old houses that decorate the banks of the Nore. Colles was a philosophical man; he wrote tragedies and to remind himself of the 'lapse of time' he had his portrait painted every seven years. His business had prospered in adversity for it was during the Napoleonic Wars, when foreign marble ceased to be imported, that he was able to flood the English market with his chimney pieces, punch bowls, buffets and vases. Then metal mantelpieces arrived and a few years ago all the blocks of marble that littered the river bank were bought by a firm which pounded them into a variegated paste, from which ten chimney pieces could be made as easily as Colles made one.

Maidenhall lies between Annamult and the Marble Works and the Griffiths, who lived there 230 years ago, were such an original couple that I have written of them separately. There are many beautiful little towns along the Nore, but since 'each man kills the thing he loves' it is perhaps unsafe to admire them. Their beauty depends on hump-backed bridges and winding streets and large trees, all of which obstruct the motorist in his race to progress. The curves of the bridge are now being straightened with cement but often you can see the great stone slabs of the parapet jutting out of the stream below the bridge.

All these little towns should have had their chroniclers, for one chronicler attracts another and a village, conscious of its history, can resist the tyranny of the government official. The Nore has not been as lucky as the Barrow. I am sure that it was the O'Learys, hereditary scribes and bakers of Graiguenamanagh on the Barrow, who attracted Sean O'Faolain to the village in 1945. As editor of *The Bell*[1] he stayed there for a week and studied the town as a good teacher studies a child. How did it begin, how was it going to develop? He found that it had been started by Wiltshire monks, planted there by the Normans. For generations they had adhered to their English ways, but had finally become assimilated. At the time of the Reformation the last Abbot was one of the Kavanaghs and their descendants still own the beautiful woods along the river bank at Borris. O'Faolain made a transparent map of the town, marking all its shops and dwellings and offices and laid it over an outline map of the old Cistercian Abbey. You can see how O'Leary's Bakery crept over the cloisters, how the refectory became a Corn Store, and Denny's Pig Scales took over the monks' cemetery. Everything changes, yet there is a core of continuity. O'Faolain traces how the very same processes which eliminated typhus in Graig and gave fresh water, sanitation and medical care, also almost destroyed the town. When the railways brought 'civilization', the bargees, the canal workers and the local craftsmen all became superfluous and got on the trains themselves. In 1841 there were 2248 inhabitants, and in 1945 there were 844. And now? Are charabancs likely to be more beneficent than the railways?

If Inistioge on the Nore is one of the loveliest of Irish villages, much of the credit is due to William Tighe of Woodstock, the large house, whose ruins lay till recently on the hill above it. For anyone who wants to know about the Nore and the Barrow, his work, *A Statistical Survey of the County Kilkenny, 1802*, is still indispensable. It has never been surpassed and never will be, because the tribe to which he and Colles and Griffith belonged, the rural polymaths, is now extinct. Tighe was a classical scholar, an archaeologist, an economist, a sociologist, a politician (a passionate opponent of the Union). He knew the names of all the flowers and all the fish of the two valleys of the Nore and the Barrow, in English, Irish and Latin, and the price of potatoes in Goresbridge in 1798 and how many 'unlicensed tippling houses' there were in Inistioge in 1800 (twenty-eight). He was a humane man and soberly recalls how melons and pineapples could be bought in Kilkenny while the poor children of Iverk went to school 'almost naked'.

He wrote a poem in four cantos called 'The Plants' about the Oak, the Rose, the Palm and the Vine. In the manner of Virgil's *Georgics* it is intended to be diverting as well as instructive. There are 150 pages of notes in Greek, Latin, Hebrew, French and Italian, and he lists 39 species of oak. He was specially interested in the oaks of Mamre, where Abraham, Isaac and Jacob were buried, and he built a small house near Woodstock in an oak grove and called it Mamre, the name by which it is still known.

His eighteenth-century archaeology once collided sensationally with the less adventurous kind which grew out of it. On Tory Hill, in south Kilkenny, there was a large stone slab inscribed with words which he copied scrupulously on a page of his *Statistical Survey* and interpreted as BELI DIVOSE.

(ELI CIVO)Ǝ

He deduced from this that Baal and Dionysus were worshipped in Early Ireland. Nearly a generation later John O'Donovan, who was working on the Ordnance Survey, came up with a different explanation. He found people alive in Mullinavat who remembered hearing of Ned Connick, the carpenter, and how he had climbed up Tory Hill and carved his name on an ancient block of stone which had later been turned over.

Tighe had copied the inscription so conscientiously that it is only necessary to turn his page upside down and, making allowances for the roughness of the stone and Ned Connick's illiteracy, you can easily read:

ECONIC 1731

William Tighe's sister-in-law, Mary Tighe, whose effigy by Flaxman is housed behind the church at Inistioge, wrote a long poem called 'Psyche', or the Legend of Love. She died young but, published after her death, 'Psyche' received considerable critical admiration. It is based on the story of Apuleius about the love of Cupid and Psyche.

The burning of Woodstock House, the home of poetry and learning, in 1922, was one of the saddest of Ireland's tragedies. But the beautiful plantations survived and there is scarcely in all Ireland a more charming walk than that which runs below the ruins along the Nore. On one side the river with its swans and water lilies, on the other the wooded cliffs and mossy glades sprinkled with ferns and frochans and foxgloves.

When I was young there were plenty of river picnics and neighbours visited each other by cot (long flat-bottomed boats which were used for net-fishing). It was every boy and girl's dream to take a cot to Inistioge, where the river becomes tidal. My brother and I once got as far as Thomastown and then our patience ran out and we walked to Inistioge and spent the night at a small hotel. There was a large stuffed white rabbit on a chest of drawers and at dawn we awoke scratching and observed two columns of insects advancing on us from the rabbit.

The hotel turned into a pub and small shops have come and gone but Inistioge is still the most beautiful and peaceful of villages. Not long ago I was sitting on a bench beside the bridge waiting for my grandchildren to come down the river by canoe from Maidenhall. I remember the red valerian, a broad bank of colour reflected on the dappled current. In such a place time stands still. The past comes close in disconnected fragments and I was thinking of the days when we were children and had dancing classes with the young Tighes at the Noreview Hotel in Thomastown; their mother, with my Aunt Harriet, used to run a Christian Science Reading Room opposite the Castle in Kilkenny, two spiders into whose web no fly ever came, and I remember when we went to Woodstock a side-car used to meet us at Thomastown station and the branches of the trees brushed our faces as we drove along.

The Tighes were friendly charming people who did not deserve the misfortunes that happened to them. When the war broke out Captain Tighe took his family to London, where he met his death in an accident that has never fully been explained. I do not believe they ever returned. In the spring of 1920 the Black and Tans took over Woodstock and patrolled the country at breakneck speed in their Crossley tenders. Then the Treaty came and they left as rapidly as they had come. It was an empty, undefended house that was finally destroyed.

Later in the afternoon an old man came and sat beside me, and I asked him what it was like when the Tans were in Woodstock. He was very ready to talk and afterwards I wrote down what he told me.

They were in the village too [he said] and we had them in the house next door to us. They weren't too bad. They made us have a notice on all the doors with the names of the people in the house. I remember there was a young chap, Ned Brennan, maybe eight or nine, and they stuck him up on the pub counter and asked him to sing, and he sang 'Wrap the Green Flag Around Me'! He was a young chap, you see, and it was one of the songs he'd learnt. But the Tans just laughed and filled his pockets with pennies. When he came home his mother was very angry and said it was 'blood money' and wouldn't let him keep it.

The Tans had two spies going round the village [he went on] and didn't fourteen of our chaps chase after them so that the two jumped into the river. And our chaps shot one of them and the other got out and ran back to Woodstock to tell the Tans. And after that didn't the Tans burn O'Hanrahans' farm, oh, a big place with cow-sheds and barns and hay ricks. And they did nothing to save old Mrs Hanrahan from burning, till Mrs Newport of Ballygallon – she was an Englishwoman – came and blamed them for not getting her out, and they got her out and she took her to her own place.

I have always believed that local history is more important than national history. There should be an archive in every village, where stories such as the old man told me are recorded. Where life is fully and consciously lived in our own neighbourhood, we are cushioned a little from the impact of great far-off events which should be of only marginal concern to us.

[1984]

1. O'Faolain founded *The Bell* in 1940. It published the best in Irish fiction, poetry and journalism, and led the struggle against censorship. With a break from April 1948 to November 1950, it continued publication until 1955. Contributors included Peadar O'Donnell (editor from 1946), Austin Clarke, Elizabeth Bowen, Oliver St John Gogarty, Patrick Kavanagh and Flann O'Brien. Hubert Butler was review editor under O'Donnell's editorship, and has written about the journal in '*The Bell*: An Anglo-Irish View', *Escape from the Anthill*, pp. 147–52.

THE DESERTED SUN PALACE[1]

The empty but still imposing shell of Desart Court stands at a crossroads a few miles from Callan in the County Kilkenny. This noble Georgian house was burnt in 1923, rebuilt and finally dismantled a few years ago. The Land Commission is prepared to make the shell safe and sound if any established society will take charge of it. The guardianship would be for many years to come a negligible responsibility, yet at present there is no association, either local or metropolitan, able to undertake it. A century ago the old Kilkenny Archaeological Society took abbeys and castles under its protection with the most matter-of-fact assurance, but nowadays we who live in the country, partly from modesty, partly from habit, look to Dublin for guidance and Dublin societies mostly have their hands full and can help us little. There is a danger that this fine fabric will disappear into road material.

Desart Court in its present form covers only a small plot of land and harms no one. Its avenues have been turned into roads which cross beside the house, and the huge brick-walled garden which faces it has reverted painlessly into an enclosed field and orchard. Its woods have been thinned but not devastated and are still lovely. The whole scene might be allowed to stay as it is for a few generations at least, like a rather dim but adequate illustration in a textbook of local history, recent as well as remote, for the Cuffes of Desart, who are now all gone, were active till the last.

They had been in Ireland before Cromwell, but one Joseph Cuffe distinguished himself in the service of the Protector and obtained lands that had previously belonged to the Norman family of Comerford, which had backed the royalist and Catholic side. The Cuffe history for a generation was true to pattern. They were successful opportunists, turning from republicans to monarchists, from Stuarts to Hanoverians, when the suitable moment arrived. The Comerfords, who had been more consistent, were never allowed to interfere with them. Their only

35

rivals were the Flood family of Farmley, from whom Henry Flood the orator was descended. With them they had a feud, which led to duels and lawsuits and even murders about the political representation of the borough of Callan.

Yet very early on the Cuffes showed signs of a generous, independent outlook and within the narrow limits of class loyalty they did their best. When the refugees from a tyrannical government in Geneva decided to build a town on the Waterford coast which was to become a centre of liberty, industry and enlightenment, a Cuffe was one of the principal Irish promoters of the scheme. But on second thoughts the British government of the time suddenly decided that it would be unwise to introduce rebellious and republican Genevans into this disaffected region. After Cuffe had superintended the laying of the foundation stone, the plan was shelved and the Genevans stayed at home. (See 'New Geneva in Waterford', *Escape from the Anthill*, pp. 25ff.)

There is much about the life of the Cuffes in the late eighteenth century in Dorothea Herbert's fascinating reminiscences. Her visits from Carrick to her uncle and aunt at Desart brought her into touch with the lively society which existed for some twenty years in Kilkenny during and before the Napoleonic Wars. The Desarts were highly temperamental. You can read how Lord Desart's daughter, Mrs Cooke, mourning for her husband, painted all the flowerpots black, reupholstered the furniture in sable and tarred the stables, turning an elderly visitor's white horse piebald for which he flogged the yard-boy. I wonder if the ill-omened portrait of John, Lord Desart was burnt in 1923? According to Miss Herbert it was painted with poisonous paint and the artist lost his sight, and Lord Desart and the three pets who were portrayed with him all succumbed to different diseases. His lordship died of a violent fever, the two dogs also perished and his fine horse was never any good after this fatal picture was painted. Lord Desart's end was so sudden and so much deplored that his funeral procession lasted for three miles.

They went in for high-spirited and rather callous practical jokes in those days.

One day at Desart Mr Hamilton Cuffe, who was teazingly nice dressed, took the Parson's Nose of a Duck for himself and she, my cousin Lucy, knowing his foible, laid her finger on it. A fit of romping took place, which ended in a serious Quarrel and violent Hystericks on her part. This was no sooner over than my Uncles affronted me by recommending Mrs Jephson as a Stepmother, if anything happened to my Mother. This threw Mama and her daughter into Hystericks and all the Servants in the House were dispatched for remedies before our Sobs could be abated. Many freaks passed at Desart that time which I now forget.

There is or was in Desart woods a famous oak claiming, like many others, to be the oldest in Ireland and it may well have been part of the ancient Irish forests. The woods have never been better described than by Humphrey O'Sullivan, the Callan schoolmaster, who wrote a diary in Irish twenty years after Dorothea's time, when Desart woods were being replanted.

I went to Desart by the same roads which I took on Easter Friday. We walked through dark evergreen pinewoods, through fine lane-ways, now crooked, now straight, shaded from the face of the sun, listening to the fluting of the lark in the way-side meadows. We went through Derrymore, through the Lord's Plantations, skipping like goats through Derreen to the fish-ponds of Desart. The landscape from this beautiful sun-palace is exquisite: a gaseous exhalation came from the sun, the mountains to the south were dark blue. Ballykeefe Hill near us to the north was newly planted and so was Knocknarah and all around us sheltering oak and ash and meadows smooth as silk and green as corn grass. . . . The sky was cloudless save for one cloudlet adding to its beauty as a dimple to a damsel's chin. . . . Slieve na man cloudless, Mount Leinster and the other mountains to the east reclining on a couch of fog, raising their heads and nodding to the sun like a gentle young bride to her husband. It is in the heart of this valley that the head-mound and capital city of Ireland ought to be.

There seems to have been an unbridgeable gulf between the accomplished and benevolent Cuffes and the people of whom Humphrey O'Sullivan was the informative and sensitive interpreter. He is a remarkable figure with his home-made education and his passionate loyalty to the last remnants of the Irish traditions and language which he knew to be dying. Much of O'Sullivan's huge diary is uninteresting and repetitive, yet it is easy to believe that he had in him some seed of truth, some zest for life, which in a less unhappy and divided society would have flowered into poetry and prose of a high order.

Yet a deep pessimism undermined and discoloured all his thoughts. Everything he wrote was perishable for the language in which he wrote it was rapidly being outlawed. Little by little he had to renounce that dim hope which sustains the solitary writer, of being understood at least by posterity. It is not unnatural that he should often break into bitter railing, finding his sole consolation in the thought that rich and poor, oppressor and oppressed, are all equally doomed.

He may have been thinking of Desart Court, 'that beautiful sun-palace', when he wrote:

What is the good of repining? The bright walled castles will disappear and the glittering sun-palaces, the earth form elemental, the entire universe like a wisp-blaze. Will it be long till this Irish language in which I am writing goes too? Fine big school houses are daily being built to teach in them this new language, the Saxon tongue. But, alas, no attention is being paid to the fine smooth Irish tongue, except by wretched Swaddlers, who are trying to see whether they can wheedle away the children of the Gael to their accursed new religion.*

The Swaddlers to whom he refers were a group of earnest Evangelicals who appeared in Kilkenny at this time and made war simultaneously on what they considered the frivolity of the Protestants and the idolatry of the Catholics. They learnt the Irish language and to propagate their views they tried to interrupt the Kilkenny theatre season and were denounced by the Protestant bishop.

O'Sullivan would certainly have been surprised if he had known that when the fate which he foresaw had overtaken the Irish language in Kilkenny, it would be one of the Cuffes of Desart who would try to revive it. The story of Otway Cuffe and his sister-in-law ought to be told because of its interest as well as its sadness. Though it happened for the most part only a generation ago, it already seems to be of another age. Yet it belongs, like the shell of Desart Court, to the shifting pattern of Irish history, and should not be forgotten.

Lately, an exhibition, organized by the National Museum, paused for a short spell in Kilkenny Castle. It was called 'the Landed Gentry' and in Dublin it was advertised by a poster of a smart lady in a top hat and hunting kit† jumping over a bill of eviction. The show was full of fascinating items, orders for footmen's livery and for the stocking of wine-cellars and imperious instructions to farm labourers and tenants on the great estates. In order to be fair, reports of Clothing Funds were included and a note that Daniel O'Connell was also a land-owner with an estate of 30,000 acres. Yet the general impression was created that the Anglo-Irish had been, contrary to what Yeats had said, a Petty People, whose main concern had been horses and rents.

There were a few mistakes (e.g. Sheestown, a small estate near

---

* Some have compared this to Prospero's monologue in *The Tempest*:
'Our revels now are ended, .../The cloud-capped towers, the gorgeous palaces,/The solemn temples, the great globe itself,/Yea, all which it inherit, shall dissolve/And, like this insubstantial pageant faded,/Leave not a rack behind. We are such stuff/As dreams are made on, and our little life/Is rounded with a sleep.'
† In fact, a photograph of Lady Clonbrock, best known as organizer of the Clonbrock and Castlegar Poultry Co-operative, which with associated home industries and crafts, outlasted all similar rural cooperatives and only died in 1952. See Patrick Bolger, *Irish Co-operative Movement*, p. 287, for a different photograph of her.

Kilkenny, where Otway Cuffe had lived, was wrongly located in Co. Waterford), but it represented well enough the skeletal structure of a civilization outwardly as dead in Ireland as that of the Hapsburgs in Bohemia. If there had been more than a spark of life left today, surely some voice of protest would have spoken of the Grattans, Floods, Edgeworths, Parnells, Plunketts and a thousand others, who had built that Anglo-Irish civilization, which is still, battered and hiding behind a Eurocratic façade with neo-Gaelic trimmings, unchangingly ours. It is only the heirs of those who created it who are doomed. J. C. Beckett in his fine book, *The Anglo-Irish Tradition*, declared that in the Anglo-Irish community even the will to survive appeared to be fading and predicted that, before the end of the century, Protestantism, their prevailing religion, would be virtually extinct in the Republic.

In the exhibition there was a photograph of the fourth Earl of Desart and his Countess who lived at Desart Court near Kilkenny. It was taken from a London illustrated paper and the caption under Lady Desart's picture explained that she had 'a good seat on a horse' and tackled 'Pat's fences' with the same grace with which she rode in Rotten Row. There followed a humorous story of how she tricked 'Land-Leaguer Pat', who had thrown stones at the fox-hounds, into playing 'God Save the Queen' on his harmonica.

I knew Lady Desart when I was young and she was old and she was not in the least like that. She was a plump and plain little Jewess with high intelligence and spirit, a guttural voice and very strong pince-nez. She would have looked ridiculous on a horse, though she may have pretended to like them because her husband, whom she loved, was MFH and had even written a novel called *The Honourable Ella of Foxshire*. He died in 1898 and was succeeded by his brother, a distinguished London barrister, and there was then no longer any need for his widow to model herself on the Honourable Ella. As she was very rich, she felt free to follow her own ideas or rather those of her youngest brother-in-law, Otway Cuffe, who was a disciple of a well-known writer, Standish O'Grady. Cuffe had led a wandering life outside Ireland, but when he realized that he was likely to succeed his brother as sixth Earl of Desart, he had, under O'Grady's influence, begun to take very seriously his responsibility to his country.

Of O'Grady, whom the Cuffes had brought to Kilkenny, W. B. Yeats was later to write: 'Whatever should come out of Ireland in the future will owe itself to two books, O'Grady's *Bardic History of Ireland* and Ferguson's *Poems*.' The *Bardic History*, in George Dangerfield's words, released Cuchullain and the other heroes of the Ulster Cycle from the grip of a scholarship, which had preserved the Irish myth, like a splendid fly in a kind of philological amber.

'In O'Grady's writings,' said AE, 'the submerged river of national culture rose up again, a shining torrent. It was he who made me conscious and proud of my country... He was the last champion of the Irish aristocracy and spoke to them of their duty to the nation as a fearless prophet might speak to a council of degenerate princes.'

When in 1898 Cuffe urged O'Grady to take over *The Kilkenny Moderator*, the Unionist and Protestant weekly, from Mr Lawlor, the Editor, who had to look after a sick brother in Bournemouth, nobody but he could guess the storms this dynamic character might precipitate in a stagnant community. All that Mr Lawlor knew of O'Grady was reassuring. He wrote in his valedictory editorial:

Mr O'Grady is among the first rank of the Irish gentry; he is first cousin to Lord Gort, second cousin to the present Viscount Guillamore and near relation to the Persses of Roxborough, the Wallers of Castletown Waller...

Then followed more names of distinguished families all of which have long disappeared and a list of medals and other distinctions he had won at Trinity.

Furthermore, Professor Lecky of Trinity and Lord Castletown of Upper Ossory have subscribed to bring over an eminent artist from England to paint his picture.

What could be more reassuring than this? In fact, the portrait was by an Irishman, John Butler Yeats, W. B.'s father, and O'Grady, though a fervent champion of the 'Landed Gentry', was also one of their most savage critics.

In one of his books which few in Ireland could have read, he had addressed the leaders of Anglo-Ireland in the manner of Carlyle.

Your ancestors who raised the noble classical buildings of Dublin loved a classical quotation, but could one in twenty of you translate the most hackneyed Latin tag in a newspaper? Christ save us all! You read nothing, you know nothing. You are totally resourceless and stupid... England has kept you like Strasburg geese which are kept until they can hardly stand without support and so slow and sleepy that they are scarcely aware when they are killed. As I write, the Protestant Anglo-Irish, who once owned all Ireland from the centre to the sea, is rotting from the land in the most dismal farce-tragedy of all time, without one brave deed, without one brave word.

He predicted that unless they could

reshape themselves in a heroic mould there would be anarchy and civil war, which might end in a shabby, sordid Irish Republic, ruled by corrupt politicians and the ignoble rich,

and he told them that they gibed at Ireland and everything Irish:

What native, I ask you, with the spirit of a rabbit would bear forever such an aristocracy as ours?... Yet bad as you are you are still the best class we have. You are individually brave and honourable men and do not deserve the doom which even the blindest can see approaching.

You are hated to an extent you can only dimly conceive. The nation is united against you. In your hands the Irish nation once lay like soft wax ready to take any impression you chose and out of it you have moulded a Frankenstein which will destroy you.[2]

As Editor of *The Kilkenny Moderator*, with Otway Cuffe and Lady Desart behind him, he maintained for two years a highly original provincial newspaper. Mr Lawlor, like most provincial editors, had flattered his readers. O'Grady challenged them.

He looked to the Ormondes for a lead, for in one of his books he had recalled the centuries of struggle during which they had built up their princedom.

Love, labour, sorrow and fighting, consultations many with the wise, close intense study of the characters of men, recruitments and dismissals innumerable before a Butler could write the proud title 'Capitanus Suae Nationis', have a nation of which to be captain and a territory on which to sustain his nation.

And he asserted that only by dedication like this could the Anglo-Irish recover the authority which was their due. Only under their guidance could Ireland be true to her history, part Gaelic, part Norse, part Norman, part Scottish, part English, but distinctively Irish and united. He was supported by all those writers, most of them Anglo-Irish, who had created the Abbey Theatre and the Literary Revival and by the Gaelic League, at that time a non-political and non-sectarian body, whose president and founder, Douglas Hyde, was, like Standish O'Grady, a rector's son. Many of them wrote for *The Moderator*.

When O'Grady came to Kilkenny the landed gentry were still outwardly at least immensely influential. The Ormonde supremacy was securely based on history. In the muniment-room of Kilkenny Castle one of the greatest collections of historical documents in the British Isles still survived. In drawers and pigeon holes were charters heavy with the wax seals of the Plantagenets, the title-deeds of monasteries that had long been dissolved and of kindred families that had been dispossessed by Cromwell or William of Orange. There were still Van Dycks, Lelys and Knellers in the Gallery.

The Ormondes had never seemed more splendid. The third Marquess and his wife had just been visited by the Duke and Duchess of York (later George V and Mary), and were shortly to receive Edward VII and Alexandra; they had been to Potsdam and the Kaiser had given Lord Ormonde the Order of the Crown of Prussia, First Class. Socially the Desarts ran them close, for the fifth Countess was later to be sister-in-law to the Princess Royal. They were all good landlords and because of the Irish love of sport they seemed to be very popular, and even though the genius of the first Duke (1610–88) and his capable son may have trickled away in Hanoverian times down obscure branches, the Ormondes still brought a breath of majesty and feudalism to puppy shows and agricultural gatherings. They had it in their power to drape ordinariness, even their own, with some of the glamour of the Middle Ages. It is unlikely that any of these people had ever heard of O'Grady.

His first year in Kilkenny was the centenary of the '98 rebellion and there were processions to commemorate a Wexford man called Hammond who had been executed in the town for manufacturing pikes. In demolishing an old house a pike was found in the wainscoting. It was regarded as an omen and it was urged that it be put in the Tholsel (town-hall) in place of Gladstone's bust. But O'Grady maintained, in *The Moderator*, that the date to celebrate was not 1798 but 1782, for it was then that the Volunteers had assembled at Dungannon in Ulster and had extorted from England those concessions which had made Grattan's Parliament possible. The Commander-in-Chief of the Volunteers had been an Ulsterman, 'the Good Lord Charlemont', and Irishmen of all creeds and classes had, for the first time, been united for a single purpose.

Now, O'Grady maintained, an analogous situation had developed. In 1782 the Volunteers had seized their opportunity, because England was at war with France and welcomed their offer to defend the Irish shores. In 1898 England was at war with the Boers. O'Grady, in *The Moderator*, refused to speak on the moral aspect of this war; all he saw in it was an opportunity for raising a new national army. If such a force were mustered now, the two opposing factions in Ireland could unite for the defence of Ireland, and Dublin would quickly take the lead from Kilkenny as once it had taken it from Dungannon. Thirty thousand British troops, which were garrisoning Ireland, could be relieved for service in the Cape.★

★ On the eve of the First World War, Sir Horace Plunkett made a similar proposal for the conversion of the two private armies of the North and South into units of a Territorial Army.

O'Grady, looking round Kilkenny for some military potential uncom-
mitted to Boer or Briton, had to overlook the Kilkenny Militia and the
local branch of the Irish Brigade, who were drilling to fight each other
in the Transvaal; he could see nothing but those two embryonic armies,
the Catholic Boys Brigade and the Protestant Church Lads Brigade, and
that phantom of a cavalry force, the Kilkenny Foxhounds. He managed
to collect recruits from the two boys' brigades and got Otway Cuffe, a
former army officer and equerry to the king, to drill them. He said
prophetically, 'If we do not act now, a very dangerous class of men will
take over the drill financed from the other side of the Atlantic. Our
natural leaders, the Irish Gentry, must step forward and lead.'

O'Grady saw another way in which the Irish people could rally round
those whom they had formerly revered. The Childers Report had
revealed that since 1880 Ireland had been overtaxed by £250,000,000
and it was calculated that of this sum Kilkenny County had been annually
overtaxed by £135,000. A Financial Relations Committee had been
formed with a Kilkenny branch under the leadership of Lord Ormonde.
They had met in the Courthouse and O'Grady had declared that if the
Anglo-Irish headed the crusade for financial justice, they could once
more become the legitimate representatives of the people. Men of education and breeding could still, as in the past, influence the destinies of
their country. There must be no delay.

But the committee members had other things to attend to and in the
autumn O'Grady wrote,

Of the sixty Kilkenny gentlemen, who trotted down High Street en route for
Knockroe last Monday, every man is a member of the Financial Relations
Committee, yet it has never met since its appointment 11 months ago. What
artillery can ever penetrate our subterhuman torpor?*

Yet O'Grady and Cuffe were not discouraged. To advertise and pay
for their new volunteers they started a gymnasium and club, and there
were frequent concerts at which Irish songs and dances alternated with
gymnastic displays.

O'Grady believed in reviving in each county all the old cultural
societies and industrial enterprises, which had been killed by the cen-

---

* Yeats in this way, explained in his autobiography their strange apathy: 'Landlord
committees were formed in every county and Lord Castletown made a famous speech
declaring that Ireland must imitate the Colonists, who flung the tea into Boston Harbour.
Protestant Ireland had immense prestige, almost every name sung in modern song had
been Protestant. Yet they lacked hereditary passion and whatever corporate action was
attempted, the show however gallant it seemed, was soon over.'

tralizing policy that had followed the Union. He was proud that *The Kilkenny Moderator*, Protestant, Conservative, Anglo-Irish, was the first significant Irish paper to print a weekly Irish lesson. Soon they started in Kilkenny a branch of the Gaelic League with Cuffe as President.*
Douglas Hyde, invited down to address the Gaelic League, told his audience that no Act of Parliament could bring them a national identity. They themselves must create a cultural uniqueness strong enough to resist the pull of sectarian and political fanaticism and to rescue them from the ocean of vulgarity in which the English press was submerging them.

Lady Desart here interposed that her own people, the Jews, had revived a forgotten language and were using it to bind together the disparate branches of her race.

Cuffe referred to the ancient Irish system, which was patriarchal, regional, communal. Though primitive, it contained in itself the germ of a society happier than ours. To help our neighbour should not be a duty but a love: 'As for myself, if I devoted all my thoughts and hopes to my near surroundings the field would still be far larger than I could cover. Yet I could do more for my country if I kept to this field than spread myself over the universe.'

It was a time of excitement and hope, which was suddenly arrested by what was called the County Scandal, a war between the Ormondes and the Desarts. This became of more interest to the Kilkenny citizens than the Boer War itself and, maybe, it had more significance for them.

Here is the story: The Colonel of the Kilkenny Militia, the popular and sporting Charlie Gore (this is not his real name), had been the fourth Earl of Desart's agent and it had been discovered on Lord Desart's death that he had appropriated £6000 belonging to the family. Charlie Gore's family, a much respected one, had paid what was owing and Charlie, though dismissed, was not taken to court. Then, as time passed, he saw an opportunity of clearing his name. The missing money, he said, had really been owed to him by Lord Desart, an unpaid racing debt. To save Lord Desart's reputation he had adjusted the matter himself.

Lady Desart and her two brothers-in-law reacted strongly. Not being

---

* They were following in an old local tradition, for Henry Flood of Farmley, near Desart Court, the great orator of Grattan's Parliament, had in his will left most of his fortune for the foundation at Trinity College of a chair in Irish history and language and the purchase of all Irish manuscripts. The Kilkenny Archaeological Society, whose aims were even broader, was founded in 1848 and rapidly became the most famous provincial archaeological society in the British Isles. The founders were the Rector of Ennisnag, a Kilkenny parish priest and a predecessor of O'Grady's as editor of the local Unionist paper. It was a disaster for Ireland that Flood's relations successfully contested his will.

litigious people, they persuaded their friend, O'Grady, to print a letter telling the true facts in *The Moderator*. In this letter Ellen, Lady Desart, called the Colonel a 'thief' and challenged him to sue her for libel. The Colonel, after a long delay, had contemptuously replied that the matter had been settled up long ago by reference to the Lord Chancellor, the Commander of the Forces and the Marquess of Ormonde. The fifth Lord Desart had then replied that the Lord Chancellor had assured him that he had made no enquiry at all and, if the Marquess and the Commander of the Forces had given a decision, they had done so without reference to a single member of the family against whom the offence had been committed. The Cuffes demanded that the Colonel be relieved of his responsibilities as a magistrate and the command of the Kilkenny Militia.

O'Grady accompanied the letter with an angry editorial and Lord Ormonde, already enraged that this upstart journalist had dared to reprove him and his friends for their neglect of the Financial Relations Committee, decided to reinstate the Colonel as publicly as he could.

When the Bishop, Dr Crozier, asked Lord Ormonde as Lieutenant of the County to review the Church Lads Brigade in the large grounds behind the Palace, he had brought the Colonel with him as ADC and at a suitable moment asked the Colonel to step forward and address the boys. The Colonel spoke and the Bishop replied, 'in terms', wrote O'Grady, 'of eulogy and approbation'. (The Bishop was later to say that he was not addressing the Man but the Office and that he had not invited the Colonel to the Palace.)

O'Grady was beside himself. All the pillars of society, which he had hoped to strengthen, the Church, the aristocracy, the army and, worst of all, the Butlers, appeared to be collapsing. He rushed to his desk and wrote a scorching editorial. He concluded:

Now for this blazing scandal I do not blame the poor Colonel, whose weak good nature may have led him into these courses. I blame the bad and dishonourable men, who, out of sheer perversity and worse motives, backed him up in the maintenance of his commission and have undertaken to see him safely through this affair. Those men who have betrayed the honour of the county are the Marquess of Ormonde, the Protestant Bishop of Ossory and the Master of the Kilkenny Hounds.

How the third of them, Sir Hercules Langrishe, comes into the story I do not know. But in the next editorial O'Grady focused all his fury on Lord Ormonde, who had disappointed him most. He began:

We are not at war with the Bishop, but with the great and dominant social power in our midst, reaching up to the Throne and down to the smallest Kilkenny huxter, a power which has almost obliterated a sense of honour and public morality in the minds of the few and dulled and paralysed the conscience of the community [and he referred less explicitly to others] who had weakly followed the line of least resistance and afforded support to a stained reputation.

After that he printed a detailed summary of what had happened and sent copies of *The Moderator* to the colonels of all the regiments on Salisbury Plain and one to the Duke of Connaught. The Kilkenny Militia was at that time on manoeuvres in North Kilkenny and it is said that he urged them to mutiny.

In a very short time a writ for libel came from the Bishop. He asked for £2000 and had engaged 'six eminent counsels'. Further writs were reported to be on the way from the Marquess of Ormonde and Sir Hercules Langrishe, who were yachting at Cowes, and from others, whom O'Grady had accused of shielding the Colonel. At a special meeting of the Kilkenny Club, of which Lord Ormonde was President, O'Grady was asked to resign.

It would take too much space to carry on this story to the end of the Boer War, to O'Grady's departure from Kilkenny, saddened, but not discouraged. Yet there were many fascinating incidents. I should like to tell how the Kilkenny Militia, in their red tunics, spiked helmets and snowy bandoliers, set off a thousand strong, to embark at Waterford for training on Salisbury Plain. At their head was Colonel Charlie, on their heels a straggling Kilkenny mob, screaming: 'Hurrah for Kruger and Lady Desart!' and throwing stones and bits of coal. 'Nature abhors a vacuum,' O'Grady wrote. 'If the leaders of society betray their trust, new centres of influence will arise.'

O'Grady left and Mr M. W. Lawlor returned from Bournemouth and took over *The Moderator* again. For many months he wooed back its affronted subscribers among the gentry with philippics against O'Grady and his 'wanton, wicked and libellous attacks against one of the most exalted, popular and esteemed Peers of the Realm, whose popularity in the hunting fields of Kilkenny and in yachting circles in England and America is so well known. He brought about a state of things', he declared, 'which should bring a blush of shame to the face of even a strolling play-actor, if such a person were capable of blushing.' He spoke of his 'slanderous wagging tongue' and his 'Silly-Billy publication, the vehicle of idiotic drivel.' He revealed that O'Grady was only 'collaterally' related to the Gorts and Guillamores and that a lot of kitchen utensils had been sold at his auction, which had never

been paid for. 'A man of failure,' he summed it all up, 'at everything he touched.' Finally he sent him a bill for printer's ink and another writ.

It was the Cuffes' letter to *The Moderator* that destroyed O'Grady's paper and so I have no doubt that it was Ellen, Lady Desart, who rescued him from financial disaster. She and Otway Cuffe continued vigorously the work which he had inspired and started. The list of their enterprises is scarcely believable. They built a theatre, a hospital, a model village with a Woodworkers Factory at Talbot's Inch, a public library, a recreation hall, a woollen mills, a tobacco farm and many other small co-operative ventures. There was a little bridge across the Nore to link Talbot's Inch with the Woollen Mills. Cuffe became Mayor of Kilkenny and you will see his name carved on John's Bridge, which was rebuilt in his Mayoralty, underneath that of his forbear the Earl of Desart, who was Mayor when the previous bridge was erected. They were trying to domesticate and regionalize the dragon of international industrialism, at a time when almost everyone was directly or indirectly in the pay of the dragon.

The story of the slow decay of all these enterprises, one by one, through strikes, fraud, arson and under the unchanging pressure of politics, religion and social jealousy, would have value as a small-scale model of a universal phenomenon. Trouble started almost immediately.

In the Kilkenny Woodworkers they needed a cabinet-maker and Cuffe after long advertisement had to accept a non-trade union worker from Glasgow. Thereupon 18 men out of 100 went on strike. The Glasgow man was a Jew and this incensed the strikers still more. They struck him and chanted in chorus, 'Clear out, Ikie!'

None of the strikers, the Kilkenny papers defiantly declared, were Kilkennymen and they underlined the mean ingratitude to Cuffe and Ellen Desart, the Jewess, who had poured money into the Kilkenny industries, regardless of profit. The English trade union officials backed up the strikers. There came a sharp letter from Alexander Gossip, General Secretary of the National Amalgamated Furnishing Trades Association of Finsbury Pavement. He said he was 'not prepared to tolerate unnecessary grievances of kind indicated'. He trusted that Cuffe 'would at once see that end was put to same'. Representatives were sent to Kilkenny but Cuffe refused to see them, and answered all their letters with haughtiness. The interference from England, the flare-up of anti-Semitism and the threat to that community, which Cuffe was trying to build up, not upon impersonal officialism and scheduled rights, but on personal relations, all this cut him to the quick. He refused all mediation and started to replace the strikers with men from outside. He knew they might be stopped by picketers at Kilkenny station, so he had them met at the station before it, Gowran. One morning a little man called Flanagan got out of the train at Gowran with his trunk and found the draughtsman there with a jennet trap. They set off together, when suddenly a side-car loaded with strikers lurched down on them. 'That's your game, is it?' they screamed. 'Get out, you white-livered little scamp!' 'I'm only doing my duty,' said little Flanagan, but he was dragged out of the trap and the box flung on the road. Finally box and Flanagan were hoisted onto the side-car and cantered off to Kilkenny. A procession of tradesmen and a piper met them in John Street and with the piper playing a victory march and the tradesmen cheering, they drove their bewildered captive and his trunk through the town. That was the first of a series of disasters.

When after years of disappointment, Cuffe died in Australia, all the shops in Kilkenny were closed and the flag on the Tholsel was flown at half-mast. He had seen the doom that was approaching and had tried to reverse it, but it was too late. Meanwhile O'Grady in Dublin continued a journal, *The All-Ireland Review*, which he had started in Kilkenny and in which, as always, he tried to reconcile the old ascendancy with those who were groping towards the recovery of a national identity. He never retreated from his Anglo-Irish and Protestant background. In one of his novels his hero was an Irish Protestant, who fought for William of Orange. From its legendary past to its confused present, Irish history was to be seen as a unity based on diversity.

Few of his disciples understood this. He had brought a new theme to Anglo-Irish literature, and new ideas, like sparks in a time of drought, can purge or destroy. Patrick Pearse and Thomas MacDonagh, who were executed in 1916, produced at their school, St Enda's, one of O'Grady's Ulster plays. Cuffe organized another at Sheestown; it was acted by the Cave Hill players from Belfast. Both were well attended.

Could anyone have guessed at the explosive force of poetry and ideas? Why does it so rarely happen that those who lay the fire are allowed to light it? Yeats had said 'O'Grady's *History of Ireland* had been the start of it all', and George Dangerfield observed that the book was 'somewhere at the heart of the Easter Rising in 1916. Cuchullain was one of the shadowy heroes who fought side by side with the living in the General Post Office.' Yeats in his old age never ceased to wonder at the effect of his own poetry.

> Did that play of mine send out
> Certain men the English shot?[3]

O'Grady's health broke down soon after the Rebellion and he left Ireland to join his son in an English rectory. Then came the Black and Tans and the Treaty and early in 1922 the British Army left Kilkenny in trains with 'Back to Blighty' chalked on them, as the crowds cheered and the church-bells rang. The soldiers added to the noise by ringing from the carriage windows the large bells, which they had used on the Crossley tenders.

Many of the Anglo-Irish, who accepted the new Government, as did Ellen, Lady Desart, took office in the new Senate and, when the civil war broke out, they became the target for the Republicans, who rejected the compromise of a Free State from which most of Ulster was excluded. The houses of 37 Senators were burnt and one night in February masked men broke into Desart Court, hacked the furniture and the doors with axes and, making a huge pile, sprinkled it with petrol. Some furniture survived in an untouched wing. It was sent by van to Kilkenny, but it too was stopped on the way and burnt. Presumably this was to punish Senator Lady Desart, who was not in fact the owner. Between January 1922 and March of the following year 139 country houses were destroyed, many of them treasure-houses of great beauty, with fine libraries, whose owners had shaped Irish history. When on 28 June, the Four Courts, where the archives of centuries had been stored, was bombed, it was like the end of a civilization. In May 1922 Kilkenny Castle was taken by the Republicans* and relieved after a few days by the Free Staters. Thirteen years later all the contents were sold and for thirty years the dry-rot invaded room after empty room.

But no purely cultural impoverishment could matter so much as the withdrawal of a whole historic class. Though O'Grady had called them degenerate, outworn and effete, and had prophesied with accuracy what would happen to them, they were stupid and defenceless simply because since the Union they had exported all their brightest and their bravest to England. They had generalled her armies, governed her provinces, dominated her newspapers and her theatres, written her plays. Many of those who remained behind had been educated in England and knew nothing of Ireland's problems.† Waterloo may or may not have been won on the playing fields of Eton, but Ireland was certainly lost there.

* The fifth Marquess of Ormonde has told the story in the *Journal of the Butler Society*, Vol. 1 No. 4.
† Characteristically those who defended Anglo-Irish values most vigorously after the Treaty were those who had previously criticized them most severely. When a bill was brought in to repeal the right of divorce, which England had introduced, Yeats in the Senate gave his famous No Petty People speech and Lady Desart supported him.

AE wrote of O'Grady:

When a man is in advance of his age, a generation, unborn when he speaks, is born in due time and finds in him its inspiration. O'Grady may have failed in his appeal to the aristocracy of his own time but he may yet create an aristocracy of intellect and character in Ireland.

[1978]

1. As printed here, this essay incorporates 'Anglo-Irish Twilight', first published in *Escape from the Anthill*.
2. First published in O'Grady's broadside *Toryism and the Tory Democracy* (1886), this exhortation was reprinted in his *Selected Essays and Passages* (n.d.), pp. 221–2.
3. From 'The Man and the Echo' in *Last Poems 1936–1939*.

DIVIDED LOYALTIES

In 1984 Ireland is so deeply divided that few now talk of a *modus vivendi* between Unionist and Nationalist, between Catholic and Protestant. You never read that ancient newspaper cliché about a 'Union of Hearts', or think as I did when I was a boy, and read AE's *Irish Statesman*, that Ireland might become the central focus of our love and loyalty.

Nobody ever investigates how these ethnic and religious love-affairs, which occasionally occur, are conducted. It is obvious though that while they can be easily frustrated, they can only very warily and deviously be promoted.

Opposites often attract each other but the attraction seldom lasts if the full extent of the opposition is ignored. It is as neighbours, full of ineradicable prejudices, that we must love each other, not as fortuitously 'separated brethren'.

I became an Irish nationalist when I was very young. I had to return to school at Charterhouse some days after the Easter week rebellion and to pass barricades near O'Connell Bridge. I had to show a pass signed by the sergeant of the RIC in Kilkenny. There were still wisps of smoke coming from Sackville Street, the names of Pearse and Connolly meant nothing to me but I felt it was my war in a way that the war in which I was being prepared to fight in the Charterhouse OTC was not. When I came home for the holidays I argued ignorantly with my parents about it. Most of our Protestant neighbours, diminished in numbers and in spirit by the everlasting brain-drain to England, were solidly Unionist. They got their little jokes about Ireland from *Punch* and *The Morning Post*.

As far as I was concerned, the first crucial discussion occurred when my slightly older cousin, Theobald Butler, came to stay. He had been head boy at Charterhouse but had become an Irish nationalist and,

51

refusing to fight in an imperialist war, had taken a job in a school in Co. Down. He had first done relief work in Serbia with a friend, Eric Dodds, who, for the same reason, was teaching at Kilkenny College. Dodds had won the famous Craven Scholarship at Oxford. There were heated arguments when they came to lunch. Sometimes after this, if I made a nationalist remark, my mother said, 'Oh, you got that off Theo and Dodds. They'll scuttle back to England the moment the war is over.' And that indeed is what they did, for England has a magnetism for the Anglo-Irish intellectual that very few can resist. Sometimes even a few acres of Irish soil can give us an unreasoning obstinacy and the illusion of security, but Theo and Dodds had not an acre between them. Before he died Theo had a full inch of London legal achievements after his name in *Burke's Peerage*, and Dodds became Regius Professor of Greek at Oxford. In his autobiography, *Missing Persons* (1977), he has described the missing person, the Irish nationalist he once was, and the disillusionment endured by all Anglo-Irishmen who had given their first love to Ireland. 'The birth of a terrible beauty has ended with the establishment of a grocers' republic,' he wrote.

But, if you are heir to some trees and fields and buildings and a river bank, your love for your country can be more enduring. It is a not too blameworthy extension of self-love; you feel qualified to influence its destiny on a small scale and you are not content, as so many of the Irish are, to radiate goodwill to Ireland from across the sea. We were minor gentry and our activities were all minor, but my father had brought the village creamery to Bennettsbridge and was the committee's president, and my mother ran a Boot-and-Coal Fund and a committee connected with tuberculosis, both subsidized by annual jumble sales and concerts. My aunt had founded the Kilkenny Horticultural Society and used to drive a fat pony round the country judging cottage gardens; I used to think she judged the cottagers as well as their gardens. She had a bossy manner and this seemed to me suitable enough.

AE had believed that, as the co-operative movement developed in Ireland, a real village community would grow round every creamery and that the principle of sharing would extend into every branch of life, spiritual, economic, cultural. The communal marketing of eggs and butter would lead to more intimate and domestic forms of sharing. AE saw the hedges planted with apple trees and gooseberry bushes, as in Germany, and gymnasiums and libraries, picture galleries and village halls, to which each man or woman made his contribution according to his powers, so that each village became a focus of activity and debate.

Sixty years ago, an ingenuous young person could really believe this would happen. There, anyway, was the new creamery on the edge of the village and it stood till 1983 when it was bulldozed away. To make all these creameries AE had travelled hundreds of miles on his bicycle and Plunkett, a sick man kept alive by his burning zeal, had made these long journeys which he records in his diaries: 'A two hours crawl in the Major's brougham to Longford. Did good I think but, oh, how boring and tiring! Two long speeches to two small meetings. My thoughts germinate in other brains and when the brains are attached to the proper physique the enthusiasm works.'

When I told my mother about the gooseberry bushes, she said, 'Stuff and nonsense! Those trees that the Kilkenny Corporation planted along the canal-walk were all slashed down in a week. When O'Grady and Otway Cuffe gave that Irish play at Sheestown the crowds all strolled out from Kilkenny and pulled up all the shrubs and broke the tea cups.'

When I suggested to my sister, who organized the village concerts, that they should do a Synge play or a Lady Gregory or at least a George Shiels, she said, 'Oh they'd hate that sentimental Irish stuff,' and as usual, she sent for a bunch of one-act farces from Messrs French in London, and she was quite right. They vastly preferred them.

And it always happened like that. When it was rumoured in the Kildare Street Club that the creameries had become social centres where the farmers discussed sedition over their milk-churns, and when the Black and Tans started burning them, many members congratulated themselves on the hostility they had shown to Plunkett. The rest of the story runs along familiar lines.

AE and Plunkett died disillusioned, in England. Kilteragh, Plunkett's house in Foxrock, which had been the meeting-place for the Anglo-Irish who were concerned about their country, was burned to the ground in the civil war, because he had become a Senator.

I was young at the time and did not realize that I was living at the end of a relatively humane and sensible era and at the beginning of a cruel and chaotic one. Ireland had her freedom and Europe had her League of Nations. I enjoyed my holidays at home, the raids and rumours, the 'battle of Kilkenny' and the three-day siege of Kilkenny Castle, and I believe there were many young people as silly as myself.

Compared to other counties, Kilkenny was peaceful and gentle. Apart from the burning of three famous and beautiful houses, Woodstock, Desart Court and Bessborough, life went on as usual with rare interruptions.

One night, at 3 a.m., we were woken by loud knocking at the front door. My sister and I went down and found two unknown men there. We were elated rather than scared. Here was real life at last. One of the men said they wanted money for the 'dependents of the Irish Republic'. I said, 'We've no guns in the house; if you're just common thieves we can't stop you taking what you want.' He replied, 'Ah we're not that sort of chap at all,' and they went away.

Another afternoon two of them came again, asking as before for money. My mother and I were in the porch and she danced about with fury. 'I know who you are,' she said to one of them. 'You're Jim Connell. Take your cigarette out of your mouth when you're talking to me.' He took it out and I began to scold my mother for interrupting what might have been a revealing conversation. It was only the second time I had seen a Republican, and when I went back to Oxford I wanted at least to say what they were like and what their plans were. My mother answered me sharply and we started an angry argument. The two men looked at each other in embarrassment and slunk politely away.

The third occasion was an episode that found its way into J. G. Farrell's *Troubles*. My sisters and I were on our way with two friends to the St Georges' dance at Kilrush, seven or eight miles beyond Kilkenny. It was a period when everyone had to have a permit signed by the police for his car, and all those who were legally on the road could be thought of as the enemy. When we got to Troyeswood, a mile outside Kilkenny, we found a wall built across the road. In front of it stood two men with long white beards, which proved, when we got closer, to be white scarves veiling their faces; they had revolvers. Behind them lay three or four cars turned upside down in the middle of the road. They turned us out of the car and led us across the hedge into the field where already a dozen of our friends were grouped with another muffled figure guarding them. When three or four more cars had been turned over and their occupants ushered into the field, we were told: 'At the expiration of half an hour you may proceed to your destinations.'

We walked back in our evening clothes across Kilkenny. Some stayed at the Club House Hotel. I tramped back home to tell my family.

Far worse things happened in Tipperary. One night in March 1923 Graiguenoe Park, my mother's home at Holycross, was burnt. We shared her sadness for we had spent many happy days with our cousins there. It was between thirty and forty miles away, but when we were children we thought of it as in another country, much wilder, less ordinary. My sister and I used to get up early and start off with our night things on our bicycle carriers and the dew still on the grass. As soon as we crossed the Tipperary border the smell of turf, unknown to us in Kilkenny, prepared us to expect everything strange and new. Leaving behind us the familiar woods of Farmley and Desart Court, we crossed Slieveardagh and turning aside after Littleton bog, we made for Killough hill and, when it came in sight, we knew we had arrived.

The little bridge across the Suir at the approach to Holycross had been rebuilt by an ancestor of my father, James Butler, twelfth Baron Dunboyne, and his wife, Lady Margaret O'Brien, in 1624. There is a Latin inscription on it and an appeal in verse to the passer-by:

> Dic, precor, ante abitum,
> verbo non amplius uno,
> evadat Stygios
> auctor uterque lacus.

> Pray, traveller, before you pass, offer one prayer only,
> that the two builders may escape the Stygian lakes.

This interesting pagan fancy has been christianized in the Tourist Board translation into 'Hell'.

James Butler had given a miraculous statue of the Virgin Mary to the Abbot of Holycross. It had come from a wrecked Spanish galleon and was said to cure toothache and keep rats from the grain.

Even Graiguenoe itself, a large early Victorian house built by my great grandfather beyond the ruins of Holycross Abbey, had romance and mystery for us. My uncle had been boycotted in 1910 and there was a police barracks on his property and for a time a general store. His farm workers had stood by him and could buy their food there when the shopkeepers in Thurles, intimidated by the Land Leaguers, refused to supply them.

Some years ago there was a dramatic dynamiting of the ruins of Graiguenoe in the presence of a photographer from *The Tipperary Star*, and the stones were used in the reconstruction of Holycross Abbey. When I went there soon after, there was no trace of the house except for a broad band of daisies that wound through the field where the avenue had been. Tom Nolan, the coachman's grandson, still lived in the lodge and I found that the new proprietor farmed a thousand acres more than Uncle Charlie had done.

Some twenty houses of the Anglo-Irish were burnt at this time in Tipperary. Most of them vanished without record, but many letters must have been written like the one which follows. It is from the housekeeper at Graiguenoe to my aunt, who was in London at the time.

March 31. 1923

From Mrs A. Good, Housekeeper, Graiguenoe Park, Holycross, Co. Tipperary, to Mrs Charles Clarke.

Madam,

By now you know the bad news how Graiguenoe is burned down. Oh it was terrible to see it blazing away!

Just at 5 past 12 on Wednesday night the bell was rung. I was only just in bed, so I jumped up and called the girls and went to Nolan; but he was up. They never stopped ringing till Nolan and I went to the hall-door; and there were two men with revolvers and demanded to know why we did not open before and come out; so I said, 'Surely you will give us time to get our things.' He said 'Yes, If we were not too long.' He wanted to know how many there were in the house. I said 'Three girls more.' He wanted to know who were all those inside there. I said, 'That is yourself in the mirror.' He thought (when he saw our reflections in the glass) that a lot of people were there. So we all got our things put together as quick as we could, but all of us had to leave a lot of things as they kept asking, 'Are ye ready, as we are in a hurry', so we got out. Nolan saved three pictures out of the dining room and your dressing case and a small case under the bed and Mr Clarke's dressing bag, but they did not want him to take anything only his own things. He also saved the harness; he worked like a nigger but he could do nothing more. He also tried to save the harness room by throwing buckets of water on the inside and the roof; but no use. The fire got too firm a hold on everything before those demons left. They had petrol, straw and hay so they made a good job of it. The only place not burned out is the scullery and Mrs Curtin's room. We were in the coach house watching it blazing. The flames were very high but the wind was in our favour, or the outhouses would also be in flames.

The Laundry Basket (Dublin) was in the passage and the man asked us was it ours and I said Yes, so he let us take it; also there is a basket at Thurles laundry, which I expect will come back on Monday. Will the things be sent to you? They could be packed in a box. Also we managed to grab some coats off the rack in the dark. They turned out to be your grey coat and the brown. Will I send them on also? There were about seven or eight men through the house but they told us not to stir from where we were for at least half an hour as the house was surrounded and we may be shot. They left before one o'clock so you see we got no time. We stayed all night.

It was heartbreaking to see the house burning where we were living so long. But we were thankful Mr Clarke was not there for the story was bad enough and he may be shot. They asked several times where was the Boss. We all came up to Mrs Hilton's at 7 o'clock in the morning. Bridget has gone home, also

Maggie and Josie. I am staying here with Mrs Hilton for the present. I will never forget the sight and experiences of Wednesday night. I feel sorry for you and Mr Clarke, but I'm thinking there will be no gentlemen's places soon.

> Hoping you and Mr Clarke are well,
> I am, Madam, yours respectfully,
>
> A. Good

> I can't find a pen so please excuse pencil.

Did the Anglo-Irish deserve the fate which was so often predicted for them? Wolfe Tone had written, 'They have disdained to occupy the station they might have held among the people and which the people would have been glad to see them fill. They see Ireland only in their rent-rolls, their places, their patronage, their pensions. They shall perish like their own dung. Those that have seen them will say, "Where are they?"'

The Anglo-Irish could have dodged their fate if their interest in Ireland, let alone their love, had been more than marginal. They recognized a duty certainly to their neighbourhood and this duty was usually intelligently fulfilled, but it only rarely happened that, like Plunkett and a few of their contemporaries, they could give their first love to their country. I believe that in a generation or two, had there been no 1914 war, no rebellion and no civil war, this duty might have turned itself into love as it often had in the eighteenth century.

Then, for a brief period, they had been able to represent something very precious. Only they could give Irishmen a sense of historical continuity and of identity. It was to be found in their bookshelves, when those who remained no longer read books, in their estate maps when they no longer had estates, in their memories when they no longer had the leisure or literary skill to write them down. The Irishmen who burnt down those Tipperary houses were sawing away the branch on which they were sitting. Clamouring that they were a distinctive people, they obliterated much of the heritage that distinguished them. The burning of the Four Courts, which swept away the records of eight centuries, was only one episode in this tale of self-destruction.

A new and more suffocating ascendancy, that of international commerce, was on the way; many of those ruined houses would have been strongholds of resistance to it, and the Anglo-Irish, with their easy-going pragmatic Christianity, would certainly have tempered the religious and political passions of our northern countrymen.

[1984]

AUNT HARRIET

When she got old and ill my grandmother grew frightened of being buried alive and she constantly asked for assurance that she would be given an autopsy. It was a persistent fear. 'She's going on about old Topsy again,' my mother said once, when coming out of her room. My mother was under great strain and I was no use to her.

I was at Oxford and found it a place of such abundance that Ireland and everyone in it, particularly my relations, were diminished. I was incessantly carping at them. In England we were nobody, while in Ireland, I maintained, if we gave it our first loyalty we could be somebody.

When Aunt Harriet, my father's sister, died, I went with my parents to keep Aunt Florence company at Lavistown. It is a small Georgian house with white Venetian blinds, built for the manager of the marble works by the founder William Colles. The marble works were still functioning in a desultory way just below Lavistown on the banks of the Nore. My father and mother slept in the big room over the dining-room where the coffin was laid on two chairs under the window. I slept in the small dressing-room off it.

Lavistown, which was four miles away from Maidenhall, was almost a second home to us; we were often there. I was very fond of Aunt Harriet, who superintended the cooking and the cook, Ellen, while Aunt Florence looked after the garden and the gardener, Donovan. We used to see more of Aunt Harriet because she had a bicycle, while Aunt Florence had to get Donovan to harness Maureen, the fat white pony. Aunt Harriet usually bicycled over with a cake in the basket on the handlebars and *The Christian Science Monitor* under it, for she was both a Christian Scientist and a Gaelic Leaguer. 'Well, chickabiddies!' she exclaimed when she saw us. The cake she gave to my mother, *The Christian Science Monitor* to us children, ostensibly because of the

Children's page, but I'm sure she thought some effluence of her faith might reach us through it. The stories were usually about dressed-up rabbits, mice, bluebottles; more moral than Beatrix Potter but less entertaining. Any message they contained was lost on us, but I was offended on Aunt Harriet's behalf when my mother said, 'Anyway, it's good thick paper; wonderful for packing eggs.'

My mother said Aunt Harriet became a Christian Scientist because a certain Dr Davis had failed to meet her under the clock on the platform at Kingsbridge Station in Dublin. She became a Gaelic Leaguer, I expect, because of the Cuffes who lived at Sheestown, a small house the other side of the Nore. Otway Cuffe was the brother and heir of the Earl of Desart, who lived at Desart Court about ten miles to the west. Mrs Cuffe was the daughter of a Cornish nobleman and they had thrown all their hereditary prestige, which in those days was considerable, into the Gaelic Revival, the development of a unique Irish civilization in-dependent of politics. His sister-in-law, Lady Desart, had, as I have related, put her vast wealth largely at Otway Cuffe's disposal for the development of local industries. Though the bulk of the Unionists were sceptical, the Cuffes had many disciples. The Gaelic movement interested Aunt Harriet, while Aunt Florence was absorbed by home industries and craft work, and they had a large framed photograph of Otway Cuffe in the dining-room at Lavistown.

All this might seem irrelevant to the story I have to tell about Aunt Harriet. It is a very brief story but nothing at all if I do not convey the closeness I felt to that body in the box. Love? Affection? Admiration? I think absolute involvement is the right phrase. She must have suspected in me, when I was quite small, some germ of heterodoxy of the kind she had nursed in herself. One day, when I was playing on the gravel at Lavistown, I fell and scraped my leg. I pointed out to Aunt Harriet that it was bleeding. 'It's nothing,' she said and put a piece of stamp paper on it. I pulled it off the moment she was out of sight and never told my mother, who would have been angry; Christian Science was unpopular in those days because a co-religionist of Aunt Harriet's, Mrs Tighe of Woodstock, refused to have a doctor for her son and he died.

My two aunts went on sketching holidays every spring to Vernet les Bains but one summer Aunt Harriet went to Boston for some special celebration of Mary Baker Eddy, the great prophetess and heresiarch of Christian Science. My mother thought she might marry an elderly Christian Scientist there and feared for our prospects. We had always held that money that you inherit, unlike money that you earn, belongs to the family. We had forebears called Kingston who owned a shipyard in Cork and, when it closed, retained the ground rents of the buildings that went up on the quays beside the Lee. The ground rents passed on to their descendants, getting less and less with each generation, together with some good miniatures of themselves in a blue velvet frame by Frederick Buck of Cork. We got the miniatures and my aunts the ground rents.

Aunt Harriet came back much invigorated from Boston. She had been also to the Niagara Falls. Mrs Eddy was dead at the time but she had seen her house and I think the cradle where she had been a baby. She had worshipped in the Mother Church of Christ Scientist and had not brought back a Christian Scientist husband. She would like to have told us more about Boston but everybody fidgetted uncomfortably when she started to talk of Mrs Eddy and asked her feverishly about the Niagara Falls.

Aunt Harriet was the strictest sort of Christian Scientist. She never admitted to any illness. She never went to a dentist but let her teeth fall out so that her cheeks contracted round three or four solitary tusks. This did nothing for her appearance. Aunt Florence had frequent small illnesses and many visits from the doctor. There must have been some snappishness between the sisters but we children never heard a word of it. We squabbled as much as most families do, but confronted by the outside world we were loyal to each other.

In those days, the Sinn Feiners were in the habit of visiting people, two by two and often by night, asking them for money for 'dependents of the Irish Republicans'. They went to Lavistown one night and Aunt Harriet had looked out of her bedroom window and said reproachfully that she would give them nothing, that she had given up the Gaelic League when it had become political and when the Sinn Feiners had started a campaign of violence. After this little lecture they went away.

I told this to a friend of my own age who lived near by. 'I don't wonder', she said, 'the Shinners got a shock and went off when Old Harriet poked her face out at them.' I took offence and told her she had no right to talk like that. She said pacifically: 'You should see my Aunt Eileen.'

I have left Aunt Harriet in her coffin a long way behind, but I am thinking of the memories she took with her; they were all unimportant but the past is a mosaic of tiny pieces, a fragment of a larger picture, Ireland in the twenties and the last days of the Anglo-Irish, and I will continue with more minutiae.

In the days before the War and the 1916 Rising, the more enlightened of the Anglo-Irish were trying desperately to identify themselves with Ireland. Aunt Harriet organized the first local Feis, an ancient festival of song and dance and miscellaneous junketting which centuries before took place at Tara. At the Kilkenny Feis there were competitions for Irish dancing and singing, lace-making, cake, jam, section honey and craft work. When it was all over Aunt Harriet was presented by the committee with a 'Tara' brooch, a richly ornamented safety pin with which the ancient Irish held their clothes together, mass produced from originals in the National Museum.

The Gaelic League was not 'political' in those days and even the British saw nothing against it. When Lady Aberdeen, Ireland's all but last Vice-Reine, came down to open our local concert hall, she defied the ridicule of the Anglo-Irish neighbours by dressing herself and the ladies of the party in emerald green with Tara brooches. She and her husband were very Scottish; he wore the Gordon tartan and they wrote a book called *We Twa*. They bred Aberdeen terriers and were Aberdonianly thrifty, and it was one of their aims to show how very Scottish one could be and yet loyal to the Crown. Why could not the Irish be the same? She entertained very little in the Vice-Regal Lodge, but started a campaign against tuberculosis with no political overtones, and motored all over Ireland trying with some success to introduce village nurses into every community.

Despite all this they were unpopular with both the more orthodox Gaels and ordinary Unionists; they were suspected of 'liberalism' which in Ireland was anathema to the traditional Unionist and one of our neighbours wrote a poem about them of which I can only remember one line: 'They cut the penny buns in half when Larkin came to tea.' (Larkin was a celebrated labour leader.)

The Cuffes and Aunt Florence and my mother all threw themselves into the crusade against tuberculosis (Aunt Harriet believed it was a delusion of the mind) and I think the Bennettsbridge village nurse was among the first in Ireland.

When Lord Aberdeen retired in 1915 he was made a Marquess and, conscious of his work for Ireland, he chose the title of Aberdeen and Tara, but the use of this most famous of all Irish placenames by a Scottish peer gave great offence. On leaving they sent photographs of themselves with an Aberdeen terrier beside them and one of the recipients wrote a letter which got great publicity: 'Thank you very much for the beautiful photograph of yourselves and your little dog Tara.' They changed Tara to Temair, which is a more ancient version of Tara but, as few knew this, no one objected.

Behind Lavistown is a big house, Leyrath, where Sir Charles Wheeler Cuffe, a distant relative of the Desarts, lived with his cousin Baroness Prochaska, an Austrianized Czech who was full of enthusiasm for home industries and handicrafts. She was very plain with projecting eyes and teeth and a gobbly Central European voice. I expect she knew the Czech language but only spoke it to her inferiors. She must have considered that the Anglo-Irish were a little like the Austro-Czechs, whose doom like theirs was only a few years away. She took up bee-keeping vigorously and prevailed on the County Council to appoint a Bee-Keeping Instructor. She had a row of hives at Leyrath with names like Peace, Love, Harmony. I don't know whether it was she or Otway Cuffe who was responsible for the Carpentry Instructor who travelled round the country villages. In Bennettsbridge he gave instruction to some twenty local boys in my father's barn once a week. I was taught with the other boys of my own age to make a small bracket on which to put a Holy Lamp. I was eight at the time and very class-conscious but had never learnt to say 'Please sir, can I leave the room?' And something awful happened that made the other boys titter and the Instructor pause to give me good advice. I thought of it with shame for months and months. This is the first time I've ever mentioned it.

The Baroness bought a horse-drawn coffee-van and got up every fair day at six a.m. and, joined sometimes by Aunt Florence, sometimes by Aunt Harriet or my elder sister, brought it to James's Green where the Kilkenny Fair was held. There they sold, very cheaply, tea, coffee and buns to the farmers, drovers and cattle-dealers. There was always a lot of money round the town on fair days, the pubs were crowded and there were men with plum-coloured faces walking unsteadily in the street. The coffee-van had an unacknowledged relevance to this. This went on for twenty years but the Baroness got ill and went to Auteven Cottage Hospital (this was one of Lady Desart's gifts to Kilkenny) and one day soon after that a lady, who was deputizing for her and had a less dominating character, was stopped, by order of the Corporation, and was not allowed in. The public-house keepers and other traders in Walkin Street, which led to the fair green, had put pressure on the Corporation. They claimed that they had a right to give drinks or proper breakfasts to drovers and that the coffee-van was depriving them of their livelihood. They said that the farmers were supporting the coffee-van because they were too mean to give their men the money for a proper breakfast.

Word of all this came to the Kilkenny Farmers' Union, an organization on which the Anglo-Irish landowners were well represented. A special meeting was held and they were all on the side of the Baroness and her coffee-van. And it was resolved that a message should be sent to her in hospital thanking her for her tireless work over the years and wishing her a speedy recovery. At the same time pressure was put on the Corporation to withdraw the veto on the coffee-van which the public-house keepers had forced them to make. The coffee-van continued as long as the Baroness lived but, when she died, it died with her.

I used to bicycle in with my father very early on the day of the Kilkenny Fair and we found the cattle from his two farms at Burnchurch and Drumherin waiting for us there, so it is not very difficult to revive all these memories, some of which are recorded in Aunt Florence's scrap book. It only slowly and sadly became apparent to my father that nature did not intend me to be a farmer. It was my younger brother, a small child then, who took over.

The Kilkenny Fair and the Kilkenny Farmers' Union ended long ago, as did the Instructors for Beekeeping and Carpentry, Lady Aberdeen's locally appointed nurse and her Women's National Health Association. I dare say they are not missed very much and have been replaced by something just as good, but some faculty of independent initiative, of overcoming apathy with an idea, has become rarer.

While Aunt Florence went to church in St Canice's Cathedral, Kilkenny, Aunt Harriet stayed at home praying and reading Mrs Eddy's *Science and Health with Key to the Scriptures*. Aunt Florence must have come back full of chat about the neighbours and their hats and the bishop's sermon. Did she have to suppress it all or did Aunt Harriet welcome this contact with the outside world?

I felt for her because at this time I was a very earnest Free Thinker, although I discovered at Oxford that my particular earnestness was twenty years out of date. I had the old nursery at the top of the house as my study and from there I could see my father and mother and two sisters setting off in the waggonette to Ennisnag church. I saw them turn down the avenue and eight minutes later I could see the top-hat of old Egan, the coachman (he sat on the box), appearing and disappearing and reappearing between the chestnut trees along the road and when it finally vanished I felt lonely but unyielding. Solitude was the price Aunt Harriet and I had to pay for our convictions. I did not change much but the world changed. In England people slipped out of faith and into indifference without mental or spiritual struggling. Earnest Rationalism like

Lecky's and Bury's is the natural child of Irish Protestantism. It is the Catholic majority that keeps most of us defiantly Protestant.

Because of this, like a jelly that has stiffened inside its jelly-mould and slid out intact, I found myself accepting the Protestant ethos and bothering less about its dogma and mythology. We respect individualism and in particular 'the sacred right of private judgment', as Grattan called it at the Convention of Dungannon in 1782. In Ireland it has played the same part in the life of the Irish Protestant as Authority has in the life of the Irish Catholic. It is frequently under attack and I have always done my best to defend it.

What was Lavistown like in January 1925? The house is still there but it has changed and I have to resurrect it by conjecture and present experience, not memory. The aconites might have been just out under the shelter of the big cypress tree that fell down many years ago, and a few tight buds of snowdrops perhaps, but the mauve crocuses, the small ones that seeded themselves under all the deciduous trees that lined the path to the garden and the back avenue, would only just have poked above the leaf mould.

The pony Maureen would have been there but would Ellen the cook? The tennis court would have been there and properly mown, and not the flat shaggy rectangle that survives still beside so many Irish country houses, recalling the days before 1922 when there were often tennis parties at different houses six days a week.

I remember the inside of the house better. Aunt Florence took in *The Queen* and used to enjoy discussing with us the Social Problem page. Aunt Harriet had a row of Irish books and Dinneen's Irish dictionary, and when I was sixteen she gave me William James's *Varieties of Religious Experience*, which did not interest me very much because I was proud to have no religious experience. It wasn't until years later that I discovered she had left a yellow ribbon in a chapter called 'The Religion of Healthy Mindedness' with a subsection on 'Mind Cure'.

I must come back to that night of 25 January 1925. We had a quiet low-voiced supper in the drawing-room opposite to the dining-room in which Aunt Harriet lay, and then we went to bed. I went first because I was in the little dressing-room. It was only the second time I had been in a house with a dead person (Granny had died the year before) and I took a long time to go to sleep, thinking of Aunt Harriet and all the things that had happened and not happened between us. It was a long chronicle of trivialities, letters I had not answered, copies of the *Monitor* with marked passages that I had not acknowledged, little openings for thoughtful conversations which I had gently closed.

Perhaps Aunt Harriet had access to some peace of mind, some freedom from pain which she had spent her life trying to share with us. But it was very difficult to think like this. It was another hour before I slept and at about four I was roused by a tapping sound. It came from the room below. It is only because my elder relations are all dead and I am an old man now, soon to go into a box myself, that I can write like this. Perhaps I should not for I have nothing interesting to relate, only what happened in my mind, and that is discreditable but not exciting.

If I could have gone downstairs directly from my room I know I would have, but to get down I had to go through my parents' room. They would certainly wake and I would put into their minds a horrifying thought, which it was my duty to confirm before expressing.

I spent the rest of the night wrestling with this problem even after the tapping had stopped. What worried me was the thought that in some supreme effort of faith she had half-conquered death, which like a wave in an ebbing tide had left her stranded half-alive on the foreshore.

I recalled Granny's fear of being buried alive. Would Aunt Harriet have woken up and not known whether she was already buried? And what could we do? Would I have to get Mr Lewis the undertaker? Where did he live? Was there a hammer and a chisel in the house?

I got up as soon as I could and as I passed through my parents' room my mother said to my father: 'Did you hear that rapping in the night? It must have been the knob of the blind cord tapping on the window pane. There was a bit of wind.' 'Yes, I expect so,' my father said indifferently. When I got down, all was quiet and the blind cord did have a knob at the end of it but the wind had stopped and I could not convince myself that my mother's explanation was the correct one. She had never believed in Aunt Harriet's faith healing. 'She could have saved herself with something quite simple like cascara,' she had said. I seldom think of that night now, though I once used often to do so. It was not a question of being right or wrong in what I thought. I had envisaged a possibility and at all costs I should have tested it. It was the first of ten or fifteen grave mistakes that I think over in the wakeful nights. I wrote a poem about them, and then found that Yeats had written some lines that were more apposite.

> Things said or done long years ago,
> Or things I did not do or say
> But thought that I might say or do,

Weigh me down, and not a day
But something is recalled,
My conscience or my vanity appalled.[1]

In the daylight, commonsense prevailed. Aunt Harriet was self-effacing and considerate. She would sooner have gone through the ordeal of death a second time than be resurrected in a blaze of newspaper publicity. Very quickly the night vision of hands battering helplessly at unyielding wood was submerged. Mr Lewis, the undertaker, arrived with the hearse and we took Aunt Florence with us to lunch at home and afterwards we met the hearse at Danesfort Cross and followed it to Burnchurch church, where my great-grandfather, once rector there, and all his family were buried. My mother said she had tried to find if there was some special Christian Science Burial Service and some special minister to perform it. Now it seems to me we did not try hard enough and that we should have urged her fellow believers to come down and do honour to their dead sister, who in a lonely way had been loyal to their principles.

Later still I felt that in view of the Cork ground rents it had been mean of us not to give my two aunts a tombstone to themselves. Instead we added their names as postscripts on the base of the tall cross put up to my Uncle Richard, who had caught cold and died after a tennis party in 1877 at the age of nineteen.

Forty years later, when I was in Boston, because of Aunt Harriet I went to the Mother Church of Christ Scientist and in a Christian Science Reading Room I found Mrs Eddy's *Science and Health with Key to the Scriptures*. I was astonished. Mrs Eddy took the offensive against philology.

'The dissection and definition of words', she wrote, 'aside from their metaphysical content is not scientific.' Extracting the 'metaphysical' content from the name Adam, she writes: 'Divide it in half and it reads A dam, as the obstacle which the serpent Sin would impose between Man and his Creator', and elsewhere she writes: 'Adam and his race are a dream of mortal mind because Cain went to live in the Land of Nod, the land of dreams and illusions.'

Was this the way Aunt Harriet and thousands of others reasoned? And yet I had to acknowledge that, as newspapers go, *The Christian Science Monitor* has many merits.

I learnt in Boston that Mary Baker Eddy had many enemies and critics there. One of them has related that some of the more ardent of her disciples thought she had conquered Death as well as Pain and that, when she proved to be mortal after all, one of them impersonated her and drove round Boston for several days in her well-known carriage till the faithful were ready to accept the truth.

Goodness often blossoms like roses on very rickety trellis-work, and beauty can grow out of nonsense. There are no grounds for supposing that one can live a life without pain and sadness, but is it wrong to believe that somehow, somewhere, this is possible?

Two years after Aunt Harriet, Aunt Florence eased herself out of life slowly and securely by many small illnesses. I got the Cork ground rents but after a few years the Post Office bought half the buildings on the site of the Kingston Shipyard and claimed to be exempt from ground rents. My two sisters got Lavistown. The gate lodge on the back avenue, where Donovan lived, belongs to my niece, who sold Lavistown to friends, who have made it a study centre. Students come there to learn about the flora and fauna of the Nore valley. The cows there produce special cheeses and the pigs special sausages. It is still a place where it is easier to believe in happiness than in pain.

[1987]

1. From 'Vacillation' in *The Winding Stair and other poems* (1933).

THE BRITISH ISRAELITES AT TARA

All my life I have heard how a band of British Israelites dug into the mounds of Tara in order to discover the Ark of the Covenant, and so muddled up everything for future excavators. The story has been used as a cautionary tale about the evils of unauthorized excavation and to justify the official regulations prohibiting it. These have always seemed to me to favour the farmer and the miner, who may demolish ancient earthworks in order to grow turnips or export minerals to Germany, and to insult and discourage the local antiquarian, who is assumed to be a barbarian. So I was delighted to learn in 1969 that the whole story was fictional from beginning to end.

My informant was my old cousin Synolda French, who like myself belonged to the lesser Irish gentry and was one of the Butlers of Dunboyne. I will relate our conversation just as it occurred, because she had a lively mind and an excellent memory and because the Meath of her childhood now seems as far away as Melchizedek, who, it is said, brought the Ark to Tara. It all took place in 1898, when Cousin Synolda was just grown-up.

'Tell me, Cousin Synolda,' I asked, 'about the band of British Israelites who excavated the mound at Tara.'

'Well, there wasn't any band but just one young student, and he was not a British Israelite and he didn't excavate the mound.'

'How did you come across him?'

'When Uncle Whitty died my father came to live at Staffordstown near Navan, but my mother died when I was seven (she was one of the Rothwells of Rockfield) and, as my father had difficulty about governesses, I went to live with Aunt Mary at 3 Leeson Park, Dublin, where I went to school, and only came home to Staffordstown for the holidays. I was born in 1881 and I was just seventeen when our neighbours, Cecil and Shirley Ball, told us about the young man from

London. Cecil's father was a retired captain who hunted and farmed at Gerardstown Castle (that place is now gone); his wife was a Humphries from Ballyhaise in the north of Ireland. They were tickled to death about this young man, Mr Groome he was called, and we were all very interested.

'You see he was lodging in a hotel in Navan and he enquired there how to get to Tara and they told him he must get in touch with G····· Briscoe at Bellinter, who was a great friend of Cecil and Shirley's.'

'Did Gussie Briscoe own Tara?'

'Yes, he came by it in an odd way. You see old Mr Preston of Bellinter had one daughter; she married a Mr Smith and had two or three children. He and his wife and children got scarlet fever, which was very hard to cure in those days, and they all died. Mr Preston was very lonely in the big house and when Mr Briscoe, the rector of Bective, died, Mr Preston asked his widow and her little boy, his godson, to come and live at Bellinter. And Mr Preston made Gussie his heir.

'We were great friends with Gussie's children. They are all dead now except the youngest, Baby or Bay she was called, but I think her real name was Muriel. Now Bay would be able to tell you a lot about that Ark of the Covenant. I was just engaged to be married at the time and, of course, I was thinking of other things.

'So this Mr Groome took a side-car out to Bellinter and told Gussie he wanted to dig for the Ark of the Covenant. Gussie was fascinated and said "Of course!" and told two of his men to dig for him and paid their wages, for the young man hadn't a penny. And they dug three big holes near the wall of the Protestant church at Tara a long way from the mounds. We were all highly delighted and amused. There were all kinds of jokes. We were very hard up at the time and we were saying that we would turn Staffordstown into a hotel for all the Jews who would come to see the Ark and we would make a lot of money. Shirley and Cecil hid all kinds of things for the young man to find, teapot lids and so on, and Shirley hid Lady Dillon's napkin-ring. But the young man was very good-humoured and just laughed.'

'Did he explain to you what he was after?'

'Yes, he did. Everyone laughed at me for taking him seriously but I was interested. One day we had tennis at Staffordstown and Cecil and Shirley brought him along. He was very gauche and badly dressed and he tried to make excuses for not playing tennis. He hadn't shoes or a racquet. But we said we'd lend him them. He played very badly and I was sorry for him; he looked so odd. He had a grey shirt with red braces and all the others had white flannels and I said, "Won't you come and see the garden?" So we walked off but I could see he wasn't at all interested in the garden either. So I said to him, "Tell me about the Ark of the Covenant." And after a bit he saw I was really interested and not just laughing at him as the others were.

'It was this way. He had been studying hieroglyphics and he found that there was a record that, wherever the Ark had rested, a stone with a certain hieroglyphic on it had been set up and these stones had been traced all the way from Palestine to the Atlantic coast. It had ended in mystery. Then one day he had been rummaging through some second-hand books on a stall and had found a small fat illustrated book about Freemasonry and there, on one of those ornaments that the masons wear, he had seen the very same hieroglyphic. He had gone then to the British Museum and found that there were stones in Ireland reaching from near Dundalk to Tara with the same hieroglyphics on them. So he'd come to Tara. He never said one word about the British Israelites. There was just himself and he'd no money. If they'd sent him, surely they'd have given him some?

'Well. Mr Groome was digging by the church wall just the right distance (he had all the measurements) from the stone which he thought must be the one locating the Ark, when an old man called Richard Wilkinson, whose father had been killed in the '98 rebellion, came up to him and told him that the stone had originally been the other side of the road on Lord Somebody's property (I forget his name) but it had been moved over near the church to commemorate the men who had been killed at the battle of Tara. Their names are on it. So Mr Groome saw he had been digging in the wrong place and he wrote to Lord Somebody asking him if he could dig on his land and Lord Somebody had just written back, "Go to Hell!" So the poor young fellow went back to London having wasted his time and found nothing.

'But when we told Dr Praeger[1] and the others that this was what had happened, they just wouldn't believe us. And some of them got quite angry about it. They'd made up their minds that Tara had been messed up by the British Israelites and nothing we said could make them change it.'

The old story cropped up in *The Irish Times* before she died and Cousin Synolda wrote contradicting it. But I don't think she made much impression, as one still hears it again and again.

[1948, 1949, 1956]

1. Robert Lloyd Praeger (1865–1953): Librarian of the National Library of Ireland, botanist, topographer, author of *The Way That I Went* (1937) and *Natural History of Ireland* (1950).

GRANDMOTHER AND WOLFE TONE

Brian Inglis, former editor of *The Spectator*, is one of the most articulate of living Anglo-Irishmen. This is not saying much, for that once voluble people seems now to be stricken with aphasia. The title of his book, *West Briton*,* was a name which, in their late prime, attached itself to the more corrupted of the Anglo-Irish. As their fortunes declined, they tried to shed it but it had stuck and in the days of their collapse it was flung as a taunt at the whole community. Now Mr Inglis, a sophisticated, guilt-ridden exile, wears it as a sort of comic hat. His swan-song of the West Britons in Malahide is first-class. He is amusing, impartial, compassionate and his book is as cheering to the remnant that still hangs on in its native land as a nice cup of Ovaltine to the victim of disseminated sclerosis.

I read *West Briton* on the Barcelona express, but was not sure what was wrong with it till I picked up a discarded French literary magazine from the seat, and read an article, 'Où sont les polemicistes?' The writer complained that paralysis has overtaken us all because we have made an idol of 'objectivity'. No educated man now dares take up a cause till he has mastered 90 per cent of the facts and all the background. 'Would Zola ever have defended Dreyfus, if he had been objective? No, he would have waited till he could examine all the files at the French War Office.' It seems we cannot move without a professional lead, so we wait for an academic to lose his temper. But an academic is *ex officio* never angry. He is paid to be objective. While he is being scrupulously fair to the Romans and making allowances for the Jews and balancing the claims of law and order against those of charity, the thirty pieces tinkle unnoticed and unneeded in his letter-box. Then, this sour Frenchman continues, Professor Iscariot, Ph.D., gives his trifling windfall to the Save

---

* Brian Inglis, *West Briton* (London 1962).

the Children Fund and settles down with relish to a *fait accompli*. Once more he has facts and dates to handle instead of the chaos of unregulated passion through which the rest of us must pick our way by the flickering light of indignation or sympathy.

While reading this engagingly objective book, I listened for the familiar tinkle and heard it once or twice. Inglis does not betray a country or a cause but has he not sometimes consciously and frankly betrayed himself? Let's leave that till later and begin by repeating that the Malahide story could not have been better done. In that prosperous little Dublin suburb they talked of Fairyhouse and the Fitzwilliam Lawn Tennis Club and Gilbert and Sullivan, and reached for Ireland through George Birmingham and Percy French. They were proud of the width of Carlisle Bridge, the size of Phoenix Park and the world supremacy of Guinness. They disapproved strongly of the Black and Tans. But Grandmother told the children how a despicable gang of cowards and cutthroats had shot policemen in the back and driven away Uncle So-and-so, who had always been so good to his employees. Consequently they cheered madly for the English Army Riders at the Horse Show and jerked the hats off the seditious who did not stand up for 'God Save the King'. They prided themselves that the word 'Dunleary' never cross their lips and made jokes about 'Erse' and 'Telefón' and 'Aerphort'. What dull provincial jokes they were! Surely the Anglo-Irish could have found a place for these sad cinders of a once blazing enthusiasm in the overflowing ash-pit into which whole centuries of their own misdirected idealism had been thrown? For whereas the Irish nationalists had been wrong about most things, the Irish unionists had been wrong about everything. Had they any option, a defeatist might argue, except to fade away – or become editor of *The Spectator*?

No whisper of self-criticism was ever heard in this tight little society and characteristically it was when he was studying the Irish Famine for an Oxford essay prize that Inglis first became aware that Kingstown had been called Dunleary till George IV set foot in it and millions had in fact died and emigrated through English incompetence so gross that recent English historians have had to explain it as the genocidal yearnings of the subconscious mind.

Family loyalty and class loyalty are not so obsessive as we grow older. For an Irish Protestant, national loyalty is a difficult and fragile growth. It may bolt into useless flowers like a summer lettuce or it may germinate hardly at all. Brian Inglis cherished his nationalism, once he had discovered it. His pages on *The Sham Squire* show what a good historian he can be and, though what he says of Galway and the Irish countryside could have been written by any English tourist after a summer holiday (the Little People, Grace O'Malley and so forth), his account of working on *The Irish Times* is unique.

His analysis of the slow social transformation of Malahide is also fascinating. He describes how the West British of the Pale got 'mixed' and how it came about that natives slid into the cavities of its decaying golf clubs. Impeccably well-born Britons, fleeing from the Labour government and unconscious of the gradations of Irish society, had swept into all the social sanctuaries, carrying with them in the backwash of their wealth so many people who were 'not our sort' that 'we' had become hopelessly contaminated. The rot had set in.

Having apparently vomited up Malahide, Inglis found that he had exchanged a firm loyalty for a wobbly one and that life is full of strain and misunderstanding and frustration for the hybrid, who works in Westmoreland Street and is expected to call it West Moreland Street. (In fact, of course, West Moreland Street is just as ignorant a solecism as Drogheeda or Yoggle!)[1] If he is a defeatist, he at least earned the right to be one by fighting his battles on Irish soil. I think he is a defeatist, because he once wrote in *The Twentieth Century* that, even if the Anglo-Irish were to vanish from Ireland, it would not greatly matter so long as the important contribution which they made to London journalism were sustained. I do not think he wrote this because he is an important London journalist, but because if he were to justify his retreat to himself, it was comforting to look 'objectively' at the handful of old country crocks, retired British servicemen, civil servants and suburban car salesmen in whom the spirit of Anglo-Ireland has its contemporary incarnation, and to assume that it would die with them. With an odd mixture of modesty and arrogance, he is oppressed by the lofty superiority of the dedicated romantic heroes of Protestant nationalism, Fitzgerald, Emmet, Parnell, but tries to bring Wolfe Tone, whom he finds the most congenial, 'within his reach' by lowering his stature a little. He suggests that Tone's Irish patriotism derived from pique with Pitt for ignoring his scheme for colonizing some Pacific islands, that like Inglis himself he tried to get a job in England, that he drank more Burgundy than was good for him and made a messy, unsuccessful attempt to dodge hanging by cutting his throat. But he misses the whole grandeur of Tone. Tone never allowed himself to be paralysed by 'objectivity' but forged a philosophy for himself out of the confused and conflicting aspirations of his day, out of his own untidy impulses and selfish ambitions, and having forged it, adhered to it and died for it.

Tone would remain great even if it were proved that his ill-success had delayed Catholic Emancipation and precipitated the Union. The only extenuation for the feebleness of the Anglo-Irish today is that no strong challenge is ever presented to them. Mr Inglis's account of his experiences in 'the real army', as Grandmother called it, illustrates this. When he was training for the RAF in Rhodesia, he decided that, supposing the British invaded Ireland to recover the ports, he would present himself for internment as an untrustworthy alien. But was he really untrustworthy? Would he ever have used his aeroplane to bomb the British out of Spike Island? If he had been interned there would have been so much gentlemanly understanding about it that the distance between Theobald Wolfe Tone and Brian Inglis could be measured only in light years.

Clearly Inglis accepts in a general way Tone's social philosophy. Tone's political ideals are now largely realized and would inflame nobody; his unorthodox Protestantism is that of most British intellectuals today. Yet in that one direction where Tone's leadership is still needed, Inglis and most of his compatriots hang back as though they were paralysed. Obviously Tone, who had seen the American Revolution and its consequences, would have been in favour of the absolute separation of Church and State, which for the first time brought religious tolerance to America and made the United States possible. Can one doubt that every Protestant revolutionary nationalist who has ever lived, Emmet, Fitzgerald, Davis, Parnell, would have favoured it? In our century, Horace Plunkett and Yeats and the Protestant rebels of 1916 would have agreed that it was the only way to end partition and annihilate bigotry, both Catholic and Protestant.

I think that Inglis believes this too, for he says that 'the future relationship of Church and State is sooner or later going to become the most serious issue in Ireland', and he hints at the possibility of future bloodshed if the problem is not solved. And anticipating his own departure from Ireland he says: 'What else was there to retain our interest in politics if the subject of the future of Church and State was barred?'

Why should the subject be barred? There appear to be two reasons according to Inglis. Irish Protestants have lost their stamina and no Protestant or Anglo-Irishman, being an outsider, can help solve the Church-State relationship: 'Irish Catholicism must be left to come to terms with itself.' He does not see that the principal evidence that the Irish Protestants have lost their stamina is that they so constantly reiterate this paltry excuse for apathy.

Irish Protestants constitute 25 per cent of the population of Ireland, north and south, yet those of the Republic enjoy telling each other and being told either that they have no stamina or that they would 'only do harm by interfering'. In this way they can free their minds from the unglamorous complications of Ireland and the dreary forms of bloodshed which they foresee. They have an excuse for whatever form of dis-engagement may be comfortable and for devoting themselves agreeably to what they call 'wider issues' in a larger society. But for a small historic community can there be any issue wider than survival and the prevention of bloodshed?

'Outsiders only make things worse by intervening.' Chicago gangsters have grown fat on this repulsive old sophistry ... moral cowardice dressing herself up in a diplomat's bemedalled frock-coat. The great Protestant nationalists did and said what they thought to be right and never argued that they could help their friends best by withholding their support from them. Nor did they consider themselves 'outsiders'.

The argument for non-intervention is ignorant as well as base. Jeffer-son and the Founding Fathers who introduced the separation of Church and State, did so in an atmosphere of tense religious rivalry. They could have been called 'outsiders' for Jefferson and John Adams, at least, were Unitarians, but if they had left it to the orthodox and the respectable to compose their differences nothing would have happened and America would be a more deeply divided country than Ireland is today.

Nor could a move to separate Church and State be called sectarian if the Anglo-Irish supported it, for hundreds of Protestant ecclesiastics, north and south, would oppose it passionately, as did their colleagues in America. Nor would it lead to 'irreligion'. Of all the great powers the USA has the highest percentage of churchgoers.

There are in fact only two forms of escape from the dilemma of the Anglo-Irish who wish to express themselves freely. One is that chosen by Mr Inglis: 'Go to England!' The unpopular alternative still remains: 'Go back to Wolfe Tone!'

Mr Inglis rightly places a great deal of blame for our dilemma on Grandmother, a totem-figure beside every Protestant hearth. She would have detested Wolfe Tone, who stabbed the real army in the back and chose a messy, unchristian death. But Inglis takes the wrong way of exorcising her since it ends in disengagement. He follows the will-o'-the-wisp of objectivity, saying: 'How could we Irish Protestants blame our fellow countrymen for bigotry? We had taught them how.' This argument which appears to lead to unity and brotherly love really leads to London.

Besides it is false. Grandmother with the real army behind her had, as a Catholic, oppressed the Irish for four centuries; as a Protestant she had oppressed them for only three. When Inglis says that, because of the penal laws, Irish Protestants can never give disinterested advice he is only searching for an excuse for not sticking his neck out. If Tone and Emmet and all the others did not by dying close that chapter, what profit is there in Mr Inglis's cosy penitence? And where does 'objectivity' begin? Where does it stop? The Catholic Church prides itself on its universality so it must be judged by its universal and not by its local activities. Why not say the penal laws started not in Ireland in 1688 but rather in France three years earlier, when after the Revocation of the Edict of Nantes several hundred thousand Lost Sheep were bayoneted back into the Fold? Why not recall that at the battle of the Boyne William III had eleven hundred Huguenot officers with him, fugitives from a Catholic persecution which, unlike the relatively tolerant affair which he instituted, was genuinely annihilating? Why not admit that scarcely twenty years ago countless Lost Sheep of Central Europe were driven back into the Fold with a Belsen-model crook and that their sufferings, though briefer, far surpassed those of the Huguenots or the Irish Catholics? Mr Inglis has seen the reports of their leaders; he knows them to be true, but considers it 'injudicious' to publish them.

All these facts prove is that collectively even kind and intelligent men are always ready to put pressure on their neighbours to make them conform, that Catholics and their 'separated brethren' still have excellent reasons for fearing each other not as individuals but as organized groups, and that real danger only arises when the state also ranges itself on the side of conformity.

There is only one way out, the way of Jefferson and Tone. In the North the Protestant Parliament for the Protestant people must go and in the South the separation of Church and State must be introduced and adhered to absolutely. Through not recognizing this, Inglis wandered down many strange bypaths before he admitted himself lost. He was a rebel without a cause, since, rejecting all those offered him by the Malahide Golf Club, he could find none in his warm, honest heart. So he window-gazed in Ireland in a discriminating way, but in the late forties each exhibit seemed more shop-soiled than the last. Yet Ireland still offers opportunities to the countrymen of Tone. On the way to them there is a rich crop of slights and misunderstandings to be harvested, but it is better to be arrogant like Yeats and to stay than to be deprecating like Inglis and to go. As Yeats knew, Irish independence, like American, was primarily the notion of a small Protestant minority. It is in stark opposition to the imperialist universalism of the English and to the Catholic universalism of the Irish and derives from a handful of unpopular Trinity students and a few Belfast radicals. Similarly, American independence was principally the work of some unorthodox Anglicans from Virginia, some unorthodox non-conformists from Massachusetts and Thomas Paine, a renegade English Quaker. The two groups made contact in revolutionary France and their affinity has often been underlined. When, for example, the American War of Independence broke out, Belfast Protestants lit bonfires and sent congratulations to George Washington while Dublin Catholics sent loyal messages to George III. Ireland might not be the dull, divided little island which it is today if those groups, north and south, to whom the idea of national independence is chiefly due, had played a greater part in its realization.

But the longer Inglis stayed in Ireland the further he strayed from his hero, Wolfe Tone. One of the causes which he adopted on behalf of the Civil Liberty Association, that of Baillie Stewart, is intelligible only as a hysterical come-back at dead, defeated Grandmother. When Irish liberals campaign on behalf of the illiberal and secure an Irish passport for Artukovitch (as Foreign Minister he introduced gas chambers into Yugoslavia) and country refuges for Skorzeny and sympathy for Lord Haw-Haw and Amery and Baillie Stewart (Inglis thinks that all these three were badly treated), they have started to sell their freedom and it will not be long now before Grandmother is called back from the shades and, heavily shrouded by NATO or the Common Market, once more takes things in hand.

Fortunately for Inglis, deliverance from all this came in the shape of the managing director of Associated Newspapers, who enabled him to transfer from a good Irish newspaper, *The Irish Times*, to a bad English one, *The Sketch*. *The Sketch* was a low rung on a lofty ladder, which led to a distinguished editorial chair and to the view that the Anglo-Irish, except for export purposes, are as good as dead.

The last words but six in this sad and honest book are 'an assured monthly cheque'. They are deliberately ironical.[2]

[1962]

1. Drogheda, pronounced Drāwda, and Youghal, pronounced Yāwl.
2. This essay provoked an exchange of letters with Brian Inglis in *The Kilkenny Magazine*, reprinted in *Grandmother and Wolfe Tone*, pp. 86–9.

EOIN 'POPE' O'MAHONY

There is still every year a commemorative service and a dinner in Dublin for Eoin O'Mahony. He was known to everyone from his schooldays onward as 'the Pope', but why this was so no one knew. He was a great Irishman whose greatness lay in a field that he had made peculiarly his own.

When he died in 1970 I wrote an appreciation of him in *The Irish Times* and, as he is still remembered, I will repeat it here. I had a special reason for admiring him which I did not express at the time. He had seen in the extended family a blueprint for what life might one day be like. Perhaps some generations or centuries from now groups of people, linked together maybe as kinsmen, maybe as neighbours, will feel a special responsibility for each other, based on a closer knowledge and affection than is possible in our faceless and centralized society.

In forming the O'Mahony Society, Eoin was following an ancient pattern. The O'Mahonys had been a closely knit Irish clan, which history had dispersed. In contrast the Butlers were merely a group of families, sometimes closely, sometimes remotely, sometimes not at all related. Yet when the Butler Society was formed we discovered for ourselves French and German cousins, and there were intermarriages. We had the advantage of the O'Mahonys in the abundance of our historic records, which reach back to the first coming of the Normans. The Butler Society started when the sixth Marquess of Ormonde gave Kilkenny Castle to the Irish nation, the O'Mahony Society much earlier. Yet despite all their differences the two societies developed along parallel lines. We felt we were exploring the past in order to illuminate the future. Eoin wanted to restore richness and variety and friendship to lives that our civilization has sterilized and, within the compass of one man's powers, he succeeded.

Eoin never had any great triumphs or disasters and yet he liked pomp and ceremony and relished life's vicissitudes. But he kept his celebrations small and personal and on a do-it-yourself scale, and he used pomp and ceremony not to magnify the great but to make ordinary people interesting. If one went to one of his gatherings or one of those dead parties which he brought to life by attending, nobody was a spectator, everyone was a participant. Nobody came away feeling he had surrendered to mass banality, as can happen at those public functions where everything proceeds smoothly towards a well-regulated climax. At any event that Eoin organized, the Organization Man, whom American sociologists rightly regarded as the Satan of the sixties, was sure to be routed ignominiously, and the Natural Man would take over. Eoin had such faith in him that he could make the sketchiest of plans, change them at the last moment and sweep on, not to the anticipated conclusion, but to an even better one.

I only attended one O'Mahony rally, but it had a wild spontaneity, a happy, confident chaos that must have had years of practice, megatons of spiritual buoyancy, behind it. Only a great artist in social intercourse could have brought it off.

Eoin had issued hundreds of gold-embossed invitations to the O'Mahony rally at Dunmanus Castle in the name of the Vicomte and Vicomtesse de O'Mahony, a nice young barrister and his wife, who live at Orleans. The Vicomte was the elected Chieftain of the Clan, and probably owed his election to Eoin, who did not bother to tell him about the invitations.

A shower of them fell on Fleet Street and a reporter from the *Daily Express*, attracted by the idea of an invitation from a vicomtesse to dance in an ancient castle on a remote promontory in West Cork (he swore that the word 'Dancing' was written in the left-hand corner), had packed his white tie and tails and, taking a day off his holidays and a ticket to Cork, had arrived at Dunmanus at the same time as ourselves. An English family with a tent and a caravan were encamped within the castle ruins and had just before been astounded by the arrival of an advance detachment of clansmen, bearing on long staves the banners of the O'Mahonys, and of all the nations that had given them refuge in the days of their exile.

They had planted their flags all around the caravan, and very soon a thousand other O'Mahonys had followed them and the small alien encampment, amazed but entertained, had been politely and totally submerged. Soon Eoin was in the thick of it all, booming eloquently in three languages, kissing continental hands, explaining and introducing. The O'Mahony rank-and-file and their friends were then planted on one side of a broken-down moat and the Vicomte stood on the other with Eoin beside him to interpret.

'I have to apologize,' began the Vicomte in high good humour and in French, 'that this is not my castle, and that it has not any roof, and that we are not able to dance in it, and that it wasn't I sent out that invitation.' Eoin translated all this jovially, and then we quickly passed on to serious matters, the long history of the O'Mahonys of Carbery and Kinelmeaky, their kinship and rivalries with the O'Sullivans and MacCarthys. Only the journalist sulked. When there was a pause in the narrative, he went up to Eoin and said: 'I understood there was to be a dance.'

'Well,' said Eoin, 'there's an excellent hotel in Skibbereen. Very nice people indeed, and, if you tell them you want to dance, I am sure they'll be delighted.' Eoin was then swept away by his kinsmen, and the journalist went and sulked on a lump of fallen masonry. He grumbled to some bystanders that he had been brought to West Cork on false pretences, that this was his holiday, not a job. But soon he observed that the O'Mahonys were entertained rather than touched by his mis-adventure. They were pointing him out to each other – 'Do you see that fella? Did you hear what he has in his suitcase?' – and he saw that he was becoming a stock character in a new version of a traditional Irish story, the innocent Englishman, who had never heard of Pope O'Mahony.

So he moved off to Skibbereen and, drinking himself into a good humour in the hotel, wrote a charming account of the rally for the London daily.

That was a typical O'Mahony occasion. It was an everyday setting, the ruined castle, the rocky shore, the drifts of bog asphodel, the gorse, the pools of water lilies, white as well as orange. And there were everyday people there. There were solicitors from Cork and a garage proprietor from Killarney and hospital nurses and a camp counsellor from Massachusetts. More notable was Rev. Jeremiah O'Mahony from Palm Beach, who was President Kennedy's chaplain and pronounced his name O'Mahóney. The most surprising clansman from America was coal-black. Or could he have been like myself a mere O'Mahonyphile?

Without the magic of Pope O'Mahony to fuse us and transmute us, it would have been the dullest of sea-side outings. But like a watchful cook stirring the jam, Eoin was introducing them all to each other the whole time. He could glamorize even the dullest. This one's aunt had swum the Channel, that one's brother had been in the San Francisco earthquake or as a girl she had known Fanny Parnell. Sometimes a stray sentence expanded into an immense anecdote, breeding other anecdotes, startling and complex but never malicious. If one of them were to end sadly like 'then the poor fellow took to drink and fell down a lift shaft in Las Vegas', it was like a wreath laid on a tomb. To be remembered by Eoin was to be honoured.

His great genius was to use the splendid in the service of the simple. Once I made myself hugely unpopular by flouting received opinion and became a local pariah. My friends rallied to me, but Eoin's support was the warmest and characteristic of him. He packed a shirt the next day (I think it was a shirt, not pyjamas, in that small, odd brown paper parcel), bussed to Naas, and hitch-hiked the rest of the way. He came out from Kilkenny on a creamery lorry, whose driver, he found, was a distant cousin of his. I do not think that we talked about the row at all. He was not much interested whether I was right or wrong. As with the prisoners, whom he was always trying to release, he had his own way of judging matters and always liked official verdicts to be reversed, and personal ones substituted. The next morning he spent at a table in the porch writing about thirty letters on notepaper headed with the address of a smart Dublin hotel, at which he often entertained his friends. For even if it meant starving himself later he liked to be hospitable in the grand manner.

One, I observed, was to a Cardinal, one to her Serene Highness Somebody. He was asking them no doubt to use their influence, either for the prisoners or for building a bridge to Valentia Island, and some may have been letters of introduction for friends going abroad. (He once gave me a package of eleven.) Then he put the letters in the brown paper parcel and hitch-hiked back to Dublin. A day or two later an announcement appeared at the very top of the Social and Personal section of *The Irish Times*: 'Mr Eoin O'Mahony, B.L. K.M., has been staying with Mr Hubert Butler, B.A., in Kilkenny.' He probably sent it to the London *Times* as well. I have never before or since appeared in that illustrious column, and I have always made a special thing of *not* being a B.A. But I immediately saw the point. Eoin was showing his solidarity, not with my opinions, but with me, in the most public and ceremonious way he could contrive.

I have just been listening to the Radio Éireann recording of an earlier O'Mahony rally at Castlemore Castle. It was so clear and characteristic, it was almost as though Eoin and his wonderful personality had been embalmed for eternity. But ten years from now, how would it sound to those who never knew him? I think, though he left so little published writing, Eoin may wear better than most of us. For the Faceless

Organization Man, whom Eoin combated, though he looks so vigorous, is really already a deader. Very soon we shall be searching for the scraps of the human personalities which he has pounded juggernaut-wise into the dust, and trying to piece them together. That is where Eoin and those he influenced will come into their own again. The seeds he sowed will begin to germinate in the vast and mouldering technological rubbish heap.

Being proud of him, we can be proud of Ireland too, for it is one of the few countries in which so eccentric a genius could be so warmly appreciated and so deeply regretted.

[1970]

ENVOY AND MR KAVANAGH

A Frenchman who was asked why a number of French writers and artists had collaborated with the Germans, replied with an indulgent smile: 'Writers and artists are children when it comes to politics. What can you expect?'

Perhaps that is specially true of poets and in an over-stable society maybe their childishness has value. It is like a window pane being broken in a stuffy room. Shelley in Dublin inciting the poor against their oppressors or in Oxford scandalizing the dons with revolutionary pamphlets is dear to us because he trusted the impulses of the heart and was indifferent to consequences. Swinburne, a little later, threw his stones with greater effect. Though society still stood four square, a good many windows had been broken in the meantime and what had been a pleasant freshness became an ominous draught. The more settled shivered apprehensively, in the deep Victorian afternoon.

Then came d'Annunzio, who strutted and declaimed like Swinburne, but by this time society was shattered and rocking and the child poet with his toy state of Fiume, his flags and flamboyant rhetoric, needed more than a spanking. Poetry, like a neglected adolescent, had become vicious and self-willed. It had met with bad companions. After that chaos followed, a few heads bob up, posturing and ranting, Pound, Montherlant, Roy Campbell, and in the east the former *enfant terrible* became not only a tolerated but a subsidized figure. For a moment or two the Shelleys sat in judgment on the dons. Then a new donnishness, more anti-poetical than anything before conceived, overwhelmed them.

What has happened to the rebel writers in Ireland? Fifty years ago their focus was Irish nationalism. It gave them unity and direction and the power of collective creation. They created the Abbey Theatre and the *Irish Statesman*, which was a bridge between literature and social endeavour, between Coole and Kilteragh.

83

Then something happened to this idea of an Irish Nation, which was fastidious but generous. It collapsed and by degrees everything else collapsed with it. What becomes of the ivy when the tree falls down? It doesn't die immediately. For a time it seems freer than before, thrusting out tendrils in all directions, choking some undergrowth, being choked by others. It is some time before it is finally suffocated.

Many Irish writers today seem pleased that nationalism is in decay. They think that art is liberated from a restricting preoccupation and can range like the ivy over the whole earth, not over a single tree. But does this happen? Has it happened anywhere? Is it possible that a rotten tree is better than no tree at all? What is the truth?

It might be helpful to conduct a post-mortem on the defunct monthly *Envoy*, for this was the organ of Ireland's rebellious writers. We might learn what they were rebelling against, and if and why the rebellion failed. It was a well-produced magazine with many brilliant writers. I don't think we can argue pessimistically from its death, which even its critics deplored. An Irish journal is like a sortie from a besieged city. Its effects cannot be measured by its duration.

As for the campaign of rebellion, *Envoy*'s objectives must be guessed at principally from the editorials and from Patrick Kavanagh's monthly diary.[1] For the editor in his final issue claimed that one of the great achievements of *Envoy* was to have given Kavanagh the opportunity of serving the cause of truth in Ireland and of scourging the untalented, who are bringing Irish writing into disrepute beyond our shores. This scourging was plainly an important part of the programme and in the valedictory number the editor and Mr Kavanagh complimented each other on having done a good job! Apart from several living writers, who had to take their trousers down in almost every issue, all the major figures of the Irish Renaissance came in for a severe beating. Matthew Arnold was told he was a 'well-meaning bore', and disciplinary measures were taken against the *Irish Times*, Radio Éireann, and the Protestants (whose 'coarseness' was the 'loutish superiority of a mediocre ruling class'). Somebody suggested to me that these were ritual flagellations, symbolic and without malice. It was like an initiation ceremony from the South Sea Islands, slightly humanized by the Church, and all it meant was that the young were ready to take over from the old. 'We shouldn't worry,' he said, 'that's life and it shows there's good stuff in them. The grandfather gorilla would only get seriously worried about his posterity if he didn't get beaten up by his children.'

But I don't think an anthropological or zoological explanation will really do. *Envoy* was a serious paper engaged on a real campaign against the Philistine and it was bad management that all the violence went on in the guard-room behind the lines, while the Philistines looked on and laughed. Compared to Patrick Kavanagh, a dashing guerrilla captain, Matthew Arnold was a great general, a tried campaigner against the Philistines, trained in all the academies of war. Rivalry was inevitable. Yet if Mr Kavanagh enjoys today a certain freedom to express himself, Arnold was one of those who guaranteed it.

Envoy had something serious to say. Perhaps it was the very urgency of the message that made the messenger so breathless. His end in the twentieth issue was tragic. It was as though he raced through the enemy's lines, bearing some tremendous news, and at last collapsed raving among his friends, whom in his delirium he mistakes for the Philistines. His lips are frothing, his pulse racing but he can only stammer out a few baleful familiar syllables, 'Mr Smyllie', 'Austin Clarke', 'Radio Éireann', 'Faugh!' He gives a last belch and dies pillowed in his own vomit, his message undelivered.

I am afraid some of the bystanders tittered at his death-bed scene. But laughter, even indulgent laughter, is out of place. *Envoy* was a good and gallant paper and its death is a tragedy. Moreover, Mr Kavanagh can be a very good writer indeed.

Envoy had been seriously schizophrenic from the start. Confronted by the fact that our best writers of a generation ago had had 'microcosmic' tendencies, the editor and Mr Kavanagh began to tug in different direc-tions. Here is an editorial manifesto, once or twice re-echoed: 'For fifty years Dublin has been the scene of the major literary Renaissance in Western civilization.' Now let's look at the hind legs of the horse, but stand well clear! It's Mr Kavanagh: 'One of the things it would be necessary to teach in this country is that the pygmy literature which was produced by the so-called Irish literary Renaissance is quite worthless.'

And then, midway in *Envoy*'s career, Mr Hogan, the Dramatic Critic, who had also been using his hooves rather wildly right and left, started to exchange kicks with Mr Kavanagh, and it was he who finally pranced on the dead body of *Envoy* in the *Irish Times*.

Yet conflict, even editorial conflict, inside a paper can be very whole-some; it is the conflict within the writer's own mind which is de-moralizing. Mr Kavanagh's mind, when he abandons poetry and fiction, is like a monkey house at feeding time. It is worthy of a careful examination because in an exaggerated form he is suffering from the same disorder as many other Irish writers. *Ex uno disce omnes.* Mr Kavanagh is highly gifted and the fact that he has to tell us so himself is in our grudging society no proof of the contrary. There is much excuse for his antics.

The perversion of the national ideal has forced Irish writers into spiritual and intellectual acrobatics for which there are few parallels outside central Europe. Many of those who thirty years ago encouraged or condoned the expulsion of the Anglo-Irish are today talking for the BBC and would not shrink from doing propaganda for the British way of life through the British Council.

Nor can we moralize about this. AE and the Anglo-Irish nationalists of a generation ago were not subjected to the same trials and temptations, and it is scarcely fair to claim that they were more consistent in their loyalties. Under stress the artist has to make the strangest recantations (they never appear as recantations since the adjustment is by stages). Our minds run a little ahead of our gross material needs and, when the economic pressure comes, it finds us spiritually conditioned. Alas! Is not Chekhov's widow, the greatest of Russian actresses, quite proud of her Stalin prize? But adjustments, though they are inevitable and gradual, may still be painful. They may shake the whole machinery of the mind so that it shrieks and rattles like an abrupt and clumsy change of gear. All the shrieking and rattling that goes on in Irish literature today is surely the result of these psychological adjustments. Compare the wise and equable tone of the *Irish Statesman* under AE with the neurotic tantrums of *Envoy*.

The Anglo-Irish contribution to letters is today, as I have suggested, a chief focus of psychological disturbance. The Anglo-Irish writers who surrounded Yeats deliberately left the big world for the small one. They were more afraid of being culturally submerged in a big empire than of being stranded in sterile isolation in a small island. Time has justified them. Work of European significance was done under the stimulus of what might be considered parochial enthusiasms, and their fame is even today one of the strongest of the links that bind Ireland to the outer world. In fact while the parochialism of 1951 is sterile, the parochialism of 1901 was richly creative.

Envoy would have done good work by facing this anomaly and tracing its causes. But Mr Kavanagh refuses to face it; he will not see that the Abbey Theatre group not only nursed Irish talent at home but also created abroad a favourable atmosphere for its reception. Every Irish writer who travels to London is in their debt. Mr Kavanagh wants to repudiate this debt in order to make his case that genius always works its own passage. Confusing universalism with megalopolitanism, which the Anglo-Irish writers repudiated, he blames them for being parochial. Then he attacks their 'pygmy literature' front and rear. In an essay on F. R. Higgins he accuses Irish Protestants of trying to 'by-pass Rome on the way to the heart of Ireland', and several times he argues with different degrees of candour that you cannot be Irish if you are not Catholic. This is a light-hearted argument without arrogance and it can be answered without arrogance by a *tu quoque*. What Mr Kavanagh is trying to do is to by-pass Anglo-Ireland on the way to the heart of London. And it is sure that while Anglo-Ireland, north and south, may ultimately be assimilated (a very slow process of reciprocal adjustment), it cannot conceivably be by-passed. The Anglo-Irish were not only the cruel stepmothers of Gaelic civilization, they were also the indulgent nurses and governesses of Irish literature in the English language. They have been the mediators between England and Ireland for centuries. Mr Kavanagh suspects them also with some reason of having been the authors of Irish Nationalism. Yet he would sooner repudiate Irish Nationalism than acknowledge any cultural indebtedness to Anglo-Ireland. Watch him at work in *Envoy*.

Synge is 'a vulgarian'. 'The predominant note of his writings is hate.' 'Yeats showed his minor microcosmic mind by advising him to study the people of his own country.' 'Yeats' material was a very parochial thing, Irish Nationalism.' 'Had he been really great he would have abandoned the anaemic world of petty nationalism and followed his stomach's leanings.' 'Hyde and Davis, Butt, Parnell and Erskine Childers were all Cromwellians.' 'Shaw is tedious' and 'all lies', and so on.

Mr Kavanagh is not a bigot. He attacks his own Church roundly, its 'anti-intellectualism' and 'barbarous pietisms', and I think his attack on Protestantism is directed against the Anglo-Irish cultural incubus rather than against the Reformation. I think he really prefers O'Casey when he assails the Church of Rome from a Communist standpoint ('the real Protestantism of our time', he calls it) to F. R. Higgins when he writes sympathetically but with an outsider's clumsiness of the Mass. He sees a good counter-blast to a certain kind of Irish clericalism in 'O'Casey's genuine Protestant bigotry', but is angry with him when he writes with friendliness of the unorthodox Father Walter Macdonald, of whom, says Mr Kavanagh, he knows 'sweet damn all'. He argues that you cannot be Irish and not a Catholic, because (I do not quite follow his reasoning here) 'Catholicism is a universal concept of mankind and Protestantism was here an attempt to by-pass this universalism and to concentrate the light on a minor detail.' But does he not see that by excluding nationalism as a Protestant Anglo-Irish heresy and equating Irishness and Catholicism, he is in danger of the far worse heresy of racialism? He toys significantly with the theory that Higgins' name was really Huggins, a Saxon masquerading as an Irishman. This is a very slippery slope indeed.

These arguments are, of course, no longer very inflammatory, and Mr Kavanagh doesn't mean any harm. We use the old coloured counters to score points in a multitude of different games, social, economic, political; they are faded and paper thin, and they have different values for different games. It is not Mr Kavanagh's disparagement of Anglo-Ireland and its prevailing faith which is so disruptive; it is his loose unserious reasoning. His own faith seems to be nostalgic and atmospheric: it is by no means fanatical or precise; 'Christianity is the only frame for Pagan freedom ... there is an outside ring of ethical abnegations and professional priests, but inside the old human life dancing like children and drinking wine like men.' 'We want to go down prostrate and cry out our belief but our reason refuses' ... and so on. This does not sound very strait-laced and maybe he feels he has to establish his orthodoxy by an occasional good-humoured wallop at the Protestants. In a good cause few Protestants would grudge their backsides. But as the real menace nowadays is not theological rigorism but sloppy thinking, we cannot afford to be too indulgent. We cannot, for example, accept this alleged bond, intimate, indissoluble, between Catholicism and Ireland. What are the grounds for it? Racial? Temperamental? But the Welsh Celts adjusted themselves well enough to Methodism, the Reformation took strong root among the Breton Celts and had to be eradicated by the French. Historical grounds? Why everybody knows that Catholic Universalism was enforced in Ireland, as never before, by the Normans and the English. In the south-east, for example, the Butlers frequently used it against the Kavanaghs as a means of breaking down their strong tribal loyalties. In the Kavanagh country, as elsewhere, there was often a Pope in every parish. Their spiritual leaders, St Maedoc, St Moling, St Munnu, were all, with the doubtful exception of the last, fanatically tribal in their loyalties. Catholic Universalism was in Ireland, as in many other countries, enforced on the invaded by the invader. When at the beginning of the nineteenth century Irish Protestantism was a pro-selytizing creed, the missionaries often saw that they could not censure Catholicism without also censuring the English ascendancy, which had used it so profitably. That is one of the reasons why Irish nationalism has often been closely linked with Protestantism.

These are dead or dying controversies, only revived to prove that Irishmen are as free to choose their beliefs as any other people. Nor is nationalism, in so far as it is only neighbourliness grown a bit inflated and unwieldy, the pernicious force that Mr Kavanagh suspects. On this point he contradicts himself often. At one stage he says that only minor poets like Rupert Brooke care about their country, but later he concedes

that 'an Irish writer is lost when he is detached from his native roots'
and that 'although the real roots are in the mind and not in geography,
yet the fact is we sometimes find it hard to get at our minds through
the screen of a strange symbol. But this can be got over if one has a truly
creative faculty.' And elsewhere he writes: 'A writer cannot come across
with nonsense to an audience of his own people. The false note rings
out loudly.'

But I think the proof that we are tied in some degree to geography
is given in Kavanagh's last essay. Has anything more parochial ever been
written in Ireland? Would a man who was not inextricably involved in
a small society bother to insult it in such detail? Obviously there is love
there as well as hate.

In fact Mr Kavanagh's anti-nationalism is probably a necessary antidote to some emotional excesses of his. Most of the Anglo-Irish writers
whom he would like to have dosed had a surfeit of this medicine from
childhood.

I don't think writers should tie themselves in knots with these words
'nationalism', 'universalism'. A writer in 1951 will want the same thing
as in 1901, even though the formula for obtaining it may have altered
slightly. He will want to write about the community he knows, with
detachment and with love. He will want to be a free individual integrated
into a stable group, not a unit in a herd. Such groups are hard to find.
Do they exist? Probably not. Yet they are more likely to be foreshadowed
in County Monaghan than in Fleet Street. That is the explanation of the
'microcosmic' tendencies of the Yeats circle, and perhaps also of Mr
Kavanagh's own fine creative achievements.

Or is Mr Kavanagh perhaps merely thinking of 'opportunities', 'publishers, literary lunches, stimulating conversations and contacts'? These
are of great though secondary importance but have nothing to do with
anti-nationalism. The BBC, which is a fairy godmother to so many
Irish writers, is a strongly national organization and its ramifications
extend through the whole of English literary society. Mr Kavanagh has
nothing but scorn for an organization such as the Pen Club, which aims,
however ineffectually, at by-passing nationalism. In fact, Mr Kavanagh's
universalism is all a cod.

No artist need be a nationalist or a universalist, concerned with the
drawing or effacing of political frontiers. But cultural frontiers exist, and
a good artist will respect them whether or not they are drawn on the
map. Most of them are not and could not be, since the social and
economic groups which they define are widely scattered and segmented.
Kavanagh says that O'Casey, like Higgins, is incompetent on a Catholic

theme, yet he is worse on an English one. Irish Catholics who write
about the Anglo-Irish are also at sea, though they are their next-door
neighbours. O'Faolain's book on Countess Markievicz is only justifiable
as a revenge for Mrs Conyers and G. A. Birmingham. In one of O'Connor's books I recollect an Irish Protestant welfare worker who might
have been described by an intelligent Chinaman. The more sensitive,
the better an artist is, the more he betrays himself when he ventures
outside the tiny zone in which he is at ease. To take a great writer,
E. M. Forster, how bad the 'inside' view of Italy is in *Where Angels Fear
to Tread* compared with the outside view in *A Room With a View*. *A
Passage To India* is a great work because the Indians are almost always
depicted two-dimensionally, as they appear to the English eye. They
and their country are little more than a backcloth against which an
English middle-class drama is staged.

Of course there are writers like Koestler who have inherited a 'universalist' outlook, but their books are not novels but Baedekers of contemporary life. Mr Kavanagh writes more permanently himself. And as
for Catholic Universalism in art, I have been hoping that Mr Waugh or
Mr Greene would write a book about Catholic Ireland, because then
their true stature as writers would become apparent here. Mr Waugh
has, I am glad to say, written a story about Anglo-Ireland. Short and
slight as it was, it was more than sufficient as an index of his universalism.
In his practical advice to the Irish writer Mr Kavanagh contradicts
himself again. In the last instalment of his diary he urged them not to
write at all if they had not genius. 'Genius alone counts.' 'The rest of
the world must accept its own sterile fate... Better not write at all than
write mediocre verse.' 'The rest of the world should be satisfied by
loving God, by praising his works and the greatest work of God on this
earth is the dancing flame of the poet's imagination.' And he tells us that
there are only about twenty of these dancing flames in Europe.

But elsewhere in his diary he says just the opposite. He tells us that
the 'worst frustration is intellectual and artistic' and that 'deaf mutes go
mad'. 'We *must* express ourselves' and 'nobody need be a mediocrity, if
he is himself'.

One might accept these contradictions as half-baked poetical aph-
orisms shortly to be fused together over a dancing flame, if so much
solid material, denunciations of Radio Éireann and the like, had not
been flung into Mr Kavanagh's crucible. Clearly his advice is meant to
be practical, and the ordinary Irishman of literary inclinations is faced
with the dilemma of either going mad in silence or else becoming the
twenty-first genius in Europe. This cannot be.

These diaries were meant for speech, not print. At their best they are paradoxical challenges flung out to stimulate thought, but in a monthly the challenge cannot be met, and the effect is chaotic.

There were many good stories and poems and constructive essays in *Envoy*, and it always gave a generous hearing to its own critics. A memorable letter was published from Matthew Horgan in which he urged that 'the work to be done here is not by the angry men but by the quiet voices which drone on behind the animal cries', and he was not afraid to appeal for 'minor works of literary value'. This modest claim is more likely to be answered than Mr Kavanagh's, who is so sure that genius will flourish in the desert like a rose, that he wishes to sterilize the soil of minor talents, or so he said. On the contrary, a long and laborious task of irrigation confronts us and a whole forest of minor talents may have to flourish and die before our soil is rich enough to sustain a single genius.

[1954]

1. Patrick Kavanagh (1904–67), poet, novelist and controversialist. Recognized as a major talent with *The Great Hunger* (1942), much of his work (like the novel *Tarry Flynn*, 1948) at once railed against the frustrations of Irish rural life and celebrated its poetry. Besides contributing to *Envoy*, he launched *Kavanagh's Weekly* in 1952, offering a lively and splenetic critique of current Irish affairs.

BOYCOTT VILLAGE

Fethard-on-Sea is a small village of about a hundred houses on the Wexford coast. It is not a seaside resort, for the muddy creek, which brings the houses to an end, can surely only be called 'the sea' to distinguish the village from the less notorious Fethard in Tipperary. The ancient hotel near the creek is now Mr Leslie Gardiner's General Stores, but neither he nor Miss Betty Cooper, who sells cornflakes, sweets and newspapers on the opposite side of the street, expect much from the seaside visitors. Tourists, of course, pass through, but they are mainly the self-sufficient kind with picnic-baskets in the boot. They are bound for Baginbun, a short distance away, where there is a charming secluded shore, rock-pools lined with emerald seaweed and, on most days, no one else. It was at Baginbun that the Normans first landed in Ireland eight centuries ago. They had been invited by Dermot Mac Morrogh, the great chieftain to whom all Wexford belonged. He had stolen another chieftain's wife. There had been unpleasantness and reprisals as a result and so he had asked for English help. The English came and they stayed. So much so that today men of English blood predominate in Wexford.

And now there has been turmoil there again about another truant wife and things have happened that have shocked all Ireland, north and south, and made the hope of unity recede still further. It is not a parochial squabble; it is not exclusively an Irish one. It is a collision between human nature and the 'immutable' principles of the Roman Catholic Church. Such collisions happen somewhere every day, but this one has been watched with such breathless interest, because in Ireland we still have the primitive power of focusing our minds like burning-glasses on tiny patches. Just as bird-watchers go to the Saltees, those three un-inhabited islands which lie off Baginbun, so men-watchers should come to Ireland to see how men, not yet trapped in the mental zoo of the

92

television set and the Sunday press, still think and act in a natural untamed state.

In the spring of 1957 Eileen Cloney had reached the age of six. She lived with her parents and her baby sister in a bald grey castle just outside Fethard. It is 600 years old but it has been liberally renovated with concrete and has rather new-looking battlements and a turret. There is a huge barn beside it, whose corrugated iron roof has grown rusty in the salty air. There are elm trees and sprawling hedges, where in late June, when I first saw Dungulph, the blackberries were beginning to flower, the last bells were still clinging to the tips of the foxgloves and the first ones climbing up some stray mulleins. It seemed an enchanted place in which to be six years old. But Eileen Cloney had reached school age and Father Allen and his curate, Father Stafford, were insistent that there must be no further delay. She must go to school. They were emphatic about this, because Mrs Cloney, a strong-minded woman, showed signs of wanting to send Eileen to the small Protestant school, where there were twelve other pupils, children of local farmers and of Leslie Gardiner. Though her husband was a Catholic, Mrs Cloney was the daughter of a Protestant stockbreeder of Fethard. I have never met Sean Cloney or his wife, Sheila, but they seem to be a likeable pair and their marriage appeared to be a happy one. The sudden split, which occurred in the middle of April, arose out of Eileen's schooling. It is disagreeable to discuss the characters and lives of quiet modest people like the Cloneys, who have never courted publicity, but circumstances and, in particular, Father Allen and Father Stafford, have decreed that their private lives are no longer their own. Sean Cloney, in his press photographs, looks a pleasant, good-looking, easy-going young man. He has that amused, cynical, shoulder-shrugging appearance that is common enough in Ireland. Sheila Cloney, who has hitherto escaped the press photographer, seems to have been more vigorous and dominating. Immediately after her marriage she started to make the 116-acre farm at Dungulph pay, wrestling herself with the tractor and the accounts and achieving such success that last year they bought a combine harvester. She was as devoted to her own Church as to her home and, when she came in from the fields, she often went with broom and scrubbing brush to the Protestant church of Fethard. It was being redecorated this spring and she was among the most tireless of the volunteers, who every night tidied away the builders' débris.

It was on May 13th that the squabble became public property, but it is not yet clear who was squabbling with whom. Was Sheila at war with Sean or was she warring with Father Allen and Father Stafford, while Sean, shrugging his shoulders, looked on? Certain it is that Sheila on April 27th took the car and the children to Wexford, where later it was found abandoned in the street. Three days later a barrister came from Belfast with 'terms of settlement'. They were drastic terms, suggesting an extreme state of feminine exasperation. Sean was to sell Dungulph Castle and they were to emigrate together to Canada or Australia, where the children were to be brought up as Protestants. 'No one influenced her in her decision,' Sean declared to a reporter. 'Once Sheila gets an idea into her head, a regiment of soldiers wouldn't change her.'

The news was received with consternation in Fethard. There was a thunderous pronouncement from the altar, and the next day a boy-cott started of all the Protestants in the neighbourhood. There was a Catholic teacher in the Protestant school, a Catholic sexton in the Protestant church; they both resigned. The elderly music teacher, Miss Knipe, lost eleven of her twelve pupils, Mr Gardiner's General Stores and Miss Cooper's more modest emporium were rigorously boycotted. So were the Protestant farmers who sold milk, and from one of them a Catholic farmhand walked away. The boycott, the priests declared, would continue till Mrs Cloney brought back the children.

For the first week the better-disciplined Catholics refused to greet or to look at their Protestant neighbours, but here and there a rebellious one gave a furtive smile when no one was looking. At the end of the week, either because a breath of Christian charity forced its way through some crack in the united front or because it was better to abate the rigour of the boycott rather than betray any lack of unanimity, the boycotters began to smile and nod. But there was no relaxation of economic pressure.

By this time the newspapers of Dublin and Belfast were headlining the news from Fethard. It was anticipated that very soon a word from the local Catholic bishop, the Bishop of Ferns, would put an end to what was becoming a national scandal. But the ecclesiastical intervention, when it came, was more astounding than what had preceded. On Saturday, June 30th, the Annual Congress of the Catholic Truth Society was being held in Wexford, and at the Church of the Immaculate Conception Cardinal D'Alton was received by the Bishop of Ferns. In front of them and five other bishops of the Roman Church, including the Archbishop of Dublin, the Bishop of Galway preached a sermon defending the boycott.

There seems [he said] to be a concerted campaign to entice or kidnap Catholic children and deprive them of their faith. Non-Catholics with one or two honourable exceptions do not protest against the crime of conspiring to steal the children of a Catholic father. But they try to make political capital, when a Catholic people make a peaceful and moderate protest.

In the same newspaper which reported this apology for a 'peaceful and moderate protest', we read that two of Mrs Cloney's brothers in Fethard had been obliged to seek police protection, because a shot had been fired at one of them near his home. At the same time a young Protestant teacher from Trinity College arrived to take charge of the Protestant school, which had been closed since the teacher had abandoned her pupils. He found a warning nailed onto the school-door:

SCABS! BEWARE OF THE LEAD IN BOYCOTT-VILLAGE!

No prominent Catholic had come forward to condemn the boycott except a barrister, Mr Donal Barrington, who in his address to a Catholic Social Study Conference in Dublin, said that the boycott was doing damage to the cause of Catholicism. 'It is', he said, 'the most terrible thing that has happened in this part of the country since the Civil War,' and he went on to say that he was only echoing the opinion of all the intelligent Catholics, laymen and priests, with whom he had discussed the matter. But their opinion had been given in private and he felt it his duty to speak publicly. 'There is a time in the affairs of people, when nothing is necessary for the triumph of evil but that good men should maintain what is called a discreet silence.'

No other Catholic made so bold a comment, till a week later Mr de Valera himself declared in the Dáil:

If, as head of the Government, I must speak, I can only say from what has appeared in public that I regard this boycott as ill-conceived, ill-considered and futile for the achievement of the purpose for which it seems to have been intended, that I regard it as unjust and cruel to confound the innocent with the guilty, that I repudiate any suggestion that this boycott is typical of the attitude or conduct of our people, that I am convinced that ninety per cent of them look on this matter as I do and that I beg of all, who have regard for the fair name, good repute and well-being of our nation, to use their influence to bring this deplorable affair to a speedy end.

Mr de Valera was right. The Irish are not by nature bullying or ungenerous; they are indulgent to human weaknesses and disinclined to totalitarian judgments. This essay, therefore, is not about bigotry, but about the ineffectuality of ordinary people with nice intentions and neighbourly instincts. This has often been demonstrated before in totalitarian countries, but only the last stage in the suppression of the amiable, when they are being finished off by threats and violence, has been closely observed. The earlier stages of coercion by 'peaceful and moderate protest' have never had the same attention, yet they are more important. For the handful of free spirits, who in any community are the last-ditch guardians of freedom, are not defenceless till the amiable majority, which forms an inert but not easily negotiable obstacle in the path of tyranny, has first been neutralized. How is this done? It is not difficult. The events in Fethard show how eagerly the amiable will cooperate in their own extinction.

It is now fifty years since the *Ne Temere* decree, which condemns the Irish nation to live in two mutually distrustful camps, was first applied to Ireland. It has broken up many homes besides the Cloneys' and brought an element of hypocrisy or perjury into every marriage between Irish people of different faith. Yet never till now did the whole Irish nation observe and deplore the cruel tensions which it has created. It is doubtful whether de Valera lost a single vote by championing the boycotted. For the Church of Ireland is much more than a vast complex of emptying palaces, rectories, cathedrals. In Ireland it is still the spearhead of the Reformation and few people are ready to renounce the liberties won at the Reformation, even when they repudiate the reformers. Father Stafford and his anathemas are as much an anachronism in Ireland as the Anglo-Irish ascendancy.

Yet this time the Protestant hierarchy made a scapegoat of Mrs Cloney and did not reiterate those protests against *Ne Temere*, which our primate made long ago and more recently republished. He and others had denied the validity of a promise 'extorted under pressure', and such denials undoubtedly influenced Mrs Cloney in her decision. Weakened perhaps by the emigration of vigour and intelligence, our clergy counselled appeasement and that 'discreet silence', which Mr Barrington saw as the prelude to the triumph of evil. By inference they accepted the *Ne Temere* promises as valid; they deprecated excessive newspaper publicity, condemned any lay attempt to organize aid for the boycotted Protestants as 'senseless retaliation' and, in our diocesan magazine, gave retrospective approval to a strange undertaking given by Mrs Cloney's father, Mr Kelly. Speaking 'on behalf of the Church of Ireland community', he had pledged it to do all it could to bring back his grandchildren to Fethard, and published this promise in the Irish papers. Tactfully he said nothing about the boycott, which is known locally as 'Parish Co-operation' and was described by Father Stafford in the press as 'this grand, dignified, legal profession of our Faith'. By implication

Protestants were committed to act as watchdogs for the observance of a decree directed against themselves. It was assumed that, as a *quid pro quo*, the boycott would be called off, but the Church of Ireland bit the dust in vain. The boycott continued and our clergy, returning from their Munich, gave themselves over to exhortation against mixed marriages, and the social intercourse that might lead to them. Canute, rebuking the waves, was not less profitably engaged. In the countryside we have dwindled to two or three per cent of the population (the rector of Fethard controls five amalgamated parishes); if we are to mix exclusively with ourselves, we are condemned to social isolation, to celibacy, inbreeding or dreary marriages of convenience. But can we really believe that our duty to our neighbour is to avoid him socially, lest we love him as ourselves and forget the dangerous contagion of his faith? For that is the way in which the gospel precepts appear to have been revised.

This ecclesiastical advice will not of course be followed, but nor will it be repudiated for, as in the early days of the Brown Shirts in Germany, respectable people put their faith in the healing properties of time. We like to think that, left to themselves, our difficulties will all 'blow over', 'peter out', 'die down'. There is a rich range of synonyms for the spontaneous disappearance of evil and we seldom commit the folly of sticking out our necks or poking in our noses. And, in fact, if we only have patience, the victim of injustice will probably emigrate and cease to embarrass us with his tedious lamentations.

Irish Protestants are generally 'broad minded' about belief. They tend to judge other religions as they judge their own, by its social consequences. Having sometimes a hereditary interest in property, they are impressed by the Catholic defence of property. A true instinct also informs them that the Catholic Church is basically as unsympathetic to Irish nationalism as is the average Irish Protestant and might at any moment barter its support of the Irish Republic for a favoured position in the Commonwealth. This emerged clearly at Fethard. The Bishop of Galway, in his Wexford address, deliberately gave arguments to the Northerners against the abolition of Partition and cannot have been dismayed by the repercussions in Belfast. A united Ireland, in which there would be a twenty-five per cent heretical minority, might seem to present the Church of Rome with problems insoluble, except in the vast dilution of the Commonwealth. But to declaim against Irish unity would be unpopular; the Orangemen could safely be left to do all the declaiming, for Ulster eyes are dim with gazing on far-off imperial horizons and cannot focus clearly on what goes on under the nose. A fund was raised for the boycotted Protestants and a Northern MP sent to distribute it. On July 12th not a single Orange orator failed to mention Fethard, but, as interest on the large 'political capital' derived from the boycott, the dividend that went to Fethard was small.

Some weeks ago Father Allen bought some cigarettes at Gardiner's. This momentous act did not mean the end of the boycott, but it has cast a rose-pink veil over its origins and the responsibility for its continuance. An irreverent person, peering through the veil, would see that the boycott can never now end. The lost customers have found other tradesmen, eager to supply their needs, a new newsagent bicycles round with the papers to Miss Cooper's former clients, a new milkman goes the rounds and the old schoolteacher and the old sextoness will never return. Nor will Miss Knipe's pupils. To end the boycott more unpleasantness and fresh dislocations would be necessary, and these are things which in Ireland we always avoid if we possibly can.

[1958]

POSTSCRIPT I (1978)

In the past years there have been some verbal concessions about the *Ne Temere* decree but very little effective change. Yet I am confident that had Protestants listened to Primate Gregg's 'Resistance in God's Name is the Duty of us all' and acted with courage and unity, they would have caused the total abolition of the decreee in 1958.

At that time we were doing up our house in Co. Kilkenny, which was fifty miles away, and we bought all our putty, paint and as much else as we could at Gardiner's Stores and Miss Cooper's Fancy Goods Shop. In two journeys we spent twenty or thirty pounds and I wrote to *The Irish Times* suggesting that if all the Protestants within fifty miles of Fethard did all their shopping there, the boycott would be over in a week. I wrote anonymously, as one often did in the fifties.

However, our bishop, Dr Phair, wrote in reply that this would be 'senseless provocation' and that was the end of my campaign. As he had always been friendly to me I might have forestalled this, had I the wit to sign my name.

Ne Temere came up in *The Irish Times* fifteen years later, when the Rev. R. C. Johnston declared that Fethard had been a turning-point in our history and that Protestants in their spinelessness had left the defence of their liberties to liberal Catholics like Noel Browne and humanists like Owen Skeffington. In reply I recalled Gregg's words and insisted that had Dr Phair encouraged us rather than the reverse, there would have been such an avalanche of Protestants from Wexford, Waterford and Kilkenny as would have kept all the boycotted in plenty for the rest of their lives and secured the repeal of *Ne Temere*.

Dr Phair was dead but his widow was much hurt; she wrote to me privately and said that those who suffered were aware of their prayers and that £1754.10.4 had been subscribed to the Fethard Relief Fund in the Bank of Ireland and that his behaviour had met with general approval. I am sure it did but it seemed to me as though the Protestant leaders were trying to buy us off our duty with cheques and as though the welfare of some shopkeepers and dairy farmers was at stake and not our children's freedom and the Protestant right of private judgment.

A great common gesture would have given us courage and confidence and arrested the sad slow Protestant decline. It would have reminded the northern Protestants that we belong together and that they belong to Ireland.

Success would have been inevitable, for the decree, only imposed on England and Ireland in 1908 and not extended to Germany, was in no way infallible. It could, in Gregg's words, be 'withdrawn at any time or thrust into the capacious waste paper basket kept at Rome for the reception of Papal utterances that have miscarried'.

Here is the conclusion of the statement made by the House of Bishops of the Church of Ireland soon after the application of *Ne Temere* to Ireland in 1908: 'We, the archbishops and bishops of the Church of Ireland, appeal on behalf of the oppressed and helpless to all lovers of justice and liberty to do their utmost by all lawful means for the redressing of a grievous wrong.'

POSTCRIPT II (1984)

In the past six years Irish Protestants, faced with a real possibility of extinction before the end of the century, have reacted more vigorously than before to the demands of the dominant majority.

In November 1983 the Irish Catholic Hierarchy issued a new 'directory' about mixed marriages. Couched in conciliatory terms, it left the situation much as it was before, except that the promises made by the Catholic parent to bring up the children as Catholics could be oral and not written. The House of Bishops of the Church of Ireland was deeply dissatisfied; in their view a promise is a promise, whether written or spoken. The Protestant bishops also complained that 'God's Law' was being invoked to support the Catholic claim: 'We do not know where in God's Law there is support for a promise to ensure the Roman Catholic upbringing of all the children.' The directory claimed that in some areas of Ireland the Protestant spouse was frequently only nominally so and therefore had no difficulty in agreeing to the Catholic ruling. The Church of Ireland reply was that in other areas the reverse was true. They were surprised, too, that whereas the directory regarded the Protestant attitude to divorce as an impediment to mixed marriages, an exception was made for the Orthodox Church, which also recognized divorce. I would suggest that the reason for this is practical not spiritual; since the Russian Revolution the Orthodox Church has been so weakened and divided that it presents a tempting mission field. There was every reason to be conciliatory.

There had been an earlier confrontation on a different issue. The Constitutional Amendment of September 1983, whose intention was to guarantee beyond all possibility of change the existing law against abortion, was passed by a majority, which was deceptive, as only half the electorate voted. It split the country as it had seldom been split before. The Protestant Churches, galvanized by Dean Griffin of St Patrick's Cathedral, took a prominent part in the resistance. Accepting that abortion is an evil, they still saw no necessity of copper-fastening a law whose observation it was impossible to guarantee. Many felt that the publicity given to the Amendment would be counter-productive. The evidence that between 3000 and 5000 woman were going annually to England to have abortions revealed how easily the law could be defied. Many, too, asked themselves what advice they would give if someone dear to them was raped or told by her doctor that she would bear a hopelessly handicapped child or was forced by circumstances to give her fatherless child to others to rear. To them it seemed that the Amendment was the negation of the Protestant right of private judgment.

There is some truth in the directory's argument about nominal Protestantism. Although there is far less vocal 'unbelief' today than a century ago, when it was based on biblical criticism and caused heart-break and alienation, there is wide-spread indifference in both Churches. On the other hand there are many who long for spiritual guidance but cannot accept it in the form in which it is offered. They see how in our materialistic and deeply divided society the Churches have lost their mediatory power. There are sectarian murders, which have nothing to do with a conflict of principle. Great blocks of hereditary conformities, which owe nothing to the movement of the individual mind, jostle each other in inflexible hostility. The arguments of the ecumenists at no point touch these embattled certainties. The leaders of rival Churches have come together and, forgetting their differences, have preached against violence. Their united voices have had no effect. They are addressing themselves to a small but powerful body of men, superbly armed and subsidized from many sources, who are confident that, if they crush their adversaries, and win, they will ultimately be accepted. History, they know, is on their side; in country after country *coups d'état*, brought about by violence, have later received ecclesiastical sanction.

The only future for the Churches in a time of mounting violence is to forget all their dogmatic differences and the supernatural claims with which mass unanimity is cemented and to concentrate on the Christian teaching of brotherly love, which applies to all our neighbours and all our countrymen, whatever their faith. This is the only catalyst that can break down every consensus, which has outlived its day, and free that teaching from sectarian overtones.

Christianity was born in a small community and it was to small communities, no bigger for the most part that Fethard-on-Sea, that St Paul wrote his epistles. The New Testament precept, 'Thou shalt love thy neighbour as thyself', was not purely allegorical. It was not impossible then to identify oneself with those with whom one associated and to feel a deep concern for them.

Today the idea of neighbourly love has been diluted till it covers all humanity. We grieve for distant events and people with sympathy as thin and ephemeral as the newspaper in which we read about them. We suffer from a disease so widespread as to seem incurable. Yet where the diagnosis is obvious, the cure cannot be for ever beyond our reach.

Is it possible that in some far-off day Christian society, responding to human needs, will gradually be structurally transformed?

THE EGGMAN AND THE FAIRIES

━━━

You can see Slievenaman from my fields, though it is across the Tipperary border, a pale blue hump with the soft, rounded contours of ancient hills whose roughnesses have been smoothed away by time. Starting after lunch you can climb to the tip and be back by summer daylight, though it is over 2000 feet high. It can be seen from five or six southern counties and is one of the three or four most famous of Irish hills. Finn MacCool lived there and so did Oisin and Oscar, and fifty beautiful maidens, who give it its name, 'The Mountain of Women', embroidered garments for them there, or so they say. The top of the mountain to within a couple of hundred feet of the cairn of stones is bare except for an odd patch of sphagnum moss and heather. Below it there is more heather, well grazed by sheep, and a few frochan clumps, but except for some piles of stones that might once have been a house and a rough track for carting turf, there is not much sign of human traffic. I had always supposed that the Clearys' house had been in one of these ruined stone heaps upon the mountain side, because I could not associate their uncanny story with the prosperous and populous plain below. But one day I went to look for Ballyvadlea, where they lived at the foot of the mountain. A hurling match was being broadcast from Dublin and the cottagers came reluctantly from their wireless sets to direct me to the 'fairy-house'. It was almost indistinguishable from their own, except that it was bare and without flowers or shrubs, an ugly cement building rather smaller than the county council houses of today but of the same type. It was only a couple of hundred yards from a main road and, though it suggested poverty, it did not suggest mystery, remoteness, primaeval superstition. Farmers and gentry driving past the door to Fethard or Clonmel will in 1895 have been talking of Dreyfus and Cecil Rhodes and some of these, who took part in the Ballyvadlea tragedy, may be still alive. They belong to our age and clime. The fairies are, if not exactly at the bottom of the garden, at least only a few fields and a few years away.

It is not very easy to build up a consecutive story out of a court case, for the end is always told before the beginning, and the central episode, seen differently by different witnesses, is often blurred like a negative several times exposed. But roughly this is how it happened.

In the spring of 1895 the Clearys were living at Ballyvadlea below Slievenaman. Michael Cleary was a labourer and his young wife, Bridget, was the daughter of a neighbour, Patrick Boland. Michael and Bridget were fond of each other and never quarrelled. They were religious people believing in the mysteries of the Catholic Church. But they also believed in the fairies and Michael was persuaded that, many years before, his mother had changed her nature. A fairy had entered into her body and once she had disappeared for two nights and it was known that she had spent them on the fairy-haunted rath at Kilnagranagh. It lay above John Dunne's cottage on the low road, and when Bridget too began to talk, like his mother, of Kilnagranagh and often to walk towards it of an evening on the low road, the old dread took shape in Michael's twilit mind. And some contagion of his fears spread to all his neighbours and all his relations, the Kennedys, the Bolands, the Dunnes, the Ahearns and Burkes, paralysing their wills and dulling their sensibilities. A whole community seemed to be bound with the spells of fairyland and powerless to extricate themselves. They appealed to the priests and the peelers to save them from themselves, but no external power was stronger than their obsessions. 'It's not my wife I have,' Michael told John Dunne, 'she's too fine a woman for my wife. She's two inches taller than my wife.' And even Bridget Cleary herself talked to her cousin, Mary Kennedy, as though she were bound with spells. 'I've a pain in my head,' she said, 'he's making a fairy of me now and an emergency. He thought to burn me three months ago.' She began to suffer from nerves and her illness was to Michael yet stronger proof that she was possessed. Dr Creary, the local doctor, declared it was due to dyspepsia, but he carried no conviction, and Michael went to Denis Guiney, the herb doctor, who prescribed a decoction of herbs and milk to be cooked in a saucepan and fed to the possessed woman.

But Michael had not much faith, either, in this innocent herbal remedy. He was convinced that there was only one way in which his Bridget could be restored to him. The fairy must be burnt out of her and then he would go to Kilnagranagh, and he would find the real Bridget there. She'd come out of the rath, riding a white horse and bound by cords to the saddle. He'd have to cut the ropes and then, if he was able to keep her, she'd stay with him.

But I should have mentioned that Michael Cleary once casually told his cousin John that Bridget on her evening walks to the fairy rath sometimes met an eggman on the low road. He used to go the rounds of the Tipperary farmsteads with his car, collecting eggs for a wholesale distributor in Clonmel. When the story was all told in the Clonmel Court House the eggman was only mentioned once and never again by judge, jury, witnesses or prisoners. For all the relevance he appeared to have to the story he and his cart might well have been swallowed up into the fairy mound. Yet these oblique and tender-hearted people had a habit of hiding their thoughts from themselves, and perhaps they sometimes thrust upon the fairies the guilt for desires and jealousies whose crudities they shrank from facing. It is possible that Michael suspected his wife of a tenderness for the eggman and just as a grain of grit will provoke an oyster to secrete a pearl, so the eggman from Clonmel unlocked the door to fairyland.

When Michael Cleary's father died he was waked in a house eleven miles from Ballyvadlea and on their way to the wake, the neighbours assembled the evening before in Michael's house. Patrick Boland, Bridget's father, was there and the Kennedy cousins including William, aged sixteen, and William Ahearn and several others. Bridget's cousin, Hannah Burke, was still washing some shirts that were needed for the wake and Mary Kennedy, young William's mother, went off to feed their hens, but when the others started to walk off for the wake, Michael Cleary stopped them. He said he would not leave his wife's sick-bed and that 'he did not care the devil about his father whether he was alive or dead'. 'No and ye won't go either,' he said to them, 'until I give her a little of the business I have to give her. Wait, boys, till you see her, till you see what I'll put out the door. I haven't Bridgie here these six weeks.'

So they did not leave for the wake, but stood about till midnight watching with mild exclamations while Michael tried to drive the fairy out of Bridget's body. Her father, Patrick Boland, raised some objections which Michael dealt with impatiently. 'Haven't you any faith?' he said. 'Don't you know it's with an old witch I'm sleeping.' 'You are not,' said Patrick Boland, 'you are sleeping with my daughter.' And telling about it later in the Clonmel courts, he, like the other witnesses, preserved a trance-like calm, as though he were watching a tragedy in which he was doomed to be a spectator, knowing the truth and yet powerless to intervene.

It is Johanna Burke who gives us the most coherent account of it all. She came back from washing the shirts about 7 p.m. on this first day of fairy exorcism, 14 March 1895. She found the Clearys' door locked and two neighbours called Simpson standing outside unable to get in. Through the window they could hear a voice saying, 'Take it, you witch or you bitch!' And when the three of them were at last let in she found the three Kennedys and John Dunne holding Bridget down on the bed, while Michael tried to give her herbs boiled in new milk from a spoon. Mary Kennedy, returned from feeding the hens, had brought some wine with her, and Michael threw it over Bridget's face and breast, exclaiming 'Are you Bridget Boland, in the name of God?' while her father echoed, 'Are you Bridget Boland, in the name of God, the daughter of Patrick Boland?' But Bridget was exhausted and speechless and the liquid was pouring down her chemise. So, while the Rosary was recited, the men raised her out of the bed and put her onto the fire. It was John Dunne's suggestion. 'We raised her over it,' he explained to the courts, 'I thought it belonged to the cure.' Hannah had just been putting sticks on the fire to make them a cup of tea and when Bridget, in the men's arms, saw her, she exclaimed in a mournful voice 'Oh, Han, Han!' She was wearing, Hannah recollected, a red petticoat and navy-blue flannel dress, green stays and navy-blue cashmere jacket, and Hannah, a conscientious witness, said of her later: 'When she was taken out, she looked like one that was silly, she looked wild and deranged and had not her own appearance. She looked different. She looked worse when she was taken out of bed than when I went into the room.' She was just 'tipping the bars' and her father and Michael Cleary were questioning her urgently in the name of God. It was too much for Hannah, she shouted out, 'Burn her away, but let me out and I'll go for the peelers.' She got out, but she did not go for the peelers.

That was the first night of burning; though there had been thirteen people in the house, we do not know much else about the remaining five hours before the visitors walked off to the funeral, except for what Patrick Boland told the court. About the first night he was very reassuring. 'Indeed,' he said, 'the fire wouldn't do anything the first night, 'twas no fire I might say.' He had left with the others at midnight and returning with them from the wake the following day, he had found nothing to complain of in Bridget's condition. 'She was grand then when I came back from Michael's father's wake, and the next night after that she was grand and the night after that she was grand until we were all taking a cup of tea.' At this point the old man broke off in tears; he tried to tell what happened on the third night in a few disjointed phrases.

It appeared that Michael had gone to his wife with the dish of herbs and milk and said: 'I'll make you take it, you old witch! I have herbs that there's nine cures in. It will be very hard to make her take these.' He struggled to explain what followed but failing to articulate, wound up: 'I had to run away from the smell. So 'tis all the way to make a long story short he burnt her.'

The witnesses all rambled incoherently backwards and forwards between the two nights of burning, lingering over what seems to us trivial, suppressing what appears to be relevant. They lived in a fairy-haunted world, whose thoughts and feelings can be measured by no ordinary rule. The poet is apt to over-estimate its charm, the moralist its cruelty. The mere chronicler is exasperated by his powerlessness to sort out the events of the successive nights. Of all the witnesses Hannah Burke is the most easy to follow. The peelers to her were almost as real as the fairies, she had actually thought of going to fetch them, and her chronology is the same as ours. After Bridget had been on the fire the first night, Hannah Burke had returned and put on her a fresh nightdress, which she had been airing for her and she had examined her body. Like Patrick Boland, she agreed that Bridget was 'grand'. 'I saw no marks on her except the size of a pin and a little blister on her hip not the size of sixpence, and a couple of little spots of burns on her chemise and a red spot under her chin. I thought it might be from the pin in her chemise so I put a safety pin there instead.' She stayed on with Bridget after the men had left for the wake and gave her some new milk, whey and claret wine, but when she left at 2 a.m. Bridget was still awake.

Hannah came the next morning with the fresh milk and her daughter Katey for company. She laid the milk on the window, and Michael gave her a shilling for it. But he said that Bridget had taken the shilling back from Hannah and, putting it under the blanket, had rubbed it against her thigh, a fairy trick, before returning it to Hannah. But when Michael had accused her of doing this, she had denied it. 'No, I am not a pishogue.' Yet she was aware how easily one might become a fairy, and for her, too, the borderland between fact and fantasy was very ill defined. 'Your mother gave two nights with the fairies,' she argued gently, 'that's why you think I'm one.'

Michael Cleary then went to the parish priest, Father Ryan, and asked him to come and say Mass for his wife. We know that in health she was 'grand', so it was surely because she was a fairy and had rubbed the shilling on her thigh that he appealed to him. But Father Ryan, doing his duty, appeared to have no inkling of the turmoil that was going on in the hearts of his parishioners. The court seemed to think it strange that he should know so little and it is difficult not to feel that Father Ryan, depending on the time-honoured formulae and ceremonies of his Church, felt excused from those simple movements of the mind and heart which might have saved the Clearys. Michael told the courts that Bridget, when she had received the sacrament, had removed the wafer from her mouth, refusing, fairy that she was, to swallow it.

To this Father Ryan replied reproachfully: 'I wish to add that if any Catholic saw Bridget Cleary remove the Blessed Sacrament from her mouth, he would be strictly bound to tell me at once so as to enable me to save the Sacred Species from profanation.' I cannot altogether blame the Clearys if it was only the supernatural claims of Father Ryan which impressed them. They appealed to him as a magician, whose magic had world-wide power and authority to reinforce it, to stand up against a more ancient magic whose power was waning. And they were deeply disappointed in his failure. The fairy failed to come out of Bridget and they were thrown back again on their own resources.

The next evening Michael tried Bridget once more with the herbs and boiled milk. He was very resolute this time. Hannah had made them cups of tea and the fire was blazing brightly. Young William Kennedy held the candle for Michael to work by, an oil lamp stood on the dresser and Patrick Boland and all the neighbours were there as on the former night, all of them distressed and friendly and solicitous. There was bread and jam and claret wine as well as cups of tea. Bridget kept saying that she was not a pishogue and that she was not turning into a fairy like Michael's mother, and her father and husband kept appealing to her in the name of God to say whether she was Bridget Boland or not. And once she asked for Tom Smith and David Hogan, 'two honest men', and she said she'd do anything they said. Smith and Hogan appear to have come and gone without altering the situation very much. And once, shifting inexpertly to the everyday world of crime and detection, she said: 'The peelers are at the window. Let ye mind ye now!' But everyone knew they were not and the observation had no consequences.

It was midnight and young William Kennedy had gone to sleep in the back room with his brother James, but they were roused by a sudden hullaballoo in the front room. Michael had taken from under the bed what was called in the Clonmel Court House 'a certain utensil' and poured the contents over his wife, then, seizing a burning log from the grate, he had forced her to lap up the herbs and milk from the saucepan, while young William once more held the candle by the bedside. Then Michael forced bread and jam down her throat, crying out all the while: 'Are you Bridget Cleary, my wife, in the name of the Father, the Son and the Holy Ghost?' while Mary Kennedy demurred, saying: 'Leave her alone, Mike, don't you see it's Bridgie as is in it?' Then Michael locked the door so that no one could leave and put the key in his pocket. Then he put Bridget on the floor and threw the lamp on her and some oil from a half-gallon oil-can from between the table and the dresser, so that Bridget was in a blaze of fire and the house suffocated with smoke. All the neighbours stampeded to the door and tried to break it down, so great was their dismay, but Michael told them they were not to leave till he had got his wife back. 'Are you Bridget Boland in the name of the Father, and Son and the Holy Ghost?' shouted Michael once more. 'Hold her over the fire and she'll soon answer!' Someone seemed then to have found the key in Michael's pocket and Patrick Boland escaped. William, a delicate boy, dropped the candle and fell down 'in a weakness' and his mother threw Easter water over him. There were signs of renewed disapproval from the neighbours, but Michael silenced them, saying: 'Hold your tongues! It isn't Bridget I'm burning. You'll soon see her go up the chimney!' Reassured by this, some of the neighbours came forward to help him and, in the words of Hannah Burke, 'They placed Mrs Cleary in a kind of sitting position on the kitchen fire, her body resting on the bars. The fire was a slow one. Mrs Cleary's appearance was greatly changed.'

After that there is mention of a large sack-bag with a dirty sheet in it, which Michael laid on the floor. Knowing what he had to do, he laid what was left of Bridget on it, on her back with her feet bent up. 'It's not Bridget,' he repeated. 'As I couldn't drive the devil out through the chimney, I'll drive her through the door.' He asked Pat Kennedy to help bury her somewhere till she could be put by her mother's side. At first he said 'No', but then he agreed and at 2 a.m. Michael and Pat went out and buried the body. Michael had lost his confidence now: 'She's burned now,' he said, 'and God knows I didn't intend to do it. It's Jack Dunne I may thank for it all.'

Mary Kennedy went round to the Clearys' cottage the next morning and found a little group of neighbours already assembled. Hannah was there and old Pat Boland, Bridget's father, was on his knees, lamenting. 'Now that my child is dead,' he said, 'there is no use in saying anything about it, but God help me in the latter end of my days!' Michael was wearing the same light suit of clothes he had worn when Bridget was being burnt and it was badly marked. He had stayed back from work to clean it. 'I saw him,' said Hannah, 'scraping the stains like of grease off the ends of his trousers, and says he to me, "Oh, God, Hannah, there is the substance of poor Bridget's body".' But he still considered that it was her body only, for he told them again that his wife had gone to Kilnagranagh to see the fairies and that they were to come there that evening and help him lift her from the white horse and cut the ropes that bound her to it and persuade her to stay with him. And in fact that evening and later evenings, till he was arrested, a crowd of people did go with him to the rath. He carried a bread-knife in his hand to cut the ropes. But fewer and fewer went and John Dunne, declaring now that it was 'all moonshine', urged him to go to the priest.

Michael's mother, she who had given two nights to the fairies, also gave evidence. When she reached his cottage she had found him, she said, still scraping himself, 'scraping the juice of the poor creature off his clothes.' 'Mike,' said I to him, 'if you were scraping your clothes for ever and if you cut them off you, God would never let the stains go out of your clothes, the stains of your poor wife.' And then she had said: 'Acorrah, go down to the police barracks and tell them what you have done.'

'No, mother,' he had answered, 'because people would be calling you a prosecutor.'

Michael asked them then to come and help him bury Bridget and one of the Kennedys said he'd come and help if she was to be buried in consecrated ground, but Michael had gone away, and without him to direct them, the neighbours wandered round the kitchen garden, hunting for the body.

Michael Cleary was at confession. Kneeling at the altar, he had torn his hair and cried would he ever be forgiven?

When the priest came out into the chapel yard, John Dunne, he who had helped to lift Bridget on to the fire, because he thought it 'belonged to the cure', accosted him. 'They burnt her to death last night, Father,' he said, 'and I have been asking them all the morning to take her up and give her a Christian burial.'

Hannah Burke ended her evidence abruptly: 'That's all I have to say and sorry I am.'

Michael from the dock said, 'You did that well, Han.'

'I did so, Mick.'

'I hope you will do it in Heaven as well as that.'

'I will with the help of God, Mick.'

When the nine prisoners from Ballyvadlea were taken for trial in Clonmel, there were demonstrations in the streets and in particular against Denis Guiney, the herb doctor. They received, however, a merciful sentence and commentators on the case in the Dublin and London periodicals were on the whole more tolerant than the Clonmel neighbours. The reaction against Victorian rationalism had started and there was a new reverence for the supernatural when it had a respectable ancient tradition behind it. Folklore had become a science, and in Ireland Standish O'Grady, by his poetical reconstruction of the Irish past, had prepared the way for Yeats and AE and the Celtic Twilight. I do not think that the fairies suffered any serious set-back by the happenings at Ballyvadlea.

In *The Nineteenth Century* E. F. Benson wrote an essay on the trial, which was typical of the period in that he covered a great deal of ground with very thin speculation. He drew analogies from the Hottentots, who try to shake out the spirit of disease from the dying, and the Zulus, who believe in Amatongos or ancestor-spirits, and he offered the Clearys a respectable place in the *Encyclopaedia of Primitive Superstition*. But to those who live around Slievenaman such a diagnosis seems as inadequate as it is pretentious. There is no need to call in the Zulus and Hottentots. A woman had been burnt to death for witchcraft in Kilkenny in 1324 on the instigation of the bishop, an English Franciscan, the only known instance of such burning in Ireland. Such catastrophes often happen when reason is in bondage to Fear of the Unknown, even when such Fear calls itself Faith.

In fact the Ballyvadlea tragedy had quite a sophisticated and civilized background. Everyone was perfectly familiar with priests and peelers, doctors and prosecutors, and for many centuries they had been subject to the laws of England and the faith of Rome. Nor were they altogether outside the current of world affairs. Some years before in the little village of Mullinahone, where the Clearys did their shopping, twenty-eight volunteers had set off to defend the Papal States against Garibaldi and had returned from Sardinian prisons to a welcome with bonfires on the mountain and triumphal arches.

All the Clearys and their neighbours lived in that perilous region of half-belief which the sophisticated find charming because they are more acquainted with its tenderness than its cruelty. It is a no-man's land of the imagination, in which fantasy, running wild, easily turns into false-hood and ruthlessness. It has still in the twentieth century its appeal and highly civilized people, as well as simple ones, claim access to it.

In the past in Ireland both the Churches and the Anglo-Normans often tried to harness the fairies to their ecclesiastical and political designs, and the results were often so delightful that the guard upon the frontiers of fairyland has sometimes been unwisely relaxed.

In an old Irish poem about Slievenaman, St Patrick raised Oisin, the famous hunter, from the dead and said to him:

Oisin, sweet is thy voice.
Tell us how many deer fell upon Slievenaman?

And Oisin answered:

We killed six thousand deer
In the glen which lay in the mountain,
O cleric of the clerks and bells!
A thousand hounds with their collars of gold
Fell before noon by one hundred hogs.

In fact St Patrick did not dispel the spirits of the mountain but became
one of them himself. The fairy goldsmiths made chalices and fonts for
Patrick and the saints as readily as they made collars for the hounds of
the Fianna. The result is that cultivated Irishmen will often have the
same ironical, indulgent smile for the mysteries of their faith as for the
legends of Fionn. And simple people, like the Clearys, not so skilled at
walking the tight rope between belief and disbelief, are at the mercy of
some temporary spasm of credulity. None of them consistently believed
that Bridget was a fairy. Even now and then the voice of reason insisted:
'Don't you see it's Bridgie as is in it?' but reason could make no headway
against Michael's passionate conviction, whose origins Michael himself
maybe did not rightly understand.

The great Norman castles on the flanks of Slievenaman, Kilcash and
Kiltinan and the others, have long ago fallen into ruin or decay, and the
noble lords whose horses and hounds evoked memories of the Fianna
have vanished. Life has been drab and poor for many generations and
poets like to transfigure it with the myth and magic of fairyland. A
couple of centuries ago a native of Slievenaman, Father Lalor, wrote a
charming and sophisticated elegy in Irish on the death of his friend
Archdeacon Kavanagh. He saw the Archdeacon, like St Patrick, among
the fairies on Slievenaman and the fact that these two solitary priests did
not believe in the fairies makes their need of them more poignant. The
poem starts gaily:

As I one time was travelling the province
Airily, cheerfully spending my youth;
Some time to gamble I bestowed and to drinking,
And a small, short time I devoted to knowledge.

Then Father Lalor describes his visit to the fairy palace on Slievenaman,
the wines and the clothes and the servants, and how he asked the fairy
queen why the mist had swept up from the Nore enveloping Dunane
and Barnan-Ely, 'What makes the side of Carnduff impenetrable to the
sun?' And the fairy queen had replied that it was because

A steady pillar of the church has died
Who was the friend of the poor and needy...
The friend of idiots without reason's light,
Who in the Lord's vineyard laboriously toiled.
He was an example to the whole diocese,
He never spent his time on lands or flocks,
He never raised the price of land by bidding against the labouring classes.
Now the white hand which distributed the sacrament
Is stretched without the power of motion by his side, alas!

Then the damsel had vanished and the splendid palace with her and there was nothing left on the mountain side but the mist, the gorse and the heather.

I doubt whether Archdeacon Kavanagh was quite as good as they thought him on Slievenaman, or Bridget Cleary so bad, or Oisin so splendid a hunter. A great deal of Irish poetry and romance is born of isolation and the nostalgia of those who escape it. Eyes that are dim with tears are not particularly perceptive; focused on the fairies they never give the eggman his due. Indeed I have read through hundreds of verses about Slievenaman without finding a single reference to him. And as for the Clearys, nobody, of course, since E. F. Benson, has mentioned them at all; though they were poetical people, they are out of harmony with what the poets tell us of that fairy-haunted mountain.

In purple robes old Slievenaman
    Towers monarch of the mountains,
The first to catch the smiles of dawn
    With all his woods and fountains...
There gallant men, for freedom born,
    With friendly grasp will meet you;
There lovely maids as bright as morn
    With sunny smiles will greet you
And there they strove the Red above
    To raise Green Ireland's banner –
There yet its fold they'll see unrolled
    Upon the banks of Anner.

[1960]

ERNEST RENAN:
THE STATUE AND THE CALVARY

Very few people are interested in Renan now. Perhaps his brand of scepticism, which was eager and voluble, is out of date. In the West, religious disbelief is so widespread that it seldom has to be defiant or even articulate. You do not have to repudiate ideas to which you are indifferent. Only in the remote or very conservative parts of Europe, where the old orthodoxies survive unchallenged, can you startle people by disbelieving. But in most other places, particularly in England, religious controversy is tame and gentlemanly.

Renan was born in Brittany and came back there in his old age. Spiritually he never left it. He could never dissociate himself from the simple, unquestioning faith which he had challenged. That challenge had been the Open Sesame to a magic world, where truth, complex and progressively revealed, was adored with all the devotion that the Bretons gave to myth and pious legend. Renan was almost fanatical in his pursuit of the truth. He asked that *dilexi veritatem* (I loved the truth) be written on his tombstone. Truth, as he saw it, was friendly, not hostile, to the imagination; it was only ruthless to those fabrications which had grown inflexible with age and were cramping to the intelligence and the will. He saw danger and cruelty in them.

I think that Renan differed from other great sceptics like Voltaire and Lucretius by his sensitive, unscornful handling of the ideas which he had rejected. He was neither a revolutionary nor a self-sufficient scholar. He was a Celt whose emotions were swayed by memories and personal loyalties. He loved the Church to which he owed the learning and the dialectical skill which he later turned against it. His childhood and the childhood of his race and all the villages and institutions of his native Brittany had developed under its care. He was bound with a cord which was precious to him; its knots and tangles had to be untied and not cut.

Renan believed that the faith of his childhood must be transcended, not simply by-passed. But the leaders of his Church preferred that their faith should be ignored rather than tampered with; they dreaded heresy more than infidelity. And that, I think, explains the fury and the fervent love which the memory of Renan can still rouse in his native Brittany, and the indifference with which he is regarded in the wider world where there are no strong tensions because there is no strong faith.

His clear and careful prose is today found sentimental and unctuous. The devout find him insidious, the sceptics find him insinuating. They do not understand what Renan was trying to do. He believed that Christianity is a still living faith, but, if it is to survive, a delicate and skilful operation must be performed on in. Renan had once operated on his own soul, amputating many passionately held convictions. After the torment of his young manhood he had reached happiness, unclouded by doubt or regret, a measured confidence in the powers of the human mind that was proof against disillusionment and catastrophe. He believed that Christianity could survive the loss of all its supernatural accretions.

I think it was partly because of this confidence that he decided to live among the Bretons, to match their fervour with his own and prove to himself that he had not broken with his past but fulfilled it. That is why, as an old man, a scholar of international repute, he chose to settle on the Breton coast, near Tréguier, where he was born and studied for the priesthood. And though Renan died nearly a century ago, he is still loved and hated there. He is a figure of controversy and a dynamic force. When, as happens every now and then, there is a celebration in his honour, it is hard to tell whether it is a challenge to the living or an act of homage to the dead.

Tréguier is a small sleepy town, but it was one of the great early Christian centres of Brittany. It was founded by the legendary half-Druidic St Tudwal, who in Saxon times led a group of refugees out of Wales. The celebrated St Yves was born there some seven centuries later. And all around there are innumerable Breton saints of marked individuality and doubtful orthodoxy. Renan himself belonged to the family of one of the most eccentric of them, St Ronan or Renan. Renan, despite his assault on the supernatural, had a tenderness for these cantankerous Breton saints whose cult had been for centuries the focus of local pieties. What he feared was not the credulity of the simple in which so often true history is enshrined, but its manipulation in the interests of orthodoxy and uniformity. When he was visited by Rhys, the great Welsh archaeologist, he sadly told him how the old statue of St Budoc had been defaced and the curate had collected a subscription of 40 francs to replace it with a Virgin of Lourdes, *ce triste miracle moderne*, to the dismay of the pious, conservative villagers. In many ways Renan, the revolutionary thinker, had a greater love for tradition than the ecclesiastics themselves.

While denying the divinity of Christ, Renan believed in the Christian traditions of brotherhood, selflessness and conscience. He believed that the Reformation of the sixteenth century had once safeguarded these by eliminating much that was idolatrous and heathen. Yet he thought that a yet greater reformation was needed which would embrace the whole of Christianity. 'The spirit of reformation', he declared, 'is being rapidly overtaken by rationalism, which knows nothing and which will destroy all that which awaits reformation before it has been reformed.' 'The reformers', he added, 'could only save Christianity by attaining to absolute rationalism themselves and joining hands with all the emancipated spirits, who will accept the Sermon on the Mount as the code of conduct.'

You can imagine what consternation these opinions caused in the Church. Long after Renan's death the battle was still being fought. And in Tréguier itself the clash of wills is immortalized in stone. Outside the church door in the centre of the square Renan's statue was erected in 1903 in the presence of Anatole France and many other leading intellectuals of France. It was a challenge which could not be ignored. A group of country people had agreed to come in and stop the unveiling, but they were prevented by a tremendous downpour of rain. A few years later, in protest against the statue, a great monument was erected called the 'expiatory Calvary'. It stands at the base of the Rue Ernest Renan, within a stone's throw of the house where Renan was born and his mother kept a small grocer's shop. Below it is inscribed: *Vere hic homo filius Dei est* (Truly this man is the son of God). In front of it, with other saints, the stone figures of St Tudwal and St Yves stand on guard. Renan's house had been a museum for a long time and some years ago it was reorganized. There was a ceremonial opening with M. Herriot from Paris, the Mayor, a naval band and a banquet for seven hundred guests. Belief and disbelief in the supernatural are in France still real issues, dividing men's minds. Evasiveness and compromise are not honoured. If this is responsible for bitterness and deep social fissures, it is also surely the source of France's cultural and intellectual pre-eminence.

Through long experience the antagonists have learnt to make graceful contact across the abyss. They can be courteous even when intransigent. I am thinking in particular of the letter Renan wrote on his first return to Tréguier, asking to be allowed to visit his old seminary and his teachers, whose favourite pupil he had once been. It is a masterpiece of delicacy and tact. But in the Principal's reply, a refusal, there is sweetness, too, as well as firmness. Perhaps the worst quarrels occur on the fringes of conviction. Renan and his teachers were not so much hostile to each other as completely unintelligible.

Renan was, of course, attacked as well as defended in an uncivilized way. He had indiscreet champions. But I think his bitterest enemies were those who never came within range of his happy, serious, friendly personality. Renan made himself loved by his Breton neighbours. He was a good man and a good Christian; on that point, their intuition was sound. But beyond the friendly circle there was no understanding or sympathy with his work. It needs generosity as well as genius to cut across the current of your age. Renan advanced fiercely unpopular opinions and yet remained smiling and unperturbed, though he was regarded by many as Anti-Christ and the Incarnation of Evil. I only know of one occasion when Renan lost his temper. He was asked to use his influence on behalf of the son of some Breton cousins of his. He paid a visit but learnt afterwards that the armchair on which he had sat had been sprinkled carefully with holy water by the boy's mother. She sent him, however, a present of some oysters. Renan had the oysters very conspicuously thrown on the manure heap.

Renan, old as he was and declining in health, by his mere physical presence in that remote corner of Brittany gave courage and confidence to many, and in particular to that small band of Breton scholars and poets who had urged him to come home to live. He had loved Brittany and the Celtic peoples and in spite of his unpopular theology there were many there to welcome him. He was the greatest Breton of his age. A heretic? Yes, but hadn't there been plenty of Breton heretics before him? Pelagius, perhaps, and Abelard and Lammenais certainly. The faith of the Bretons, he declared, had always been detached from books and forms, orthodoxy had been imposed through French bishops and concordats made with the French. For centuries there had been no Breton-speaking bishop. The Reformation had once taken a firm hold on the Bretons and it was only an accident of politics that they had not, like their kinsmen in Wales, remained under its sway.

Renan was looking in Brittany for some affinity of spirit that did not rest on scholarship, and, if one is to judge by the small public demonstrations that were made in his honour, I think he must have found it. Once when he was so crippled that he could not walk, he was entertained on the Island of Brehat; as usual on these occasions in France, there was a canon and a mayor and a naval band, a fleet of little painted boats and a banquet and lots of little girls dressed in white with bunches of flowers. When their boat reached the shore he found that a victoria, the first carriage ever seen on the island, had been ferried across the night before to receive him. With the simplicity of genius Renan spoke to the gathering of his father, the sailor, of his neighbours and friends of his childhood. Renan would like to have felt as at home in Brittany as in the Collège de France. He believed in the natural pieties of home and fatherland. 'The memory of our native land is for each of us', he said, 'a part of our morality.' He believed in the power of natural goodness, which can in time replace that precarious goodness, as he would have considered it, which requires the support of a supernatural system. Was he anti-clerical? It is not so simple as that. 'Fatherland', he said, 'and family are the two great natural forms of human association. Both are essential, but they cannot suffice of themselves. Side by side with them must be maintained an institution in which the soul can be nurtured and receive consolation and counsel, in which charity may be organized and spiritual masters and directors found.'

Though Renan was isolated and frustrated, yet he had confidence. He thought that one day he would be justified. Though Christianity appeared inseparable from forms and ceremonies, from established hierarchies and supernatural beliefs, these things belong to the childhood of reason, while we are accustoming ourselves to the naked truth. One day we shall dispense with them. What did he mean though, by the 'institution for nurturing the soul', or 'the spiritual directors and masters'? In what respect would these differ from the Church and its ministers? It is a point that Renan has not made clear. I think he would say that certain men have a clearer vision than others of the truth and can walk undazzled in the light of it. They are the true spiritual directors, whose task it would be to nurture the soul. But the Church will have none of them. They are feared and hated. It is even asserted that the Christian virtues themselves would collapse if the supernatural origin of the Church was repudiated. Renan denied this.

In fact Renan's enemies gave constant proof of the precariousness of this supernaturally fortified goodness. When his body was laid to rest in the Pantheon, and later, when his statue was erected at Tréguier, a flood of malice poured from the press. I can think of one book, similar to many, whose author dwelt with satisfaction on the last painful months of Renan's illness. 'It was proof', he said, 'that God had deserted him, as he deserted Voltaire and Arius the Heresiarch' who died of a haemorrhage in a privy at the moment of his triumph, an answer to the prayers of the pious bishop Alexander. 'The apostate', says the writer, 'was hustled away to die in the grim fortress of the Collège de France, so that he might be out of reach of the pious Bretons, whose faith he had assailed and whose conviction it was that he had been devoured by lice.' And he perfects the parallel with Arius; 'The apostate', he says, 'was a humiliating spectacle in an old coat like a soutane and a sort of ecclesiastical hat tottering in the garden, coughing, spitting, puffing, groaning, trembling, crying like a soul in pain. Two valets followed him bearing a commode shaped like an armchair.'

So the statue of Renan at Tréguier was, in a sense, expiatory like the Calvary. In the words of the French Minister at the unveiling: it was to 'repair the unjust ostracism to which the apostle of toleration had so long been submitted on the soil of his native Brittany'. The Mayor of Tréguier declared in 1903, 'This statue proclaims in the face of the whole world that our old province has not been absolutely abandoned to fanaticism. To attack this statue will be to attack the glory of France and to do a deep injury to the dignity of human thought.'

But the statue has never been attacked. It is as safe as the Calvary in this civilized little town. The citizens are deeply divided in their loyalties, but they can cherish their differences with dignity. Renan, according to one of his biographers, will never attract followers. To have disciples is the destiny of those who *croient lourdement*, like Paul and Luther and Wesley. All the same I think that the picture of Renan, the smiling sceptic, aloof, ineffectual, impregnable, has been overdrawn. Renan the fearless enquirer, the fighter for the truth, has been underestimated. He followed the truth without misgiving as to where it would lead him. He saw that what he had written would bring release to some, but pain and bewilderment to others. Would the ill-disposed profit by what he, in good faith, had said? He did not ask.

Renan's faith in human destiny was a very individual, almost aristocratic one. It was proof against the disillusionment that may overtake all our democratic enthusiasm. 'Idealists like us', he said, 'must approach these fires with precaution. The chances are that we'll lose our head or our wings in them!' And he remarked on that strange magnetism which plays between the opposite poles of religious and socialistic orthodoxy. 'How often', he said, 'it happens that when a man abandons the Church, he will search for the lost absolute, the lost comfort of believing friends and colleagues, in a fanatical political faith!' And the converse happens too.

Is there something rather smug about Renan's practical sobriety? Sometimes admittedly there is. I think it was not always wisdom so much as a certain physical timidity that prevented him from dissipating his energies in unprofitable idealism, but, whatever the reason, the clarity of his vision was seldom dimmed by passion or prejudice. He believed that truth must be pursued without any reservation. He thought that man, through advancing knowledge, would acquire the power to extricate himself from the difficulties in which his too great confidence might plunge him. In one of his last writings he foretold how Caliban would turn Prospero out of his kingdom, and wisdom and goodness would have to be cherished in exile and in secret. But he thought that it would be better to endure Caliban for a space than to have Prospero restored by the forces of clerical reaction. 'Far from being a Renaissance,' he said, 'that would be in our circumstances annihilation. Let us keep Caliban.' These lines were quoted by Anatole France at the unveiling of the statue. I am sorry that he did not quote further, for Renan believed that Ariel, the spirit of religion, would survive all these vicissitudes and adapt himself to changed circumstances.

In fact Renan was convinced that Christ's teaching had a validity that needed no supernatural sanction. He thought it was only obscured by arguments based on historical facts that would always be disputed. You might entice millions into conformity by an elaborate system of beliefs and duties and catechismal phrases, but you would alienate thereby the handful of Christians who loved the truth unreservedly and were ardent and expert in the pursuit of it. Time would prove that they and no others were the best advocates of Christian love and charity.

It is nearly ninety years now since the statue was put up but I discovered in the fifties that the Breton scholar who had first appealed for its erection was still alive and still capable of inspiring and infuriating his countrymen. He was the founder of one of the leading Breton nationalist associations and, though old and half blind, was unjustly sentenced to a short imprisonment for his political opinions.

What would Renan have thought of Breton separatism? I think, like Matthew Arnold, another philo-Celt, he would have regretted that it was the lowest gifts of the Celtic peoples and not the highest, for which the modern world could find a use. Political revolt would have seemed to him merely the physical symptoms of a spiritual disequilibrium. There was no place today in the world for those excellences which the Celt had once contributed to European civilization, their gifts of imagination and of poetry, their defiance of the orthodox in thought and feeling. It would be natural that the Celts should wish to rebel against a civilization which claimed to be able to dispense with these qualities. I think here too Renan would have proved a prophet of reconciliation. For he himself had found no conflict between his love of France and his loyalty to his native land.

[1950, 1988]

GRAHAM GREENE AND STEPHEN SPENDER: THE SENSE OF EVIL AND THE SENSE OF GUILT

I

Graham Greene and Stephen Spender are like two explorers who leave the same outpost in opposite directions and travelling in a wide circle, converge on each other again. They have seen all the familiar features from opposite angles, but when their experiences are collated, the sense of contradiction disappears. Greene is a traditionalist with some wayward inclinations, Spender is a rather hesitant experimentalist. I wish it were possible to confront Spender's autobiography, *World Within World*, with something more revealing and exhaustive than Greene's short personal memoir in his volume of critical sketches, *The Lost Childhood*.* But perhaps the bleakness of this memoir is in itself an autobiographical comment. Greene is buttoned up securely into his close-fitting philosophy, while Spender is always unbuttoning his looser one. Yet I would say that their obsession with buttons brings them curiously near to each other and makes them fit representatives of their age. They are both constantly concerned with life and society and the restraints that men should and should not impose on each other. They are inseparable in their dissent, like two sisters quarrelling in the family home. The one wants the front door locked in case there's a burglar, the other wants it ajar, in case there's a fire. Or so they say. But they are arguing not from objective probabilities but from personal phobias.

Greene's autobiographical essay, short as it is, is an invaluable commentary and corrective to his astute critical essays. It is plain that he had

---

*Graham Greene, *The Lost Childhood and Other Essays* (London 1951); Kenneth Allott and Miriam Farris, *The Art of Graham Greene* (London 1951); Stephen Spender, *World Within World* (London 1951).

good reason for his belief in bolts and buttons, in social restraints and categorical imperatives. As a child all manner of strange thoughts and desires, the birth pangs perhaps of his great talents, made themselves felt and had to be suppressed. As an established writer he has not liberated himself from this fear of monstrous and seemingly supernatural intrusions. There is nothing discreditable about his idiosyncrasies or Mr Spender's but those who do not share them must dread any attempt to base on them a universally applicable philosophy. As a boy Graham Greene experimented nine or ten times with suicide. After he had run away from school his parents sent him to be psychoanalysed. His months at the psychoanalyst were, he said, perhaps the happiest in his life. He emerged 'correctly orientated' once more and yet 'wrung dry' and incapable of taking an aesthetic interest in anything. His boredom seems to have brought him to a quiet despair, from which, in a zestless way, he tried several times to rescue himself with a revolver which was kept in the corner cupboard, using it more as a stimulant (it was a six-chambered revolver with only one charge and there was an exciting risk) than a gateway to everlasting peace.

Readers of his novels may feel that this conviction that life is flat and grey has never left him and, like the fox without a tail, he has persuaded many beside himself that the only true normality is abnormality. But if we accept his philosophy as a mere mechanism of personal adjustment, it is not contagious. Like a foreign language it obscures but cannot neutralize his excellent craftsmanship.

The Greene world is stricken with an induced paralysis, as though to make it more amenable to his skilful dissection. Hope is dead unregretted, like a nagging nerve that had to be killed. Boredom and torpor are surgically guaranteed like a eunuch's passivity. They are proof against life's infinite variety and can only be dissipated by an explosive from the corner cupboard. For the catastrophes that build up the plot are irruptions from outside, they are contrived and inorganic. Mr Greene's Remorseless Destiny is a mechanized scarecrow more impressive than the old broom-handle contraptions of the Hardy school but not more true to life.

In Mr Greene's last collection of critical essays we can see this technique of self adjustment and literary craftsmanship doing duty as a philosophy. Like most makeshifts it seems to me clumsy and destructive and it is applied irresponsibly for the discrediting of Havelock Ellis and Samuel Butler, and, for some rather odd reasons, for the exaltation of Henry James. Mr Greene is often a generous and sensitive critic of those whose philosophy is alien to his own, of Herbert Read, for example, and Walter de la Mare. But on the whole his generosity is rationed rather primly, and he gives the impression of a bruised soul searching for soul-mates and resentful of those who are unbruised or have found a balm for their bruises which is not his own.

Mr Greene's scepticism about the possibility of human happiness seems to derive from an unhappy childhood. How many uncompromising and intolerant philosophies are based on childish misery! The scales are weighted then so heavily against rebellion and unconventionality that our wretchedness seems predestined and to resist it sacrilege. Sometimes we carry with us to the end of our days a quite artificial resignation to the system of oppressor and oppressed. Dickens, as Greene observes in his very penetrating essay, 'The Burden of Childhood', was one of those, a minority I think, who learnt sympathy and understanding for the whole human race from his years of defenceless unhappiness. But Kipling's Auntie Rosa and Saki (H. H. Munro)'s Aunt Augusta had a different effect on their victims to Dickens's blacking factory, filling them with indignation and hate, which boiled over in their writings. Greene compares Munro very justly to 'a chivalrous highwayman'. Behind all his stories he discovers 'an exacting sense of justice'. On the one hand 'with Kipling revenge rather than justice seems to be the motive (Auntie Rosa had established herself in the mind of her victim and corrupted it)'. He protected himself 'with manliness, knowingness, imaginary adventures of soldiers and empire builders'. Kipling had sensibility without judgment and for the most part it was on harmless people that he discharged this immense burden of resentment which he carried about with him.

One would naturally look for an Auntie Rosa in Mr Greene's childhood, but I expect that his resentment was not focused on any single human figure, or, as with Dickens, on any social injustice. Mr Greene was miserable in a middle-class, privileged way in a liberal humanitarian democracy and he is forced to condemn, not the abuses of society, but society itself. I think that, as with Kipling, his sweeping damnations are a measure of his shortcomings as well as of his sensibility. Outside his craft, let us admit it, he is not very intelligent. His essay on Havelock Ellis, for example, is written with the same assured stupidity with which Kipling wrote of the Church of Rome.

In Gothic Art you will occasionally find the serpent entwined with more Christian symbols and adapted to ecclesiastical decoration by the cross on his tail. In Mr Greene's work you will sometimes find, as in this essay, a secular malice converted by a turn of phrase to Christian usage. Havelock Ellis, who had explored the recesses of the human mind in a spirit of enquiry not of condemnation, is reproached for his lack of religion and compared to 'a Father Christmas from Selfridge's with a fake prophet's air'; his work is dismissed as 'full of case histories and invincible ignorance'. Greene's essay purports to be a review of Mr Ellis's autobiography and the fact that he had dared to reprint it is sure proof of the sickness of English criticism today. For Greene has ignored or misunderstood Ellis's account of his wife's nature, which is so lovingly and faithfully described, and attempts to charge him with having driven his wife 'to the last breakdown of health and sanity' by his 'advanced' ideas. (One recalls E. M. Forster's the Rev. Cuthbert Eager, who said that old Emerson 'murdered his wife', adding hastily 'in the sight of God'!) When we reflect that Greene declared that perhaps the happiest months of his life were spent in the care of a psychoanalyst, it is plain that the writer's attitude to 'advanced ideas' might well be the subject of a case history, a complicated tangle of love and hate, devotion and betrayal. In *The Ministry of Fear* he makes the arch-villain, who is a cowardly murderer and a Nazi spy, into the head of a psychological nursing home. Even his very admiring critics, Mr Allott and Miss Farris, detect here 'a flavour of wartime highbrow baiting'. They complain that though Greene's heroes are solitaries, he dislikes the isolation of the intellectual and in the portrayal of Dr Forester, the psychologist, 'prejudice seems to have stampeded him into accepting herd warmth at almost any price'.

But I would suspect that Mr Greene's anti-intellectual bias is a mere idiosyncrasy, a distaste for the pursuit of knowledge, which has escaped challenge and insinuated itself into respectable company because of the cross on its tail. The Greene hero is permanently out of reach of the grapes; he has wearied of intellectual independence before he has striven for it. He is the type of solitary who snarls suspiciously if he is caressed. He is like a pariah dog who has lost his pack but refuses to become domesticated. The pack, invisible and unreachable, remains the focus of yearning and mystical devotion. Mr Greene's pity for the excluded is balanced precisely by his resentment of the emancipated. It is a negative kind of pity and he sees it in others as an occupational affliction of the just and the gentle, 'the horrible and horrifying emotion of pity'. He sees it as horrible because often it leads its victim, its Rowes and Scobies, to compassionate mercy-killings, adulteries, suicides. And Havelock Ellis is to Mr Greene an ignoramus and a fake Father Christmas and he has a Selfridge beard simply because of his tendency to see these disasters as sorrows rather than sins.

Greene's speculations about sin are as esoteric as the speculations of a

Jew about a pork-pie. Is it really sin? Is it really pork? There is little moral censure about the enquiry. Sin is to violate a tabu, not to deceive or to be cruel. Mr Greene only once, I think, in these very Christian essays uses the word 'goodness', and then in connection with its tendency to 'wilt' into philanthropy and kindness. He sneers at Samuel Butler and his admirers for their determination to be Honest Men (ironical capitals), 'with an inability to tell polite untruths', and he shudders fastidiously at the Victorian progressives almost as the two Miss Allens shuddered at old Mr Emerson. The Emersons and their like stand by 'small and dingy shops' in 'scrubby stained and smelly clothes', reading 'ugly, cheap reprints from the Rationalist Press'. They suggest to Mr Greene a crippled childhood, attics, blackbeetles, a grim grammar school. Mr Greene shows such a refined and wincing sensibility when confronted with the scrubby, the smelly, the cheap, that one wonders why as an artist he is so irresistibly attracted to them. There is no warmth of love about his researches, no curiosity, no hope. What is this fastidious person looking for as he pokes the garbage over with the ferrule of his rolled umbrella? Only treasure trove or the consciousness of a mission would draw so exclusive a person so constantly to squalor and misery. These essays show plainly enough that he is looking for a Sense of Sin, which he seems to connect with a Sense of Evil. Samuel Butler had not a trace, Dickens scarcely a trace, but in the repugnant home-life of Havelock Ellis, which he explores with the toe of his boot, he seems to divine, despite the absence of dogmatic belief, a 'buried religious feeling'. He finds tenderness and love and nostalgic regret and Mr Greene has decided that these are the prerogatives of the religious but that the 'advanced' leave out of account 'all natural un-eugenic feelings'.

Mr Greene is the modern kind of Luddite. Those of the last century rejected the mechanical inventions of the age. But the modern Luddite has accommodated himself to the industrial revolution, to telephones, to the wireless and the cinema. He merely rejects those intellectual conceptions and attitudes which are the spiritual counterpart of material invention. Havelock Ellis, whom Mr Greene in his Luddite mood has charged with 'invincible ignorance', introduced into the world an engine of reform as irresistible as Stephenson's Rocket. Mr Greene is heavily committed to the modern world: he has not only endured that his books should be filmed, but he has also been successfully psychoanalysed. Yet he rushes at Mr Havelock Ellis's collected works like a Luddite at a lace machine. Surely he is trying to stir up among us the same schizophrenic conflict which rages in his own mind. Yet his problem, how to eat your cake and yet reject it with scorn, is one of his own making and he seems to solve it in the usual way, deluding himself that the next best thing to renouncing a pleasure or a privilege is to accept it ungraciously.

It is probable that we have entered a phase of history in which personal relations will at first be complicated, not eased, by new discovery and experiment. Often the old ignorance will seem preferable to the new enlightenment, which illuminates suffering and conflict but cannot yet show us how to cure them. The Churches once said that we should not tamper with the body, not even the bodies of the dead, and anatomy was long forbidden (not only Christians but Arabs and Indians have shared these intelligible misgivings), and perhaps if we could avoid violating these ancient pre-Christian tabus we should be none the worse. But we cannot. We should not waste our time trying. Only a minute fraction of the mental and physical suffering of our time could be cured by Mr Greene's revival of moribund dogma about sin.

Mr Greene's essays on Henry James reveal clearly how personal is his philosophy. He is like a refugee in a sanctuary whose inviolability depends on its repute rather than its defences. Its holiness is thrown into relief by the sinfulness of the world that surrounds it, so that those outside who see evil everywhere must be regarded as allies and viewed with special favour by the guardians and patrons of the precincts. I cannot see how otherwise Mr Greene should feel this curious sense of solidarity with Henry James, who, if we are to judge him as Greene does, by his letters and the moods of his characters, never ventured inside a Christian church without a frisson of disloyalty. And obviously James's interest in colourful rites and vestments derive more from the collectomania of the well-to-do American than from the Christian renunciation of the world. The most one can say is that the frisson was sometimes half-pleasurable as frissons so often are.

Excavating for 'buried religious feeling' in Henry James's work, Mr Greene puts his finds on the table. They are pathetically meagre. Henry James took a pleasure in a visit to St Peter's and Mr Greene draws satisfaction from the following account of the experience.

To crown my day, on my way home, I met His Holiness in person driving in prodigious purple state – sitting dim within the shadow of his coach with two uplifted benedictory figures – like some dusky Hindoo idol in the depths of its shrine... From the high tribune of a great chapel of St Peter's I have heard in the Papal choir a strange old man sing in a shrill unpleasant soprano. I've seen troops of little tortured neophytes clad in scarlet, marching and counter-marching, ducking and flopping, like poor little raw recruits for the heavenly host.

Then what other traces have we of buried religion? Strether in *The Ambassadors* used to go into Notre Dame, yielding to some impulse, 'which he amused himself by thinking of as a private concession to cowardice'. He went so that for a moment the things of the world 'could fall into abeyance'. 'That was the cowardice, probably – to dodge them, to beg the question, not to deal with it in the hard outer light; but his own oblivions were too brief, too vain to hurt anyone but himself.'

Rowland Mallet, another character, in 1875, found in St Peter's 'relief from most contrarieties ... from a heartache to a Roman rain', and Mr Greene finds in 'The Altar of the Dead' a promising, though ill-informed interest in prayers for the deceased.

And that is almost all. In the last analysis it is on Henry James's Sense of Evil that Mr Greene bases his tottering hypothesis. And to convince us of this sense of evil Mr Greene uses paradoxical interpretations that he would censure surely as over-intellectual in a Marxist or a Freudian. For example Mr Greene is fascinated by broad hints of an obsession with evil in 'The Turn of the Screw'. Unfortunately James has explicitly stated of this story that it was 'a fairy tale pure and simple ... an amusette to catch those not easily caught', and Mr Greene admits, 'So a valuable ally must be relinquished.' But *can* Mr Greene relinquish this ally? Not he! In two other articles he uses 'The Turn of the Screw' as evidence of his theory. James was 'blinding his reader with a bold sleight of hand'. He was not being frank. 'One cannot avoid a conviction that here he (James) touched and recoiled from an important inhibition.' Mr Greene worries away at it like a dog with a rubber bone, picking it up and dropping it in an ecstasy of self-deception. Yet I cannot believe that he wishes others to be tormented by his unhappy obsessions. I am sure he is looking for comrades in misfortune rather than converts. The proof of that is that he is reassured rather than discomfited to find that the sense of evil which he detects in Henry James can be traced in other members of the James family but definitely allied to psychological and mental peculiarity. Henry's father 'was intermittently attacked by a sense of perfectly insane and abject terror' and his sister Alice was a prey to suicidal tendencies. To clinch the matter Mr Greene quotes a horrifying daytime hallucination of William James, who saw an epileptic idiot, which left him for months a prey to irrational terror. An ordinary student would be convinced by these instances that the Jamesian 'sense of evil' was a family misfortune like consumption or weak sight. But to Mr Greene the hereditary recurrence of these horrible obsessions is a guarantee of their validity. And by succumbing to these visions the gifted James family gave to them a horrible authenticity and importance.

'If ever a man's imagination was clouded by the Pit,' says Mr Greene, approvingly, 'it was James!'

But Greene tries to prove that not only had Henry James a hereditary addiction to the sense of evil, but it received a morbid confirmation in his youth, when he evaded military service in the American Civil War on an insufficient plea of ill-health. For, according to Mr Greene, with James 'the idea of treachery ... was always attached to his sense of evil'. Next we note that Greene's very able and industrious biographers, Allott and Farris, detect the same twin obsessions in his work. So it is less curious to find that Mr Greene, having identified to his satisfaction these two obsessions in James's writings, next argues that they were leading James to the same goal to which they led himself. He declares that James came very close to a direct statement of his belief in Hell and Purgatory. In fact of course Mr Desmond MacCarthy was correct in claiming that James had not a trace of religious feeling. Greene's argument remains interesting, though, because it reveals how a superficial and inconsequent philosophy will give an adequate foundation to an impressive artistic effort. How can Mr Greene continue to cherish so tenderly and proudly his sense of evil, after he has shown to us how in others it can develop out of mental aberration and cowardice? I can only suppose that he reveres it as the source of his art, the pea in the shoe that provoked him into creativity, and that he would feel lonely and disloyal without it like a Moslem lady without her veil.

He stresses elsewhere this fancied connection between art and the sense of supernatural evil, when he quotes with approval Mr T. S. Eliot, 'with the disappearance of the idea of Original Sin, with the disappearance of the idea of intense moral struggle, the human beings presented to us both in poetry and in prose fiction... tend to become less real'. And Greene considers that without the chiaroscuro of black and white (he absurdly attributes to Henry James the view that men were either 'of God's or the Devil's party'), the characters of later distinguished novelists, like Mrs Woolf and E. M. Forster, 'wandered like cardboard symbols through a world that was paper-thin'.

Have we here a prophet rebuking sin or a black-and-white artist decrying water colours? Mr Greene, like some other writers, mounts the pulpit in order to chastise Mrs Woolf and Mr Forster and to advance some questionable opinions about literature. It is hard to fight back at these opinions about without appearing to show disrespect to the venerable vestments in which they are clothed. Some time ago Miss Stevie Smith flung a brickbat or two at a group of neo-Christian essayists, accusing them, if I remember rightly, of a repellent blend of 'gaiety, cruelty and knowingness'. Those who have been cowed by Mr Greene's cleverness and learning into tolerating his sombre philosophy will draw from the evidence of his cruelty the courage to rebel. Beverley Nichols is fair game for the highbrow critic, but Mr Greene's chastisement of him is impermissible. Nichols, the man, who is as God made him, is taunted as unmasculine boys are taunted in grammar schools, while Nichols the writer, who has substituted for his real self a bestselling one, is allowed to escape.

I do not know what lies beneath all this débris in Mr Greene's mind but something that is not properly dead has been interred there. It would be justice to call up Havelock Ellis from 'the Pit' to excavate but I doubt if he would find much in his line there. Nor do I think it is some Auntie Rosa who is still giving trouble. A mere family tyrant would long ago have decomposed among Mr Greene's caustic thoughts. I think it is not a person, but an entire institution, perhaps Berkhamsted School. The ferment of his mind has acted on the place and modified it but there is a hard core of tyranny and tedium which no acid will dissolve. Mr Greene has at last had to come to terms with it and to call it the Sense of Evil, and to say that it is eternal and inevitable and to find for it analogies and apologists in the external world. But the rest of us cannot be expected to base our philosophies on Mr Greene's unhappy adolescence.

II

Stephen Spender and Graham Greene ought to be valuable correctives to each other, but the idea of mutual admonition has not I think occurred to either of them. Spender's solitary reference to Greene in his autobiography is polite and Greene says not a word about Spender. Certainly Greene would find *World Within World*, as he found Havelock Ellis's *My Life*, 'far too intimate for general reading', yet I doubt whether he will ever say so. I think they are both of them conscientious members of the artists' trade union, whose senior representatives do not attack each other, till they are dead. Is there nobility in this mutual tolerance or is there collusion? Why does one think of those French and German armament factories, which were said to guarantee protection for each other in Franco-German wars? If Mr Greene and Mr Spender were serious about their philosophies they would know they were handling explosive as lethal to society as we know it as anything produced by

Krupp or Hotchkiss. The supporters of the Liberal society, as Spender conceives it, are the deadly enemies of the Catholic society championed by Mr Greene. Readers of the two books I have quoted cannot be unaware of this implacable opposition. Yet I doubt whether either Greene or Spender have committed themselves with more than a fraction of their minds or that the armaments, which they have been piling up, were ever meant for war. Like Krupps and Hotchkiss they may find tension more rewarding than conflict. Their art and their reputation would not, I think, survive a real *kulturkampf* in which first principles were not only invoked but applied.

In the meantime Spender, a representative of what he calls the 'Divided Generation', is rather a drooping figure to oppose to the more dogmatic Greene with his nicely tailored moralities and his upright carriage assisted by ethical corsets. I think that Spender reveals the liberal creed most clearly in an admirable reference to the philosophy of E. M. Forster, 'his almost pagan amorality combined with his minute preoccupation with moral issues, his love of freedom combined with his impressive self-discipline'. It is surely true to say that the liberal is always engaged on this expert dovetailing of freedom and discipline. He is always paring and splicing, taking in a bit here, letting out a bit there; he has no plan of campaign beyond day-to-day solicitude and conviction that by foresight and ingenious contrivance men can be made happy and free without hurting each other. I doubt if Spender, though, has ever been a liberal in this meticulous way. He seems to have practised very conscientiously the pagan amorality but he does not appear to have studied how to integrate his philosphy of self-expression into society as it is or might be.

Sometimes idealism is more like a physiological phase than an intellectual conviction. It is time-conditioned and starts to flag when the hair grows thin and the dentist begins to talk of a plate. The very attractive portrait of himself which Mr Spender uses as a frontispiece, an open collar, a sun-beam on his ruffled hair, and the shy side glance of a fawn, is dated 1932 and gives a misleading period air to what would seem to be his deepest convictions. It made me revolt against the modern practice of illustrating seductively the story of our heart as though it was a packet of seeds. The search for lost time, if it is serious, begins well below camera level. Like Proust and Joyce and the great ones, we should leave our faces behind, as we leave our overcoats when we go down a coal mine. Mr Spender is a serious investigator but I think that in *World Within World* he makes the mistake of supposing that the inner and the outer world overlap and merge, whereas as a general rule they alternate and cannot be contemplated together. If in a train journey at night we wish to watch the flying fields outside, we must totally exclude the bright static images of ourselves upon the window pane. Mr Spender tries by a trick of the eye to see the two worlds at once and, though he often achieves it, it is at the cost of clarity and sense.

I think we diminish writers by our habit of classifying them, but Mr Spender is ready to be considered as a spokesman of the Divided Generation, a sad and yet somehow romantic group like the Wild Geese or the Mohicans. He and his friends take a bitter-sweet satisfaction in the thought that a certain phase of human hope and endeavour exactly synchronized with the progress and passing of their youth. The illusion is pardonable, for in 1932 for some reason (it may have been because of the death or disillusionment of an earlier generation in the 1914–18 war) the belief in a changed world had linked itself provisionally with youth, with open collars, with bronze bodies and forest camps and hazardous applications of revolutionary theories of sex. The young people thought of themselves as pioneers in a new world but in fact most of them were only the luxury tourists who follow in the wake of the explorer when the ground has been cleared and the routes marked. The Divided Generation contributed extraordinarily little beyond some well-written poems and stories to the emancipation of the human spirit; the youth movement itself, which had centred on Germany, ended in appalling catastrophe. The pioneer work had been done by a previous generation, the bearded philosophers and the crusty eccentrics with 'scrubby, stained and smelly clothes', in whom with such sound intuition Mr Greene recognized his enemies. So that Mr Spender's belief that an important epoch ended with his youth is only partially true. The age of emotional tourism had yielded disappointing results, but the findings of the explorers, who preceded it, have not been seriously challenged.

The Divided Generation was cliquey and in love with itself. It fell from the heights of over-confidence to the depths of despair. Now Narcissus has scrambled out of the pool and stands, damp and discouraged, looking at the muddied water. But instead of saying, 'I am vain,' he says, 'All is vanity!' Indeed otherworldliness is popular with many writers today simply because a collective avowal of original sin is less bruising and intellectually exacting to the individual than a sober consideration of avoidable follies.

I think that Mr Spender, even when he was expressing his individuality most abundantly, was still anxious to keep open this loophole of escape into collective guilt and atonement. The philosophy of Mr T. S. Eliot is a curious link between Spender and Greene. When he was young

Spender rebelled tentatively against Eliot's 'escapism into the past', as he dared to consider it, but he repented of this and came ultimately to admire Eliot's notion that the past was in some way 'integrated', while the present is 'fragmentary'. He considered that Eliot was one of those happy few, who had secured his survival by detaching himself from liberalism and resisting 'the imprisoned preoccupation of his age with its own time'. The pivot of Eliot's philosophy, which Spender does not now find repulsive, was despair about the material world, somewhat relieved by backward glances at history. Eliot confessed to him once that for the future of mankind, he saw nothing but 'internecine conflict' and that 'what matters is whether I believe in original sin'. That is to say, acquiescence in the incurable nature of human ills is a necessary stage towards that Eliot resignation which Mr Spender seems to commend.

Pessimism has become a virtue, but it is pessimism of a rather recondite sort. 'However much the individual might be committed to social tasks, he belonged to an eternal order of events, where he was not the product and victim of his time.' This seems a mere juggling with the dimensions of time and place in the interests of equanimity. Of course we do know that against the background of prehistory our best and foulest deeds dwindle into insignificance. But equally, looking through the other end of the telescope, we can see our most trivial act or thought setting up an infinite chain of repercussions. Every sneeze is weighted with consequence. These ideas are valuable in certain circumstances, as drugs and stimulants, but a wise man will not become an addict to either. Mr Spender, an impressionable person, is strongly susceptible to both forms of auto-intoxication. He ends the book in a trance of solipsism, induced by an overdose of these ideas of the 'smallness of human life compared to the infinitude of time'. All that remains is the 'desire to love and be loved', just because we are 'ignorant and miserable and surrounded by unknowns of time and space'. And 'like shipwrecked people upon a sea... the only sanity must lie in helping one another'. So we are back where we began. The book is rounded off with an admirably written description of the author's schooldays. There is no doubt a parable here, but I don't quite know how to read it. Has Odysseus come back to Ithaca and the domestic pieties? Has Narcissus come back to the pool with a new suit of clothes on? Will some Daddy-figure, some Auntie Rosa in the form of a categorical imperative, slip back on to the empty throne where the Liberal Ethic once reigned?

Mr Spender sees that 'sense of social guilt' as one of the mainsprings of the revolutionary impulse in the bourgeoisie, and no doubt he is right. But it is an unreliable emotion, misdirecting the goodwill which it calls to its aid. The knowledge that he had £300 a year and that he was raised above 'those marginal existences, whose lives registered as delicately as the needle of an instrument booms and slumps', drove him into politics, yet made him 'unable to criticize a thief or a blackmailer'. 'I could never,' he explains rather foggily, 'feel within myself the rightness of a social system which would rebuke the wrongness in others.' And he reproaches himself with this attitude: 'I should have been tougher and more cynical, accepting my own position in the world and expecting others to accept theirs.'

If he can reject in this way the sense of social guilt without any feeling of intellectual recantation, he must acknowledge that it is purely subjective. What is its origin then in the mind and the reason of its great influence? Only a handful of the possessing classes is ever seriously incommoded by this sense of guilt, yet it has always been an important phenomenon. In one generation a few youthful writers affected by it, headed by Auden and Isherwood and Spender, managed to give its special character to the 'Pink Decade'. Why do such people so often love the proletariat, when the proletariat so seldom loves them? Those who gibe at 'parlour pinks' usually attribute their pinkness to ignorance and affectation. Yet Spender, like the others, was exceptionally clear-sighted and straightforward; he knew quite well that the proletariat bored him though his description of his war-time associates is the reverse of boring. I think too that he would have agreed that privilege develops the faculties and sharpens the sensibilities and that therefore the rule of the unprivileged for the first generation of its establishment would be crude and insensitive. But the heart has its reasons. Many of the Pinks felt a bitter dislike of their own class and milieu and the proletariat had at least done them no harm. We judge people by the injury they have done us, not by their capacity to injure our descendants. The English bourgeois intellectual has often an abiding and legitimate grievance against the society in which he grew up. Otherwise it is hard to explain the passionate recoil (in opposite direction) of Greene and Spender from bourgeois traditions. Greene is the more bitter of the two, since he sees the whole world as evil, not merely the section of it that bred him. The sense of evil and the sense of social guilt show us two publicly approved methods of discharging a burden of private resentment and shame. To the conventionally progressive an orgy of social guilt may be as com-forting as an abject general confession can be to the conventionally devout. On the surface this collective contrition seems respectable enough, but does it not often require a closer analysis?

Mr Spender is so honest, observant and uninhibited that we have abundance of evidence here for judging the Divided Generation if we knew how to use it. The question arises, were they ever liberals in the sense that Stephen's father and his uncle were? Had he or his friends ever bothered themselves as the elder Spenders did with the problem of extending to wider and wider circles the privileges of the higher classes? I think they were mostly in rebellion against these alleged social advantages, their education for example. The revolutionary changes they wished could not be effected by any political party. As this book reveals they made, in the name of the free individual, far more sweeping demands on society than the elder Spenders would have made even for themselves. When they elected for Communism, as Stephen Spender and others of them did, it was the destructive negative side of it which appealed to them, the overthrow of the bourgeoisie and the cruel régimes in Italy, Germany and Spain, which had been reared in its defence. I don't think the positive Communist programme attracted them in the least and when later it was forced on their attention they repudiated it. They were really passive anarchists, hoping, in a mystical way, that the liberties they wished for would grow up in the fissures of a shattered society, like ferns in a crumbling wall. That was why dissolving Weimar Germany held such an appeal for them and why their political activities disquieted Virginia Woolf and the leaders of the Bloomsbury circle.

The Bloomsbury group had in fact lodged itself satisfactorily in a crevice of the still intact fabric of society, against many of whose canons it was in revolt. Ethically it was like a self-governing republic within the framework of an empire. Its members enjoyed already some of the privileges of self-expression, which the Divided Generation desired, but its authority, its security, depended on a certain exclusiveness. As Spender says, it was rather snobbish. The crevice could not be indefinitely enlarged without imperilling the structure of society and alarming its guardians. That is to say the exacting Bloomsbury ethic operated in a more or less closed circle, focused on two or three distinguished households. It drew its sanctions from the mutual trust and affection which united its members, who had freed themselves from many of the social conventions, not by a social struggle but by their assurance that they were an aristocracy sometimes of birth and wealth, always of intellect. They were too self-sufficient to crusade for their convictions. For example, it is hard to imagine Virginia Woolf campaigning very confidently on behalf of the legalisation of suicide or euthanasia, yet when she found herself faced with the decay of her intellect, she consulted her own sense of what was right and took her life.

This Bloomsbury way of life was not, as Mr R. F. Harrod shows in his recent life of J. M. Keynes, for export. Divorced from personal solicitude, the intimate analysis of feelings and motives to which the group subjected each other would become cruel and gossiping; its unflinching vocabulary would become a weapon of malice. Inevitably there would be a recoil towards Victorian reticence and suppression.

The Divided Generation inherited from Bloomsbury its belief in persons rather than in principles, its difficult code of moral freedom tempered by self-discipline, yet it has less focus and friendly solidarity, less faith. I suppose their leaders were insubstantial figures, compared with the Woolfs, Keynes, Stracheys and Russells, not so intellectually confident or materially established. Perhaps too the spectacle of social collapse tempted them to think that the barriers were everywhere breaking down and that a whole new world would enter into relations with them. They need not be satisfied with a tolerated enclave in the old one.

To Communist critics, like Christopher Caudwell, these left-wing poets seemed to be Lone Wolves, whose chief value to the party lay in their destructive hatred of bourgeois restraints. It was plain that they would reject Communist discipline with equal defiance. In a previous century they might have formed their own sect or school, but they lacked even the cohesion of Bloomsbury, not recognizing themselves for what they were, a minority group, whose strength lay in concentration and not in diffusion. They preached their gospel of individualism and self-realization round all the Messianic communities but without success. A few of them became Communists or Churchmen or members of mystical communities, most of them were deflected in some degree from their individualism by the mass movements which they tried to influence.

The Bloomsbury group were sensitive interpreters of foreign cultures. Their successors, more consciously European, seemed happiest on the crumbling margins. Berlin in the Weimar days was rather like Corinth in early Christian time, a cosmopolitan dunghill, in which delicate flowers and rank weeds could flourish side by side. The artist prospered there as he did in Russia in the first chaotic years of Bolshevism. Mr Spender says of it: 'When I was living a life dangerous to myself and impossible to justify to others I was writing my best early poems', and he says that he and others used Germany 'as a kind of a cure for our personal problems'. Referring to the same period, he says: 'I sought to discover my real self by behaviour, which outraged my ideal self. The result of this was a series of relationships undertaken in a spirit of opportunism. Yet I was too much an idealist to maintain a cynical attitude.'

I think these quotations show that, if any of the reformist spirit of his liberal forbears had descended to Mr Spender, it would have expressed itself more naturally in the ethical than in the political sphere. For the Divided Generation felt indulgently towards many ethical heresies. When, as in the Spanish Civil War, Spender's revolutionary ethics came in conflict with his revolutionary politics, it was the rebel of the outer world who capitulated to the rebel of the inner one. Yet Spender has done all his public crusading in the, to him, less important sphere of politics. (This displacement of ardour is not usual. How many secret streams flow into the broad river of political discontent?) But now his inability to justify to others his way of life, to relate it to society or to a rebel group within society, makes him as defenceless as an alien without a passport. His candour and his scruples will not by themselves establish the innocence of which he feels assured. That is the tragedy of the individualist; some niggling fastidiousness, some pride in his uniqueness, will often prevent him from co-operating in the construction of an impressive dogmatism behind which to shelter his non-conformities.

In the case of Mr Spender a more reasoned apologia is needed to raise his autobiography from the level of the curious to the significant, from the case history to the critique of contemporary ethic. As it is, he will not even succeed in annoying Mr Graham Greene, as Havelock Ellis did, for the authoritarian is always indulgent to amorality of an individualistic cast. What rouses his wrath is the moral person who flaunts a private code of ethics. To be wise without paying tribute to the source of all wisdom is worse than folly. It is a graver offence against society to own an illicit still and be sober than to be drunk in the streets. Mr Spender will be scolded and then forgiven for the lesser sin of intemperance. Will he ever, like Auden, lump together his ethical with his political heresies and renounce them both?

Mr Spender tells an anecdote which shows perhaps that he prides himself on his romantic inability to fit his emotional impulses into a social framework. At his wedding in a burst of spontaneous generosity he thrust some silver toast-racks, trays 'and so forth', the gifts of his wealthier friends, on the poorer wedding guests, as they left. That is the act of a large-hearted Caliph, not of a middle-aged liberal. If you are conventional enough to have a wedding, you must observe the rules of weddings. Presents are tokens of regard and to give them away is to rebuff a gesture which you appear to have solicited. Mr Spender's assault on the proprieties often has a loud echo, because it is contained by the four walls of conventions which he has failed to breach. We are all of us tethered to our past, or, if you like, to our social background, but it is only the more adventurous who find this out by straining the tether till it is taut. The others believe themselves free. Mr Spender's frolics, abandoned as they may seem, never took him far enough from the tethering post for a real test of strength.

None the less this book is of great importance, because it shows how very feeble were the attempts which the Divided Generation made to co-ordinate the inner and the outer world. Their incursions into politics were more like plundering raids than serious attempts at engagements and in ethics they were emotional buccaneers, not reformers.

What is the wider significance of the collapse of the Divided Generation? Does it mean the bankruptcy of the liberal revolutionary spirit? I think it means merely that the intellectual cliques which have so long been the standard bearers of liberal thought, have lost their *raison d'être*. As a clique the Divided Generation had a clear heredity through the Bloomsbury group to Leslie Stephen and the Victorian Rationalists and through them to their immediate predecessors, Wilberforce and the Clapham Evangelicals. Each stage in the descent marked an evaporation of influence as the state closed its ranks more solidly against the intellectual and as the clique became more heterodox and more loosely knit.

The modern bureaucratic state is as impervious to minority enthusiasms as any autocratic régime of the seventeenth century. In those days the sect rather than the clique was the vehicle of revolutionary liberalism. Its members repudiated society because they despaired of reforming it. The sects offered a refuge from the inhumanity of the state, not, as later, an armed camp for its subjugation. Sometimes it looks as if those days might return. Freedom, the freedom of the inner world, might seem to have its best guarantee, not in legislation extorted from the government, but in pledges of mutual support and tolerance exchanged between individuals in the shadow of the state.

[1951]

MARIA EDGEWORTH

There are some Irish writers who are so precariously balanced between England and Ireland that an Irishman often has to do a bit of special pleading in order to claim them for Ireland at all. If I had felt that Maria Edgeworth was one of these borderline cases, I might have been tempted to concentrate on her Irish stories, *Castle Rackrent*, and *The Absentee* and *Ormond*, and to treat her other work, her educational tales and English novels, as in some way secondary. But in fact from the time she was fifteen and returned to Edgeworthstown with her father, Ireland became her home and Irish life her major preoccupation. Yet though she lived in Ireland, she was far less provincial than many of her great English contemporaries; she was accepted on the continent as a European in a way that Jane Austen, a much greater novelist, never was. The Edgeworth Way of Life, expounded by her father and herself, had found them disciples far and wide. Friends in Paris once urged them to set up a salon there in rivalry to Mme de Staël, for it was thought that the Edgeworths and their philosophy of rational conduct would be a wholesome antidote to the brilliant romanticism of the de Staël circle.

All this led Maria to speak condescendingly of Jane Austen, who had found all the material for her art ready to hand in a Hampshire village, and whose novels never touched on the social problems which agitated the Edgeworths. 'One gets tired', said Maria of Jane, 'of milk and water, even when the milk is of the sweetest and the water the purest.'

One cannot wholly blame Maria for this undervaluation or for the havoc the once-fashionable Edgeworth notions made of her own talents as a novelist. Ireland in those days offered a challenge to the heart as well as to the head, and in warm-hearted intelligent people like Maria and her father it was bound to stimulate ideas of justice and reform. The Edgeworths found arrogance on one side and poverty and ignorance beyond belief upon the other, and a deep social fissure which it seemed to them only education and mutual trust could bridge. They had a passion for social justice and they could not be content to be chroniclers of country manners like Jane or like Maria herself in *Castle Rackrent*.

In her old age Maria recognized clearly what had happened. She admitted that her best-conceived characters were those, like Sir Condy of *Castle Rackrent* and Thady Quirk, which she had created with a minimum of what she called 'philosophical construction'. 'Where I least aimed at drawing character,' she wrote, 'I succeeded best.' She would like to have gone on writing about Ireland but she said that passions were too high and there was no place for a writer who wished to hold the mirror up to nature. The people would smash the mirror and that would be the end.

If she was often very didactic it was because she was an invincible optimist, believing that there was no evil to which experience and self-knowledge could not discover a cure. In this she was no mere echo of her father, dominating character as he was. R. L. Edgeworth was certainly dynamic. He invented springs for carriages, 'Macadamized' roads and early types of bicycles and telegraphs. He was an enthusiast for education and domesticity, which his twenty-two children and five wives did not succeed in quenching. As a young man he had been a disciple of Rousseau and for a time had brought up his eldest son as a child of nature. But the more he saw of the miseries of Ireland the less respect he had for primitive simplicity and for Rousseau, who had sung its praises When the Edgeworth philosophy took its final form, I think it could be summarized in three words: 'Learn by experience', or perhaps 'Think for yourself'. That was the refrain that recurred through scores of Edgeworth novels and tales.

Perhaps it is easier for us than it was for our parents to understand how such a chilly platitude could become a slogan in a crusade. For if there is any truth in the theory that history repeats itself in cycles, have we not come round again to the problems of the Edgeworths and their friends? Then, just as now, civilization had rocked and men were slowly recovering from the intoxication of tremendous dreams. The magic of the dreams had faded but they had not relaxed their hold upon the mind. Men of opposing factions were mobilized to think in blocks and there was a stigma of treachery attached to those who chose to be independent. Edgeworth was one of those whose pride it was to think for himself into whatever eccentricities this might lead him, and Maria had inherited some of her father's uncompromisingly experimental spirit. The Edgeworths and their circle despised nothing so much as intellectual timidity. If you had a belief you must also have the courage to practise it. Maria's brother-in-law, Dr Beddoes, for example, a well-known physician, used to terrorize the landladies of Bristol by driving cows upstairs to his patients' bedrooms. Why? Simply because the doctor was convinced that in pulmonary complaints nothing was so wholesome for an invalid as a cow breathing on him. And is not health more important than stair-carpets?

Her father was more cautiously experimental than this and the success of his methods was to be read in his well-run estate, his contented tenantry and his happy children. The large plain house in the Irish midlands became famous in Europe and a focus of pilgrimage almost like Mme de Staël's house at Coppet or Tolstoy's at Yasnaya Polyana.

If you think I exaggerate, look up the Edgeworthstown chapter in Mr and Mrs Hall's famous *Travels in Ireland* and you will find those two quite hard-boiled pilgrims almost inarticulate with emotion. They seem to be on tip-toe from the moment they enter County Longford, fearful to violate this sanctuary of family happiness but at the same time anxious to draw from their visit and share with the world all the enlightenment they could.

For from this mansion [they wrote] has issued so much practical good to Ireland and not alone to Ireland but to the whole civilized world. It has been for long the residence of high intellect, well directed genius, industry and virtue. It is a place that perhaps possesses larger moral interest than any other in the kingdom.

Mr and Mrs Hall, like so many others, saw Maria working at her stories in the general living-room, children in and out the whole time, for in addition to some dozen brothers and sisters there were nephews and nieces, but her mind was so attuned to domesticity that they did not disturb her. Indeed in one of her letters she writes that she was taking her writing desk into her sister Lucy's room for Lucy, while in bed, liked to hear the sound of Maria's pencil. In most modern writers distraction like that would be almost unintelligible but with Maria it was no affectation. Affection for her family and friends was the fuel which kept her mind in motion.

Maria and her father, much more than Rousseau or Montessori or any one else, were the progenitors of the progressive school with its educational toys and uninhibited ethic. And it was as an educational reformer that Maria first acquired a European reputation. I wonder if it is her fault or ours that no modern child has an appetite for the sort of story she wrote. This may be an accident of fashion, for though to us her stories seem steeped in the most austere morality, the Victorians did not find them moral enough. Or rather they complained that the

Edgeworths used all the wrong arguments for inculcating virtue, basing it on neighbourliness and reason and common sense rather than the Ten Commandments. They did not, like Charlotte M. Yonge, the Victorian favourite, link virtue to the eternal verities. Indeed *The Quarterly Review* printed what her friend, Dumont, called 'an infamous and calumnious attack' on Maria. The writer complained of 'the deplorable omission of expressions of devoutness, which from its persistence it is impossible to believe to be accidental'. Elsewhere the Rev. R. Hall wrote:

Her books are the most irreligious I have ever read. She does not attack religion but makes it appear unnecessary by exhibiting perfect virtue without it. No works ever produced so bad an effect on my mind as hers.

But what our children miss is fantasy. The Edgeworths had no use for it. Maria's stories about little Rosamond are crisp and logical, like a proposition in Euclid. There are no fairies, pirates or bunny rabbits' tea parties. Particularly about rabbits was Rosamond very rational. She discussed with her mama the idea that it was wrong to kill and eat rabbits, but rejected it as unreasonable. And when a rabbit nibbled a shrub that her mother had given her, her brother made her a humane and ingenious rabbit trap. I haven't a doubt that if Rosamond's mother lived today she would blame myxomatosis on Peter Rabbit. She would argue like this: 'If you grant to animals false feelings that they have not, you will finally forget the true feelings which they have.'

How can one explain the immense appeal that these uncompromising stories had for the children of 150 years ago? Maria tried to give a plain unadorned view of society and its obligations, scaling it down to a child's vision. She never bluffed or condescended. Children felt they were being initiated into the secrets of the grown-up world, its tabus and dangers, and perhaps this was as thrilling to them as mystery and adventure are to children today.

'Rosamond and the Purple Jar' is the best known of these stories. It exemplifies so well the remorseless but benevolent Edgeworth logic that I'll relate the plot.

Rosamond, going out shopping with her mama and a servant to carry the parcels, inevitably wanted to buy almost everything she saw in the fascinating shops, but her mama countered all her excited suggestions with cool prim logic.

'Nay, Rosamond, I have a pair of buckles, I do not want any more,' or 'Yes, Rosamond, the jewels are pretty but what use are pretty baubles to me? ... You say I would discover a use, but I would rather find out the use before buying.'

And then they come to a chemist's shop and Rosamond can scarcely be drawn away from the delirious contemplation of a purple jar in the window.

'Oh, mama, but it would be useful. We could put flowers in it.'

'You have a flower-pot, Rosamond, and that is not a flower-pot.'

'But I could use it as a flower-pot, mama.'

'Perhaps, if you were to examine it closer, Rosamond, you would be disappointed.'

'No, indeed, mama, I am sure I shouldn't.'

A little later Rosamond starts to limp on the pavement. 'Oh, mama, there is a great hole in my shoe and a stone is got in. My shoes are quite worn out. I wish you would be so very good as to buy me another pair.'

'Nay, Rosamond, I have money but not enough to buy shoes, buckles, pretty baubles and purple jars.'

But the limp becomes worse, really cruel, and they have to go into a shoe shop, dark and smelling horribly of new leather, but they find a pair of shoes that exactly fits. And Rosamond is given her choice. She may have the shoes or she may have the purple jar and wait till the end of the month for the shoes.

After reflection she decides, 'Oh, mama, I *think* I can wear the bad shoes till the end of the month. I would *prefer* the flower-pot if you will not think me very silly.'

'Why, I cannot promise not to think you silly, Rosamond. But when you have to judge for yourself, you should choose what will make you happy and then it will not signify who thinks you silly.'

'Then mama, I am sure the flower-pot will make me happy.'

You will remember or can guess the rest. When the servant arrived with the purple jar, Rosamond finds to her dismay that it is just a plain glass jar full of nasty purple liquid. And every day her shoes get worse and worse so that she can't jump or dance or run. She offered to exchange the jar with her mother for a pair of shoes, but the calm logical answer came back, 'Nay, Rosamond, you must abide by your choice.'

Rosamond's mama would be attacked from a dozen different angles today. A woman, we'd say, who could afford a servant to carry her parcels, should be ashamed to let her child hobble round in broken-down shoes and there would be medical talk about permanent injury to the instep and so on. But the key to the Edgeworth doctrine surely lies in the mother's remark. 'What does it signify who thinks you silly, if you choose what will make you happy?' The Edgeworthian parents never, like the Victorian paterfamilias, put themselves on pedestals. They seldom preached and never punished. But nor did they hasten headlong,

as we should do, to protect their children from the educative consequences of an unwise choice.

The stories themselves don't sufficiently explain the little world of
mutual solicitude and patience, which Maria assumed as a necessary
background to these chastening adventures. Mr Edgeworth's letters and,
much more so, Maria's, make things clearer. For instance there is his
letter to Maria about little Fanny who had asked him what a section was
when he was busy. He tells Maria to buy a lemon for her and get a small
cylinder of wood turned. Then Maria is to demonstrate with a knife
what a transverse section is and then what a longitudinal section is. The
Edgeworth educational system demanded a warm and constant intimacy
between elders and children. Boarding schools were regarded as an easy,
inadequate way out. It was only because Mr Edgeworth was dead and
Maria old that the youngest of the brood was sent to Charterhouse.

Many little sisters – there were ten of them – went to the making of
Rosamond. And that rather abstract little girl becomes more intelligible
if we set the reality beside the fiction. It is a little daunting to read of
Maria's young sister Harriet coming in before breakfast at eight a.m.
every morning to read her Mme de Sévigné, but turn a page or two
and you will find Maria taking Harriet and Fanny to visit Sir Walter
Scott at Abbotsford or to Mme de Genlis, Lord Edward's mother-in-
law, decaying in a Parisian garret. Or dressing them up for a dance at
Almacks. And then coming home again and helping Maria make a
gutter in the main street at Edgeworthstown, her own idea, her own
plans and 'twenty men', Maria claims proudly, 'employed for three
weeks'. Those returns to Edgeworthstown were always happy. 'We look
to our dear home for permanent happiness,' wrote Maria. 'We return
without a regret for anything we have left behind except our friends.'

A few days pass and we read of Harriet again. She is taking the part
of a fire-eater in a charade and devouring lighted spills; 'she only burnt
her lips a little'. Or listen how the children organized a *fête champêtre* at
Edgeworthstown in 1805 to celebrate old Mr Edgeworth's birthday.
First of all they contrived to get their elders and the babies out of the
way for the afternoon.

I had little Lucy in my arms [wrote Maria] and, after the chaise, on horseback
came rosy Charlotte all smiles, and Henry with eyes brilliant with pleasure. We
came home with no suspicion of what was prepared, when our ears were
suddenly struck with the sound of music and as if by enchantment a fairy festival
appeared upon the green. An amphitheatre of verdant festoons suspended from
white staffs with scarlet streamers. Youths and maidens in white, their heads
adorned with flowers, were dancing while their mothers and little children were

seated on benches round the amphitheatre. William danced a reel with Harriet and baby Sophie, and Kitty served cakes and syllabubs and then William at present in the height of his electrical enthusiasm proposed to the dancers a few electrical sparks to complete the joys of the day. Everybody flocked after him to the study and shrieks of surprise and terror mixed with the laughter. And when we came out the grass-plat was lit up by boys waving flambeaux, illuminating the beauty of green boughs and flowers.

You see it was part of the theory that when Rosamond had learnt to reason for herself and had discovered that purple jars might not be purple, she should use her intelligence and daring to its utmost limits. Not only could she play with fire, she could swallow it if she chose. So you can understand Maria's indignation when Mme de Staël gibed at the 'triste utilité' of the Edgeworth educational system. There was no evidence that it produced either prigs or pedants.

Their educational schemes had of course their setbacks. Maria's brother, Lovell, put into practice an old dream of his father's, and with the support of the Catholic priest and the Protestant rector of Edgeworthstown started an inter-denominational school there. This experiment, a unique one in those days, went well for ten years. But Lovell's business capacity was not equal to his educational zeal. He bankrupted the estate and Maria had to take it over and run it herself from her literary earnings.

It would be hard certainly to claim that even in her novels Maria was not excessively didactic. The book of hers which I prefer, *The Absentee*, is more propagandist even than *Uncle Tom's Cabin*. It is like the most entertaining sermon that was ever written. All the characters are tilted slightly from the plane of reality towards the central argument of the book: 'An Irish landlord must live among the people from whom he draws his subsistence.' Because they neglect this principle, Lady Clonbrony lives beyond her income, trying to buy her way into fashionable London society, while fashionable London merely laughs at her provinciality and vulgar Irishisms. For the same reason Lord Clonbrony is *désoeuvré* and feebly resentful. He exaggerates his Irishness from defiance. Meanwhile in Ireland, unknown to the absentee landlord, the bad agent of the Clonbrony property prospers, the good agent is squeezed out by intrigue. And among the humble tenants, we see virtue discouraged and vice triumphant all because of the canker of absenteeism.

But fortunately the young lord shares many of Mr Edgeworth's views about estate management. He travels to the family estates incognito. There is a superb account of social life in Dublin and the provinces in the years after the Union. The young lord reveals himself and establishes the rule of reason and order. And the earl and countess drive home to Clonbrony Castle to the cheers of their tenantry.

Maria's plots are complicated and ingenious as is fitting in an inventor's daughter. Sometimes one seems to hear the pulleys creak and the ropes strain as virtue is hoisted on to her pedestal. One recalls Mr Edgeworth raising by a new device his patent metal spire on Edgeworthstown church and how a bugle blew when the hoisting started and when at last the golden weather cock settled into position, a flag flew and the congregation cheered. And how that did not prevent a murmuring among the devout: 'Yes but is Mr Edgeworth really orthodox?' Maria's enthusiasm and ingenuity are no answer either to a parallel question: 'Is Miss Edgeworth really a novelist?' Compared to Jane Austen, I don't think she is, but she was a writer of great and significant books, and her integrity if not her art should secure her a place among the immortals.

Her last book *Helen* caused her much misgiving. It was rewritten several times and is as far removed as possible from the spontaneous ease of *Castle Rackrent*. Her father had been dead seventeen years, during which she had written little, and those who blame him for turning her from an artist into a moralist have to explain why the book which she wrote without any encouragement from him should blaze with such moral fervour. Maria had a horror of half-lies, of innuendo and evasion, and the plot of *Helen* hinges on a very charming lady's inability to make an awkward admission. Little lies breed big lies and at last the truth can only be vindicated by a lady as downright and disagreeable as Rosamond's mama. This lady hears the whole slanderous story from her dentist, as she sits in the dental chair. Such is her indignation that she bites his finger, and, with her toothache still raging, sets off to expose the falsehood.

These last novels seem today very archaic in construction but I think they have the same importance as some of Mr Edgeworth's mechanical contrivances, those dim foreshadowings of the bicycle and the telephone whose debris were found not long ago in an out-house at Edgeworthstown. They were experiments which, had he not been so pre-occupied with moral problems and perhaps with Ireland, he might have brought to perfection. I don't mean by this that either he or his daughter failed in what they attempted, but that their proudest achievements must be looked for in their lives rather than in their art.

Maria Edgeworth was a brilliant and sociable personality who gave only half her genius to her art. As with her father, her ambition was as much to change society as to observe it. And though she left little imprint upon public life, who can set a limit in space or time to the influence of a happy and dynamic personality? Scott and Turgenev recorded their debt in print, for they said that it was *Castle Rackrent* that first inspired them to write as they did about Scotland and about Russia. But how many others had no opportunity of acknowledging what they owed to Maria! One debt to her, as a writer of children's stories, was paid in a way that delighted her. When the great famine was at its height and Maria, an old woman of eighty, was launching appeals on behalf of the stricken people of Edgeworthstown, a present arrived for Miss Edgeworth to distribute, 150 barrels of wheat and rice from the children of Boston, who had loved the stories of Rosamond and Harry and Frank.

Maria was a great family woman, so I can't do better than finish with a family tribute. In the home circle one is most likely to get impartiality from one's in-laws, and Richard Butler, the Dean of Clonmacnois, a scholar and antiquarian, was married to Maria's sister Harriet. Here is what he wrote to a friend after Maria, in the last years of her life, had paid them her annual visit.

We have just had Maria Edgeworth with us, as cheerful and as fresh as ever. Having her is like having the sunshine always about you and I think she is more in her element and puts out all herself more in strictly domestic life than any other. Her constant flow of gaiety is one of the most surprising things in nature. Neither sadness nor malice nor anything very bad can stand long in her presence.

[1954]

INFLUENZA IN ARAN

When I arrived in Aran by the *Naomh Eanna* at Kilronan I was sneezing and by the time I had raced to St Enda's church at Killeany and seen the stone on which he had floated in from Connemara I was feverish and coughing. I spent the rest of my time in bed reading the only two books on Aran and its saints which I could find, a big one by Mr Ó Síocháin and a small one by Father Scantlebury.★ I also studied Irish with my landlady's daughter, a little girl of four called Teresa. These lessons started when she had her hands behind her back and said, 'You can't see my fingers!' I said, 'No more I can! But say it in Irish!' She replied immediately, 'Ní féidir leat mo mhéaranna a fheiceáil!' And so it went on. She was as instantaneous as an interpreter at the United Nations Assembly and she asked no salary. She taught and I learnt with pleasure and indeed joy. This is how Irish should have been. Yet in 1987 40,000 Irish are leaving Ireland every year, cursing their elders who forced them to learn Irish instead of something 'useful' like business management or word-processing or nuclear physics.

But to come back to those two books: Father Scantlebury is cautious and a little dry, Mr Ó Síocháin is exuberant and daring. He says that Aran might well be the tail-end of Hy Brasil, the wonderful island which, like Plato's Atlantis, is lost beneath the sea. He adds that Aran was once 'the greatest spiritual storehouse the world has ever known'. When the Celts first settled there, they had a mighty empire in Europe behind them and 'centuries of civilization of the highest order'. Of St Enda, the doyen of the spiritual storehouse, Mr Ó Síocháin says: 'He was probably one of the greatest teachers the Church has ever known.' Father Scantlebury says the same thing more cautiously. There is much

★ P. A. Ó Síocháin, *Aran Islands of Legend* (Dublin 1962); Rev. C. Scantlebury, S.J., *Saints and Shrines of Aran Mór* (Dublin 1926).

of interest in both these books. Mr Ó Síocháin writes perceptively of John Synge's brief but memorable sojourn in Aran, and of the many owners who collected rents from the islands but never visited them.

I too am tempted to use the language of hyperbole about Aran. It seems to me one of the most enchanting and interesting spots in Europe since it has held on to a precarious beauty and simplicity which the rest of the world is disastrously discarding. But it is St Enda and the spiritual storehouse that chiefly arouse my curiosity. When my friend Dr Simpson came out from Galway to visit me on the Whit Monday excursion I hoped to communicate some of my enthusiasm to him but I failed miserably. He dismissed Ó Síocháin scornfully and Scantlebury patroniz-ingly, and talked to me in terms of the Latin *Life of Enda*, of conflations, collations, recensions. After a glance or two he slapped both my books down on the counterpane. 'I see they repeat that old error, which Zimmer exposed, of Conall Derg being the father of Enda. Conall was a purely fabulous person.'

'Of course,' I agreed, 'he was the wicked King of Clogher, who brought the poisoned ox to St Lassar on Devenish Island.' (I should explain that I enjoy the ancient Irish habit of explaining with an enter-taining anecdote any proper name that puzzles them, as so many do. Devenish [Damh Inis] on Loch Erne, means Ox Island.)

'But surely,' I added, 'even if it were a different Enda who was son of Conall Derg and spent his youth burning churches and plotting to murder his grandfather, did the real Enda of Aran ever do or say anything that we would recognize as even faintly Christian? Weren't he and all the other saints of Aran merely very successful magicians?'

He dodged this and talked instead of folklore and comparative religion and then his voice tapered away into something about the charm of innocence. We both of us began to yawn and after a bit he got up to catch his boat.

He left me with the impression that Enda is sliding gently out of history on the heels of Conall Derg and that the whole spiritual storehouse is in danger of collapsing. Just as Enda had much in common with his church-burning namesake, so many of the other saints of Aran had either a sinful past or a sinful namesake. Moreover they are almost all Enda's relations and so are the saints of Wales, Cornwall, Scotland and Brittany. Three generations ago Father Shearman accommodated all the most important ones into three or four intertwined family trees. If one goes, and there are many hundreds of them, they all go. For they support each other like a house of cards in which no single card can stand alone or can safely be pulled away and if Enda, the greatest teacher in the greatest spiritual storehouse, were to go, a hundred spiritual storehouses would collapse with him, leaving a forest of interrogation marks behind.

For different reasons, romantic, religious, academic, tourist, no one wants this to happen. If Enda and his storehouse were to disintegrate, they would do so without any sort of explosion. No tremors would be recorded on Aran. *Naomh Éanna* would not sink or have to be renamed. Nor would Dr Simpson bother to force his new perceptions on Father Scantlebury or Mr Ó Síocháin.

This absence of explosion is a proof that learning, which in Ireland has always flourished best in the country, is dead. It has not transplanted well to the universities. Real learning is dynamic, dangerous, exhilarating. It is built on curiosity, not on knowledge. When it explodes, someone feels liberated, someone else is hurt. At present in place of curiosity there is textual criticism, and philology and scientific excavations, which are all highly skilled crafts like apiculture and hairdressing. No bombs are thrown at Atlantis or the spiritual storehouse, but there is much silent and salaried sneering.

Dr Simpson and the textual critics are at present working on Enda. When they have amputated what is fabulous or corrupt, there will be almost nothing left of the great teacher and saint. But because of their fine finicky methods, his will be an almost painless extinction. Every sentence is analysed separately and any attempt to judge truth by everyday criteria is deemed amateurish.

Mr Ó Síocháin argues like this too but more artlessly. He relates how Enda in his warlike, church-burning phase had tried to abduct a virgin from his sister St Fainche's convent and how the virgin, on a hint from Fainche, had said she would prefer to be the bride of Christ and had composed herself on a couch and died. Mr Ó Síocháin finds this too extreme and says that it was a clever little trick of Fainche's to make Enda repent. The girl was not really dead; her deathly pallor was due to shock and the dim conventual light. In fact he euhemerizes her as Dr Simpson would say. Enda repented and built his sister a church in Co. Louth which, rather oddly, he called after himself, Killany. He built several such churches.

Were Enda and his colleagues just 'folklore', the unmotivated fabrication of country people? I do not think so. The travels of the saints, their friendships and quarrels, their kinships, their prophesies and cursings, have a close-woven consistency in which a pattern is dimly discernible. They cannot be the product of local and arbitrary fantasy. Behind the fiction lies truth of some kind. What is it?

I have a rough idea of what happened and Enda, like the others, offers clues. His story, though odd, is not chaotic. It is like the agitated and mysterious shadow thrown by a tree on a windy, moonlit night. In the daytime the mystery disperses; the tree is seen to be earth-bound and all its movements occur in a prescribed orbit. Our predecessors wrote history in a primitive picture-language. How is one to interpret it? My guess would be that the saints were the fabulous pre-Christian ancestors of pre-Celtic and proto-Celtic tribes and amalgamations of tribes, and that in their pilgrimages and pedigrees and in the multiplicity of their names, nicknames, cult-centres, we can read the true story of the wan-derings of tribes. But since on this early pattern of history-writing later patterns have been superimposed, we have a palimpsest that is very hard to decipher.

Was Enda or Enna, as he is often called, an ancestor? And if so, can one guess what his tribe was? Before the Celts came to Gaul and it was populated by Iberians, Ligurians, Ilyrians, who knows what tribes invaded Ireland? After the Celts, it was the Eneti-Veneti who had easiest access to Ireland.

Thomas O'Rahilly, speculating in his Rhys Lecture on how the Q-Celts came to Ireland, since he knew of none in Gaul, suggested that in the mass migration of the Q-Celtic Helvetii from Switzerland, which Caesar had arrested with immense slaughter, a remnant might have escaped to Ireland, ferried across by the Veneti.

In this many-tiered conjecture what interested me was that so dis-tinguished a scholar accepted the travels of the Veneti to Ireland quite casually. However, in his book *Early Irish History and Mythology* he took it all back, acknowledging that the Helvetii were not Q- but P-Celts and that there *were* Q-Celts, the Quariates, in Gaul. His manner of saying 'I was wrong' is interesting.

'My suggestion', he wrote, 'had the fatal merit of picturesqueness, which impressed itself on people who were not in a position to appreciate my arguments.' If his lecture were reprinted, he said he would relegate it all to a footnote 'in the hope of preventing the less experienced reader from drawing lopsided conclusions'. But if the Helvetii were not, as he thought, Q-Celts, why mention them at all?

If the Veneti, who were also called Eneti, never came to Ireland and had nothing to do with Fintan and Enda, well, I was wrong and I apologize for my lopsided conclusion, but a few years later they did have a better reason for coming than transporting the Helvetii. They lived on the coast of Britanny leaving their name at Vannes. They were the most accomplished navigators in Gaul. They had a fleet of over 200 ships and, when Julius Caesar attacked them, they were able to summon allies from Britain and all the maritime tribes of northern Gaul. They felt themselves to be invincible and dared to imprison the two ambassadors that the Romans sent. This was an unforgivable outrage and, when Caesar had built a more formidable navy than theirs at Bordeaux and defeated them, none was spared. In his words (he always writes in the third person):

Caesar thought that punishment should be inflicted the more severely, in order that for the future rights of ambassadors might be more carefully respected by barbarians. Having, therefore, put to death all their senate, he sold the rest for slaves.

So he says, but there were many thousands of Veneti and I do not doubt that many escaped to Britain and to Ireland. Gwynedd in Wales is supposed to owe its name to them, and some have suggested Fenit in Kerry and Fanad in Donegal.

Early tribes had eponymous ancestors: the Moabites had Moab, the Hittites had Heth, the Ionians had Ion, the Persians Perseus, and we do not doubt that the Gaulish tribes had them too, though the Romans, intending that Roman Gaul should be unified, aimed at the suppression of all the old tribal loyalties, in which the Romans showed no interest at all. Caesar did not view the Celts as Mr Ó Síocháin does. The Gauls to him were all just 'barbarians'.

Yet we know that the Esuvii had Esus as ancestor, the Lepontii had Lepontius, the Salassi had Salassus. Who was the ancestor of the Eneti-Veneti? Surely someone like Enetus or Venetus. But we know these proper names only in their Romanized form where the singular ended in -us, the plural in -i. The Gaulish form could easily have been, or become after several generations in Ireland, something like Enna or Enda and Fintan.

When St Enda arrived on his stone in Aran he found a very wicked King Corban in control. When St Enda approached, Corban's subjects all fled in wonder and horror to the coast of Clare, 'for the sun cannot abide with darkness nor heathendom with the light of the Gospel'. Only Corban himself stood his ground, 'a second Pharaoh, *obduratus in malicia*', but finally even he was convinced by a miracle and Enda took over the island. He divided it at first between nine other saints but then, to their anger, decided to keep half for himself. This and some other questions about procedure were settled by two doves flying from Rome. One dropped a missal into St Enda's lap, the other flung a cape over his shoulders to indicate his primacy. Only St Brecan at the Kilmurvey end of the island disputed this.

A different story is told of the division of the island between St Enda and St Brecan. They agreed to start Mass at the same time, one at Cill Éanna, the other at Teampall Bhreacáin. They were then to walk towards each other and where they met the island was to be divided between them. But St Brecan cheated and began Mass before St Enda and so was able to start sooner. However, St Enda quickly caught on to the deception and prayed to the Lord. As a result, when St Brecan and his disciples reached the sea at Kilmurvey their feet stuck fast in the sand and Enda came up to them and so got his fair share of Aran.

Who was this Brecan who held onto his corner of Aranmore when Enda routed Corban and his followers? The late Anne O'Sullivan, my dear friend Neans, edited a poem put into the mouth of a supposed Brecan of Aran. He was pictured as an old bishop dictating his life-story to a young man with special reference to the dues owed by the various families, especially the O'Muldowneys and O'Hallorans, to him and his successors. He relates how his original name was Bresal and his first mission was to Aran where he once destroyed the reigning idol, Brecan, and himself took his name (*Celtica*, Vol. XX, p. 28).

The story delights me for I have always maintained that the Irish saints were tribal ancestors Christianized, and here we see it actually happening.

The newly sanctified Brecan had said, 'The fierce Brecan was in Aran before me, I undertook to expel him and I sanctified his place.'

Anne O'Sullivan suggests that the 'fierce Brecan' was 'an idol', but in the pre-Christian saga there is little talk of idols and much of ancestors. St Brecan and St Enda, competing for territory with Corban and his flock, are behaving like tribes, not like individuals, and in historical retrospect the ancestor, a revered figure, symbolizes the tribe and when in time the tribe dissolves the ancestor, still a revered figure but without a vocation, easily turns into a saint. In Gaul the ancestor, losing his tribe under the Romans, became a god. Thus the god Esus was ancestor of the Esuvii of Normandy, while the goddess Nantosvelta was surely the amalgamated ancestress of the Nantuates and Svelteri of south-east Gaul.

Another inmate of the spiritual storehouse was St Grigóir of Aran. The great Celtic scholar, Rudolf Thurneysen, was baffled by an ancient prophecy that Pope Gregory the Great would be descended from the tribe of Curoi Mac Daire, the famous chieftain of the Dingle Peninsula in Kerry. '*Wie der Verfasser auf diesen Gedanken gekommen ist, ist unbekannt,*' he wrote. It is not, however, at all unknown. Father Shearman, a Victorian country scholar, knew all about it and wrote at length in 1876 in the *Kilkenny Archaeological Journal*.

He writes that there was an Irish St Grigóir or Gregory, a native of the Blasket Islands opposite the Dingle Peninsula, who went with another saint, Faelcu, to Rome; he dismisses as idle talk the story that while in Rome the pontiff died and a dove settled on Faelcu's head and he was offered the papacy, but he believes that on return they settled in Inishmaan in the Aran Islands, where as canons regular they founded Cill na Cannanach, or the Church of the Canons.

It was natural, he thinks, that because of this visit to Rome the Aran islanders should confound their St Gregory with Gregory the Great, and make him share a feast-day, 12 March, with the great pope. And it was not surprising that they should call after him Gregory's Sound, the strait between Inishmore and Inishmaan, through which he and Faelcu passed on their return from Rome. And he says that in 1876, when he wrote, the fishermen who voyaged down the sound on their way to Galway still lowered their sails in homage to the Irish pope

Father Shearman thinks it quite natural that in Kerry, Grigóir's native land, the strait between the Blasket Islands and the Dingle Peninsula should also be called Gregory's Sound and that St Gregory the Great should be given the Kerry pedigree of his Irish namesake.[*]

Father Shearman has done better than Thurneysen but his argument should be carried a little farther into regions where he would be unwilling to follow me. Opposite Aran on the Clare coast were the Grecraige or Gregraige, with one ancestor called Grecus and another called Grec mac Aarod. There are Grecraige on Lough Gara in Co. Sligo and their territory is called the Gregories, so obviously Grecraige turns easily into Gregory and makes St Grigóir-Gregory look like a Christian incarnation of the pagan ancestor Grecus.

But to learn more about St Grigóir-Gregory I must go back to Kerry, his native land, and the southern Gregory's Sound. At the base of the Dingle Peninsula is Castle Gregory and inevitably I would claim it for St Gregory, but an Anglo-Norman family called Hoare once lived nearby and it is alleged that one of their number was called Gregory. Yet St Gregory's claim is stronger because he was patron of a church at Glenbeigh in the next barony of Iveragh and in Father Shearman's time his feast-day was observed there on 12 March. But even here, like mocking spirits from the pre-Celtic and pre-Christian past, the Grecraige are recorded in Inis Grecraige or Beare Island, a few miles off in Bantry Bay.

The Grecraige appear in many forms in many parts of Ireland with

* You will find the great pope's Kerry pedigree in Shearman's *Loca Patriciana*, p. 273.

many ancestors and heroes and saints. To mention one of each, there were Gracraige in Munster with Grac as their ancestor; as hero, there was King Grig of Scotland, the ancestor of the Macgregors, who was also confused with Gregory the Great; there was St Colman Grec of Fermoy, whom Canon Power, the historian of the Decies in Co. Waterford, thought at first must be a Greek but then decided was one of the Grecraige.

I made it my duty to hunt them all down, but I must come back to Aran and the spiritual storehouse.

St Cybi (also called Cuby) was a Cornishman who founded several churches in Cornwall and Wales and then went to Ireland, where he spent four years in Aran. He took with him two disciples, Maelóg (31 Dec.), the son of Caw, and Cyngar (7 Nov.), an elderly relation of failing health who could take no food but milk, so St Cuby brought a cow and a calf with him.

They straightaway fell out with an irascible saint called Fintan. Maelóg quarrelled with him initially by digging the ground outside his house and they had to get Enda to make peace between them.

Then Cyngar's calf strayed into Fintan's cornfield and Fintan's people tied it to a great tree. Cuby sent one of his disciples to beg Fintan for the return of the calf but Fintan refused. Then St Cuby prayed that the calf should return to its mother, for without it the cow would not give milk and old Cyngar would die. The Lord heard his prayer and the calf returned to the cow dragging the great tree by the roots behind it. Fintan then prayed to the Lord that he would drive away Cuby from Aran and an angel of the Lord came to Cuby as he slept, advising him to go eastward. And Cuby answered, 'May God destroy Fintan from the island!' And the angel said, 'So shall it be.'

Then Cuby went eastward to Meath and on the way he built three churches; the third was the great church of Mochop. But Fintan pursued him farther east till he reached the sea and Fintan said, 'Cuby, go beyond the sea.' And Cuby turned on him and said, 'All thy churches are so much deserted that there are scarcely three to be found in the whole island of Ireland where there is singing at the altar.'

So Cuby and his disciples built a boat and Fintan said to prove he was a saint he must cross the sea without covering the planks with hide. The Lord aided Cuby and he crossed in a skinless currach to Anglesea. His adventures in Wales and back to Cornwall were many and varied. To commemorate his Welsh activities, there are Caergybi at Holyhead, Llangybi in Carnarvonshire and Llangybi in Monmouth.

Two aspects of this are interesting. Another version of the story describes Fintan not as a saint but as a rich landowner. Secondly, one of the churches which Cybi built while he was fleeing from St Fintan was called Kilmore Mo Cop, that is to say 'the big church of St Mo Cop' (for 'mo' [my] is said to be a prefix of affectionate respect: 'My Cop'). Now St Mo Cop has an Irish pedigree and is culted three days later than St Cybi, and it is very strange that a church which the great St Cybi founded should be called after an insignificant successor. The fact is that both St Cybi and St Mo Cop clearly belong to the great family of Goban saints, who are very difficult to distinguish from each other, and several of whom are called Mo Coppoc or Mo Goppoc Artifex.

St Gobban or Goban is usually thought the most fabulous of the Irish saints, although he only behaves as all the others do. The critics of his sanctity connect him with Goibniu, the Celtic god of smithcraft. This god had a Welsh counterpart, Goibnenn or Gwydion, who was responsible for Abergavenny, became St Govan in Pembroke and Sir Gawain of the Round Table. The critics believe that god and saint and knight developed out of the Irish word 'goba', a smith. There was a St Goban in Suffolk and a St Gobain in Picardy. In Aran St Cybi, St Goban and the virgin saint Gobnait of Inishere made a family party, for Cybi's first cousin, St David, had a sister Magna, who lived in the Galtees and was Goban's mother, and Gobnait was culted the same day as a St Goban. If they could be distinguished from each other there must have been about twenty of these Goban saints. They were mostly craftsmen and builders, and Petrie has fused them all into one real architect who built the round towers of Antrim, Ferns, Kilmacduagh and Killala. But even remote Gobans, like St Gobain of Laon, built their own churches, as did St Cybi. Order comes into this confusion only if we assume an ordinary tribal ancestor, whose name incidentally suggested smithcraft. What was the tribe?

I suggest they were the Cubi of the Upper Loira, a primitive tribe overrun by the Bituriges who gave their name to Bourges and were the only Celtic tribe in Aquitania.

Further, I suggest that in Ireland the Cubi were hard pressed by the Veneti, as in Gaul they were pressed by the Bituriges. I cannot otherwise explain why the Fintan saints treated the Goban saints so badly. St Fintan of Clonenagh once exposed his disciple, Presbyter Goban, as an appalling sinner at the very moment when he was celebrating Mass. He was ejected and died miserably and in sin.

Another Goban saint was chased away by a St Fintan in Wexford and many other saints treated them harshly or displaced them. St Abban blinded Goban, his church-builder, for overcharging. Another Goban was such an ignorant man that he had to have his hands blessed by St Maedoc before he could build.

All the Aran saints had lives as adventurous as Enda's. I must write of St Ceannfionnán, or Concannon, because Concannon was Teresa's name. His name means Whitehead and his sister Ceanndearg or Redhead is also culted in Aran, but Mr Ó Síocháin thinks she must have been a male because no nun could be called Redhead. St Ceannfionnán was the son of a king and, like three other saints of Aran, went to Rome and was offered the papacy.

Ceannfionnán was beheaded in Connemara, the only Irish martyr; many Irish heroes with 'ceann' (head) in their names had an adventure with their head. I should mention too a lake near Kilmurvey once called Stagnum Genanni or Ceannfionnán. (The Gennani, an ancient tribe, once lived in the west.) It has not been connected, though, with St Ceannfionná or the Concannons, but with a white-headed cow of St Enda's. It turned round three times in honour of the Trinity and disappeared into the lake.

Was Ceannfionnán a saint or a cow? I suspect he was neither but as no tribal ancestors come to mind perhaps someone else will take up the question.

Who was the wicked Corban who was turned out of Aran by Enda? He and his people were surely some scattered half-forgotten community. For example, in the midlands St Ciarán of Saighir also had trouble with a wicked king called Corban or Cobran, who had an evil eye. St Ciarán and his mother, St Liadán, who lived nearby, had two erring disciples called respectively Gobran and Cerpan, who died miserably. St Ciarán dealt with them all as Enda would have done. King Corban or Cobran was struck blind at Rathdowney in Co. Laois, where he gave himself and his property to St Ciarán; Gobran was redeemed from Hell and Cerpan was revived. It is natural to say that Corban, Cobran, Gobran and Cerpan never lived and their names are four regional variations of the same name. It is harder to say that they were invented for there is still at Rathdowney a place called Killcoran or the church of St Cobran. There is a large rath round the ruins of a church and a mound beside it was removed a hundred years ago and found to contain a mass of human bones. Did a saint or wicked king ever live there? Surely it is more probable that it was a settlement of an ancient, widespread tribe, submerged by later invaders, the Corban tribe in fact. Was there any known primitive tribe whom they represented? To speculate about that would take me far away from Aran.

Let us go back to Aran and St Caradoc Garb, who left his name at

Cowragh and Port Caradoc between Kilronan and Kilmurvey. I know only one Caradoc saint and he was Welsh and twelfth century and possibly real. Many saints and heroes have been called 'Garb', which means rough. In a saint, Canon O'Hanlon suggested that it meant he was 'somewhat abrupt in his manner of rebuking sin', but the early hagiographers had far odder explanations. For example, St Enda's sister St Fainche Garb is said to have got her nickname because she swam under Loch Erne to avoid a suitor and St Diarmaid, seeing her emerging with shells and pondweed clinging to her skin, said, 'That is rough.' In fact no one knows, or has ever known, what 'garb' really meant and the reason is that it meant nothing; it was a tribal element applied to the ancestor or ancestress of the tribe by his or her descendants. There were two saints and a pagan hero called Senach Garb and the mountain in Kerry, which is called after the latter, had three other heroes called Senach Garb on it and a river Garb nearby. But the proof that it was tribal is offered by a Scottish hero, Fergna Garb, who was the eponymous ancestor of the Garbraige tribe. Now, however rough his manners or his skin may have been, a whole tribe would not be called 'the rough' on his account. So we must ask not 'What does "garb" mean?' but 'Who were the Garb-folk originally?' Since a certain hero Garb was also called Carpad, the best guess I can make at the moment is that they derive from the Carpetani, a very large Iberian tribe of the Upper Tagus.

I wrote, of course, most of all this when I got home. I worked out my general theory about Enda and his colleagues in Aran itself but developed it when I got back to my library in Kilkenny. The book which I have used most and enjoyed most is *Silva Gadelica* by Standish Hayes O'Grady, published in 1892. It is a collection of ancient Irish tales in two volumes, the first in Irish, the second in translation.

Till recently, I had not read his introduction and realized what a highly idiosyncratic and independent-minded man he was. His biography has never been written but I have heard that, a great Celtic scholar, he lived in London and worked in the British Museum. Here is a short passage from the introduction:

This work is far from being exclusively or even primarily designed for the omniscient impeccable leviathans of science that headlong sound the linguistic ocean to its most horrid depths, and (in the intervals of ramming each other) ply their flukes on such audacious small fry as even on the mere surface will venture within their danger. Rather is it adapted to the use of those weaker brethren who, not blindly persisting in their hitherto blissful ignorance, may be disposed to learn, if but a little, of an out of the way and curious branch of literature.

It would be no less instructive than easy to point out how and where lordly Cetaceans of philology, enviously invading shallows in which the humble Celtic whitebait sports at ease, lie stranded (as Milton has it) 'many a rood in length'.

He calls himself 'a humble quarryman' who brings up the raw material for the 'Keltologues' and 'philologists', the folklorists and others: 'Personally, I cannot boast of being anything that ends in either -logue or -ist.'

Did he have some grievance against them? I don't think so. The other Standish O'Grady, as I described in 'The Deserted Sun Palace', had a vision of a society which in our century and here in Ireland was governed by intellectual aristocrats. Standish Hayes O'Grady believed that Irish scholarship could be liberated from the combination of the -logues and -ists and that the impeccable omniscient leviathans of science should work fraternally with those who merely rescue the past without bothering themselves unduly about the language within which it is recorded; the whale would disport itself with the whitebait.

I believe O'Grady might, had he lived, have seen O'Rahilly as 'a lordly Cetacean lying stranded in the shallows'. As a humble whitebait he might have had sympathy for me.

I started this investigation in Aran so I shall end it in Aran. I decided that, when I passed through Galway on my way home, I would try and goad Dr Simpson into some interest in all this. He was very friendly but nothing came of it. I was embarrassed by not being sure how to pronounce Fainche and finding that he had scarcely heard of her or, for that matter, the Carpetani. They were gatecrashers, like myself, at a party to which only the Celts and Celticists were welcomed.

'I gather', he said, 'that you are saying that toponyms are frequently tribal in origin. That of course has been allowed for. But certainly the systematic study of onomastics has often been helped on by free-wheeling methods like yours. Splendid! But see that they don't degenerate into uncontrolled folk-philosophizing like poor Ó Síocháin's. Names have no more generality of behaviour than the pertinent dimensions of the specific culture of which they form a part.'

Simpson always expresses himself with great lucidity, but he has a curiously numbing effect on me. He paralyses the curiosity on which my confidence is based. My convictions do not seem wrong but in the wrong place. Corban may have felt like that when the fierce light of the gospel beat down on him, but he may have stammered out a few unpleasant things before he disappeared.

'But what about the spiritual storehouse?' I said.

'My dear fellow,' he answered a little irritably, 'all that you are arguing is really very old stuff. You'll find that Jorgensen of Wisconsin noted the chronological difficulties about Enda and others in *Gelehrte Anzeigen* fully forty years ago. As for Gobban, I wrote only last week for the Bollandists that it is no doubt a hypocoristic form of "goba", smith, with geminated b.'

'Then Ó Síocháin is wrong?' I persisted. 'There weren't really any saints?'

'Ó Síocháin!' he snorted. 'What in the world does he know about anything? Ó Síocháin is utterly unimportant.'

'Well,' I answered, 'about a thousand copies of his book are sold to one of yours. Would yours have been published at all without a university subsidy?'

He looked very much hurt and so I did not finish what I was going to say, that country scholarship had deteriorated hugely since archaeology was professionalized.

Neither of us wanted to quarrel so he did the only thing he could do, which was to pour me out a geminated whiskey and say that I must look after my cold.

As I walked to the bus I reflected that Jorgensen and his colleagues had made a vast gulf between life and scholarship, between living and knowing, and that it would take a generation or two to fill it in. Educated Irishmen are now bored with the saints, who intrigued so intensely the sceptical antiquarians of our great-grandfathers' day. The question, 'Who were the saints?' had aroused curiosity then. There were theories and counter-theories and local societies had grown up as arenas in which fierce battles could be fought about them. Now all is still and dead, and the saints have been laid away in lavender in a bottom drawer. And curiosity has no status unless it is paid.

Yet for the Irish people to forget the saints is for them to forget their childhood. We are emotionally and intellectually committed to them. They beckon us along a private road that leads not only to the Irish past but to the past of Europe. It is through them that we can learn about the youth of the world and the infancy of religion. Whether they really lived or not, they belong to us more than to anybody else.

[1987]

BOUCHER DE PERTHES:
THE FATHER OF PREHISTORY

Some years ago I was looking at the earliest records of the old Kilkenny Archaeological Society which I had recently revived in our neighbourhood. It had been started in 1848 by our rector, Mr Graves, with the help of some doctors, newspapermen and country gentlemen. Though it was later to attract the antiquaries of Dublin and finally to be absorbed by them and moved to the capital as The Royal Society of Antiquaries of Ireland, these first journals belonged to its obscure and rustic infancy. I was surprised therefore to find that two years after its foundation the Society had already captured the interest of a Frenchman. He was given the title of Honorary Foreign Corresponding Member and his name was M. Jacques Boucher de Crèvecoeur de Perthes, President of the Société d'Emulation at Abbeville (near the coast some 135 kilometres north of Paris).

Boucher de Perthes (1788–1868) was the son of aristocratic parents from Abbeville. His father, liberal enough to keep his post as a Director of Customs throughout the Revolution, was an enthusiastic botanist and the founder of the scientific society of which his son was to be president; his mother's family claimed descent from that of Joan of Arc. Boucher de Perthes adopted his father's profession and was made Director of Customs at Abbeville in 1825. Becoming interested in the geological strata of a local gravel-pit, he gradually collected a large number of hand-axes and other flint tools, undoubtedly man-made, of the kind known later as Abbevillois. These artefacts were present, with the bones of extinct animals, in strata described by the geologists as Antediluvian (before the Flood). From 1838 onwards he sought to convince the scientific world that man had existed thousands of years earlier than anyone had supposed: he had in fact discovered the Old Stone Age. He was met with the same total indifference as was later to be the lot of Mendel when he approached the leading specialists of his generation. He did receive some encouragement from the great Danish archaeologist Worsae, and eventually one of his leading detractors, Rigollet of Amiens, excavated the gravel-pits of St Acheul in order to refute him but discovered the tools now called Acheulian, and in 1854 published findings in agreement with Boucher's. However, it was not until 1859, more than twenty years after he began to publicize his discovery, that the antiquity of man and the work of Boucher de Perthes himself finally received the stamp of official scientific approval.

In France he is honoured today as 'the Father of Prehistory', but in 1850, though he had already published the volume of *Antiquités Celtiques et Antediluviennes* (1847) in which his great discovery was announced, almost no one had read it. He was still regarded by the pundits of London and Paris as a ridiculous old provincial bore. For many years he had been pestering them to visit Abbeville and sending them parcels of flint implements and bones and books. Some of the implements seemed fakes and the accompanying diagrams were very unprofessional. How could anyone believe this tedious person when he said he had discovered the implements beside the bones of extinct animals during the digging of a canal near Abbeville?

And how had it come about that our obscure Society had been the first of all the learned bodies in the British Isles to honour M. de Perthes? Were there perhaps, I speculated, champions of Antediluvian Man in Kilkenny? I looked up the *Journal* of 1859 for evidence of their triumph, for in the spring of that year Sir John Evans and Dr Prestwich had at last visited Abbeville and a month later communicated to the Royal Society their official recognition of Antediluvian Man. The old gentleman, after years of arduous campaigning, had been gloriously vindicated.

I found nothing of all this in the *Journal* for 1859. When after his victory the Honorary Foreign Corresponding Member visited Ireland, he did not come to Kilkenny. So I concluded that it was as the president of an exemplary regional society and not as the Father of Prehistory that he had been co-opted. His father had founded the Société d'Emulation in the Revolutionary year VI (1795) and he himself had revived it, when it was almost moribund, in 1825. To the Kilkenny Archaeological Society it must have appeared as a model, for both groups gloried in being provincial and were proud to have created in two intellectually decaying corners of Europe two lively, critical and fearlessly speculative associations.

It may have been Boucher who took the initiative. I found in the appendix of an early *Journal* a list of donations which included one of Boucher's famous parcels. It must have caused some surprise in the Irish

Society but it was characteristic of Boucher and throws light upon the birth of a science. It contained, besides the momentous work on Antediluvian Man, samples of Boucher's philosophy, poetry and folklore, and even a satirical comedy called *La Marquise de Montalle*. The Kilkenny Society was by no means as austere as it later became and must still have been conscious of its own origins in local sentiment and belles-lettres. Evidently they did not laugh at M. de Perthes (but nor, I suspect, did they read him). Without comment, they co-opted him.

It is curious that even today the Father of Prehistory continues to irritate his spiritual children. It seems to them intolerable that fate should have selected this discursive old dilettante, who grew prize pears, wrote poems and plays, organized a swimming bath and, though a customs official, advocated Free Trade, to carry through a major revolution in geology and anthropology. Had they not dedicated their entire lives to these pursuits? And since collective jealousy is more potent than the individual kind, being laced with professional *ésprit de corps*, some have almost managed to delude themselves that Boucher de Perthes never existed. When I looked him up in my *Chambers Encyclopaedia* (1935) I found that everything was forgotten about him except the jaw-bone of Moulin Quignon, which he found in 1863 and which is now regarded as a trick played on him by his workmen. For many scholars the science of prehistory did not open till 1859, when tardily and condescendingly Prestwich and Sir John Evans accepted the invitation of Boucher to Abbeville. For those who might consider this English chronology as odd as that of the Old Testament, which the prehistorians overthrew, Miss Joan Evans, daughter of Sir John, explained in a long article on Boucher de Perthes (*Antiquity*, 1949): 'Belief indeed became possible when it was an experienced geologist, and not Boucher de Perthes, who presented the case.' In other words, truth has no status till it is endorsed by an 'expert'.

Miss Evans' article is the most agile exhibition of professional solidarity and filial piety I have ever seen. She deplores Boucher's 'horrid little outline plates' with which he tried to convince the sceptics, and, following the Parisian critic Aufrère, she says that Boucher in his auto-biography re-wrote his own early correspondence so as to ante-date by some decades his theory of prehistory. On a lower plane, she says that when he offered his collection of antique Picardy furniture to the museum at Cluny, 'it was to secure for himself more consideration in the city', and to get an excise post in Paris, a marble plaque and a gallery bearing his name. When he suggested that a local painter should paint a picture of all the celebrities of Abbeville, 'he doubtless expected to find himself in the front row'. When he claimed to have visited practically every excavation near Abbeville in the past ten years, 'the claim may be well-founded for he was an idle man and a good walker'.

Some of this is partly true, yet all is wholly false. Certainly Boucher's discursiveness could be irritating, but only in our dullest moments do we pursue knowledge for its own sake. 'Science', he wrote, 'helps us to prove but prevents us understanding.' In the Age of Science many scholars wear their learning as a well-trained carriage horse wears his blinkers. As an archaeologist Boucher was remarkably modest and open-minded. It seemed to him that it was just because he had a rather vagrant mind that he hit upon the truth, which seldom frequents the highways. 'I know about as much science as a donkey does of music,' he wrote. That meant that he had fewer misconceptions to eradicate. 'Ignorance', he wrote, 'is a field in which the nettle and the thistle never took root, so they do not have to be grubbed up.'

Boucher fully grasped that the knowledge to which he aspired could not be deep if it was to be wide. 'My science', he wrote, 'is only foresight', a form of intuition based on wide-ranging reflection and experiment in a dozen arts and sciences, and his triumph was perhaps the last and the greatest of the old polymathic humanism. He took it very lightly indeed: 'This victory proves that often it is good to be obstinate and that conviction, united to perseverance, can take the place of knowledge.'

Boucher gloried in being an autodidact, an attitude that sometimes reduced his critics to helpless exasperation. Aufrère comments on the scientific innocence of Boucher's five-volume *De La Création*, but he does not quote this extraordinary passage from the introduction.

Perhaps what I am writing is a repetition of what has already been said, for I am completely ignorant of all that has been published on the matter. No scholar has talked to me about it and I have not read the relevant books.

Boucher claimed later that in these volumes he anticipated the discovery of Antediluvian Man, but Aufrère cannot trace him there. In fact the concept of Antediluvian Man was not the child of geology but was hatched in a densely woven cocoon of miscellaneous speculation. In the same way the idea of evolution is thrown off casually in a footnote to Vol II, p. 362, of *Antiquités*, where, two years before the publication of *The Origin of Species*, Boucher suggests that as the sea retreated, marine animals may have modified their shape by jumping with their flippers. But, as a humanist, Boucher was more concerned with the implications of his theories than with the theories themselves. He sometimes called himself a Pythagorean, for he believed that the power of God is manifest in every living thing, moulding transitory forms and then discarding them: 'The creative power is great, for it is that of God himself.' This consciousness of divinity is present in every being, so that there can be no such thing as an atheist. The word is meaningless.

As for De La Création, Boucher said that only ten people besides himself ever finished reading it and that he never gave it to his friends so that the obligation of reading it should not weigh upon their minds. Yet Aufrère says that Victor Hugo and Lamennais had drawn inspiration from it without acknowledgment, and that it had delighted the followers of the socialist writer Fourier.

Though she gives it an individual twist, Miss Evans gets most of her disparaging comments on Boucher from Aufrère, who is in his own right an interesting character. Obliged to work for some years in Boucher's museum at Abbeville, and impatient with the traditional idolatries of the little town, he scrutinized all the drawers and cabinets in which the old bachelor had stored the debris of eighty years. In the end the Father of Prehistory came to fascinate him more than prehistory itself. He read all his novels, plays, philosophy, folklore and travel. He compared the rough drafts of letters with their published variants. He collated the labels on the exhibits with the records of their discovery. He proved (and no one can now disagree, because everything was destroyed in the bombardment of May 1940) that Boucher, in the cause of prehistory, cheated quite a bit. 'In order to get the truth accepted, he was often less than truthful himself.'

At the bottom of a drawer M. Aufrère found, ticketed as carefully as a mammoth's bones, a tooth and a chestnut curl. The curl was in a metal frame, embossed with the arms of the de Perthes and the de Crèvecoeurs, and was inscribed, 'hair of M. de Boucher de Perthes, April 1853'. Beside it was a tooth in a little box labelled, 'last molar extracted from upper jaw by the dentist, M. Catel, March 2, 1855'. Combining this with the evidence of the novels, Aufrère deduced a strong vein of narcissism or at least a preoccupation with self, which was hardly normal. He found too that Boucher's early novels were inspired by a love affair, real or fanciful, with Napoleon's sister, Princess Pauline Borghese, and he has commemorated this in the reconstructed museum at Abbeville. In the middle of a case full of Boucher's antediluvian artefacts, Aufrère has set a plaster model of the Princess's hand. This is meant, I suppose, to symbolize the intimate association of science and sentiment in Boucher's lifework. I value it more as evidence that Aufrère too was, like Boucher, an ingrained original and hence capable of appreciating the unique blend of obstinacy, clowning and ecstatic vision, in which the science of prehistory was born. Aufrère does justice to Boucher, the prophet-scientist, when he writes:

Making a discovery is not just making a lucky find, it is being susceptible to the splendour of an idea. That was what he was, for his thought is rich in resonances. It was through ruminating and writing on the history of man, his arts and sciences, that Boucher had pushed back the frontiers of human history.

But does Aufrère make sufficient allowances for the pathological quirks which may be induced in us by decades of unmerited neglect? Also something more than ordinary vanity is needed to make a man keep and label a decayed molar. What was it? If we knew, we might come to understand better the long solitary life from which prehistory was born and Boucher's Pythagorean belief that the body was the transient lodging of the eternal spirit, which moulded it and would discard it. For his beliefs and his discoveries and the shape of his life were not dictated by his birth and circumstances. He was sociable, rich and vigorous. He had been handsome. He longed to marry, to see his plays staged, to live in Paris. But some irresistible introversion rooted him to Abbeville and to womb-like speculations, which he could share with few.

And is not the learned resistance to prehistory also very interesting psychologically? A congress of scientists had been held at Laon, only a couple of hours by train east of Abbeville. Boucher had as usual bombarded them with parcels and invitations to his gravel-pits. They had discussed Antediluvian Man and rejected him, without inspecting the gravel-pits, reading Boucher's books or visiting his collections.

I am far from considering myself a savant [he wrote] or even a very clever man, but I am not blind. What seems to me ten times worse than criticism is this obstinate refusal to look at the facts and to say 'It's impossible!' without going to see for themselves.

But many times he wrote about it more passionately and surely justifiably: 'Hate and persecution at least offer you a chance... but indifference is a wall between you and the light, it burns you alive. I'd sooner an enemy who flung Truth back into her well and crashed the bucket down on her head.'

The English geologists, Falconer, Prestwich, Evans and many others, who came to Abbeville after 1850 to pay their respects to Antediluvian Man and to the Father of Prehistory, were all of them pleasant, well-educated men, as their long letters to Boucher which have survived the bombardments testify. Yet they would all have agreed that, when you have a revelation of the truth and wish busy experts to accept it, you must draft your propositions in a brief business-like way. Prestwich, announcing Boucher's discovery to the Royal Society, explained his failure to convince them earlier 'as politely as he could'. This phrase is Miss Evans', but none of them would have thought it inappropriate. The contrast of their busy lives and Boucher's leisured dilettantism is one on which Miss Evans loved to dwell. When Falconer at last accepted Boucher's invitation to Abbeville, he was a day later than he said; the house was all shut up and Boucher himself was sitting in his carriage ready to drive away to the country. Instantly the Father of Prehistory leapt out, cancelled his visit to the country, had his house opened up again and laid himself out to make a convert of Falconer. He succeeded; and a few weeks later Prestwich and Evans, urged on by Falconer, were at Abbeville too. Boucher was at their hotel soon after seven a.m., and when they returned, converted, from the gravel-pits, he gave them what Miss Evans calls 'a sumptuous fork lunch'. This sounds excessive, almost vulgar. In contrast Prestwich, displaying Boucher's implements and expounding Boucher's discovery to a distinguished gathering in London eight days later, 'entertained them with his legendary sherry'. For busy men this was just right.

Hugh Falconer in a letter to Prestwich strikes the precise note of amused condescension with which the learned world allowed itself to be convinced by a donkey!

I have a charming letter from M. Boucher de Perthes, full of gratitude to *perfide Albion* for helping him to assured immortality and giving him a lift, when his countrymen of the Institute left him in the gutter. He radiates a benignant smile from his lofty pinnacle on you and me – surprised that the treacherous Leopard should have behaved so well.

Yet it was just the fantastic element in Boucher's character, which, allied to his practical earnestness, made him assert the impossible and maintain it doggedly against the experts. Falconer, Evans and Prestwich could have spent a lifetime classifying their tertiary pebbles and sipping their legendary sherry, but they could never have taken that great leap into the inconceivable that the customs officer of Abbeville accomplished with bravado and relish. If they had been capable of such a leap they would have taken it years before, for they had all the evidence beside them. In 1797 John Frere had reported the same combination of artefacts and antediluvian bones in Suffolk, and a dozen other such discoveries had in the intervening years been recorded. The geologists were responsible, gregarious people; industrialists consulted them about seams and measures. Probably they instinctively shied away from that solitude in which subversive discoveries are made. And deep in their subconscious there may have been some apprehension of the explosions that could be triggered off by Antediluvian Man. First there was the War with Moses, as Boucher called it, and round the corner they might have caught a glimpse of Evolution and 'Godless' materialism, and the sinister pseudo-science of Social 'Darwinism'. These premonitions cannot have been clearly defined, but they may have clouded that zone of sensibility that Boucher was trying to inflame, and decided them against opening the door to Antediluvian Man. Boucher himself was not at all frightened by him; there had long been a comfortable place prepared for him in his many-chambered humanist philosophy.

One could find dozens of passages in which Boucher tried to placate the professional scientists; but his main offence was that he had been right, so the more he abased himself and called himself a donkey, the worse it became. If it proved that a scientific revolution could be introduced by a donkey, all the academies in Europe would totter.

Undoubtedly many of Aufrère's semi-genial assaults on Boucher's integrity are unfair. He complains that Boucher tendentiously 'edited' the correspondence from which, as an old man, he composed his eight-volume autobiography. But, in fact, he explained in his preface that he had rewritten from memory such letters as he had not copied or could not recover. The bulk of the letters are as they were written, and give a charming picture of the life of a scholarly eccentric in a provincial town. They are fertile in imagination and invention and French scholars still glean ideas from them. Lately, for example, M. Roger Agache used a long and detailed letter from Boucher, written 150 years ago, to illustrate a thesis about the 'crop marks' visible from the air in northern France (*Revue Archaeologique de-l'Est*, 42, 1962).

Miss Evans insists that the man who really introduced prehistory was not Boucher but his dead friend, Dr Picard. 'He wore Picard's mantle', she writes, 'with such dramatic effect that he soon forgot it had not always been his own.'

Yet all the evidence for this comes from Boucher himself via Aufrère and I do not believe that Miss Evans could have distilled so much poison from Aufrère's book if that distinguished work had been wholly sweet-tempered. Are there perhaps traces in it of the old jealousy between the paid scholar, who lacks freedom, and the independent one, who lacks status? Certainly Boucher's great friend and disciple Dr Picard had taken the first steps towards the discovery of prehistory, but it is from Boucher himself, who gave Picard every encouragement till his early death in 1841, that we draw most of our information about the young doctor. It was Boucher's Society which printed his theories and gave him a forum for discussing them. In the first draft of his *Antiquités*, composed in 1844, Boucher had written a page attributing everything to Picard, of whom he claimed to be no more than an inadequate interpreter. 'He was starting his career when I was ending mine.' Why did he later leave out all but a sentence of this touching tribute? He was getting on for seventy. Recognition seemed far away and maybe he felt that by his obstinacy he had earned the greater part of such applause as his book might gain. In fact it gained none. Less than a hundred copies were sold of the book which ushered in the new science of prehistory. The booksellers begged him to take back their stock. He sighed not only for his masterpiece but also for the fine quality paper which had had to go to 'the writers' cemetery, the butter-merchant'.

Moreover in the third volume of *Antiquités* he gave ample justice to all those who had preceded Picard and himself, John Frere of Hoxney, Father McEnergy, Schmerling and many others. 'I abase myself before labours like these. All that I can say for myself is that I have been the most obstinate.'

Miss Evans asserts that after his victory Boucher was 'more anxious for his own reputation than for the scientific implications of his discoveries'. Yet if you read the letters he wrote in the triumphant year of 1859, you will see how little his reputation was bothering him. When in 1908 the Abbevillois erected a statue to him, they inscribed on the base PALAIONTOLOGUE ET PHILANTHROPE, but in 1859 the Philanthrope was in the ascendant. There are long, painstaking letters about the cure for drunkenness, the rescue of horses from burning stables, and the agricultural use of a freshwater mussel which he had discovered in the Somme.

Boucher was a great giver of prizes and medals. He offered awards for examplary working women in a dozen towns in Picardy, dispensing in this way during his lifetime 100,000 francs, and bequeathing after his death a further 150,000 francs. It would have been strange if he had not accepted medals and prizes himself, but he took this casually enough. He once wrote: 'They wanted to make me a municipal councillor... and even a deputy, but I was like that old soldier, who was taken prisoner by the Turks. He said: "They offered me all the offices, Bey, Pasha, Vizier, ... even Eunuch, but I refused them all."'

In 1860 Boucher set off for the British Isles. He describes his visit in one of his travel books, which cover all of Europe and some of Africa.

He writes as unaffectedly as he must have conversed. For an old gentleman who had recently extended human history by many millennia, he was on this journey remarkably unassuming; he expected and received no acclamation whatever.

When he reached London his distinguished friends were as kind to him as if he had been their old uncle just up from the country. Prestwich asked him to supper to meet his sister and Falconer gave him lunch at the Colonial Club and took him to the Zoo. At the Athenaeum, to which he had sent one of his parcels, he met 'M. Th. Huxlevy' (he seldom got any English name right) and was given a month's membership. Most of the time he wandered round by himself, as he had done in Kiev and Belgrade and Algiers. He visited 'Kesington', 'Pale Male' and 'Hyde Parck'. He changed his linen twice a day because of the dirt and, watching rain from a hotel window, he composed one of his sad rhymes about London cut-throats and pickpockets (he had seen one of their victims running and shrieking 'Policy! Policy!'), and a young prostitute, who was killed by a resurrectionist. His happiest day was when he went to 'Escher' for a memorial service to Louis Philippe, who had always been kind to him (the Comte de Paris had accepted Antediluvian Man). The train at Esher was two hours late; he had left his overcoat on the wrong platform and, in retrieving it, was nearly run over by the train. Aufrère says of him that he was 'a man of great gaiety, with no luck!' Boucher describes these episodes with so much humour, zest and philosophical comment that the loneliness in which prehistory was conceived can only be guessed at.

Miss Evans cannot bear to agree with Aufrère that Boucher wrote extremely well and that it was often his fearless championship of liberal causes that prevented his plays, which were usually satirical, from being performed. She dismisses them with scorn and in his other writings she grudgingly allows him 'facility' and 'a capacity for eloquence, not uncommon in men brought up on the windy rhetoric of the revolution'. Yet Aufrère says of his plays: 'They had verve and observation and had a happy turn of phrase. And if he had not been dogged by ill-luck, he would have made his mark as a playwright.' And he relates how the greatest of French comedians, Potier, was an ardent champion of Boucher's plays against the censor.

In fact in an easy unpretentious way Boucher was an admirable writer fully deserving Aufrère's many comments on his excellent French and the graceful purity of his style. The problems to which he addressed himself sometimes no longer puzzle us, but his books are not all period pieces. In 1961 his *Petit Glossaire*, a satirical attack on the French administration was republished in paperback 126 years after its original appearance. A delightful anthology could still be made from his auto-biographical volumes and his travel books.

Archaeology in 1850 was still considered to be a bridge between humanism and the physical sciences. Boucher planted prehistory at the humanist end of this bridge and defended it against all aggressors. The bridge has long ago been blown up and prehistory has been built into the fortress of science. It flourishes there but disturbing things have happened which would not, perhaps, have occurred in the old days of provincial humanism.

Boucher had greatness because he was a crusader for the unity of knowledge in an age when its fragmentation was already far advanced. His appears to be a lost cause but it is one that will always have adherents. Fighting his own battles, he was fighting for others too, the individualists, the provincial, the scholar who refuses to specialize. As that ill-organized community cannot now even recognize its own champions, it is good that in Abbeville at least the Father of Prehistory is still greatly honoured.

[1987]

LAMENT FOR ARCHAEOLOGY

I. THE LAY PRETENDERS

We live in the age of the institution and the expert and mostly consult them with respect and gratitude, but archaeology is the latest of the sciences to be institutionalized and the authority of the expert is still frequently challenged.

A few years ago the site of a Danish settlement in Dublin, Wood Quay on the Liffey, was threatened by the Corporation building surveyors and it was planned to erect municipal offices on the half-excavated site. There was an unprecedented outcry not only from Dubliners but from interested people all over Ireland. They were outraged that ancient traces of Danish Dublin should be revealed only to be covered over again. There were big demonstrations, headed by the vigorous and devoted Father F. X. Martin, and busloads of people from the provinces came up to take part in them.

I believe in demonstrations. In the past two or three years two of our principal Norman mottes in Kilkenny, at Tibraghney and Knocktopher, both associated with English kings, John and Richard II, have been bulldozed away for agricultural purposes, and three or four eighteenth-century bridges have been partially destroyed. Only in the case of the beautiful Thomastown bridge did we have a demonstration and if we had acted earlier, I believe, we might have saved it. The Corporation received our belated deputation kindly, and, like everybody else, we used a bit shamefacedly the tourist gimmick and told of the increasing number of foreign canoeists who are using our lovely rivers, the Nore, the Barrow, the Suir. From the river there is a secret charm in sliding under the dark arches of the high-parapetted bridges and finding our little towns concealed behind them. Now, with the bridges broadened for lorry traffic, we just see a moving panorama of legs and wheels.

So at Wood Quay I was shocked that there was no unqualified support for the demonstrators from the 'authorities' in the National Museum and the universities. It was said that all the available evidence had been collected from the site and that there were other sites from which corroboration could more easily be secured.

Yet the demonstrations went on and the Corporation scheme was delayed for months. Had the defenders of Wood Quay had the support of the experts, the Danish site would have been saved. Their final failure was tragically significant. The disagreement between the supporters of office blocks and of archaeological sites does not need investigation. It is the conflict between the demonstrators and the experts that is of permanent interest.

Of this conflict we had revealing evidence at the time. An expert from one of the universities, in an article in *The Irish Times*, attacked the demonstrators, describing them as 'lay pretenders'. He suggested that they were survivals from the romantic antiquarianism of the nineteenth century, which held Irish archaeology in its grip till rescued by a tiny band of devoted men, who sometime in the thirties 'secured a respectably high position for Irish archaeology among related sciences throughout the world'. Judging by reports of what is happening in the National Museum and the fate of various small collections stored there in the basement and at Kilmainham, we are now at the nadir of Irish archaeology. The peak was sometime in the 1850s. I am convinced that when the experts talk of 'romantic antiquarianism', they are thinking of Vallancey and Betham, Beauford and Beaufort, who pioneered Irish archaeology at the end of the eighteenth century. Yet it is manifest that their intellectual influence had totally faded by 1833, when Petrie scourged them in his book on round towers (rather uncharitably, considering how fanciful and dogmatic he could often be himself). In Irish scholarship few disputed the supremacy of O'Donovan and to a lesser extent O'Curry, both of them Petrie's colleagues in the Ordnance Survey. In the Kilkenny Archaeological Society, which after 1848 became one of the leading provincial archaeological societies in the British Isles, I can find only one reference to Vallancey which is not disparaging, a comment at a General Meeting: 'Despite Vallancey's questionable theories, he had done much good in arousing attention to Irish archaeology at a time when it excited little interest.'

After Petrie, as is well-known, came Graves and Prim, Wakeman, Brash, Lawlor, Westropp, Todd, Reeves, Standish Hayes O'Grady, Richard Butler, Wilde, Windele, Prendergast and many others. Most of them were good classical scholars who saw Irish history in its European setting. Those of them who were Irish scholars seldom pretended to subtleties of understanding they did not possess. The antithesis of professional and amateur had scarcely been invented, yet which of these men was 'a lay pretender'?

In the 1850s many provincial societies flourished and carried out functions that now have to be shared between several government-subsidized departments. They considered themselves the guardians and recorders as well as the interpreters of their own antiquities. Not only did the KAS watch over and publish the vast collections in Kilkenny Castle muniment room and much regional material that was later removed for greater safety to the Four Courts and burnt there; they arrested also the decay of Jerpoint and Clonmacnoise, and prosecuted vandals. Graves himself, in a famous and fiery correspondence, tackled Lord Templemore's agent, who claimed that by taking down a portion of Dunbrody Abbey he was 'only improving it'.

Had the Society after the death of Graves and Prim confined its activities to its corner of Ireland, it might have survived there. But the temptation to become a nation-wide society was irresistible. When that happened it was not long before museum and library headquarters were transferred to Dublin, and the influence of the Society slowly retreated from Kilkenny, where it had been born.

A century ago it would have been less easy for the Tibraghny and Knocktopher disasters to have happened. When in 1850 Sir Richard Langrishe of Knocktopher heard that a tenant of his was about to destroy the huge Ballyboodan ogham stone, he promptly stopped him. The KAS had to contend with the same barbarism and it is due to their patient efforts that, till about ten years ago, farmers still had a respect for the antiquities of their neighbourhood. When in 1848 Graves and Prim heard that the local landowner at Dunbell was digging up one of the numerous raths that lie between Bennettsbridge and Maddockstown, they discovered that his workpeople had smashed up the two famous Dunbell ogham stones into small pieces. Graves detected, however, that the ogham stones were made of red sandstone while the prevailing local stone is blue limestone. After hours of careful labour he and Prim managed to sort out the fragments from the dump and tentatively piece them together. When they returned the next day, the workmen, realizing the fragments were valued, had concealed them and would not give them up unless they were paid £30, a huge sum for the young Society to pay and an appalling precedent for future discoveries. By tact and firmness the ogham stones were after three weeks recovered and lodged with many other Dunbell finds in the museum.

They stayed there till, after the deaths of Graves and Prim, the rot had set in. They were then transferred with everything else to the National Museum.

As they were on loan I hoped they would soon be returned to Kilkenny when we tried to revive the Society as it had once been and started a small collection which was ultimately transferred to Rothe House. Far from it. Even when some years ago the whole area, which Graves considered to be rich in archaeological promise, was taken over by Quigley Magnesite and subjected to open-cast mining for dolomite, I could not persuade the National Museum to send down the objects which had been found at Dunbell, for local display. Therefore, I made xerox copies of Graves' drawings in the *Kilkenny Archaeological Journal* for 1852 of sample finds in wood and stone and jet, bone and flint, and gave them to the manager. He was entirely co-operative, but space-age machinery precludes detailed investigation and nothing has turned up.

Apart from their great intellectual achievement, these provincial societies were a source of harmony and reconciliation. The KAS, by its Rule 7, excluded 'all matters concerning our political and religious differences' from its papers and discussions. Through the stormy days of Church Disestablishment and the Land League, when its members, outside the Society, freely expressed loud and contrary opinions, complete harmony prevailed within. Yet Graves was a Protestant clergyman, Prim the editor of a Protestant newspaper, the organ of the landed gentry. Explosive material lay about but no explosion occurred inside the Society.

It occurs to me that the post-Treaty scholars would like to believe that their illustrious predecessors had never existed. Not long ago on the radio an Irish scholar maintained that societies like KAS depended on 'large expensive private libraries, which when social change redistributed wealth, could no longer exist'. This is nonsense. The KAS library was founded by John Prim, a country newspaper proprietor, and James Graves, the rector of a small country parish. Graves, because of his devotion to archaeology, lost promotion in his Church, earning nothing till he was old and got a civil list pension of £100 a year from the British Government. The Society was not exclusive as anyone who could pay his subscription was welcome. There were, of course, great house libraries but scholars were given ready access to them. In this county they were mostly burnt in the twenties as in Woodstock, Desart Court and Bessborough, or sold as in Kilfane and Kilkenny Castle.

As for 'the respectably high position that Irish archaeology has now reached among related sciences throughout the world' it is true that just before the war we had an eminent Nazi prehistorian, Adolf Mahr, as Director of our National Museum (suspected by Military Intelligence of being a spy), and another eminent prehistorian, Dr Sprockhoff, a protégé of Himmler, was invited to join in the centenary celebrations in 1949 (God Help Us!) of Graves' and Prim's great achievements. Yet surely we were more in touch with international learning, indeed ahead of it, when in 1852 the KAS made Boucher de Perthes, 'the Father of Pre-history', our 'Honorary Corresponding Member'. This was five years before his 'discovery' of prehistoric man had been internationally acknowledged. Boucher sent several volumes of his writings to the KAS simply because he recognized the Society as of the same calibre as his own Société d'Emulation at Abbeville, in which one of the great discoveries of the nineteenth century was made.

When transferred to Dublin, Boucher de Perthes' gifts to the Society were lost; similarly, the contents of the Kilkenny Museum were mixed up with everything else in the National Museum and are now irretrievable.

Boucher de Perthes was a customs officer at Abbeville, who grew prize pears, organized a public swimming bath, and wrote poor plays and lively travel books. He was the quintessential 'amateur' or lay pretender and gloried in it. 'I know as much about science,' he wrote, 'as a donkey does about music... Ignorance is a field in which nettle and thistle never took root, so they do not have to be grubbed up.'

Boucher and the other two great nineteenth-century pioneers, Schliemann, the indigo merchant, and Arthur Evans, the Balkan war-correspondent and rebel, who revealed the Mycenaean and Minoan civilizations, could also in their day have been called 'romantic anti-quarians'. Their great discoveries were hatched in a cocoon of lively guess-work. Ventris, who nearer our time deciphered and revealed the Greek affinities of Linear B, was an architect, who 'did a bit of Greek', he admitted, at Stowe School. Archaeology, in fact, owes an incalculable debt to the lay pretender, and when professional integrity had died, as happened lately for long periods over much of Europe, the lay pretender survived.

When some time in the eighties of the last century the experts removed a vast quantity of our parish registers and other valuable material to the doomed Four Courts for safe-keeping, they were only robbing us of paper. What they are doing now is robbing us of men and women. In the last century those who had a sense of the past used it so that, in Camden's phrase, they should not be 'Strangers in their own land and forrainers in their own cities.' Now it opens the door to a university course in archaeology and 'a job'. And if there is not one in Ireland they look for it in some English or American university.

All those who see that they can make a career out of what used to be called 'a sweet food of the mind' are irresistibly tempted away. If they come home again it is as talent-spotters, and we have in many cases to get 'forrainers' to teach us about our own city. Urban pundit and country puppet nourish each other. There are, of course, brilliant exceptions, men and women who struggle against the tide. There is nothing unique to Ireland about this. It is happening all over the world and meeting varying degrees of resistance.

II. DEATH OF TWO SISTERS

It is a platitude to say that the pursuit of science is no longer of necessity an honourable one. Most sciences have now been institutionalized and though half of man's mind may be on the discovery of truth, the other half is on chairs and grants and exams and whatever great power endows the institutes. One thinks first of physics and the scramble by the British and Americans to snatch Wernher von Braun from Krensburg prison before the Russians got hold of him. It was he who had launched the twenty-seven V2 rockets on London from Peenemunde and it was Himmler who had equipped him with assistants from the concentration camps. They worked, for security reasons, in stinking caves under the Harz mountains. But knowledge, of course, 'belongs to the world' and when von Braun, handed over to the Americans, turned his brains to 'the conquest of space', everyone was delighted with him. There were those who wanted him awarded the Nobel Peace Prize.

It was not long before the dark shadow that had fallen on physics and its related sciences had enveloped them all.

The subject is richly documented. The best book I know about it, Frederick Lilge's *The Abuse of Learning: The Failure of the German Universities*, was published soon after the war and is still highly relevant. The Germans were pioneers in Scientific Method which the rest of the world soon gratefully adopted. The Higher Learning, with its rigorous Teutonic ideal of *Wissenschaft*, spread to America after the Civil War. Knowledge, there, was and still is in danger of disintegrating into multiversities, where degrees are given for pastry-making, and the Higher Learning shone down upon this trackless confusion like a beacon of Integrity and Truth. For many years it was wonderful and great institutes like the Johns Hopkins were founded and prospered.

Then suddenly a terrible disease fell upon the Higher Learning in the country of its birth and spread, in a less virulent form, to America and the rest of Europe.

Lilge's diagnosis is that the tradition of 'scholarly objectivity' and 'the neutrality of science' made the academic the slave of the governments and corporations, which alone had power to pay for abstract studies; these could never, like pastries, pay for themselves. Freed from economic cares, from moral and spiritual responsibilities, the academics shared out the Quest for Truth among themselves as if it was a pork-pie.

They had [writes Lilge] the happiness of permanent employment and of concealing from themselves the futility of their efforts and their lives.

Departmentalism unleashed all that competitiveness, that currying for favour, that attention to public relations, that scrambling for students, that pettiness and jealousy, which made the university indistinguishable from other organizations.

Obviously it is in Germany where it began that the rise and fall of the Higher Learning can best be studied and of all the sciences the degradation of the sister sciences, Anthropology and Archaeology, are the most revealing for they are the most related to Man and to Human Life. The most damning evidence comes from before the war, when intellectual resistance was still possible, and I know no better account of what happened than that by Eva Lips, the wife of the curator of the Anthropological Museum in Cologne and an anthropologist herself. She wrote in 1938:

The anthropologists of Germany, at the outbreak of the Third Reich, hastened to destroy what they had previously revered; truth in research and freedom in teaching. The sphere of activity of these men of science was the world. No science was so well fitted as anthropology to protest against the madness of classifying races according to a scale of values. But they knew also the sacrifices and dangers that a public stand for truth would entail. Not a single man rose up to lift his voice for truth and freedom in science, content to face the certainty of want and persecution if he could but retain his honour.

This, of course, is a world tragedy, not a German one. In the days of Voltaire and the Encyclopaedists it was possible to talk of Science having no frontiers, but this became the emptiest of slogans as soon as learning was officially subsidized. Anything that is paid for by the state is the concern of the state, and in a time of crisis it is easy to justify any form of capitulation or connivance. 'If I go to prison, what happens to my library, my laboratory, my half-classified collection?'

Listen to the advice that Herr van Rautenstrauch, the founder of the Cologne Anthropological Museum and a stalwart enemy of the Nazis, gave to Professor Lips:

Your attitude strikes me as neither practical nor wise. I would avoid everything that would irritate those now in power and place obstacles in the way of mutual understanding, whereas if you will now wholeheartedly agree to all reasonable requests, I am confident that you can continue your scientific activities indefinitely at the museum.

I believe that is the way in which all directors of all institutes would react in times of stress. Frau Lips calls them 'co-ordinated jellyfish' but it must be admitted that for the purely physical survival of a cultural organism, the jellyfish tactics are best. Professor Lips, as an alternative, tried a silly-clever experiment but failed. He installed as his successor a jellyfish so loathsome in his ignorance and venality that he was sure the authorities would come to their senses. But, of course, he was wrong. Institutes that depend not on men but on administrative machinery will go on churning out degrees and chairs, Festschrifts and journals, though the air is thick with the smell of corpses.

The museum survived but its complicated mechanism was put neatly into reverse. Anthropology, whose object had been to stress the unity of mankind, had become a neat dove-tailing of disparate technologies and it was possible for it to be turned upside down without falling apart. The museum was henceforward used to demonstrate that mankind is in fact so varied that some races can be reckoned as subhuman and treated like animals.

In a very short time, to reinforce the new message, Himmler, who was the most generous patron of Anthropology and Archaeology Germany had ever known, had established at Strasburg an SS Institute for Anthropological Research, under the supervision of Professor Hirt, Director of the University's Anatomical Institute. Hirt had a magnificent collection of skulls of all the races of the earth, but it was defective in Jewish and Russian specimens till the war in the east offered an abundance of excellent quality. Edward Crankshaw has printed Dr Hirt's fascinating instructions to the Wehrmacht for the collection and dispatch of the heads of Jewish Bolshevik commissars. The commissars were to be treated with great care, photographed, measured and all relevant facts recorded, before the heads were expertly severed by a Wehrmacht physician and sent in cans of preserving spirits to Strasburg.

Professor Hirt was later hanged, but in fact he was little worse than a thousand other scholars who at the price of silence bought governmental support for the advancement of learning. The commissars would have been killed in any case. Had not Himmler in his speech at Weselburg dwelt on the necessity of exterminating 30,000,000 Russians? The professor's concern for their skulls may have saved them preliminary discomfort.

By 1933, eleven per cent of all the university faculty members of Germany had become nazified and the others argued no doubt that Science and Culture were beyond politics and that Art had no frontiers. They were surely victims not of German history or temperament but of an occupational disease, which is now afflicting all universities everywhere.

Their own scholars had predicted it generations before. Von Humboldt, for example, who became Prussian Secretary of Education in 1809, believed that 'the aim of all scientific work is not knowledge but the enlargement of man's character'. What you learn must be integrated with all that you know. 'As soon as a man deludes himself that knowledge does not depend on creative imagination but can be put together mechanically, all is irrevocably lost.'

By 1933 all was lost.

Unfortunately there is no Frau Professor Lips to tell us how archaeology died and when. Was it when Himmler made twenty-five new chairs of archaeology and found twenty-five learned men to fill them? Was it when he sent Sprockhoff to dig for Aryans under Vidkun Quisling? Was it when he sent an expedition to search for the traces of Aryanism (Tokharian?) in Tibet?

I think myself that archaeology did not really die till all international scholars decided that it would be wise and generous to let bygones be bygones. After that all the eminent scholars of Europe, America and Russia, and even a Jew or two, signed a Festschrift in honour of Professor Sprockhoff's sixtieth birthday and he was an honoured guest at conferences such as ours in Kilkenny.

The point that Humboldt, Ortega y Gasset, Lilge and others have made is that the departmentalization of learning had destroyed it. It had ceased to be an integral part of an educated man, transfusing everything. It was detachable, and profound studies about skulls could be pigeonholed in the mind separately from the question of severing and pickling them. In this way archaeology, which had been born beside ruined abbeys and whose purpose had not been knowledge but to keep alive in a small community the sense of the past and the continuity of history, became one of the whore sciences whose poxy favours can be bought by any government prepared to pay for them.

In fairness one must admit that knowledge basely acquired has once or twice been destroyed. When the allies reached Dachau they burnt all the valuable evidence that Dr Rascher had acquired about high altitude flying – he kept prisoners in ice-cold water tanks or special vans from which air could be extracted till they died of haemorrhage. But probably that was because no 'expert' was present.

Listen for instance to Dr Grahame Clark on this subject:

Though the motives of the Nazi leaders were nefarious yet they showed a clear recognition of the value of archaeology for enhancing solidarity. . . nor need we find it difficult to admit that some of the research they made possible was of a high technical standard and yielded solid results.

Should we not, therefore, respect 'solid results', however acquired?

Unlike archaeologists, anthropologists have shown themselves ready to admit that their science is dead. Kathleen Gough, a Canadian university lecturer, writes that anthropologists, through claiming that their science is 'ethically neutral', have lost sight of the human goals to which it was once directed. They have ceased to be its masters and become its slaves.

For example, in November 1966 the Association of American Anthropologists passed a resolution which was tantamount to a condemnation of the war in Vietnam. Yet some score of anthropologists were sent out east because their knowledge of primitive customs could be useful in the American counter-insurgency programme, Project Agile. By offering to the military their knowledge of primitive people, they bought themselves out of the job of killing them.

As a human science I do not think archaeology is half as dead as anthropology, simply because we have the example of a century ago to guide us. At the present time, to recover what we have lost is an almost insuperable task. In Ireland the old county societies were linked with a variety of social circumstances which no one would wish to restore even if that had been possible. Yet revivals of earlier ways of thinking have often been adapted to changed circumstances and we need not despair.

[1984]

ZHIVAGO'S CREATOR

I

To those with some acquaintance with Russian literature, Pasternak has been a well-known name for thirty or forty years, but not till the publication of *Dr Zhivago* did his fame extend beyond a very small circle of initiates. It was easy for the Russians to say that the award of the Nobel Prize was a political act and to be sceptical when it was explained that it was his entire work that was being crowned at Stockholm, and not *Dr Zhivago* alone. And in fact it may have been admiration not for his literary works but for his courage and integrity, it may have been indignation at the way he was treated, that brought him the prize. Pasternak is not a typical Nobel Prize winner. Two of these three books show him to have been far more like James Joyce, whom the adjudicators ignored, than like Pearl Buck, whom they crowned.

These works,* except for the autobiography, which is recent (1954) and rather stilted and slow, as though a grasshopper were trying to walk, are very hard to read and as much in need of glossaries and commentaries as *Finnegans Wake*. While Joyce dismembered language, Pasternak tried to dismember experience. The pattern of their work shines out (as in a kaleidoscope) from a swirl of fragments. Yet in one way they are in startling contrast. Joyce, in his early work, was a social and spiritual rebel and he wrote as lucidly as Ibsen, whom he revered. It was when he rejected the society that he satirized that he began to tunnel like a care-free beaver beneath the foundations of speech and the fragile conventions of human behaviour.

* Boris Pasternak, *The Last Summer*, Introduction by George Reavey; *Prose and Poems of Pasternak*, Introduction by J. M. Cohen; *An Essay in Autobiography*, Introduction by Edward Crankshaw (all London 1959).

Pasternak followed a contrary course. It is as an elderly man that he comes out of his tunnel. He writes with indignation and faith. Forgetful of his old preoccupation with the winding ways of thought and feeling, he writes simply what he thought and felt.

In his new mood he dismisses his old one more curtly than we can: 'I would not lift a finger to rescue more than a quarter of my writings from oblivion... I dislike my style up to 1940... I dislike the disintegrating forms, the impoverished thought and the littered and uneven language of those days.' He complains that his ear had been vitiated by 'our verbal whirligigs and the twisting and chopping of all familiar things'. He and his friends 'were then so tongue-tied that we could only be original despite ourselves and make a virtue of our inarticulateness'. He condemns 'the affected manner, the besetting sin of those days', in which his early autobiography, *Safe Conduct* (here published by Benn) was written.

Pasternak was the child of Imagism and Symbolism, period names for the artist's perennial revolt against the Philistine acquiescence in commonplace values. Associating these values with the bourgeoisie, one could easily become a revolutionary and join in the Fascist or Communist assault upon the bourgeois and his cosy conventions. But this special cosiness, which the artist scorns, does not appear to be politically conditioned. It survives social revolution, and many of these literary rebels suffered a shattering disillusionment. While in America Pound found refuge in a mad-house; in Russia Mayakovsky, Yesenin, Fadayev, Tsvetayeva, all killed themselves long before Stalin's purges had begun.

Pasternak had not committed himself so deeply. He was the type of fellow-traveller whom left and right condemn as a parlour-pink, and in Russia the pinks seem to have kept their colour, their principles, their dignity, much better than the reds, the whites, the blacks, the browns. Pasternak in his disillusionment had only to throw overboard the idiom of literary rebellion. Yet that idiom was a stage in his literary development and these early books, which illustrate it, cannot be ignored as he would wish us to do.

Only a very devoted coterie could read the prose of these first two books with pleasure. Pasternak's individual vision is smothered with 'individualism,' with tropes, metaphors, conceits. Yet we often meet laboured anticipations of those graceful images, which decorate and only occasionally obstruct the narrative of *Dr Zhivago*. Did he perhaps in the end owe something to Soviet Russia, that harsh step-mother to the imaginative writer? Lucidity was perhaps born of suffering. His early prose certainly suggests that some mighty inscrutable masterpiece was on the way, had not Lenin intercepted it, some portentous Russian version of *Finnegans Wake*, which a generation of foreign translators would have prowled around despairingly.

Observe in these books his obsession with trains. A volume of verse was called *On Early Trains*, and there is hardly a story without its train. They were to culminate in that magnificent train journey in *Dr Zhivago*, unsurpassed in literature; but these early Imagist-Futurist trains were cherished for the tricks they played on vision. They moved through the world of confused senses and drowsy children. Or rather *they* did not move, the landscape did, as it does for trains at fun-fairs – but very pretentiously. Tunnels are mountains that creep over the carriages, a terminus is a reef that leaps on a train and extinguishes it. 'A little later the rushing embankment was suddenly held in check by the brakes. . . . The stations flew away to the end of the train like stone butterflies.' On a journey through the Alps the train does actually move, but very oddly: 'Overhanging jags leapt onto the train and, settling themselves on the carriage-roofs, called to each other, waving their legs, and abandoned themselves to the free ride.'

In those days he seems to have cultivated his individual vision by looking at things upside-down or back to front; if it helped him later to resist the iron conformities of the Soviets, the discipline may have been a good one.

A story called, rather oddly, 'The Childhood of Luvers,' is an epitome of all the merits and defects of the early Pasternak. Zhenia Luvers is a small girl and for an adult to see the world through her unsophisticated, non-rational mind, many constrictions and contortions are necessary. Often he succeeds: 'One of the metal globes on the bed gleamed like a single bead. The other was extinguished because a garment had been thrown over it. Zhenia screwed up her eyes, the bead moved away from the floor and swam towards the wardrobe.'

More often the wheels of imagery turn, the words fly off in a shower of sparks, but nothing happens. Whose fault is this – ours, Zhenia's, Pasternak's, the translator's? Here is Zhenia looking at a small back-street: 'It shone like something in a dream, brilliantly and minutely illuminated and noiseless, as though the sun, wearing glasses, was scrabbling in the chickweed.' Pasternak, as he peers sympathetically over Zhenia's shoulder, and gropes for images, has completely blotted out the little girl.

The coterie which the early Pasternak fascinated vanished without a trace; so did the bourgeoisie, which he shocked and mystified. He wrote no prose for twenty years. Then he wrote with something of the economy and lucidity of a man crying for help. The problems of speech and sensibility to which he had dedicated his youth and middle age seemed secondary. Things had happened to himself and to the craft of letters, which had to be told. It is not always easy for a complicated man to express himself with simplicity, but in Dr Zhivago this difficult *tour de force* was almost achieved.

II

Not long ago a successful Soviet author explained to me that the position of the unorthodox writer in Russia was not so bad as one had heard. 'You can't stop a man writing a book,' he said; 'if it can't be published now, well, he'll put it in a drawer, and, if it is good, some day it will be printed.' Headmasters, advising their pupils with literary ambitions not to 'coddle their talents' but to go into the civil service, normally argue in this way too: 'If the right stuff is in you, it will come out, however unsympathetic the environment.' In fact they visualize literary genius as an explosive natural force, which nothing can repress. Judging by Dr Zhivago their optimism is only half justified.* Here is a sublime masterpiece that has been kept for ten or twenty years in a drawer. It has all the marks of irrepressible genius but it also has grave blemishes, which suggest that while it is not easy to neutralize creative gifts, they can be damaged and distorted by public indifference or hostility.

Dr Zhivago is a work of great beauty and consummate integrity but it should have been many books, not one. The thoughts and experiences of a lifetime have been crammed into an elderly man's first novel (for Boris Pasternak was born in 1890). Though in general the narrative flows freely, the track seems often to be choked with an accumulation of feelings, descriptions and observations which should have found expression decades ago. The digressions have the air of inhibited short stories and towards the end of the book new characters make brief hasty appearances like customers before closing time. Yet as a story of the Russian Revolution and its impact on a few strong personalities, it can have no equal. Yury Zhivago belonged, like most of his friends, to the prosperous intelligentsia, which sympathized with the Revolution

* Boris Pasternak, Dr Zhivago, translated by Max Hayward and Manya Harari (London 1958).

and tried to preserve intact and untarnished through the years of disillusionment and terror that vision of equity and justice which had inspired the early revolutionaries. Some succeeded better than others, but they all betrayed their principles more easily than they betrayed their friends, and politics are seldom more than a stormy background to the drama of personal relations. The friends meet and re-meet in Moscow, on long train-journeys, in Siberian woods and villages. Some had become zealots, others vagabonds or opportunists, others were guilt-tormented slaves, idealizing their own bondage. Zhivago himself clung to his personal independence with a tenacity beyond his powers, losing his health and seeing his wits grow dull and his heart cold, but retaining his integrity.

Pasternak is, of course, primarily a poet and an overflow of poetic sensibility which should have found its proper channel seems to have flooded some pages with obscure symbolism. There are uncanny coincidences, justified forebodings and in casual episodes a hint of 'deeper significances'. For the most part the novel moves on a clear sunlit Chekhovian plane but these sudden plunges into the twilight of Dostoievsky tilt the story needlessly towards unreality.

Dr Zhivago was accepted for publication in Russia during that brief thaw which ended with the Hungarian revolt and its suppression. Its rejection was a great disaster for Russia and for the West, for its publication would have made it difficult for us to taunt the Russians with their harshness towards their internal critics. That the thaw was a very real one, many pages of this book give evidence. For Zhivago the Revolution had been 'like God come down to earth from heaven', yet a few years later, he was saying:

Those who inspired the revolution aren't at home in anything except change and turmoil... For them transition periods, worlds in the making, are an end in themselves... Yet Man is born to live, not to prepare for life. Life itself is such a breathtakingly serious thing! Why substitute this childish harlequinade of adolescent fantasies, these schoolboy escapades?... Revolutions are made by fanatical men of action with one-track minds, who are narrow-minded to the point of genius. They overturn the old order in a few hours or days and for decades thereafter, for centuries, the spirit of narrowness, which led to the upheaval, is worshipped as holy.... There is nothing more self-centred and further from the facts than Marxism.

Yet in his contempt for 'the slinking bourgeois breed', Zhivago was at one with the revolutionaries. It seemed to him that their boasted 'habit of independent thought' was a mere by-product of their leisure and their privileges and that, when these were lost, their moral fibre collapsed too.

If another thaw were to come and more manuscripts were to be taken from their drawers we might find that Russia in its essentials had changed very little. Though winter alters the outward face of everything, when spring returns even small and delicate things are seen to have survived. One had thought that the childlike candour and freshness of Russian literature, its spontaneity and subtlety, were gone for ever, yet here they all are again.

The translators do their work well. Pasternak uses homely images, which easily in translation sound crude or comic; yet though something is lost much of eternal Russia remains. The thick black ice is chunky like the bottoms of broken beer bottles. The starry sky throws a pale blue flicker like the flame of methylated spirit over the black earth. The aspens have the scent of fresh toilet water and pale thin hollyhocks gaze into the distance over the fences like women in their night shifts, whom the heat indoors has driven out for a breath of air.

As in the old Russia the writer still has power to undermine pomposity with humour and irony and to tame the vast distances with detailed and intimate sketches of the things nearby.

[1959]

ENDNOTE

On 18 February 1959 Hubert Butler chaired a meeting of a literary society in University College, Dublin, when the topic for discussion was *Dr Zhivago* and the award of the Nobel Prize for Literature to Boris Pasternak. He had already reviewed the novel in *The Irish Times* (second section above) and was shortly to discuss Pasternak's earlier prose (first section).

The topic, even by the exacting standards of Ireland in the 1950s, was uncontroversial. Introducing the discussion, Butler spoke for about ten minutes and stressed Pasternak's links with the pre-revolutionary intel-ligentsia and his affinity to Chekhov in certain regards:

Chekhov had to compromise with his conscience many times, but when he saw an opportunity of making an effective protest, he did so. For example, he resigned from the academy when Gorki was ejected for political reasons; and at the time of the Dreyfus case in France he quarrelled with the reactionary and anti-Semite paper which published his stories, even though this meant quarrelling with his bread and butter... I think that Pasternak may have acted as he did in refusing the Nobel Prize fully alive to what would follow, and in no way surprised. He seems to have Chekhov's unfrightened realism and he may be finding what has happened more entertaining than alarming. He has lived as an honoured figure behind the iron curtain for the greater part of his life. He knows all about it. Now that he has punctured quite a large hole in it, he is probably quite pleased with himself and would be puzzled by our sympathy.

This sympathy was not echoed universally. Immediately after the debate a notice appeared throughout the College above the name of the Registrar, J. J. Hogan, intimating in capital letters that 'NO PERSON NOT A MEMBER OF THE COLLEGE MAY BE INVITED TO TAKE PART IN OR BE PRESENT AT ANY MEETING OF A COLLEGE SOCIETY WITHOUT THE PERMISSION OF THE PRESIDENT'. At the time Butler felt that this retrospective rebuke had been caused not by his discussion of Pasternak – 'which was innocuous' – but by his attitude towards the Compulsory Conversion Campaign in Croatia (see 'The Sub-Prefect Should Have Held His Tongue' below). In fact, several notable figures were *personae non gratae* in UCD during these years, and the Pasternak debate was neither a major nor an isolated incident. (*Ed.*)

RIGA STRAND IN 1930

Once a week in the summer months, a pleasure steamer berths in Reval harbour and for a few hours troops of excited English tourists swoop down on the town, swarm up the hill, and penetrate in charabancs as far as Pirita and St Brigid's abbey. It is a charming spot; the views, the churches, the crooked narrow streets, compact, accessible and picturesque, are just what is required. Though they straggle off unshepherded in fifty different directions, they meet each other in a few minutes with glad cries in antique shops and cathedrals where everybody speaks English. When the hooter calls them back to the ship they have seen everything and yet are not exhausted.

The same ship wisely seldom stops at Riga. Riga is big and sprawling and new looking; it has clean, cosmopolitan boulevards, public parks, and large exhausting museums; the few tourists have a harried look and the hours pass in catching trams, changing money and haggling with droshky drivers. There are, it is true, a great many English people in Riga, but they are a serious, residential tribe, the complete reverse of the sightseers of Reval or Helsingfors. The Riga Britons are homesick and resentful business-men who have come to buy timber and find that the Letts don't want to sell it, or bored and studious soldiers who have come to learn Russian and find that the Letts don't want to teach it. Their subsequent stories of Riga and Latvia are naturally coloured by their experiences. The timber merchants are confronted with the petty officialdom of a young nation, proud of its new independence and snatching at all opportunities of asserting it. The officers are met with blank surprise; their shy, stumbling sentences get no encouraging response from the Letts, for Russian is out of favour and they find their society restricted to the English Club and a few embittered Russian aristocrats to whom Latvia is only a rebellious province, governed by the lower orders. No wonder then that officers and merchants have no

187

rosy memories of Riga; grudgingly perhaps they repeat the legend that
the Riga air is very good and that Schwarz's is the best café between
Berlin and Tokyo, though they've never been to Tokyo and Schwarz's
is very much like other cafés; they bring home amber necklaces and
caviare and polished birchwood cigarette cases, but they don't conceal
that they are thankful to be out of Riga and would gladly never return.

All the same Riga Strand must have a fascination for more leisured
visitors, who have time to be interested in the past and the future of the
small republics which rose from the ruins of the Russian Empire. It is
the holiday ground not only for Letts but for all the newly liberated
peoples of the Baltic. There one may meet Estonians and Finns, Lithu-
anians and Poles, bathing side by side with Germans, Russians and
Swedes, who were once their masters.

Of all the Baltic nations perhaps the Letts have suffered the most, yet
their story is typical. Their nationality and their language have survived
a double conquest and many centuries of foreign rule. From the west
came the Teutonic knights bearing with them a German culture and
occupying the ancient territories of Lett and Lithuanian and Estonian,
as far as the Finnish marshes and the empire of the Tsars. Russia too was
expanding. Peter the Great was casting covetous eyes upon the Baltic
and at last the 'Baltic Barons' in their turn, and all their possessions,
passed under the Russian eagles. The Letts now found that they had not
one master but two, for the Russians respected the Barons for their
solidity and thrift and good husbandry, and confirmed them in their
possessions, giving them in return for their loyalty high places at court
and in the army. Ever since Peter the Great had first turned the eye of
Russia westward, German culture and methods had been admired and
imitated. Catherine the Great was a German, and she and her successors
often chose advisers from their German subjects. The Baltic Barons
found that they lost nothing by their incorporation in the Russian
Empire.

If the Barons were the most privileged of the Tsar's subjects, the Letts
whom they oppressed were the most wretched... their very existence
was denied, the name of Latvia was abandoned, and the Baltic lands
divided into Russian provinces in which the racial differences were
carefully ignored. The Letts had no appeal from the caprice of their
masters; an early law limited flogging to thirty-six strokes, but humane
legislation did not go much further and the Letts remained all but serfs
till late on in the last century. Lettish schools were closed and Lettish
newspapers prohibited, even old songs and customs that might remind

them of their national past were suppressed. Every year in the old days there had been a great festival of song, the rallying point of national feeling, and every town and village had its band of singers. But the rulers recognized that a song can be more dangerous than a sword and the festival was rigorously proclaimed.

Many Letts joined revolutionary organizations and, when the Revolution of 1905 broke out, the great rehearsal for the Revolution of 1917, there was an abortive revolt in Riga. A Lettish Republic was declared and for a few days maintained. The Tsar was alarmed, concessions were promised, and, when all danger was averted, forgotten: the Barons, momentarily panic-stricken, recovered their composure. But the Letts persevered, their time had not yet come, and the Great War found them still trusting in the clemency of the Tsar. It was an occasion when all the subject races must be rallied to the Russian cause, and the Baltic peoples, who were disaffected and lived upon the frontiers of the enemy, must at all costs be conciliated. The German emperor had promised to establish a Lettish Republic, and the Barons, who took this with a grain of salt, were many of them ready to welcome a German invasion. The moment was propitious for a generous gesture from Nicolas II. He agreed to grant a request hitherto persistently refused; henceforward the Letts might serve under their own officers as a separate Lettish unit. Lettish regiments were formed and graciously permitted to defend their fatherland and promised that when they had beaten the enemy they would enjoy equal rights with the Barons. There were rejoicings in Riga, and the credulous Letts believed that at last the day of their deliverance was at hand; but those who were more discerning guessed that whoever won, the Letts would be the losers, the Barons would not be shifted and the emperors would find good reasons for forgetting their solemn pledges. But as often occurs the most discerning were wrong. The unexpected, the impossible happened: both sides were defeated, Kaiser Wilhelm lost his throne and the line of Peter the Great came to a tragic end at Ekaterinburg. Yet at first it seemed as if Latvia would merely be smothered in the collapse of the two empires. By the Treaty of Brest-Litovsk Russia treacherously abandoned Latvia to Germany and after the Armistice the Allies allowed the Germans to remain in Riga to keep the country safe from Bolsheviks.

Then followed eighteen months of terrible suffering for Latvia. The Letts drove out the Bolsheviks in the east only to find the Germans in their rear, and a third enemy appeared suddenly, for an army of White Russian exiles, mobilized in Berlin, tried to conquer Latvia as a base for an attack on Russia. White and Red and Balt and German alternately

ravaged the land, for their landlord barons made common cause against
the Letts. But the Letts fought like tigers. At last, after foreign intervention and unheard of struggles, peace was restored, boundaries were
traced by English colonels and professors, and the Latvian Republic was
proclaimed.

Now at last the Letts are masters of Riga Strand, and on a June morning
the sands are alive with holiday-makers. Where do they all come from?
Outside Riga the pinewoods and the wastelands stretch empty and
interminable, dotted here and there only with a few ramshackle wooden
huts, and Riga itself does not suggest an unlimited supply of pleasure-
seekers. Granted that some of them come from abroad the answer is that
a seaside holiday is not so much a luxury in Latvia as a necessity. There
is scarcely a clerk or artisan in Riga too humble to have a rickety wooden
dacha for his family during the summer months, and from there he
commutes daily.

A great broad shore fringed with pinewoods sweeps round the gulf
of Riga as far as eye can see: the sea is almost tideless and yet the beach
is always deep and soft and clean, for the wind blows away the bus
tickets and the paper bags and buries orange peel and match boxes deep
in the sand. Then during the long winters the snow and the frost scavenge
round the shuttered dachas, there are mountains of ice and the whole
Gulf is frozen over, so that a year or two ago two men skated forty
miles across the sea to the small island of Runo, but when they got there
they did not recognize it for it too was covered with ice.

June when it comes finds the scene completely changed: the syringas
are in blossom, the railway is opened and the post office and the post
mistress are established; there are bands and cinemas and charabancs, and
people run about the shady streets in dressing-gowns. Riga Strand is
awake again. It is an annual metamorphosis, a conspiracy between man
and nature that has started afresh every season since the first dacha went
up in the pinewoods. There is a story that it belonged to a Scottish
merchant and that he called it Edinburga thus giving its name to one of
the seven villages of Riga Strand. Another of the villages is called
Dubbelin though the Irish merchant who founded it is only a legend.
In any case the villages bear little resemblance to their namesakes. Behind
them, parallel to the shore, flows the broad river Aar; in front of them
stretches the coastline. There is nothing to interrupt the long monotonous
shore; one may walk and walk and still the landmarks keep the same
place upon the horizon. There are no rock-pools nor seaweeds nor shells
nor birds; sea and land meet each other with a minimum of detail and

complication. One might walk to Lithuania and meet scarcely anything but water and sand and trees and sky.

There are three sandbanks that stretch round the whole of the Latvian coast as if to grade the depths for bathers; children can splash about in front of the first, while their parents sleep contentedly on the shore, but only the most intrepid swimmers venture beyond the third. In general, though, the Letts are very well used to the sea and the attendants have placed the long line of basket chairs with their backs to the waves, so that the occupants can watch the stream of people passing by under the restaurants in striped Turkish dressing-gowns and bathing-dresses far too modish to bathe in. The serious bathers do not wear bathing-dresses at all, for the beach belongs to the men till eight o'clock in the morning, when they must give place to the women, who have it to themselves till midday.

The villages themselves are scattered among the trees, long grassy tracks run parallel to each other, criss-crossed by others and fringed with wooden dachas. Here and there is an outcrop of cinemas and dance-halls. There are more pretentious buildings too with archways and gardens; they are empty and dilapidated but not with age for carved in the stone doorways one can often read 1905 or 1908 or 1912. Those were the great days of Riga Strand when wealthy merchants from Moscow and St Petersburg or noblemen who did not despise Russian resorts came here with their families. Mineral springs and mud-baths were discovered and exploited; though Riga Strand was not beautiful like Finland yet it was close at hand and it was not as expensive or as exclusive as the Crimea; at least it only excluded the Jews and they were excluded as a matter of course from every chic imperial resort. There was an imperial decree forbidding them to Riga Strand.

For a decade or more all went well; new wings were constructed, new gardens laid out, fashionable specialists built up practices, more and more medicinal baths were opened – then all at once the same fate overtook the villages of Riga Strand that extinguished all the pleasure resorts of Western Europe. But the Great War, which cast only a passing blight upon the others, eclipsed for ever the brief splendours of the Latvian shore. The Baltic lands fell out of favour with the Russians, their 'barons' were suspected of intriguing with the enemy; for years it was discovered they had been employing German spies as their foresters and now from being courted they were shunned.

Then began the long campaign among the swamps and forests of Northern Europe... slowly the Russians fell back and their armies melted away; Bolshevik and German and White Russian swept over land and devastated it. In Riga telegraph wires were pulled down; rope had run short but there were still men to hang.

Riga Strand has emerged from the terror now and there are visitors there once more, but the clients for whom the casinos and the dance-halls and the rickety palaces of 1910 were built are gone for ever. Where now are her wealthy St Petersburg patrons, where is St Petersburg itself? Even if they wished to come, there are barbed wire entanglements six foot high, manned by armed sentries, that can only be crossed with a stack of passports. The Japanese garden with its little bridges and artificial jungles is knee-deep in groundsel and toadstools; there are trenches still and tangles of rusty barbed wire round the sulphur springs at Kemmeri, and the fashionable specialists have no prodigal Caucasian Princes to diet in their sanatoria, they have to haggle with Jewesses about mud-baths and superfluous fat. The disinherited have come into their own, the Jews have descended like locusts on Riga Strand... for them it has the fascination of a forbidden land. Synagogues begin to oust the gleaming onion towers and Assari, the farthest of the resorts, has almost become a Jewish village. Jewish ladies emerge with blonde curls from the hair-dressers, for there are two or three 'frisetavas' in every street and Lettish gentlemen prefer blondes. But the Jews have still to mind their step, for the Letts have inherited many of the prejudices of their masters; they too fear and despise the Jews, just as they themselves were despised by the Russians.

In the afternoon the sun beats down scorchingly on Riga Strand, the pinetrees are too far away to lend their shade and even beneath them the sand is parched and burning. There are a few boatmen, a few bathers, some ladies stretched in deck-chairs under the shady walls of a sanatorium, and in the long coarse grass between the pinewoods and the sand the day-trippers lie like logs. It is so quiet that one can hear a baby crying in the next village, the hoot of a steamer on the Aar, a man knocking the sand out of his shoe upon an upturned boat. It is nearly five o'clock and soon the bells begin to ring for tea in all the pensions and lodging-houses along the beach. The sanatorium bell clangs like a fire-engine, the ladies in the deck-chairs clap their hands to their ears and scream at the matron, but she has been preparing the tea while they were sleeping and swings it all the harder.

After tea the beach becomes awake again, the dacha residents come out with watering-cans and make puddles in the grey powder of their flower-beds. The earth has forgotten how to drink and for a moment the water sits in a curved bubble on the surface or forms little pellets with the sand. In any case a garden in Latvia is an unnatural thing... the flowers in the dachas are tenants for the season like their owners. None of them looks permanent or settled; geraniums and petunias flush up a dizzy scarlet or purple for a month or two like a local inflammation, and die down the moment the owner and his watering-can have departed. The big restaurants do not even bother about bedding plants but on a gala night, the night for instance of the firemen's ball, a cart arrives from the country piled high with branches and in half an hour the café is embedded in a luxuriant forest and flowers and shrubs have sprung up out of the dry sand. There are no gardens in the country either; sometimes someone will stick a peony or a dahlia into the grass, but if it does not look after itself, no one else will – and its life is usually a prolonged battle.

As the night falls more people stream out on to the strand, for the air is cool and the sinking sun has spilt a pink light across the shore. It is the hour for the evening stroll, and from dacha and sanatorium the same familiar figures emerge. There are three robust Finnish ladies, the wives of foresters, a German financier and a Lithuanian governess. There is an Estonian gentleman who is very popular with many different ladies in turn; he has friendly charming manners and is always beautifully dressed and carries a cane. He varies the ladies not because he is fickle but because sooner or later they each of them discover that he is stupid almost to mental deficiency. There is a Swedish lady who has come over to cure her pale small son from vomiting. She has a jealous husband who condemns her yearly to dull provincial watering places and Riga, she thinks, is the dullest of them all. She has a new dress for every meal but her evening parties with kisses for forfeits are not well attended. She started to have English lessons from a British officer and amid shrieks of merry badinage learnt 'I luv you so' and 'keessmequeek' and then she got bored again. All the upper classes are bored on Riga Strand. 'Ochen skoochno!' 'Sehr langweilig!' 'I'm bored stiff!' It is only good form to be bored.

A more independent type is the Russian lady who lives with her widowed mother in a dacha up the strand. She is severe, uncompromising. Every morning she does Catherine wheels, nude, on the beach for the good of her figure and in the afternoons she mortifies herself by giving Russian lessons to French and English officers. It is a degrading occupation for an aristocrat, and she slaps down her instructions with callous, disdainful efficiency. They want to study Bolshevik idioms and the new alphabet and she has forced herself to master even that. In the back room she stows away her lonely garrulous old mother and the Lettish husband, whom she married to get out of Russia, and sometimes when she is late for a lesson, the old mother slips out and gossips with the pupils. What revelations! What merry undignified chuckles! She is delighted to have someone to talk to but suddenly she hears her terrifying daughter outside and slips back shamefacedly into her room.

There are many other Russians on Riga Strand, the remnants of the wealthy patrons of former days. All that they could save from the Revolution they have brought with them but they have no homes or estates to return to; they have to be thankful for a refuge from their own countrymen among a people they have always despised, and to get jobs in Latvia they set themselves to learning Lettish, a language they have always regarded as a servant patois. Life is very hard but they contrive often to be gay and self-confident and outrageous. They still take short cuts across flower-beds if they belong to Jews, and are condescending to Letts at tea-parties. They are ingenious at finding ways to restore their self respect.

There is also a Soviet Commissar holidaying on Riga Strand, but it is unlikely that he will join the crowd that watches the sunset in the evening. He is neither gay nor sociable. Even at meals he talks to no one but gazes intently at his plate of food, frightened to look up in case he should intercept a glance of hate. He is pale with enthusiasm or under-nourishment and he obviously enjoys the fleshpots of Riga Strand.

As the evening grows colder the strand empties, and a group of boys come out of the pinewoods where they have been collecting sticks, and build a bonfire on the shore. The rest of the sand sinks back into the night and they are islanded in the firelight. As the flames burn higher it is easier to see their keen Jewish faces. They have not yet lost the colours of the Mediterranean, though it may be many generations since their ancestors travelled up from Palestine to the shores of the Baltic. The leaders are a woman with loose black hair and a Messianic youth of seventeen. Are they making speeches or telling stories? The eyes of twenty boys are fixed, black and burning in the firelight, on the woman as she cries passionately to them in Yiddish. Three or four boys reply to her and they sing strange, unhomely Eastern tunes. Only a few yards away are the cafés and the sanatoria but in the darkness the sand seems to stretch away interminably and the Jewish scouts seem to be the only creatures alive on the shore, a nomad tribe camping in the desert. They are of the same race, the same families perhaps, as the predatory blondes in the beach costumes, but the spirit that fills them now is alien from Riga or from Europe. Persecution has hardened them and given them strength to survive war and revolution and even to profit by them and direct them. Perhaps it is they in the end who will decide the future of Riga Strand.

At last the fire dies down, the boys make ready for sleep, and once more the small, scarcely audible sounds of the waves break upon the silence.

[1930]

PETER'S WINDOW

No. 59 Chernishev Pereulok was a large plum-coloured block of bour-geois flats near the Yekaterinsky Sad (the Catharine Gardens), and the Archangelskys' flat was on the fifth floor. The lift had not worked since 1917 and sat in the well of the staircase, full of tram tickets and old newspapers. There was still a large gilt mirror on their landing, though all the others had been removed by the Jacht or House Committee. Darya Andreyevna, the former owner of the flat and its 'responsible tenant', set great store by all these traces of former grandeur and the Jacht had yielded before her fury when the mirror was threatened.

When my wife, Peggy, and I and our friend Archie Lyall, first came to Leningrad in 1931 on the *Alexei Rykov*, a tourist ship, the Archangelskys had made a special effort to welcome us. We brought news of Nikolai Mihalitch's old friends in England with whom he had had no contact since his wife, Connie, and baby son had left. They had gone home three years ago when the NEP period had given place to the rigours of the Five Year Plan and milk and baby-foods became scarce. We got the introduction to Nikolai Mihalitch through my cousin, Willy de Burgh, Professor of Philosophy at Reading University. Nikolai's father had been a priest in Tiflis and they had fled from the Bolsheviks to the Crimea (for a short time in White Russian hands). There, his sister had married an Englishman, an officer in the British interventionist forces, whose home was in Reading. When the Bol-sheviks seized the Crimea, Nikolai was sent to England and became one of the most brilliant of de Burgh's pupils. It was there that, later, he married Connie, a fellow student, and influenced by the left-wing intellectualism of the time, they became Communists and decided to join his widowed mother in Leningrad.

When we first called there were biscuits and tea with hot milk, and strawberry jam in saucers, and his mother was in a state of collapse

compounded of hospitality and suspicion. Nikolai had asked a friend of
his, Major Tihomirov, a teacher in the Military Academy, to meet us
and a colleague of his own, Baroness Garatinsky, was anxiously awaited.
Nikolai Mihalitch had told me her story. She had been an old revolutionary and in 1917 her peasants, who had taken over her estates in
Central Russia, had made her their manager. Five years later her position
had become impossible and she was now teaching languages in Leningrad. Through the open window we saw her limping slowly up the
street, pausing and glancing up and down to see that it was empty before
she turned in. 'It isn't very safe for us to visit each other,' he said; 'in
any case she doesn't like the stairs with her lame leg, but this is a special
occasion.' He told me that because of her origins, she was suspect
politically. She had a daughter in exile in Siberia and a son in Solovietski
Island. In Goskurs, the Polytechnic where she taught, she was the victim
of petty persecution. 'Women are the worst,' he said, and he was
explaining how in Leningrad an arts education was more accessible to
the female than to the male bourgeois, when the baroness walked in.
She paused in the doorway, leaning on her stick, and diverted with a
smile his mother's effort to introduce us and give her a chair. 'Later,
later, Nina Gavrilovna.' To us she said, 'Women are allowed a bit
more licence, because even here they aren't taken seriously. Masculine
unreliability matters more.'

She had a sharp rather cantankerous manner but spoke English well
in a beautifully clear voice. She always talked rapidly and provocatively
when she was manoeuvring into chairs or difficult positions, as if to
distract attention. She looked coldly into people's eyes when she talked
to them. She herself had a lack of personal inquisitiveness that was almost
unfriendly. It was as if she could only argue or disagree and did not
waste time in liking or disliking.

Nina Gavrilovna was a crushed, dark little woman. She followed our
English talk anxiously with her bright black eyes, interrupting her son
with nudges and murmurs, when she could: 'Kolya, ask the lady after
the Professor's wife's health!' 'Kolya, you are talking so much you have
not noticed the lady has nothing on her plate!' (Only Nikolai's mother
called him Kolya, as I will for brevity, but actually everybody in the
flat was very formal and used patronymics. Even his closest friends called
him Nikolai Mihalitch.)

She guessed correctly that her son was being indiscreet but could
never learn that it made him worse to interrupt. The baroness, seeing
her agitation, said to me, 'You mustn't think that because we have much
to complain of, we are enemies of the Revolution. The Revolution had

to happen, it was the result of generations of suffering and plotting. All
the great Russians of the past have played a part in it. It is a historical
fact, a great convulsion of human nature. If we are to go on living we
must accept it, and I have always done so gladly.'

Before we could reply Tihomirov succeeded in changing the conversation. He spoke English in the genteel, mincing way of some educated Russians. He had gold teeth and a moist, glinting smile.

As we left, Kolya said to me, 'When you come back from Rostov,
you must stay with me. I will get you a job teaching.' He translated this
to his mother, who gave a glance of agony. 'But there is no bed. What
will Darya Andreyevna say?' He ignored her. 'I will arrange. I will get
you a bed. You must stay a term.'

We went down the Volga and visited Moscow and Rostov. Archie
Lyall wrote a book on our experiences, *Russian Roundabout*, which
became a classic for all earlier travellers by Intourist. I came back fearing
that Kolya's mother would have dissuaded him from inviting me to stay
on. I was wrong. We spent a few days in Leningrad before the *Rykov*
sailed back and it was plain Kolya counted on my staying. Smiling and
bowing, Alexander Ivanitch Tihomirov came to our hotel and together
we went to the military stores, where, under his guidance, I bought
myself a camp-bed for forty roubles. The next day the *Rykov* sailed.
Kolya, Tihomirov and I went to the docks to see off Peggy and Archie.
It was a strange departure, for there was a young woman among the
passengers who had had a nervous breakdown. She had been recommended a 'complete change' and she and her parents could think of
nothing better than a trip to Russia. While there she had gone mad and
had to be dragged aboard kicking and struggling and finally lifted up
the gangway, screaming.

That afternoon I installed myself in Chernishev Pereulok. It was the
name-day of all the Sonias and Nadjezhdas, and their friends were
hurrying up and down the streets carrying bunches of overblown dahlias.
A few foreigners were still bathing on the broad strand by the Peter and
Paul fortress but the melon pips, which had started to sprout by the
water's rim, had been nipped by an early frost. Workmen were wrapping
up the heads of delicate shrubs in the Summer Garden in balloons of
paper and taking in the cactuses and coleuses, which ornamented the
lawns with hammers and sickles.

In the Archangelskys' flat the Jacht had sent a chimney sweep to clean
the flue. Everything I saw was coloured and penetrated for me by the
thought of the Revolution. Even commonplace or inevitable things had

a bloom of special significance because they had matured at such a time
and in such a place.

I pitched my camp-bed between the stove and the window in the
room where we had our tea-party in the summer. Kolya had a divan
covered with drab fusty material in the opposite corner. Everything in
the room was shabby and dark. There were large patches on the wall
where his son, Misha, a couple of years before had peeled off the
wallpaper and scribbled on the plaster. Over the whole flat there was
that sweetish, musty smell of black bread and benzine and scent and
galoshes that Russians seem to carry with them, even into exile. I felt
lonely and ill-at-ease. Nina Gavrilovna plainly did not want me there.
She refused to believe that being foreign I could understand anything,
unless she shouted at me with plentiful gesticulations. Her bed was in a
widening of the passage, which was screened off by a dark curtain.
Beyond that were two rooms, where invisible factory-workers lived.
To the left was the room of Darya Andreyevna and her husband. In the
dark passage outside our room near the front door, Lyubotchka, the
Archangelskys' maid, used to sleep on her trunk. Till I had practice I
stumbled over her every time I came to bed late. At the far end of the
passage was the kitchen, where each tenant had his private Primus, and
off that there were two windowless cupboards, the bathroom and the
WC. Darya had asserted her authority in these two rooms by pinning
up the pictures that decorated the flat when it had been hers, 'Stags at
Bay', 'The Imperial Palace at Gatchina', family groups. They bulged out
from their drawing-pins with all the fluff and dust that had accumulated
behind them. No one dared to remove them, but during the paper
shortage hard-pressed tenants had torn jagged strips from them and from
their cardboard mounts.

Kolya had exchanged his Russian white summer suit for a Norfolk
jacket and grey flannel trousers. Before he was like an Italian but now
he was like a Bloomsbury Asiatic. He had a dark thin fanatical face and
abrupt, vehement movements. He did not like to explain or to have his
explanations questioned.

My first day I spent alone in the flat writing letters and examining
Kolya's books. They were neatly shelved on a pair of skis that he was
storing for his elder brother, an engineer. I saw F. H. Bradley, Hegel,
Bertrand Russell, Aldous Huxley, D. H. Lawrence. Of Russian writers
he had only Lenin and his commentators.

I was interrupted constantly by the telephone. His mother would slip
in and answer it, looking at me through the corners of her eyes. 'Ne
doma,' she would say bitterly, 'Ne znaioo!' 'He's not at home.' 'I don't

know!' This happened two or three times. Then she took out her basket and went marketing, and I was left to answer the next call myself three-quarters of an hour later. It was a lady. 'Where is Nikolai Mihalitch?' From my way of answering she guessed I was English and she went on in English. 'Where can he be? He was due to give his lesson here half an hour ago and I rang up Techmass, but he hadn't given his class there, and at Goskurs it was the same.' I couldn't enlighten her.

At six o'clock his mother let him in and there was a voluble conversation in the passage. He came into the room without greeting me. He looked completely exhausted. 'It is arranged,' he said, but hearing his mother at the door leapt up and seized a plate of over-cooked vegetable marrow from her. 'Isn't your mother going to eat here?' I asked. 'No, it would be better not. She does not understand the English.' Even when it was irrelevant, I made a point of saying I was Irish not English. I made things worse by saying once that the de Burghs were Irish too. It was as a visitor from England, where he had been so happy, that Kolya was welcoming me. For years he had been waiting for an opportunity to return the kindness which had been shown him. Even for his mother the syllables Dee Buggs had some mystic significance. He did not want to be put off by details.

'What is arranged?' I asked, when he seemed ready for a question. 'Your classes are arranged,' he said. 'You will have four classes every evening from eight till midnight. I've made out the list. You will be a member of our brigade. Then there is Olga Kulgachev two hours and Engineer Stavrogin three hours in a decade, and you've already fixed up with Alexander Ivanitch. They will start next week.' A decade, which sounded to me an eternity, meant ten days. Brigades were groups of friends, who shared out pupils or jobs between each other. There were other brigades for house decoration, theatre craft, translating and all the more specialized arts and crafts. 'But did you spend all this time looking for work for me? You must have missed all your classes.'

'That is of no importance.'

For the next few days he once more gave up all his classes in spite of my protests, and we tramped and trammed from one end of Leningrad to the other, interviewing passport officials, professors, pupils.

One day as we were queuing up outside the offices of the Lensoviet, he tried to explain himself to me: 'I am a Caucasian from Georgia like Stalin, with the same theological background. He was a theological student. He believes like the Manicheans that there is Good and Evil, Black and White, a dichotomy. All this which he thinks Good is Evil.' He waved his hand at the Lensoviet and the long queue.

'Why do you like the English so much then? They are not Manichean. They play down all the major issues of good and evil. They are loyal to small obligations, not big ones. I can't imagine an English teacher neglecting all his classes to help the friend of friends, who were once very good to him.'

He looked hurt, as if I had accused him of being un-English. But I had meant it as a compliment and I could not let the subject drop. I argued that social organization works better in England, simply because the English only made superficial impact on each other. They glide about, cannoning off each other like billiard balls. They can calculate each other's reactions accurately, because they hardly ever impinge. Perhaps the reason why the Russians are difficult to organize is because they make real contact. It's like playing billiards with bull's eyes.

'You forget I am a Caucasian. That's what I hate about the Russians, always prying and enquiring about each other.'

I found his claim to be Caucasian as irritating as he found my claim to be Irish: 'I don't think Russians could ever be detached in the tepid, unemphatic English way. You would merely isolate yourselves.'

After a pause, he said: 'Darya Andreyevna was catechizing my mother about you today. She thinks you are a spy and wants the House Committee to turn you out. She has been to the Upravdom [the President of the House Committee]. Lyubotchka did her best for you. She said she thought you were a harmless idiot because you smile when you talk to her.'

'I only meant to be friendly.'

'Yes, but real Russians only smile at jokes.'

I had no way of paying for my lodgings, so I suggested that Peggy should pay Connie in Eastbourne every week. He refused indignantly. I was his guest. I accepted this but asked Peggy to send suitable things to Connie instead.

But we were to have other complications that evening. Lyubotchka the maid came from Karelia near Finland where not much was known about plumbing. She had broken one of Connie's wedding-present tea cups, and, fearing to admit it, had thrown it down the W.C. and pulled the plug. Darya Andreyevna a little later found the W.C. choked and, groping with her hand, she discovered a piece of Connie's china. With me there without her permission, it was too much for her. Sobbing with rage, she burst through the door and flung the horrible handful on the floor.

In the fury about the tea cup my problem was forgotten. Nobody ever again thought I was a spy. But after that, Darya and Kolya never went to see each other. They communicated, when they had to, by telephone. When our door was open, we could hear Darya Andreyevna's real voice through the passage wall almost as clearly as her telephone voice. Though she lived in the next room for many months, I never saw her again, nor did I ever see her husband though we were incessantly aware of each other.

Darya's husband had been a colonel in the Tsar's army, a very tyrannical one, Kolya told me, and his wife had been an opera singer and quite famous. After the revolution she had sung Soviet songs and had been awarded the rank of 'Naoochnaya Rabotnitsa' or 'Scientific Worker'. Because of this she had first-category food rations and the right to a certain floor space in her old flat. In relation to the Jacht she became 'the responsible tenant'. With her food tickets she could get, among other things, macaroni. Nina Gavrilovna could never forgive her this. A Tsarist colonel's wife got macaroni, while her son, a Marxist professor and Privat Dozent at the Oriental Institute, had to live on vegetable marrow. Incessantly nagging Kolya about this, she had made it psychologically impossible for him ever to get a first-category food ticket. All that was necessary was for him to fill in a few forms, but nothing would induce him to do so. Whenever macaroni was mentioned, his face went dead and cold and Manichean.

Soon after this my classes began. The last tourists had disappeared from the streets and I felt like a privileged member of the audience who goes home with the actors after the play. Stacks of logs were being piled in the courtyards and back streets and one heard the whine of saws. The streets got emptier and footsteps echoed. Everyone except Kolya sealed up his double windows with gummed paper and closed the phortochka, the little ventilating window by which they were pierced. Everyone bought galoshes, for the pavements were like troughs and held water.

I had no winter clothes and clothing became an obsession, for my arms were too long for everything I could afford. Kolya lent me an old coat, and I wedged a pair of undersize galoshes onto my shoes. I could never get them off again, so I used to take off shoes and all at my classes and hide my feet under the desk. Later on I put my galoshes on my indoor shoes, but I had to walk sedately or the galoshes dragged them off again.

One day, as I was walking to my classes in the twilight, I saw a large leather-coated figure lying on the pavement. He had an open dispatch-case beside him with papers scattered about. He was snoring. A woman came from the far side of the Moika river to help me lift him up. 'What

a shame,' she exclaimed, 'to see such a beautiful coat lying in the mud!'
We examined it together. 'I bet he's a commissar!' she said. 'One can
only get a coat like that with valuta.' We dragged him to the Mariinski
Theatre and propped him up, sitting against one of the columns of the
portico. I told her I had valuta and needed a coat, so she took a pencil
and piece of paper out of his dispatch-case and wrote the name of the
place where I could get one like it.

Next day I went there. There was only one possible coat but it was
still too short in the sleeves. Nina Gavrilovna did not seem to like my
wearing Kolya's coat, so I went back several times but could not make
up my mind to spend so much money on a coat that did not fit.

Kolya had brought back from England an obsession about fresh air,
and was proud that he was the only man among his acquaintances who
kept his phortochka open day and night. Alexander Ivanitch Tihomirov
told me that Max Müller had once come to Petersburg to lecture on
Fresh Air but had to postpone his lecture because he had lost his voice.
My experience was the same. I always woke up with a sore throat, but
it was a point of honour with Kolya not to close the phortochka.

Kolya had two other friends who taught English, besides Tihomirov
and Vera Garatinsky. Both of them, Yegunov and Lihachev, came of
wealthy families, who had governesses. Yegunov had had a Scottish
governess, whose Glasgow accents reproduced themselves in all his
pupils. Lihachev was in the navy and only settled in Leningrad during
the winter, when he taught at the Marine Academy. His English was
the strangest and the most fluent. Onto a precise bookish English he had
grafted a cosmopolitan sailor's slang derived from conversations in the
lingua franca at Baltic ports. He was never at a loss for a word. We only
got two roubles an hour for our classes and big deductions were made
for holidays. There were also 'voluntary' contributions, which were
compulsory; only Kolya did not pay them, as he disapproved on principle.

Alexander Ivanitch, in those days, was a bachelor with close-cropped
hair and a smart military appearance. He had been a Tsarist officer. He
was courtly and considerate. He described himself to my wife as 'very
Victorian'. But when he deplored the new ways, he did not mean
Bolshevism, but foxtrots, red fingernails, James Joyce. The Revolution
had been such an overwhelming experience that I doubt if he ever
criticized it, even to himself. All the same, to save his self-respect, he
permitted himself some tiny heresies, about women in public life, for
example. In most totalitarian creeds there is an unimportant corner, like
a game-reserve, retained for harmless scepticism and good-humoured

satire. Alexander Ivanitch knew his way about it perfectly and for some time appeared to me to be a highly emancipated person.

He had learnt English by the 'Williamson Method' and used to compare his face in a looking-glass with a series of enlarged coloured pictures of the mouth and tongue. He was very conscientious and wished to capture the spirit of the language as well as the idiom. In addition to the mouth-pictures he had a collection of English political speeches on gramophone records. Also he recited to me once a week a leader from *The Manchester Guardian*, which as an officer in the army he was permitted to take in.

He had other military privileges regarding rations of food and clothing, which he shared generously with his friends and the two devoted old ladies who looked after him. He lived in a stuffy room above a tailor's shop. It smelt of pot plants and leather and kvass. He used to put on a record just before my lesson, so as to get his ear into training. One unseasonably warm afternoon I walked with Lihachev towards his house. The loudspeakers on the street corners, which bawled out the feats of shock workers, were silent as if exhausted by the heat, and I was astounded to hear a cultured and fruity English voice echoing unchallenged through the narrow empty street. The voice came from Alexander Ivanitch's open window; it was Mr Asquith addressing a meeting in Edinburgh seventeen years before: 'We shall not sheathe the sword,' he was declaiming, 'till Belgium has recovered in full measure all and more than all that she has lost, till France. . .'

'It is rare and pleasant,' said Lihachev, 'to hear someone praise liberty who has dined well.'

Alexander Ivanitch was revising a pre-revolutionary grammar of English conversation. The questions of the new Russian tourist, instead of being inquisitive and pleasure-seeking, became didactic and uncompromising. He enquired about wages and factories instead of theatres and laundries. The rigours of his catechism were tempered by a strange jauntiness, in which Alexander Ivanitch took a special pride. 'Is a sportlike way of asking the time to say "What do you make the time?"' he enquired, 'and can one use the phrase "oneish twoish" without a preposition?'

I gave him his lessons under seal of secrecy, lest it should get about among rival teachers that he still had anything to learn. Slavs are too logical to value modesty or self-depreciation. 'If you yourself', they argue, 'think poorly of your faculties, they must be poor indeed.'

One day he told me to be very careful what I said to Nikolai Mihalitch. He was unreliable, he explained, and indiscreet. I did not mention that Kolya had given me similar warnings about him. I gathered that Alexander Ivanitch was in touch with the GPU (the Gaypayoo was the current name in 1931 for the Secret Police). In the end I came to the conclusion that almost all those whom I was able to see constantly had obtained the consent of the GPU and were under obligation to report my movements. I was flattered that they liked my company enough to go to this trouble, but I am sure that Alexander Ivanitch alone attempted a conscientious record of my unmemorable sayings and doings.

He was, in fact, the ideal spy. It was a disinterested pleasure to him to gossip, and it was a bonus for him to feel patriotic. He never did us any harm. Indeed, hovering on the edge of our little group, he was a kind of insurance that we should not be molested. He liked his lessons and wished us well. He once publicly refuted a rival teacher's allegation that I had 'a terrible Irish accent'.

Kolya had made out the curriculum for English literature in Techmass and Goskurs. It was very impressive. Every English writer who had written anything vaguely subversive was included. There were Kingsley's *Alton Locke*, Mrs Gaskell's *Mary Barton*, Charlotte Brontë's *Shirley*. Were these about the industrial revolution perhaps? But why Virginia Woolf, Aldous Huxley and E. M. Forster? Copies of the list were typed and I handed them round to my classes and asked them to bring what books they could. About twelve books came: some Byrons, Wildes, Galsworthys, and a book, author unknown, called *A Fairy Sits Upon My Knee*. A little Jewess, who, I had been told, was a political spy, brought in and insisted on reading a book by Mildred Cram about a man who married above himself in London society and did not know that you had to eat asparagus with your fingers. His wife tried to stifle the artistic side of his nature and eventually he flung it all up and returned to his old simple life. No other books could be found. As a result, most classes had to be improvised, and though my pupils were friendly and interested, there was no interval between the four classes, so by midnight I was often nearly speechless from exhaustion.

That winter the fortieth anniversary of Gorki's 'creative work' was being celebrated. Nizhni Novgorod was being rechristened Gorki, and a bombing aeroplane had been dedicated to him. Though we never talked of politics, we sometimes discussed 'ideology'. A woman said that Gorki was 'a gumanist' (our 'h' is 'g' in Russian) and that a bombing aeroplane would not please him much. I asked them to define 'gumanism'. A man said in English, 'It is what you say "namby-pamby".' The woman was not satisfied and began to protest. It appeared that about

half the class thought nambi-pambiness a good thing, but the political
spy, a kind of woman, who did not want trouble, proposed we go on
with Mildred Cram.

The classes were orderly and well arranged, the rooms clean and airy.
The Principal of Goskurs had once been Director of the Imperial Ballet
and all his staff except two or three were bourgeois, who had learnt
foreign languages from governesses and tutors. At the doorway sat
the political director, an Armenian called Guzelimian. Every time I
passed he examined me fiercely, as if he wished to catechize me;
he had a villainous peasant face and I hurried on pretending not to
notice him. One day when we were alone in the hall he beckoned me
over. 'When you go to England,' he said, 'will you get me a fishing-
rod?' Fumbling with his papers, he took out a picture. 'Like that. I
wanted to talk to you several times, but you looked so stiff I didn't
dare.'

The other teachers didn't talk to me but I felt an atmosphere of
friendliness and goodwill. Once, when a long corridor was empty, an
elderly man, who had never spoken to me, came up and presented me
with a book. 'This is my book,' he said. 'Don't tell anyone.' He bolted
before I had time to thank him. Whenever I passed him later, he
pretended not to see me.

The small blue volume was an excellent Russian-English dictionary
by C. K. Bojanus and V. K. Muller. Later Kolya told me that he was
Professor Bojanus himself, that he intended to marry Mrs Williamson
of the mouth-pictures and go with her to England, but did not want
to prejudice his chances of leaving Russia by any association with
foreigners.

Edmund Wilson (*New Yorker*, 20 April 1963) wrote that Bojanus was
liquidated and his name taken off the title page of the dictionary, but
the verb 'sostavili', 'composed', was left in the plural, though Muller is
named as sole author. I had previously heard that he escaped and worked
at the School of Slavonic Studies till he died. I reproach myself that I
never enquired about this kind, good man, or sent the fishing-rod to
Guzelimian.

Nina Gavrilovna was against me from the start and decided that I was
to blame for anything that went wrong in the flat. In Moscow I had
been given a sixteenth-century ikon of John the Baptist by Leonid
Leonov, whose book *The Thief* I had translated, and one day I showed
it to Kolya, who promptly hung it on the wall. His mother, seeing it
when Kolya was out, was appalled. 'What will his pupils say? It's pearls

before swine.' She laid the ikon reverently in the laundry-basket. When Kolya came back and saw the gap on the wall he marched unerringly to the laundry-basket. The ikon came in and out of the basket several times. Then I said to Kolya, 'I'm a nuisance here. I'd better find a room elsewhere.'

He flared up, 'Are you not comfortable here? No one would have you except me; they would be frightened even if they had room. And at the hotel you would have to pay two pounds a day. My mother will be going to Luga soon. At the New Year I will arrange that we take a few days' holiday and go on an excursion with Lihachev and Yegunov to the South. I will arrange to get teachers' tickets.'

All the same I put several advertisements in the papers and got some replies. I went round to the addresses. Nobody wanted to be paid. In fact money meant very little in Leningrad; they lost all interest in me when they heard I was not a foreign engineer, paid in valuta, and entitled to meal tickets at Quisisana, the Insnab restaurant (Insnab meant Inostranni Snabzheniye or Foreign Provision). One woman thought that as a foreign engineer I would be able to get her coat lined at Torgsin. One letter I did not answer. It was from a Pole called Vaishlé, who offered me a bed in his living-room. His aunt used it in the daytime, but she worked in the post office at night. It would be empty then and I could use it free, if I would help him read an English book on geology. One day when I came back from giving Alexander Ivanitch his lesson, I found Kolya entertaining the Pole, a small fat jolly man. He had brought his lunch and his geology book under his arm. 'I thought you might be too shy to come, so I came instead.' I was relieved to find that in the last resort there was someone in Leningrad eager to house me, and I offered to read some geology with him then and there. As he left, he said, 'I'm in this neighbourhood once or twice a week. I'll just call round and we'll read a bit of geology and I'll promise to keep my aunt's bed free for you.'

I agreed to this arrangement as a sort of retaining fee, and every now and then he came round. He always brought his lunch, but sometimes he came without his geology book just for a talk. Being a Pole, he was the first person I met willing to admit that I was an Irishman. He was greatly interested and told me that Daniel O'Connell's great grand daughter was working in a large china factory on the Neva. He seemed to take it for granted at his first glance at my surroundings that for an Irishman to live in a Russian family was a chemical experiment that might or might not succeed. 'How are things going?' he would ask. 'Remember my aunt's bed is always free.' Once, as he left, he clasped my hand and said: 'You know Russians are Asiatics, they don't understand comfort. I advise you to come to us.'

I had some £25 worth of black roubles, given me by an English sociologist who was staying at the British Embassy. He was going home and no longer needed them. So often I would ask Kolya out to lunch at one of the tourist hotels. After the season the fare was always the same. We had only one course. At the Europa there was a rich-looking paté made of game in aspic, at the October a fish called 'sudak' with Sauce Tartare. Except for ourselves and one waiter, the large dining-rooms were usually empty. The restaurant at the October was below street level and beggars would crouch on the road outside and stretch in supplicating hands through the ventilators. Kolya came reluctantly or else refused. He was very proud. When I pressed him into coming, in order to show that he had not refused from fear of being compromised, he would talk loudly in English criticizing the Soviet régime. I think he was flattered when one day an old woman came up to us outside the October and said: 'Messieurs, votre roi est le cousin de notre empereur.' He gave her a few kopecks. The old woman looked at them for a moment in hurt perplexity and then stuffed them quickly in her skirt.

In the end I believe it was the Pole and not hunger that prevailed upon Kolya to apply for a first-category food ticket. Though I was the cause of so much trouble, he wanted me to stay. He said one evening: 'I am becoming a "naoochny rabotnik". I have arranged that tomorrow there will be a proper English breakfast. There will be porridge and scrambled eggs.' And next morning Lyubotchka produced a thin custardy substance and 'grechnevaya kasha', a sort of gruel made of buckwheat. The buckwheat only lasted a week, for, learning that Kolya was a naoochny rabotnik, Nadya, one of Kolya's predatory relations, made a claim on it. 'There will be just scrambled eggs,' he said, 'but that will be a change, which is always nice.' 'Yes,' I agreed, 'but next time couldn't Nadya have the change and let us have the buckwheat?'

But he was totally indifferent to food. Once he gave up his sugar ration for a whole month so that he could buy the works of Dorothy Wordsworth, of which a consignment had reached Leningrad.

One day the first snow came and the waters in the canals moved turbidly below a film of ice. Lihachev, who had been in Armenia, was back and we talked of going to ski at Pavlovsk. Everybody became cheerful and excited, the streets were gay and sparkling, and tiny children, so tightly buttoned into shubas that they looked like small sheep, pulled each other about in packing cases in the Yekaterinsky Sad. Once or twice a week we had free evenings and there were theatres and ballets and impromptu parties.

I was the only one who could buy at Torgsin, the foreign currency shop, but my black roubles were running out so I seldom went there or to the hotels. But for our parties I got bottles of sweet Caucasian wine. I had a pupil behind the counter who helped me dodge the queues. In the markets there was always plenty of bread, and different delicacies swept over the city in waves; honey or cheese or stiff black cranberry jam crowded the shops for a few weeks and then disappeared in a night as quickly as they had come. Instead came sock suspenders or celluloid tooth-brush cases and, in the window, a red cloth with a bust of Lenin on it. There were no containers for the honey and Kolya in his English mood refused to carry his jug in his hand down the Nevsky. Inevitably, Nina Gavrilovna blamed it on me that everything in his attaché case, books and lecture notes, was covered in honey.

Baroness Garatinsky came back from a visit to her son, who was imprisoned in Solovietsky Island; every day for five minutes she was allowed with all the other visitors into a long corridor, where behind an iron railing their relations were waiting to see them. So as to be heard, each tried to talk louder than his neighbour and, when it was impossible, they had to communicate by gestures. 'I felt we had stopped being human and become monkeys. Perhaps we have always been monkeys.'

Lihachev usually came with Yegunov, who taught English with him at the Marine Academy. He was a Greek scholar and had translated *Aethiopika*, a third-century Alexandrian novel by Heliodorus. As far as I could judge, Yegunov's translation and its ninety-page introduction would have brought him distinction in England. He was now translating Plato's *Timaeus*, also for the Academia Press, but hesitated to publish it. 'Two friends of mine,' he explained, 'were overheard at a party setting Plato above Karl Marx and they were banished from Leningrad.' 'Don't risk it then,' I said. 'Well, it was not so bad for them,' he answered doubtfully, 'they were unemployed stage managers and they were sent to Orel, where, as it happened, they got jobs straightaway in a new theatre. They sneak back to Leningrad, when they can. But I could not bear to leave Leningrad.' For though Leningrad is the least typical of Russian cities, its citizens love it as Parisians love Paris. They are unhappy away from its grave and charming avenues and gardens, its cold northern sunsets.

Yegunov had tuberculosis. Peter the Great built his city on a marsh for wealthy aristocrats with fur coats and servants with warming-pans

and stoves, or else for tough mouzhiks, who would warm themselves
with labour and vodka. A generation ago the remnants of a well-to-do
bourgeoisie lived there without fuel or fur coats to interpose between
themselves and the raw and foggy winters. How could they not get
tuberculosis?

Lihachev was always cheerful. His father had been a wealthy doctor,
who, at the outbreak of the Revolution, had invited all his relations and
friends to share his two-storied house so that they need not have strangers
forced on them. They had brought all their most cherished furniture
with them. Two uncles had been in the consular service in Africa and
had crammed the rooms with bamboo and bark and bronze and stamped
leather. He told me that when they had all in the old days lived in
different parts of Petrograd, they travelled long distances to quarrel with
each other. 'Now it's so easy, there's no sport in it.'

One day in October we were eating raw herring and scrambled eggs,
and having the last drop of the brandy flask I had brought from Ireland,
when the telephone rang. It was a girl, in the flat above. She said she
was a pupil of Kolya's at the Oriental Institute and, as they were having
a party and short of 'cavaliers', would we come up and join them? Kolya
said he had friends with him. 'Well, bring them all,' she said, so we all
trooped upstairs.

The girl opened the door herself, but when she let go the doorhandle
she slipped backwards and would have fallen if she had not clutched at
Kolya. A girlfriend beside her was scarcely steadier on her feet and,
when at last we got into the room, we saw the reason. It was an infinitely
more luxurious flat than ours, with pre-revolutionary candelabras, family
portraits and wall-hangings, and a long table heaped with grapes and
pineapples, every variety of wine and liqueur and plates full of appetizing
food. There were men in morning coats and ladies in evening dress. It
was astonishing to come from our bleak, dark and damp quarters and
to discover so much light and luxury a few feet above us, and in a room
the same size and shape as ours. Half dazed, I flopped into a chair beside
a plump lady with enormous ear-rings, who poured me out some
curaçao and talked to me in faultless English about Ilfracombe. Then
someone told me it was a wedding, and the bridegroom came and asked
me very pleasantly to bring up my curaçao and come to dance in the
next room. It was very small and corresponded to one of the factory
workers' rooms down below. Lihachev was foxtrotting in the tiny floor
and I found a partner and joined him. It was hot and uncomfortable and
I sensed that something was wrong, but I could not tell what or why.
Suddenly I discovered that the tension, which I had detected, was

emanating in dense waves from Kolya, who sat scowling on a sofa beside Yegunov. My partner suggested that we should stop and sample some of the delicious food and I gratefully agreed. Then I saw Kolya talking in a very haughty way to a lady, who I assumed to be the hostess, and who looked embarrassed. All at once he got up and swept us along with him in a puzzled, disapproving crocodile, making it difficult for us to say any thank-yous or goodbyes.

It was not until I got downstairs that I understood what had happened. The two girls, the bride and her friend, both of them Kolya's pupils and both drunk, had dared each other to ask their romantic-looking teacher to the wedding party. Brimfull of hospitality and alcohol, the bride had chortled excitedly down the telephone without thinking of consulting her Mama. She must have been appalled when, instead of the glittering cavaliers she expected, four frowsy intellectuals in shabby suits turned up. Lihachev was the best of us because he was still in his naval uniform. But the bride's mother, a dignified lady with grey hair, came up to Kolya and explained that there had been 'a little misunderstanding': 'We're not the sort of people, you know, who just ask anyone to our family functions.' Kolya had snapped back loudly that it was no pleasure for him to come but the bride had been so pressing on the telephone. A stunned silence of embarrassment fell on the wedding party for two minutes and then was skilfully dispelled by a tornado of convivial noises as we trooped away down the stairs.

Once or twice my pupils invited me to birthday parties. They were mostly easy and pleasant and uneventful. Why does one remember the embarrassing occasions best? There was Olga N. and her mother, bourgeois, still only half-adjusted to the new régime. Kolya and I arrived at her birthday party with a cake I had chosen with care at Torgsin, covered with crystallized cherries, and I was disappointed when Olga, not looking at it, grandly told the maid to put it with a pile of other unopened presents on the piano. She was a prize pupil of mine and prattled away in a low, quiet, self-important voice in very literary English. When we came in, the mother was saying, 'Oh dear, not enough tea-spoons! Where can the wretched girl have put the spoons?' Olga then said to the company in English: 'My Mother had formerly four dozen tea-spoons, but she was forced to sell three dozen. She is very old fashioned and now greatly regrets the deprivation and cannot reconcile herself to the loss. Consequently she resorts to little subterfuges such as you have just heard.' She herself was worried about the buttons on her blouse. The little red ornaments on them were wearing out, but, because they were enamel, couldn't be painted in, so she was getting a friend, a chemical engineer, to help. He was first of all going to scoop out the centres, and then...

These are the things we talked about in Leningrad in 1931: spoons, buttons, macaroni, galoshes, macaroni again. I don't believe I ever heard anyone mention Magnetogorsk or the liquidation of the Kulaks or any of the remote and monstrous contemporary happenings to which by a complicated chain of causes our lifestyle and our macaroni were linked.

Communism is said to inspire a dull uniformity, but Lihachev, who was quite unpolitical, was always seeking and finding coloured variations. In his rooms I met Negro communists and Turks, Tartars and Kirghiz, and one day he took me to the Hispano-American Society. It was held in the room of a Mexican communist, a lady, who dreaded the Russian winter. In the autumn she had shut herself and her family into her room and sealed up the large double window and the phortochka, and then fought the domestic and personal smells with powerful scents. It was not yet mid-winter, but it was plain to all the battle had been lost. Lilies and jasmine had been routed by an appalling primeval smell that was neither Slav nor Latin. Lihachev said it was Aztec. The lady introduced me to a celebrated Mexican writer, but talking meant breathing, and I appeared to him to be dumb, and he went over to Lihachev. For Lihachev, as I heard long afterwards, it proved to be a disastrous meeting. The Mexican was charmed with him, and when he went home he sent his book on Communism for Lihachev to review. Unfortunately the book had Trotskyite tendencies and he was compromised by receiving it. He was dismissed from the navy and he became a literary freelance compiling anthologies of foreign poetry, always lively and occupied. In a large new sombrero, he visited all the Leningrad publishing houses and got contracts.

That was the last I heard of him, but before I left Leningrad Vera Garatinsky had told me that in a couple of years there would be enough English-speaking proletarians to replace all the bourgeois teachers and guides and translators. 'That will be the end of us,' she said. 'It's that accursed English woman and her method. Don't let them invent any more clever methods over there, please.'

My way to Goskurs lay along the Moika, the little river that ran from the Winter Palace under the Nevsky and the Vosnesensky to the Neva. It had been a very aristocratic district once. On the far side, in a pale green eighteenth-century house, Pushkin had lived and had died painfully after a fatal duel. The quays and surrounding streets were almost deserted in the winter evenings, and very quiet except for my galoshes slapping loosely on the pavements. In the marsh air the northern sunset quivered from time to time as if it was trapped between the beautiful impassive houses. In the daytime the red proletarian trimmings held the eye and the mind, but in the twilight different obsessions replaced them.

Before I went to Russia, I had been reading Dostoievsky's *The Idiot*. It is the story of passionate people pursuing each other through the streets of St Petersburg, with love, with hate, with revolvers or bundles of roubles. Their feelings and their motives are often obscure, and Dostoievsky, standing outside his own creations, suggests different explanations of their behaviour. Through this, his characters have the freshness of reality, for mostly we only guess at other peoples' minds. Prince Muishkin, the Idiot, is the still centre of the hurricane, the personification of Dostoievsky's belief that 'the Russian heart is more adapted to universal brotherly friendship than that of any other nation'. And indeed perhaps the Russians are more perceptive and, when it is in their power, more ready than others to make allowances for the failures they perceive. The first people to give Prince Muishkin hospitality, when he arrived poor and shabby in St Petersburg, were the Epanchins, who lived in a large house on the broad bustling Sadovaya, where I caught the tram for my classes. Muishkin was at peace with himself and, despite his simplicity, this gave him a strange authority over others. To Dostoievsky he was the symbol of Russia's unconscious, unexercised power.

I do not believe that the creations of genius die without issue or that, because of a change of government, cities start to breed a different type of man. They dress differently and feed differently, and that is all.

Great writers interpret men to each other by example and analogy. The creative imagination ebbs and flows with some degree of constancy. On the one hand all men have common needs, passions, hopes, which society has to satisfy; on the other hand every man is unique and he must so manipulate society that his nature is fulfilled. The great Russian writers, Tolstoy, Dostoievsky, Chekhov, were almost always more conscious of diversity of temperament than of uniformity of needs. Then Karl Marx and the Revolution created the Economic Man, and while this wonderfully lifelike dummy is in the shop window, what hope is there for the genius that is kindled by human diversity? The fact that there are vast editions of the classics published and sold out keeps the flame alive but cannot fan it.

I once tried to talk about these things at Goskurs during the dangerous half-hour of free conversation, when my pupils and I, under cover of grammar, tried to find out what we were like. One of them helped me out with a cliché, 'ghosts of the past', which quenched what I had to say, and instead I said that Petersburg, like Alexandria and Constantinople, had the tremendous toughness of cities that were built round an idea, not a market. Peter's 'window upon Europe' had been made for autocrats and bureaucrats, but once opened it could not be shut. Marx came through as well as Dickens and Byron and George Sand and Henry George and all the strange assortment of foreign influences. Tolstoy, no less than Dostoievsky the Slavophile, had hated Petersburg and its Western culture, as the oyster hates the foreign body it turns into a pearl, but they could not ignore it. And what they had accepted and adorned, their successors could still less ignore.

The weather was getting foggy. Most Russians had sealed up their windows, but whenever I shut the phortochka Kolya opened it again. Fresh air was one of his cherished English traditions, about which he was very sensitive. His love of England was a substitute for religion and I knew that his welcome to me derived from it. There was a legend in Techmass about his 'English reserve', but in fact there was nothing English about it. He was normally impetuous and enthusiastic but in his English mood he alternated between a cold animal torpor and a passionate misanthropy. 'English dissent and socialism,' I said, 'are based on an accidental tepidity or, if you like, sobriety of temperament. Your emotional heterodoxy is something quite different.' I would not have risked saying this but my cold was getting worse and I was scared of getting stranded in Leningrad with bronchitis. The next time I shut the phortochka he looked stern but left it shut.

Once, when I was sitting over my sudak in the October, an Oxford acquaintance, John Lane-Tuckey and his wife, a sleek, self-satisfied university couple, came by. They were tired of crèches and clinics and wanted to see 'real Russians'. It seemed obvious to ask them back and Kolya was pleased. But the moment they came into the room I saw it was a mistake. John asked light ironical questions about Soviet economics – he was a sociologist. Barbara, his wife, was silent, clearly horrified by the squalor of the flat. Something in their manner and appearance turned Kolya into a pillar of Marxist orthodoxy. His open friendliness dropped and he talked to them as if he was giving copy to journalists. I took them back to their hotel. 'But you can't go on living there,' Barbara Lane-Tuckey said, 'the smell, the dark!' She was kind and worried and pressed on me what they'd brought from England and no longer needed, a packet of lump sugar, three lemons and a bottle of hydrogen peroxide to gargle. I felt unsettled, like a child at school who has had a visit from home. I tried to come back into the flat as if it was for the first time, so

as to experience what they had seen and smelt. Yes, it was unbelievable.
I shut up the provisions in my trunk. Neither of us referred to the Lane-
Tuckeys again.

Kolya had appalling moments of self-criticism. Soon after this he
stayed up a whole night reading *A Passage to India*. Closing the book at
breakfast-time, he said, 'I'm like Aziz. I'm an Asiatic.' He was sombre
the entire day, but he felt he had given himself away too much, for a
little later he started to refer to Lyubotchka as 'the maid' and to give
her lessons in waiting at table. She was always terrified of him when he
was being English. He instructed her in a cool, bitter, military voice:
'All over again till you get it right, please.' Lyubotchka reacted as if to
electric shocks. She started to jerk and dart about like a rabbit, her eyes
glazed with fear. Eating, which she had done all her life, suddenly
became black magic.

When I found someone had been rummaging in my suitcase, I kept
count of the lumps of sugar and chocolate, and found two or three pieces
disappeared every day. They were precious as gold to me in case I got
ill and couldn't go out to buy food. Nina Gavrilovna used to do all their
shopping in the market, and if I asked her to go to Torgsin, the foreign
currency shop, people might think she had been receiving valuta from
abroad or hoarding jewellery.

One day a golden-haired cousin of Kolya's called, all charm and
friendliness, but Kolya was nervous and abrupt. He obviously wanted
her to go, but she stayed on. At last she turned to me and said, 'I wonder
if...?' Kolya shot up into the air and came between us, clenching his
fists: 'No, that I forbid you to ask him! That you shall not ask! No!' She
shrugged her shoulders and left, followed by Kolya raging. The hall
door slammed. After a bit the girl came back with a bottle in her hand.
'I wanted to ask you if I could have a drop of peroxide for my hair?'

When Kolya came back I told him that she was welcome to my
peroxide but I thought Lyubotchka was stealing things out of my trunk.
He became very solemn: 'The matter must be brought before the
House Committee.' That evening the curtain flapped ceaselessly over his
mother's recess. The murmur of conversation never ceased. When Kolya
went out, she emerged and asked me if I wasn't ashamed, a greedy
foreigner, who cheated on the currency and had fine meals in the Europa,
to count lumps of sugar and persecute a poor servant-girl? And I had
lemons in my trunk too, and chocolate.

'How did you know I had lemons in my trunk?' I couldn't stop myself
asking. Oh, she crowed, she'd been digging in my trunk had she? What
would Kolya say when he heard I accused his mother of being a thief?

This I could not answer. My Russian was not good enough for me to pick my way through the tangle of misunderstandings. 'And Kolya has given up his translating in order to show you the way round Leningrad. You don't even pay for your lodgings.'

I tried to explain the arrangement Kolya and I had come to, adding, 'Perhaps he didn't fully understand?'

'So he didn't understand? He can't understand English can he? He speaks it as well as you do, if not better. That'll be news to him he can't speak English.' And then she produced her trump card. 'If the GPU knew you have black roubles... Russians have been shot for less!'

At this moment the Pole came to the door. He was very apologetic for interrupting and sincerely anxious that we go on with our quarrel and not mind him. Nina Gavrilovna went out and he produced a slip of paper and explained to me how many weeks I had earned by my translations to use his aunt's bed. But chiefly he had come to ask me to a party. He gave a ceremonious bow. It was for the Fifteenth Anniversary of the Revolution; it was going to be a very special party. I accepted and he told me I would get a formal invitation in a day or two. I had an almost permanent cold now and I kept on wondering what would happen if either the aunt or I got ill. I wished I had paid more attention to the conducted tours round infirmaries and hospitals.

When Kolya came home that night, his mother drew him behind her curtain. Then I heard him leave. He did not come back that night or the following morning. Then the telephone started to ring as it had the first day I spent in Chernyshev Pereulok, and I answered the pupils as his mother had done, 'Ne doma. Ne znaioo.'

He came back in the evening. 'I can't stay in the house with you any longer,' he said. 'I'm going to Lihachev's.' He began to pack a suitcase.

'If you think I'm to blame, I'll go.'

'You've nowhere to go.'

'I'll find somewhere!' I jumped up and put on my coat and hat and, seizing my suitcase, walked out of the room.

Kolya was out of his mind. 'That's my coat,' he said. 'I can't trust you to bring it back. You must leave your suitcase behind instead.'

I threw the suitcase down and flung the coat at him too, in a rage. When I was half-way down the stairs, the door of the flat opened and his mother came running after me. 'Come back,' she said, 'he just lost his temper. He hasn't had anything to eat all day.'

'No, I won't come back.'

'Please come back. If the GPU hears that Kolya turned you out, he'll get into trouble.'

'They won't hear.'

It was not until I was in the street that I realized I had left my passport in Kolya's coat, but nothing would have induced me to return.

Leningrad was very badly lit in the evenings and the directions hard to follow, as the new street names were usually too long to use. The Nevsky, for example, was never called its proper name, October Twenty-Fifth Street. At so late an hour I hesitated to go to Yegunov, who lived nearby. He had a single room in a vast tenement house, honeycombed with arches and passages, the entries blocked with stacks of firewood and stinking rubbish-heaps, and every arch and entry looked alike. The Pole's house was in the outskirts of the city in the Narva district, and I knew I would never find it.

There was a thin coat of snow in the Nevsky that flung back the light of the lamps. All the passers-by had on shubas, or leather coats, except for a few beggars in the archways and the old general standing as always with his tray of transfers and celluloid toothbrush cases outside the Moscow Station. Yet in spite of the snow I was so angry and excited I did not feel cold. I walked up and down the Nevsky enquiring at all the hotels, big and small. They would none of them take me. They were full up with delegates from the provinces for the Fifteenth Anniversary. In any case, as I was registered in a private house, I would have first to get my registration cancelled at the police station, and that had closed three hours earlier. At the Gostiny Dvor, the big shopping-centre between the Nevsky and the Sadovya, I ate some pirozhkies, hot cabbage pies, at a stall. There were lights in the Kazan Cathedral, where the finishing touches were being put to an historical exhibition, and outside workmen on scaffolding were nailing up strips of red cloth for the celebrations. Some others were sitting round a brazier eating food out of parcels.

Opposite the Kazan Cathedral was the British Consulate. Mr Bullard, whom I knew, got his food from a London shop. He had deep armchairs and a roaring fire. Several times I had dropped in for a chat and a cup of tea and Huntley and Palmer chocolate biscuits. He was friendly but did not approve, any more than the Russians did, of fraternization. Kolya told me that he had tried to take Connie Archangelsky's passport from her because she was married to a Russian. Rumour said that there was always someone lurking by the cathedral steps making a note of his visitors. He had good manners and would be able to dissemble his satisfaction at seeing somebody paid out for staying in a Russian family.

He himself only met official Russians and had to go to Finland to get Russian lessons.

I could easily persuade myself that I had an official claim on him, but I loathed going to him, as I would to the GPU. I thought I had the courage and skill to treat most human problems as personal ones, but the moment I appealed to authority to help me out I was like a man on a tightrope who thinks of falling. Could I convince myself that the consul was a friend as well as an official? I hesitated and all at once the light went out in the consulate. My mind was made up.

I rang the bell on the first landing, but there was no answer. I rang again and knocked. After half an hour of waiting I came down into the street. I walked on towards the Admiralty and sweeping aside by St Isaac's I tried the Astoria and finally ended up on the Neva. It was no good. When I got back to the Kazan Cathedral I was shivering with cold and the workmen round the brazier whom I intended to ask for a night's lodgings had gone. I walked back to the consulate and banged at all the doors in the building. Bullard emerged from one of them. 'You were knocking at the offices, which closed at four,' he explained. 'The private part of the house is on this side.'

I had no self-reproaches as I got into bed, for I was persuaded that I was going to be desperately ill.

The next morning I woke up feeling remarkably well. I had an English breakfast with eggs and bacon, marmalade and toast and coffee. Afterwards I went out and bought the commissar's coat with the short sleeves. The sun was shining. The palaces on the canals, freshly colour-washed in buff or pink, were framed in snow and draped with broad red banners. I felt wonderfully detached from it all. The palaces wore their banners with the patient suffering look of domestic pets wearing bows for a birthday party. About everything there was an impromptu, impermanent and almost innocent look.

It was with a feeling of insolent well-being that I returned to Chernishev Pereulok. After I had rung the bell I felt ashamed of my new coat and folded it into a bundle. Kolya was in bed. We were polite and constrained. He handed me a postcard from Vaishlé, the Pole. 'Gubert Georgievitch. Congratulations on the Fifteenth Anniversary of Socialist Construction and the termination of the fourth year of the five-year plan! I also invite you to my house for the latter half of tomorrow, the first day of the holidays.'

The kitchen was full of smoke, for everybody in the flat was having a bath for the Anniversary. No one trusted the cleanliness of the bath itself but put a stool inside and balanced a basin of hot water on the stool. Darya Andreyevna even placed in it a trough for her feet. I used to prefer to wash in the communal baths, where there was constant hot water and elderly people lashed themselves with birch twigs.

Darya Andreyevna was going to lead the procession for the theatre. Kolya was marching for the Oriental Institute. The Director of Techmass had rung up to find if I would march with them, but I had been out and did not know where to meet them. Kolya, instead of being flippant as he usually was about processions, was important and treated me as if I was Lane-Tuckey. I would never be forgiven that night at the consulate. As we went out he made a stately, unfriendly apology. He had been in a Manichean mood, he said. He insisted that I should come back that night. I agreed I would and said that I would see that his wife Connie in Eastbourne would get the same rent that he had to pay when he worked for the Soviet Embassy and lived in Torrington Square, but I said I must have the phortochka shut. We discussed the matter in a business-like way, as if Chernishev Pereulok was in fact a Bloomsbury lodging-house.

As we were going down the stairs we met the Pole coming up. He had a big peony in his buttonhole with slogans stamped in gold on each petal. 'I came to see if you had got my invitation', he said. 'Yes, and I'm coming.' 'Good! And I brought you this.'

It was another letter. Handing it to me, he bolted down the stairs and disappeared. When I unstuck it, a packet of roubles tumbled out with a note: 'Lent for an indefinite period, in case you are short for the celebration of the Fifteenth Anniversary of Socialist Construction.' I went to Torgsin and bought some bottles of wine to take to the party.

It was difficult pressing my way through the crowds in the Nevsky and, at the corner of the Sadovya, I was brought to a halt by a fresh tributary coming in from the Neva docks and the English Quay. I had to wait there wedged against a parapet for several hours. I was told that a million men and women passed along the Nevsky that day. In each group of this endless procession two men on either flank held up a flapping red streamer with a slogan on it, or grotesque figures of European statesmen. It was fully an hour before the students' and teachers' procession passed. I wanted to see if there was anyone I knew, and how they were affected by this performance. Organized in processions, those whom we have known as complex individuals shed colour and character. Also there is some unconscious tabu that we violate every time we look at our friends in their public moments, which are often the moments of deepest privacy. The violation may be easy and pleasant, but it delays us for that split second between perceiving and observing. Kolya passed close by but not till he had gone did I realize that I had seen him. A column of sailors went by and I looked in vain for Lihachev. A little later I noticed a dislocation in the procession, people moderating their step behind and on either side of the baroness. She walked slowly enough for me to watch her. Her companions on either side, keeping step, held a pole from which a banner was stretched: WE ARE MARCHING TOWARDS THE CONQUEST OF TECHNICAL EFFICIENCY IN A SOCIALIST WORLD. She did not look either ironical or embarrassed. It was as if she was half asleep but sufficiently awake to enjoy her dream. She did not seem conscious of her lameness, imposing her pace with confidence on those around her.

I have thought that just as half our physical lives passes in sleep, it is perhaps intended that our mental life should be equally distributed between the assertion of our uniqueness and its renunciation. If that trance-like state of submersion in a public or collective mood bears an analogy to sleep, it would reflect our individual and self-centred lives by very simple images and phrases in dream-like sequences. In such a way, the caricatures and slogans that floated above them would complement, like dreams, the intricate, logical natures of Kolya and the baroness. The slogans were the shadows of human thinking in which their thoughts merged restfully, just as their footsteps concurred in the broad beaten track upon the snow, and we do not expect faithfulness in tone or form or colour from shadows.

All I remember of the Pole's party is the food and a tall thin guest with a bald head, a geologist like Vaishlé. As he shook hands, he said, 'I am bald and thin because I think very much; my Polish friend is round and jolly because he never thinks. I have been prospecting in Turkestan and I will show you some photographs. Later still I will recite you some poems of the French poet, Béranger.' All happened as he predicted. As for the food, there were golubtsi (mince and rice wrapped in cabbage leaves and fried), hard cakes covered with stewed apple, soft cakes covered with poppy seeds, glasses of vodka mixed with lemonade and chilis. I saw the aunt and her bed, but I had decided to leave Russia and the desperate significance they would have had for me a week before was no longer there.

The last few weeks before the schools closed I spent at Chernishev Pereulok. Kolya submerged himself in his translation of Lenin and began to take his Communism and his professional functions much more seriously. I was a foreign critic now not a friend and he would step

coldly from argument to argument, like rungs on a ladder. His English
obsession only flared up now and again, as when every Saturday he laid
a neat bill on my bed for me to forward to my wife. Several times we
made up parties to Sestroretsk or Pavlovsk or Gatchina. He was never
unfriendly but he had become a different person, conscientious, informative and rather dull. He provoked in me all the qualities I had detested
in the Lane-Tuckeys.

I took many solitary walks under the lovely alleys of lime and maple
round Leningrad. Lihachev was away but sometimes Yegunov came
with me. He had a big dog which was in the stud book and therefore
had a ration book of its own, and despite the rigours of the Five-Year-
Plan ate more than its master. We usually exercised it in the Kamenny
Ostrov, the island in the Neva, where the wealthy merchant families,
whose houses are now rest-homes and hospitals, once lived. It was criss-
crossed by little birch-lined canals and bridges. Sometimes I went with
one or two of my pupils to the Yussupov Palace, to which as a teacher
I had access. It was a Students' Recreation Centre, with rooms for chess
and cards and billiards. It had also a small theatre. Down in the basement
in the winter of 1916 Rasputin, who was hard to kill, was beaten to
death by Prince Yussupov and his companions. The vast china chandelier
in the hall surely dated from those days. There were robins and canaries
perched on its branches, which dripped with blue convolvulus.

For my last evening Kolya decided to have a party and, setting enough
money aside for my droshki to the station, I gave him the remainder of
my roubles. I was pleased when he said, 'I will arrange it all,' and then
spent more than half on smoked fish, a favourite delicacy of his. It was
like a return to ordinary humanity. Lihachev was back home again and
when our guests had gone in the early morning, he and Yegunov spread
their shubas on the floor and slept on them. My train left very early, so
I did not bother to sleep. Kolya and I left without rousing the others.

At the station, the Pole and Guzelimian and Tihomirov and two of
my pupils were waiting. The Pole gave me a box of liqueur chocolates,
Guzelimian asked me to remember his fishing-rod. Then there suddenly
flashed into my mind, 'My blue carriage rug!' I exclaimed aloud, and
promptly Kolya said, 'I'll fetch it!' and darted away. I shouted after him,
'For God's sake keep it!' but I paused for one greedy moment before I
said this and I was too late. The blue rug, which I had brought from
Ireland, had stood between me and pneumonia; now it meant nothing
to me, but it could have meant a great deal to the Archangelsksys. They
got it in the end, but how ungraciously.

I kept looking at the station entrance while the others were talking, because I was wondering how I could keep in touch with my Russian friends. Would it be safe to write letters to each other? Could we send newspapers? I had left all this to the last moment, for I intended to ask Kolya and hear him say, 'I will arrange.' But the train went out. Alexander Ivanitch and the Pole looked at the wheels, which meant, I had been told, that they wanted me to come back.

The train went through lonely swamp, thinly wooded with birch and alder. Here and there a solitary Soviet soldier guarded the line until, as we approached the frontier, the main roads slowly became cart tracks and petered out into grass and barbed-wire entanglements.

★

In the autumn of 1956 I went with seven other Irishmen on a 'cultural delegation' to China. On the way back I parted from the others in Moscow because I wished to go to Leningrad to see if any of my old friends were alive. As the translator of Leonov's *The Thief*, I had good contacts with the Union of Writers and, when I told them my reasons for wishing to go to Leningrad, I met with understanding. They said they would look out for a guide to take me on the night train the following day. But would I in the meantime give them a talk on Irish Writing? I went back to the Hotel National and spent the day in my room writing and was ready for my appointment with them in the afternoon. There were about a dozen people there, mostly teachers and translators. They asked me searching and intelligent questions. One of them was translating O'Casey's autobiographical series and he asked me to interpret a passage in O'Casey's idiosyncratic idiom, which always seemed to me to obscure what was otherwise lucid. I did badly but recovered a little of my credit when I said that in *Sunset and Evening Star* O'Casey had written a couple of friendly pages about me and the 'Insult' to the Papal Nuncio.

As I left them I was told that my guide, Anna Shelestova, would meet me at the National late that evening and take me on the night train to Leningrad. On the train I reflected on my chances of finding any of my friends alive. There was only a thin hope. What I had heard as rumour at home had been confirmed in Moscow. In 1934, three years after I had left, Kirov, the Leningrad Party Boss, whom many thought would be Stalin's successor, had been murdered. Foreign influence was suspected and many thousands of arrests were made on the flimsiest of evidence. I heard how the elderly vet who treated the German consul's dog, and the woman who sold eggs to the Polish consul, had been hauled off to prison. It was obvious that all foreign-language teachers would be under suspicion. Five years later the war had broken out, and after that came the invasion of Russia and the terrible siege of Leningrad. It was a forlorn hope.

Almost all my friends in Leningrad had had telephones, so the first thing we did when we arrived was to look up their names in the telephone book. Only one familiar name was there, the one I most wanted to see, Nikolai Mihalitch Archangelsky. He was not in Chernishev Pereulok but in the southern suburb of Narva. When Anna telephoned, a female voice said that he was out but would be back at two.

We leapt into a cab and, as Anna was a native of Leningrad, we quickly found the Archangelsky's flat. It was in a large new tenement block and No. 32 was on the third storey. When the door was opened by a big blowsy woman, there was a babel of children's voices and kitchen smells. She did not ask us in but said that if we cared to wait, Nikolai Mihalitch would be along in twenty minutes. 'Does he still work at the Oriental Institute?' I asked. 'No, he works at the Kirov Factory.' 'That was the Putilov in your time,' interjected Anna. 'Does he write at all now?' I asked. The woman looked puzzled. 'He's an engineer,' she said. It took me a moment to grasp that there were two Nikolai Mihalitch Archangelskys, and that this was the wrong one. I could not stay there a second longer. 'Let's at least try Chernishev Pereulok,' I said to Anna. My disappointment had turned into relief, for the Nikolai Mihalitch I knew would have been miserable in such surroundings.

I was no help to Anna in finding our way to Chernishev Pereulok. All the familiar landmarks had gone, and when we arrived and stopped at No. 59 I got out in perplexity. Even in the hallway it was different. The lift was working. Could these be the stairs that I had run down with Nina Gavrilovna shouting after me that night I had spent at the consul's? It was not possible. We went up in the lift all the same and stopped on the fifth floor.

Darya Andreyevna's mirror had gone and so had the mat. A stranger came to the door when I rang the bell. No, he had never heard of anyone called Nikolai Mihalitch Archangelsky, but there was a very old lady in the flat still who had been there since before the war. She might know. 'Is it Darya Andreyevna?' I asked. 'Yes, that's her name.' I described myself and he said he would find out if she would see me. He came back and said the old lady remembered me – an Englishman – but she was bedridden and did not want to see a strange man; she'd see the woman who came with me. So Anna went alone. I waited for a long time on the landing till Anna came out. She said Darya Andreyevna remembered the Archangelskys well. The mother had died and sometime in the mid-thirties Nikolai Mihalitch had been taken away to Gorohovaia Prison for quite a short period. He had come back and after three weeks had died in the flat.

I could not leave it like that. It seemed to me that Tihomirov, as a Red Army man, was the one who was likely to have survived the purge that followed Kirov's murder. By a strange chance I had in my notebook the number of the two old women with whom he lodged, and in a moment I was talking to the one who had survived. Yes, she remembered Alexander Ivanitch talking about me, the Englishman. 'Poor Alexander Ivanitch! He died you know three years ago. I always told him he drank too much coffee.' This seemed a very old-ladyish diagnosis, but I asked her did she remember Lihachev and Yegunov and Kolya. Indeed she did, but Alexander Ivanitch had not been seeing anything of them for a very long time before he died. 'How long?' 'Oh, maybe fifteen or twenty years ago. I think something may have happened to them.' She was not going to tell me more and maybe she did not know. When anyone went to prison in those days, their relations used to bring them parcels, until one day they were told no more parcels were necessary. You were not informed whether they had died or been moved to another prison.

I had learnt very much what I had expected to learn, which was nothing. I was sad not only for my friends but for anyone who leaves the world anonymously, surrounded by hostile or uncaring people.

Anna had done her best for me. There was still half a day. What would I like to see? I did not want to go sight-seeing, and in any case most of the Intourist sights had been destroyed by the Germans. The imperial palaces in the southern environs of the city, Peterhov, Gatchina, Pavlovsk, Tsarskoye Selo, had all lain in the path of the German advance and had been looted and burned. All the trees in their parks had been cut down. 'But we're restoring them,' said Anna, loyal to Intourism, 'and we're getting all the pictures and sculptures back again, or their equivalents. And we're replanted the trees.'

In the end she took me to a hill overlooking the city and the Gulf of Finland. There was a slot-machine telescope there and with a running commentary from Anna I turned it round. To the west I saw the island of Kronstadt and the wooded coast of Finland, and Anna told me how, backed by the Finns, the Germans had flung forty-five divisions against the city. After the victory at Kingisepp, in which her brother had died, they forced their way across the Estonian frontier, confident that the city would fall to them in a couple of days, but the siege had lasted twenty-nine months and had ended in a Russian victory. Moving the telescope towards the city, I saw the Nevsky Prospekt thrusting eastwards to the Champs de Mars. The biggest fire from the incendiary bombs, Anna said, had been in the Gostiny Dvor. That was the shopping-centre in the Nevsky where I had eaten pirozhkies the night I slept at the consulate. She told me about the famine and how her brother's family had eaten carpenter's glue and yeast with hot water, till the fierce winter of 1941–42 when they had made a road across the ice on Lake Ladoga and transported food across from the east. I traced the Neva till it veered southwards by the Finland Station and the Summer Palace. To the north I saw the islands where I had walked with Yegunov and his dog. They were now called the Kirov Islands, Anna told me, and the great highway that led to them was called Kirov Avenue. Thousands of honest men and women died because of Kirov, but their names are nowhere recorded.

I have forgotten much of what Anna told me but I am more inclined to apologize for writing about great events, which touched me not at all, than for tracing again the tiny snail track which I made myself.

Is it not obvious that when through the modern media far things are brought near, the near things must be pushed far to make room for them? Imperceptibly, we become Lilliputians wandering in a Brobdingnag of our own contrivances and persuading ourselves that through contact with greatness we ourselves become greater. Then something happens to jerk us back to thoughts and people of our own size and significance. Most of the time when I was looking through that telescope, I was thinking not of the tremendous disasters that had befallen Leningrad and all Russia, but of the small stupidities, the acts of laziness or greed I had committed myself. Why had I not given the blue rug to Kolya's mother instead of leaving it behind by mistake? Why hadn't I sent Guzelimian his fishing-rod?

[1984]

Nazor, Oroschatz and
the von Berks

———

At the beginning of a revolution artists and writers find themselves in a position of unaccustomed importance. Their support is eagerly canvassed, and it is very hard for them not to be flattered by these attentions. In Yugoslavia the writer must depend on a very small public, perhaps, owing to the differences of dialect within the country, on only a fraction of the reading public, which is not large. Even though some writers are of outstanding merit, they have very rarely been translated so that, when a writer parts with his country, he says good-bye, too, to his craft and his livelihood. Painters, sculptors and musicians are less tied by their medium, and a man like Mestrovich, with an international reputation, can choose his politics without reference to economic considerations: a writer can't.

A French writer, when asked to explain why certain artists collaborated in France, said 'Collaborate? But in politics artists are just children, you know!' It would be truer to say that artists are passionate individualists and there are certain temptations to which they succumb rather easily. They will tolerate any system which gives scope to their temperaments. They are restless, discontented people in modern democracies and are unusually open-minded in regard to any change.

Pavelitch[1] and his German patrons took very great pains to conciliate the artists and writers of Croatia; a novelist, Budak, was the first President, and a number of literary papers of excellent quality were produced. I do not think the artist was much molested at the start; for example, Krleza, the best-known Croatian dramatist, lived on peacefully through the Occupation in Zagreb, though a Communist. In the early numbers of *Spremnost* there are constant flattering articles about Mestrovich and Augustinchich, the sculptors, and Nazor the poet, and the most prominent of the Croatian painters. The articles hinted, often incorrectly, that the subject of their praise was a supporter of the government. Sometimes

226

the artist or writer responded to this flattery with an ode or a picture; sometimes he contributed something non-committal to the papers. That was good enough. The editors felt they had netted him. They did not insist on ideological conformity, his name was what they were after, and because of that these papers of the occupation have much admirable material in them.

There was a curious technique if the writer or artist did not respond at all to their advances. He suddenly found himself whipped off to prison for no reason he could understand... as suddenly he would be let out; soon after some friendly, casual person would come up and say to him, 'Oh by the way, I'm getting up an exhibition (or bringing out a new number), I'd be awfully pleased, old man, if you'd let me have something.' One artist told me that he was only able to resist this technique by pretending that his mind had been unhinged by prison. Very few said flatly, 'No'. But the painters had difficulty with paint or materials or found their inspiration drying up, the producers found the plays were quite impossible to cast. The mercurial artistic temperament was freely invoked and as it was wartime, there were often plausible excuses for doing nothing. Mestrovich, after he had been in prison for some weeks, found there was only one subject to which he could do justice at the moment. He must go to the Vatican and make some busts of the mediaeval Popes. He knew Pavelitch could not refuse so praiseworthy a suggestion. On the way there he was asked to accompany the Croatian exhibition to Venice where his sculpture was to be displayed. He did so. He then made the busts in Rome, got a visa to Switzerland through the Vatican, and never returned to Croatia.

Soon after the liberation a magazine was published in Zagreb with the intention of disconcerting the government. It published various odes and declamations, photographs, busts and pictures that had appeared under well-known names during the Occupation and in which the Ustashe and the Germans were glorified. The editor pointed out that these people were now ardent Partisans and supporters of the government. It was, I believe, the last freely critical paper published since the liberation and it was very quickly suppressed. I do not know whether the editor was making a gesture against corruption or whether he was being just malicious. What he proved, I think, was that while the power and influence of the creative mind is acknowledged, only unrepresentative governments are prepared to subsidize it. They invite the writers and artists to compensate with their enthusiasm for the frigidity of the electorate.

But it was not only creative minds that the Ustashe tried to buy, it was also cultivated and educated minds. With the collapse of several empires in 1918 a number of men, product of the wealth and leisure of this society, found themselves deprived of the climate in which their talents developed and needed to be maintained. I suppose they were considered greenhouse plants in a society which could not afford a greenhouse, but, as it turned out, their talents, which needed artifice and privilege for their development, were missed in a thousand ways in the new states. Alexander during his dictatorship made a great use of the Russian émigrés in Belgrade, and under Pavelitch in Zagreb the remnant of the Austro-Hungarian ascendancy, which was all but moribund, began to show signs of life; they were, I think, not quite so militant, embittered and combative as the Russians, their days of glory were further in the past, but they could not forget that Zagreb and Croatia had once been a great greenhouse for the forcing of their talents and that the civilization of the Croatian towns had been given an indelible stamp by the Austro-Hungarians. Probably it was the most idealistic and disinterested of them who took part in the new Croatia, the ambitious would find more scope under Hitler in Germany or Austria.

I can think of one Austro-Hungarian poet who for the first time in his life found in Pavelitch's Croatia an outlet for his remarkable gifts. As an Austrian, whose family had been connected for centuries with Croatia and Slovenia, he felt himself qualified to act as interpreter between Croat and Austrian and for three years he filled the Zagreb newspapers with remarkable poetry and prose. The new Croatia was as indulgent as it dared to the old ascendancy; its temper was romantic and pseudo-mediaeval but as all the Croatian aristocracy had disappeared or been absorbed generations earlier into the Austro-Hungarian upper classes, much compromise and connivance was essential. Poets, if they can't be anarchists, are susceptible to the romance of aristocracy, and I think it must have been this spurious pretence of aristocracy, with its bogus titles and resurrected pomps, ceremonies and traditions, that seduced for a time some of the better Croatian writers. I am told that the great poet Nazor was induced at the beginning to write praises of the new régime, but though I found many articles in the Occupation papers praising his work, I could not find anything written by him.

After a year he had had enough and in the New Year of 1943 the Partisans sent a car to Zagreb for him to fetch him 'to the woods'. He was an old man in poor health, and victory for the Partisans was still a long way out of sight, so his courage in leaving his comfortable home in Zagreb and a devoted sister in order to undertake this arduous journey across the frozen rivers and through trackless mountains of Bosnia will not be forgotten. The Partisans on their side paid a fine tribute to his fame and to poetry in undertaking the task of transporting, often by stretcher, this distinguished old gentleman with eczema and digestive troubles. He had his reward when he became the Vice-President of the Federal Republic of Croatia and was the first to address in Zagreb the liberated citizens.

If it is true that romance and poetry disappeared under the Communist government in Yugoslavia, there was an abundance of both in the Partisan warfare. There cannot be many wartime descriptions to equal Nazor's; it is not ordinary reporting... the enchantment of the Bosnian woods in the early morning and the hallucinations that the interlacing branches and mists weave in the mind of a sick old man recall Turgenev. The hero-worship and the comradeship of the woods were the real kind; not till it was transferred to the streets and newspapers and the election platform did the metamorphosis begin. The process is, I think, inevitable. Nazor prints in his book the poems that his comrades wrote, often about Tito; they are monotonous and uninventive as the song of the blackbird but in the woods they have their own appropriateness. Tito is their Achilles, he has the head of a young lion, says Nazor, and like the heroes of Homer he is only partly real; he becomes the symbol of what men admire in each other and everything he does and says becomes charged with significance. It is not till the symbol has to appear on the election platform that some spell is broken. 'Tito with us and we with Tito' they scribble on all the walls. But it is not the same. Some appalling catastrophe happens which should be explained not in terms of politics but of social psychology.

Nazor's diary has great documentary interest.* As an old, bourgeois poet campaigning with young revolutionaries, his elderly attempts to share their thoughts as well as their hardships are sometimes embarrassing, but the reader gets the feeling that he is trying sincerely to interpret the virtues of the old world in which he grew up in terms of the new, and that he is trying to save a good many venerable but discredited idols from the first fury of the iconoclasts.

A staff-officer, Major Moma Djurich, looked after him and saw that he had very quiet horses and refused to allow him to carry arms. In a rebellious mood Nazor wrote him a poem:

> When will you give to me, Commandant Moma,
> Rifle and horse, not a broken old screw?
> Did you forget how Nestor of Homer
> Was older than I but a warrior too?

* Vladimir Nazor, *Partizanska Knjiga* (*1943–1944*) (Zagreb 1949).

Did you forget how, when Doichen was dying,
They strapped on his harness? Come harness me well,
And set me on horseback! I'm weary of lying.
I too would be after the black infidel!

One day they arrived at a castle in Bosnia where Tito had his headquarters. It had been built in 1902 with turrets and battlements by a
romantic landowner, Frau Isabella von Berks. She herself was of Croatian
descent but her husband's family came originally from England to
Austria during a time of religious persecution under James I. They had
been Earls of Berkshire but had been deprived of their estates, and that
may have influenced her in spending her dowry on erecting this imitation
Anglo-Norman castle on the banks of the stormy river Una. Inside it
was furnished with four-posters and rich canopies, with carved Gothic
presses and cabinets and refectory tables, no doubt in polished pitch pine.
The long gloomy passages were hung with trophies of the chase, there
were mirrors in heavy gilt surrounds, and ranks of ancestors in the
dining-room. The library was full of ancient tomes in lofty book-cases,
German and French and Italian, but there was not a single book in the
Croatian or any other Slav tongue. There was literally nothing in the
whole castle, said Nazor, to indicate the country in which it was built.
It was as if the owner had deliberately set out to ignore the people of
whose blood she was. The castle had been ransacked by all the armies
which had passed through it in the last year, Italian and German and
Ustashe, as well as Moslem fugitives, and insults about the von Berks
family were scribbled in Italian on the walls. Now it was the temporary
headquarters of Marshal Tito and Nazor describes the speed and vigour
with which water and electricity and telephones were installed by the
Partisans and Tito. 'May he do as well', he cried, 'when they come into
possession of the derelict and plundered castle which is Croatia!' Outside
there was deep snow so that the burnt and deserted villages, the unburied
corpses, were hidden from view, the stumps of the plantations along the
Una which the Italians had cut down no longer offended, even the rocks
gleamed like silver in the sunlight. On the wireless the news came
through of the victories of the Partisans in the Lika, of the Russian
armies by Rostov. It was easy to believe, in this castle, that the worst
was past.

In the night Nazor was restless with his illness and could not sleep, so
he got up and wandered round the castle. There was no one about except
the two guards on watch outside the little room where Tito was still
writing up his despatches. In the dining-room the bright snow outside

the window made such a lovely light in the rooms that he found his way around without lighting his torch. He was looking for a ghost, the inevitable tenant of an English castle, and what ghost was he more likely to see than Isabella von Berks? If she was ever to appear it would be now, when 'barbarians' were desecrating this creation of her romantic soul. There was no ghost, and he did not know which of the portraits was Isabella, but he persuaded himself that if he flashed his torch into their faces, one after the other, the proud owner would surely move in her frame, if only to turn her back on him. He had an obsession that one day he would meet her and know more about her; he would find her perhaps sitting at the head of the dining-table, reproachful and indignant, waiting for him. He felt that he understood her, for he too had a nostalgia for the past. He had lived for twenty years on his Dalmatian island in the shadow of a tower, and wherever he had moved to afterwards, conscious of being ridiculous, he had built himself a tower. He went back to bed disappointed but confident that all the same he would somehow get to know her.

The next day the doctor would not allow him to move and while Tito and his men were ranging the countryside, Nazor was confined to the castle watching from the large window the snow thudding and slipping down from the evergreens and tossed off irritably, like premature flowers, from the bare and spindly twigs of the lilac. There was a slight thaw. The Una was black between its snowy banks, and the devastation on either bank was revealed. Where were the woods in which the animals, whose heads hung in the dining-room, had ranged? Where was the bridge and little mill? When Isabella lived here and sat on the terrace the hills must have been clothed in greenery and filled with songbirds. (Now there is nothing but bleakness and in the distance the minarets of a mosque.) The voices of the villagers and servants must have come up to her. What a place for an old person to live and forget the past!

Every day, as they did repairs, something came to light in the castle; a muffin dish from behind the panelling, some candelabra from a hole in the wall, silver fruit dishes from the roof; but the Partisans had not time for a thorough investigation. Only Nazor had the leisure to explore, but that was not the sort of research in which he was interested. He wanted to re-create the life of Isabella.

He had luck, for Lisica, the wife of the caretaker, a sly and lazy person, still lived in the castle, and she took Nazor to see Isabella's room, and showed him an old photograph of Isabella, an unpretentious looking

woman in a white blouse and Edwardian *coiffeur*. Lisica told him she
was tall with blue eyes, did not talk much, and as a mistress was kind
but firm.

But Isabella sent him a second messenger, a Serbian in Tito's entourage
called Tsrni, who had lived in Soviet Russia and spoke and read Russian
and French, a hard, dry but prompt and resourceful man. Somewhere
or other he discovered the 'Stammbuch' of the von Berks, one of those
monstrous, illuminated books, all gold and azure and crimson, compiled
at the end of the last century to please the parvenu wives or unmarried
sisters of the Austro-Hungarian nobility. He also found two packets of
letters from Isabella to her son written in 1922 and 1923.

From these letters Nazor learnt that Isabella's last years had been spent
in struggles and difficulties and not peacefully and romantically in the
castle of Oroschatz. Her son was looking after it for her; his own house
in Slavonia had been burnt by the Communists (that is what he called
them but probably they were Serbian nationalists) in 1918, and she was
living with a married daughter and nine grandchildren in Germany. It
was the inflation time and they were in great poverty and wretchedness.
But she wrote with patience and courage and an utter absence of that
pride and self-dramatization which Nazor had anticipated; she seemed
to have given up all her dreams about the castle, there was nothing left
of all her romantic fantasies. 'She had only her Croatian mother's heart,'
said Nazor, 'the cold misty romanticism of the foreigners from the
North had been purged and chastened on the day of wrath, and it had
given way to our Slavonic sensitiveness, warm, plebeian, creative.'

Isabella, said Nazor, was not buried here, and it was useless to look
for her ghost, but if the hopes of Tito were realized and the castle was
turned into a holiday home for poor children or for veterans, perhaps
her kind shade would appear under the roof.

It seemed to Nazor that she had not spent her dowry in vain. 'Build!'
he exclaimed, as he ended this entry in his diary. 'Build! Even though
you do not know for whom or for what you are building!'

I had read all this with interest because I had stayed with Isabella's son,
to whom the letters had been written, at his house in the village of
Podgorac in Slavonia. I had come as a friend of his children's tutor,
Christopher Cooper, whom I had met in Zagreb. Von Berks had been
murdered early after the invasion of Yugoslavia, I suppose by the same
people who had burnt his house thirty years before and whom he called,
with more justification than then, 'Communists'. They were probably
just his neighbours and employees. He and such neighbours as he con-

sidered his equals were living precariously and resentfully on the edge of the abyss into which they were shortly to plunge. If he had been told that he would be murdered and his wife and sons have to fly, and his daughter, to whom he was devoted, only save herself by marrying a village Communist, what would he have done? I think he could have done very little, except juggle a bit more with his and his wife's investments and see that his sons got a good English education.

They all of them refused to see anything inevitable about their fate; they had a personal grievance against Destiny which had permitted them, intelligent, educated, fastidious and honourable people, to be ordered about by people of low breeding and semi-barbarous culture. Yet when I read Nazor's diary it seems to me that there is nothing inevitable about ruthlessness, that it comes from a misuse of words; that it is the business of men of education to keep words flexible and rich in significance and to keep them free of crude antitheses. Mr von Berks and most of his friends indulged freely in antitheses. There were good people and bad people, Communists and democrats, educated and uneducated, Slav and Teuton, us and them.

Mr von Berks had none of his mother's romantic nature nor was he a snob; he valued wealth and privilege for the power they conferred, not for prestige. He had been in a bank in America after the collapse of Austria-Hungary and he had a superstitious belief in science. This did not interfere with his support of the Church, which he thought exercised a stabilizing influence on those incapable of independent reflection and without scientific training. Archbishop Stepinac was an honoured guest at his table but when the parish priest came to meals this polyglot family used to joke about him in different languages and their superior education showed itself not in the power to deflect or soften the impact of cultural difference but in giving the contrast extra pungency and force, which they did with eloquence and skill. International politics entertained him, local politics hardly at all. I think that he derived his extraordinary arrogance less from his pride of birth than from scientific enlightenment and American bumptiousness.

When the Mayor's daughter in Podgorac was married Mr von Berks asked me and Christopher to the interminable banquet in the village hall. He enjoyed himself on equal terms, arguing, quarrelling, drinking in the most convivial way with his red-faced sweating neighbours. He knew all their failings, just as they knew his, but there was not a trace of real comradeship in this reciprocal knowledge. He was an individualist more than a democrat. I don't think he had any confidence such as his mother had in the glamour and prestige of his ancestors. What he admired was science and power and American nationalism which he mistook for internationalism. He regarded small nations as nonsense and was humiliated by the imputation that he now belonged to one. It was degrading to have to ask permission of Belgrade to travel through the land of the former Austro-Hungarian empire, so he had provided himself with a special stamp and ink eraser so that he could organize his own passport and travel to Budapest or Vienna without ridiculous formalities.

I think his generation, Americanized and internationalized, was less easily assimilated than even his mother's. They were of more common fibre: they could capitulate or dominate but not live on equal terms, and with the disappearance of the feudal relationship with all its vague reciprocal obligations, the stark antitheses of wealth and poverty, pretension and powerlessness, became more pronounced than ever before.

The von Berks lived in an ugly mansion at the end of the main street of Podgorac. It had been rebuilt after the Yugoslav nationalists had burnt it in 1918, as splendidly as was consistent with comfort and practical good sense. The grandeur had been laid on afterwards on the side that faced the street. At the back was a straggling garden with a large rickety greenhouse which did not look as if it were much used. Paprikas and tomatoes drying on the edge had stuck to the woodwork. There were aubergines there, some like polished ebony but most had gone a dirty brown. Obviously the von Berks took no interest in their garden.

The second day I was there the Count, a local magnate, came to lunch. I had met him at the wedding banquet and had found him a very congenial person. After we had eaten we all four walked up the street together. It was October and the broad flat fields round Podgorac were full of dried stumps of maize stalks with golden pumpkins crawling around them, some of them pale green, some frosted and rotten. Four Podolian oxen were dragging a one-furrow plough across one of the fields. The ploughman shouted at them as they reached the headland and they trudged round as if in a trance, dark-eyed and blue-grey. 'How beautiful,' said the Count. 'Horses would do this quicker,' said the steward, 'oxen for harrowing.'

I never learnt the Count's name or saw his house, but the fields at the eastern end of the village must have been his as he showed us his wine-cellar under a mound in the Turkish cemetery. 'I won't have much wine this year, I'm afraid, as I've had lumbago and I could not go round and see that the vines were properly sprayed.'

I think that, unlike von Berks, the Count was proud to be Yugoslav. He spoke Croatian, not German, to the steward. He had been born an Austro-Hungarian citizen but remained proud of his Croat nationality.

Many such had cherished the Yugoslav ideal and, when the empire collapsed in 1918, had given their support to it. The man who had earlier pioneered the Croatian revival, Lyudevit Gai, had been half-German. It often happens like that. In an empire subject peoples are ashamed of their language till someone of the imperial blood urges them to value it. That was the story of Douglas Hyde and the Gaelic League, of Yeats and Synge and the Irish Literary Renaissance. They were all Anglo-Irishmen.

As elsewhere in the formerly Hungarian parts of Yugoslavia, each cottage had a strip of land behind it. In the Austro-Hungarian days the landlord ruled the village and had the right of life and death over the villagers and kept a certain routine going, which still partially survived. At four o'clock on summer mornings the cow-boy blew a horn under the priest's window and the cows went off to their grazing. The broad street was criss-crossed with the tracks of the cows. It is very muddy in the autumn but there is space enough for the traffic to use one half of the road till the other half has time to dry.

Podgorac on my last day seemed amazingly tranquil and beautiful. Turkeys and geese strutted down the street. There were maize cobs stuck away for the winter under the tiles. There was a short, rather noisy interruption. The fire-brigade band, having got out their uniforms and instruments for the wedding, marched up and down a couple of times extra before they put them away. The second time they collided with the cows coming back from the pastures. Each cow knew its own home and made for it, but they were wildly alarmed by the drumming and trumpeting and for a few moments man and beast were helplessly interlocked.

Before I left, the Count insisted on my visiting the village school. There were little boys with books and little girls with embroidery crouched round the central stove. They must have had an imaginative teacher. He had helped them make a map of the country round Podgorac and another map of the Dravska Banovina, the province through which their river, the Drava, flows. It was constructed out of coloured matches, powdered paint and little bits of a sponge dyed green for the trees. They were growing cherry trees from cherry stones and later were going to learn to graft them. The Count had given them a drawer full of oddities from his home and also an 'orrery' to show the movements of the planets round the sun. And there were two large coloured posters on the wall, one to illustrate the growth of a lobster, the other the formation of a molehill. The children all looked lively and interested. I complimented the Count from my heart for what he had done for the school. I thought that, as he trotted away behind his white pony, he looked pleased.

Years later, when I heard what had happened to the von Berks, I wondered how the Count had fared when the Partisans arrived in Podgorac. Is it true, as a Roman poet thought, that the good man is his own protection? 'He does not need Moorish javelins and poisoned arrows.' I doubt if that applies in the post-von Berks world, where one is judged not by one's temperament but by one's presumed politics.

1. Ante Pavelíc masterminded the assassination of King Alexander by the Ustase, and subsequently returned to Yugoslavia, becoming leader of 'Independent Croatia' – initially under the auspices of Mussolini. See 'The Sub-Prefect Should Have Held His Tongue', pp. 271–282, below.

CARL VON OSSIETZKY

Many of the greatest martyrs and saints of modern times will never have their biographies written or their centenaries celebrated. Nobody knows when or how they died. Their lives are often a complex web of insignificant detail which few would have the patience to unravel. Often they have struggled in solitude against mass movements and it is inevitable that the mass media, through which we now obtain the most of our information, should ignore them.

Lately I found a grimy old pamphlet dating from the first years of Hitler. It is called 'The Case of Carl von Ossietzky' and it was the work of fifteen eminent English writers. It is an appeal to the Nobel Peace Prize Committee on behalf of Ossietzky, who was at that time in a German prison.[1]

They wrote: 'We have all tried to do something for the cause of peace, but he has done more than any of us. He has done most of all living men to deserve this acknowledgment from his fellow-men.' Because of these efforts Ossietzky did get his Nobel Prize in 1936, but a year or two later he died reclaiming marshland in Esterwegen prison camp. Nobody really knows about his death.[2]

Why does nobody care either? Germans of the East and the West are now combing history for evidence that they resisted Hitler but Ossietzky and his friends are seldom mentioned. Very few people talk of the large and honourable resistance to Hitler, which was extinguished before the war began, before Auschwitz was thought of, and which left the German opposition leaderless. The reason for this silence is clear. History is written by survivors and most of those who survived till 1939 had had to make many moral and political adjustments in order to do so. Inevitably they have encouraged us to believe that the best martyrs are diplomatists who balance one tyranny against another and choose (provisionally of course) the least repugnant. Ossietzky, who did not want

237

any tyranny at all, does not fit comfortably into this picture, and so he is honoured neither in the East nor the West. There is much competition to be numbered among those brave Germans who tried to murder Hitler because he was losing the war, but Ossietzky, who opposed Hitler because he was Hitler, and war because it was war, has been almost totally forgotten.

His fifteen sponsors seem rather out-of-date figures too, Aldous Huxley, Gilbert Murray, Rose Macaulay, Norman Angell, Gerald Heard, Bertrand Russell, J. B. Priestley, Leonard and Virginia Woolf to name a few. They all had this in common with Ossietzky: they hated the Organization Man, the mechanical dummy who does what he is told. And they believed he could be resisted. Nowadays most writers either belong to an organization themselves or else believe that the world created by the Organization Man is so obscene and ludicrous that they can only laugh at it, the bitter laughter of the defeated, of Joyce and Beckett, Albee and Genet and a hundred such others, and with a certain sad satisfaction reflect that this world is a Vale of Tears anyway and we should turn our minds to the next.

Ossietzky was different. He was the son of a Hamburg merchant and had fought with average ability and less than average enthusiasm in the First World War. Even then he had realized where German militarism was tending. As soon as he was demobilized he started a weekly in Hamburg whose aims he describes thus: 'We who are supporters of peace have a duty and a task to point out over and over again that there is nothing heroic in war but that it brings terror and misery to mankind.'

As a result of the German military collapse, there had been a great cultural revival with which the names of Einstein, Thomas and Heinrich Mann, Arnold Zweig, Gropius, Max Reinhardt, Hindemith and Bruno Walter are associated. There was springtime in the air and for a few years all Europe looked to Berlin as it had once looked to Weimar. To Berlin Ossietzky went. He started there the *Nie Wieder Krieg* movement and became editor of the *Weltbühne*. Till the day of his last arrest it was the principal literary organ of resistance, first to the reviving German militarism and then to Hitler.

Weltbühne had been called *Schaubühne* before the war, and was an organ of the theatre. It was connected with a firm that published children's books, *Emil and the Detectives*, translations of *Dr Dolittle* and so on. But soon it was clear that the independence of the actor, the writer, the artist, was about to be threatened and that the *Weltbühne*, the world-stage, required them. The paper changed its name and its character. It became militantly anti-militarist and earned the hatred of the

General Staff. For Ossietzky claimed with good reason that some of the generals were lending support to the Black Reichswehr, a secret society, directed against German democracy and defending itself by what were known as the *vehme* murders. He revealed that German commercial aviation was being used as a screen for military activities. He opposed the granting of naturalization papers to Hitler. He attacked those, who, under Nazi pressure, had banned the famous anti-war film, 'All Quiet on the Western Front'. 'Today', he wrote, 'German fascism has slain a film. Tomorrow it will be something else... Soon only one tune will be permitted, and every one of our steps will be carefully measured.'

Ossietzky was not forced into resistance by violence like the Jews, nor by political theory like the Communists. Rudolf Olden, his friend and lawyer, who was editor of the *Berliner Tageblatt*, explained him as a *Bürger*, a civilian defending the rights of civilians.

The generals were handling Hitler very gently, for they believed they could use him and had no notion how soon they would be his puppets. Ossietzky, who saw clearly what was happening, had to be silenced. In an action for slander the generals secured his arrest and imprisonment. Yet till Hitler came, a *Bürger* could still count on some justice. Over 42,000 Germans signed an appeal for his release, a brave thing to do for it was only three weeks before Hitler came to power. When for a brief period General Echleicher took over the government Ossietzky was released.

But soon the flames of the burning Reichstag lit up unmistakably the shape of the future. His colleagues on the *Weltbühne* escaped abroad and Ossietzky's friends urged him to think of his small daughter and to follow them. But he had written: 'The man who is opposing the Government of his own country and who goes across the border, speaks with a hollow voice.'

He refused to leave. The writers of my old pamphlet recall how Socrates was urged by Crito to fly to Thessaly while there was time; it was a duty to his friends, to his family, and Socrates had answered: 'The principles, which I have hitherto honoured and revered, I still honour.'

The day after the Reichstag fire Ossietzky was taken to Spandau Prison and thence to Sonnenburg concentration camp. After that there were a few rumours from fellow-prisoners who escaped of beatings and torture but nothing definite. We know more about Socrates.

Since Ossietzky was the principal leader of the German resistance to Hitler, why is his name so seldom mentioned when the whole German people is being charged with complicity in Hitler's crimes? I've suggested the reason already. It is because Ossietzky and his 42,000 supporters, who were eliminated with him, were absolutists. Hitler to them was an absolute evil, whereas to most of their contemporaries inside and outside Germany, he was only a relative evil. Effective German resistance collapsed with Ossietzky, for only relativists were left. Not only in Germany but all over Europe, millions of intelligent people believed that Hitler could be 'handled', used effectively against the Communists and then, when his work was done, discarded. One must recall that while Ossietzky was in Sonnenburg, the British Ambassador was shooting elk with General Göring, and Ribbentrop was an honoured guest with Lord Londonderry in Co. Down.

The ghost of the relativist delusion still haunts us, corrupting history as it once corrupted politics. When it is finally accepted that Hitler was wholly evil and Stalin's most effective ally, Ossietzky and the thousands who died with him will be remembered again. They were the men who would have saved us – had we supported them – not only from Hitler, but from Stalin as well.

[1964]

1. For the unsuccessful attempt to persuade W. B. Yeats to join this campaign in 1936 see Ethel Mannin, *Privileged Spectator* (1939).
2. It is now established that he was moved on 27 May 1936 from Esterwegen to hospital in Berlin, suffering from tuberculosis, and held there under detention. In mid-November 1936 the detention order was technically rescinded, but he remained under Gestapo surveillance throughout his hospitalization, which ended with his death at the Nordend Private Clinic on 4 May 1938.

THE KAGRAN GRUPPE

I believe one of the happiest times of my life was when I was working for the Austrian Jews in Vienna in 1938–9. It is strange to be happy when others are miserable, but all the people at the Freundeszentrum in the Singerstrasse were cheerful too. The reason surely is that we have always known of the immense unhappiness that all humanity has to suffer. We read of it in the newspapers and hear it on the radio but can do nothing about it.

Most people tied to a single job or profession die without exercising more than a tenth of their capacities. In the Singerstrasse for many months all my faculties were engaged and I exercised an intimate control over the lives of a great many people, and I believe I helped them.

Hitler brought into the world misery such as no man had previously conceived possible. It had to be combated. The British were slow to observe this. The Irish never did. As late as 1936 Lloyd George went to Germany and told Hitler he was the greatest German of his age. London's society hostesses flocked round Ribbentrop and received invitations to the Olympic Games which, thanks to Goëbbels, were a huge success. Predictably, the poor silly Duke and Duchess of Windsor visited the Führer.

The mood in Ireland was one of ignorant indifference. It was expressed in the Dail in 1943 by a very pious Catholic, Oliver Flanagan. 'There is one thing', he said, 'that the Germans did and that was to rout the Jews out of their country.' He added that we should rout them out of Ireland: 'They crucified our Saviour 1900 years ago and they have been crucifying us every day of the week.' No one contradicted him.

But I was as Irish as Oliver Flanagan and I was determined that Jewish refugees should come to Ireland. At the time of the Anschluss the Quakers were settled in the Freundeszentrum in Vienna and through Friends' House in London I got permission to join them. The

Freundeszentrum was a former nobleman's palace in the Singerstrasse and when I got there, together with a charming and energetic young Quaker called Mary Campbell, I was put in charge of the Kagran Gruppe, a group of Viennese Jews who had banded together for collective emigration.

My first few weeks at the Freundeszentrum were spent at a desk filling in hundreds of 'bogen', or emigration forms, for the crowds of applicants who turned up. After the usual questions about age, religion, profession, married or single, the women were asked, 'Can you cook, wash, scrub, knit?' The men had a corresponding questionnaire. Almost all the questions were answered in the affirmative. At the bottom one added one's comment. I do not know what happened to the stacks and stacks of bogen. Probably they were forwarded to the Friends' House in Euston Road and carefully filed. What would we have done if some instinct had told us of Auschwitz? Why was I the only non-Quaker there?

I think now it was obtuse of us not to have anticipated Auschwitz. I had walked along the Prater Strasse to the Prater, the great Viennese Park where bands played and stalls sold ice-cream and coffee. The street must have had a great many Jewish shopkeepers in it, because all the way down there were broken windows in front of looted shops with VERHOLUNG NACH DACHAU ('Gone for a rest-cure to Dachau') scrawled over the surviving panes, and the air was full of the mindless hatred which war, that fosters all our basest passions, would inevitably make murderous.

I speak German and French so I was shortly sent to the Conference on the problem of the German Jews at Evian, by the Lake of Geneva. The League of Nations had at last got to work and it was attended by representatives of all the countries in Europe and America. Vague gestures of goodwill were made. I talked to the two delegates from Ireland, or rather from the Irish Embassies in Paris and Berne. One remarked, 'Didn't we suffer like this in the Penal Days and nobody came to our help.'

When I got back I visited all the embassies to get visas for the emigrating Jews. There was a kindly official at the Mexican embassy who would sign an entry visa for anyone who asked. Even though it might fail to get them into Mexico it would get them out of Austria. So many applicants arrived that he had to get his wife and family in to help him.

One day I visited the Peruvian embassy. It was a splendid building with a large map of Peru painted on the staircase. I entered a spacious room with well-filled bookcases and handsome furniture. At the far end was a small figure seated at a large desk. I assumed he was the Peruvian ambassador, though in fact it was probably the consul. After the Anschluss the ambassadors had all been transferred to Stuttgart or Berlin. I appealed to him to persuade his government to admit Viennese Jews. He looked at me doubtfully and then said: 'I was wondering if you could help me. You see, I too am a Jew and want to get out as soon as possible. I've just written a letter to Churchill. Do you think that a good idea?' 'It would be much better to write to Emma Cadbury,' I replied. He bowed but looked too proud to be interested.

At this time the Bolivian consulate was one of the most thronged in Vienna. The report had got round that land was being given to agriculturalists on favourable terms, and that engineers and craftsmen were required. Of the many that applied only a very few were accepted. In the autumn a group of about 200 Jews were urged to prepare immediately for the journey. While the relief organizations hurriedly helped with the official formalities, they themselves sold their possessions with desperate haste for whatever they could get for them. They kept only the barest necessities for the journey and such goods as they could carry in their trunks to their new home. A few days before the boat was due to sail they were informed that there had been a misunderstanding between the Gestapo and the Bolivian Consulate. No visas would be given for Bolivia and the expedition could not set off. The 200 settlers, now without homes or property, had to wander round the streets looking for hospitality from their friends.

At Eichmann's trial in Jerusalem in 1961 it emerged that he personally was responsible for providing the field in which the Kagran Gruppe was trained. When he was in Vienna emissaries from Palestine had approached him for help in the illegal immigration of Jews into British-ruled Palestine. 'He was polite,' they said, 'and even provided a farm and facilities for setting up vocational training camps for prospective immigrants. On one occasion he expelled a group of nuns from a convent to provide a training camp for young Jews.'

Eichmann, like other Nazis in the early days, was sympathetic to Zionism and this lasted till 7th November 1938 when Ernst von Rath, the Third Secretary of the German embassy in Paris, ironically an anti-Nazi, was murdered by a 17-year-old Jewish youth Herschel Grynzpan, whose family had been deported to Poland. This led to Kristallnacht in November 1938, when all the synagogues in Berlin went up in flames, 7500 Jewish shop-windows were smashed and 20,000 Jews were taken off to concentration camps. This increased the tension in Vienna and ever more people joined the Kagran Gruppe.

I found a letter of that time describing the desperate atmosphere to my wife:

There was a meeting yesterday of the leading Jews. I was very much moved by their courage and seriousness and idealism and innocence, as it seemed to me. They spent about twenty minutes deciding whether they should take their mahogany sideboards and bamboo hat-racks by ship or not and describing them. They have to go first to Sweden (that is to say if anything comes of the scheme at all and they can raise £14,000) and then after they've had their 'umschulung' training in agriculture there, they go off to somewhere like Paraguay, or, if they are lucky, to Colombia, where there is some sort of community settlement already. I said that even shipping furniture from Belgrade to Dubrovnik, as we had done, was far dearer than selling it and then buying new stuff. They looked shocked and I realized I had said something hurtful and callous about their homes, and that to many its furniture was an intimate part of their lives. They had grown up with it and it was full of memories. This was 'Papa's chair and this was Mutti's' and the more stuck in their ways and the more entrenched they are, the more terribly touching it is. However, I'm glad they did decide to bring only the most cherished pieces. This afternoon when I was alone the Controller of Foreign Currency in the biggest bank but one – quite a swell with an almost complete set of gold teeth – pleaded to be allowed to join the camp with his wife and go out with them. He produced an armful of testimonials, but how could he be any use there?

But the real time for seeing people is between nine and one thirty. I see about ten and by the time one has reached the tenth one is utterly drained of sympathy and ideas and resourcefulness. I just gaze at them and put a new nib in the pen and rearrange the papers on the desk. In some cases it's just a matter of advice, how to find the address of a relation in Cairo or Cincinnati or something like that. There is a tremendous drive on now to Aryanize all the gemeindehauser (blocks of flats) and private houses along main streets where flags have to be hung on important occasions. As a result four people who came to me yesterday have had a notice to quit by August 1st and nowhere to go. They might get taken in as tenants by a Jewish landlord, but what are they to do with their furniture? Aryans who take Jewish lodgers also are liable to lose their flats. There was one old gentleman yesterday with an ear-trumpet in a state of mind about his flat. It belonged to his wife's daughter who was illegitimate and consequently happened to be Aryan, but he was terrified of disgracing her by living with her and was going to move out. Another couple had married Aryanized daughters who were very anxious to support them, but for the same reason they were frightened of embroiling them and wanted to emigrate. There was an old officer with a testimonial from his General about his bravery at the battle of Przemysl.

It's such a relief when one comes on a really nasty one, as one does, e.g. a Feinkost Erzeuger (maker of delicatessen), with a horrible Aryan wife who wanted to know if the Friends' House in Philadelphia would get her an affidavit if she became a Quaker. Then there was a young police-officer, very well-educated, and a dark scared fanatical writer on a fashion paper, dozens and dozens of Beamter, Buchalter, Mechaniker, Technicker and chauffeurs and garage proprietors. There was one young Jew who had become a Nazi and hoped to become an honorary Aryan but wasn't accepted. And yesterday at the end two women and a little girl turned up. I was so fuddled by that time I can't remember what they wanted but they suddenly quite spontaneously and untheatrically all three began to snivel.

A plump dark-haired woman, a Nazi named Baronin Rikki von Appell, was always straying into the Friends' Centre. I think her job was to keep us under observation and she was particularly concerned about me as I was not a Quaker. She knew about Quakers and remembered the good work they had done in Vienna in 1920; the Viennese were starving so the Quakers among other projects imported 1500 cows from Holland, to provide milk.

But what was I up to, a non-Quaker? She was puzzled and asked me to join her and a friend on a boating trip on the Danube. We started from Klosterneuburg and I was enchanted with the unspoilt beauty, the water lilies and scarlet willows growing beside the river bank so close to a great city. Her friend was a thin fair-haired woman with a slight limp. She told me she had been engaged to be married, but because of her limp the Nazis, for genetic reasons, refused to allow it. She did not seem particularly resentful. I satisfied Rikki's curiosity by telling her that, like the Quakers, I had come out to help the Jews. She said the Jews were parasites who had speculated on the dwindling value of the Austrian crown after 1918. I did not accept this but was too ignorant to comment.

If I'd been a Quaker I would have said that the Quakers would help anyone who was suffering unjustly. The Quakers helped the Social Democrats when in 1934 Chancellor Dollfuss, a so-called Christian Socialist or Fascist, had crushed them. In Emma Cadbury's brilliant account of this period, *A Three-Day War and Its Aftermath*, she wrote that this civil conflict in Austria was one of the main causes of the Second World War. The Nazi take-over of Austria without opposition from England or France had made Czechoslovakia, now surrounded on three sides, an easy victim which the great powers would hesitate to defend.

Had it not been for the Three Days' War Austria would have been well able to defend itself against the Nazis. Democracy had been growing there as in Germany before the collapse of the two empires in 1918, and in Austria the Social Democrats (socialists) then became the dominant power in Vienna. Emma Cadbury describes all that they did for the workers' libraries, adult education, hospitals, clinics, and above all

housing. Before the war 73 per cent of the people had been living in
two rooms or less. In 1922, 60,000 houses were built with space for trees
and grass and flowers. It was a superb achievement.

'Thus,' writes Emma Cadbury, 'life was made easier for the proletariat
and Communism found no foothold in Vienna.' But the Social Democrats had their enemies. Chief among them were the Christian Socialists,
who were strongly influenced by the Catholic Church. They were
extremely hostile to Hitler but regarded the Social Democrats as enemies
of the Church who were impoverishing the middle and upper classes by
overtaxation. The Social Democrats were ready to co-operate in fighting
Hitler but the Christian Socialists could not wait. On 12 February 1934,
with the approval of Chancellor Dollfuss, the Austrian army with the
help of the Heimwehr, the army of the Christian Socialists, and the
police made an assault on the Social Democrats. They and their army,
the Schutzbund, were no match for the forces allied against them. Nearly
2000 were killed and some 5000 wounded. Many were executed and
imprisoned. The Quakers were quickly on the scene distributing food
with funds that came through the International Federation of Trade
Unions.

The Austrian Nazis must have taken heart when they saw this great
split in the ranks of their opponents. On 25 July 1934, a group of
them broke into the Chancellery and shot Dollfuss. It was thought
that this might lead to an immediate Nazi take-over. But Schuschnigg
managed to forestall this move and thirteen of the assassins were
hanged.

Schuschnigg was summoned to Berchtesgarten and was bullied into
signing a capitulation; as he had hoped, President Miklas refused to
endorse it. Then he decided to hold a plebiscite, appealing for Social
Democratic support, promising to free their members from prison.
March 14th, 1938, was to be the Great Day.

The vote would certainly have gone against the Nazis, so on 12
March, Hitler strutted into Austria. He crossed the frontier at Braunau
and received a riotous welcome near Linz, his birthplace. Cardinal
Innitzer ordered all the church bells in Austria to be rung. Schuschnigg
was thrown into prison in the Gestapo headquarters and later was
transferred to Dachau.

It was some months after this that I came to Vienna.

Typical of many is the story of the first Austrians I brought to Ireland.
Erwin Strunz, an 'Aryan' with a Jewish wife and two small children,
had been a trade union secretary with promise of a career in parliament

in the Social Democratic Party till Dollfuss took over the government and routed the socialists. The Strunzes had no friends abroad and with a small son and a new-born baby they could not cross on foot over the mountains into Switzerland.

Erwin was advised by his Jewish friend Dr Schonfeld, President of the Austrian Atheists Association, to visit the Quaker Centre in Vienna. He had called on many Labour leaders and ecclesiastics. None of them could help. Then he remembered the work the Quakers had done in starving Vienna in 1920. With a letter from Dr Schonfeld he visited Emma Cadbury at the Freundeszentrum. It was there I first met them at my desk and filled in their two bogen. Erwin told me he was an atheist and Lisl, who had big black eyes and a lively but firm expression, said to me, 'I will be a Mohammedan if it will help my children.' I entered them both as 'konfessionslos' (without Church), which in fact was the creed of very many Viennese Jews.

Emma Cadbury gave permission for 200 Kagraners to meet in the Quaker Centre and discuss their plans. They begged her to help them emigrate and form an agricultural co-operative overseas. Erwin and Lisl went early every morning with little Peter and all the others on the long tram journey to Kagran, a suburb on the left bank of the Danube. The group worked under the supervision of armed guards from the Gestapo who relished watching middle-aged Jews, many of them once rich sedentary businessmen, cutting trees, digging irrigation trenches, making a road; men who had never before held a shovel in their hands. They worked all the summer, while Emma Cadbury, Mary Campbell and I tried desperately to get entry permits for them to Peru, Bolivia, Rhodesia, Colombia, Canada. As I had already realized at Evian, nobody wanted them.

Erwin and his wife were in great danger. They slept every night in fear of the heavy knock at 5 a.m., the hour usually chosen by the Gestapo for the departure to Dachau. The Viennese Nazi Party thought there might be leader material in Erwin so the Party solicitor offered to arrange a divorce. He would be housed, temporarily, in the factory to avoid painful meetings with his ex-wife and children, and a blue-eyed Nazi woman had agreed to marry him. He was told he was lucky as she had a house of her own and some money. He would ultimately be transferred to the synthetic petrol factory at Dusseldorf and allotted a car, a mono-plane and a villa. He could attend the university and later be drafted to the Party Leader School in Nuremberg. It was a dazzling offer so when he did not reply the Party grew suspicious. He hurriedly took sick-leave and simulated a nervous breakdown while still digging at Kagran. The

Gruppe had seemed to be a way out of his difficulties, but now the future looked very menacing.

On 16th September 1938 he was rung up after midnight: 'Erwin. You have 48 hours to get out. Your arrest and deportation to Dachau has been decided.' He recognized the voice; it was a friend who had joined the Nazi Party but worked on behalf of the underground. (There were many such.) Erwin was thunderstruck, for though he had anticipated trouble he had not expected it so soon. He came to me next day in the Singerstrasse so hopeless and dispirited he could hardly speak. I finally found out what had happened and explained the situation to Emma Cadbury. After a good deal of telephoning, somehow she obtained entry permits for England which arrived within two hours.

The Kagran Gruppe had set aside funds for the fares of emigrants which Hans Koch had entrusted to the treasurer, Viktor Strasser, and they were kept in a moneybox with two keys of which Koch had one, but when he went to get the fare for the Strunz' journey he found the box empty. Strasser had stolen it all. We were forced to apply, as often before, to the Gildemeester Fund. (Gildemeester was a Dutch philanthropist to whose outstanding generosity in these terrible times I have seldom seen any reference.) The Strunzes got off on the train to Ostend and I telephoned to Peggy, my wife, to meet them at Charing Cross. After they arrived in London, owing to the strain of recent weeks, Erwin had a genuine breakdown and Peggy took them all back to her mother's home at Annaghmakerrig in Co. Monaghan.

After my own departure from Vienna I went on trying to get accommodation for the Kagran Group in Ireland and England, but Mary Campbell, who had been in charge of it with me in Vienna, was drafted by the Quakers to other work and replaced by a woman who knew nothing of Vienna or Kagran and did not speak German, so the heart went out of the idea of group emigration. She simply selected those most easy to place. In this way she was able to dispose of Hecht, the Kagran bee-keeper, Kalan, one of the very few agriculturalists, and Weinberg, our butcher and his wife: she was delighted with herself for this achievement, particularly when she had her picture in the *Daily Mirror*.

We were left with a goldsmith, seven academics, a hairdresser, an umbrella maker, and many clerks, teachers and shopkeepers. It soon emerged that simply shelter and support in a friendly ambience was all that could be organized. This we achieved through the generosity of various private people in Ireland such as Arland Ussher in Cappagh, Co. Waterford, and Sir John Keane at Ardmore. I went to Bunnaton, a youth hostel in Donegal that was empty in the winter months. The parish priest, Fr O'Doherty, wanted to build a road from Bunnaton to Port Salon and hoped the refugees would help him. We also found places in England for three groups of Kagranners. Inevitably in Ireland the sectarian question arose and, I believe, our Irish Refugee Committee was unwittingly to blame for this. Members of committees seem always to be chosen to represent different interests whereas they should only have one interest, in this case the defence of the persecuted.

The long peace was about to end and the fate of the Jews had not precipitated that 'saeva indignatio' in the rest of Europe that would have given encouragement to the many hundreds of thousands of non-Jewish Germans who hated Hitler and, in 1944, welcomed the rising against him. Thousands must have died fighting for a Fatherland that had betrayed them.

Lately I came across a newspaper report of 10 December 1938 which I had cut out at this time. It tells of a great meeting in the Mansion House, London, on behalf of the Jews. The Archbishop of Canterbury spoke of 'the systematic persecution without parallel even in the Middle Ages', and the 'incredible mental and moral torture' to which the Jews were being subjected. Cardinal Pacelli sent the following telegram:

The Holy Father's thoughts and feelings will be correctly interpreted by declaring he looks with humane and Christian approval on every effort to show charity and give effective assistance to all those who are innocent victims in these sad times of distress.

The tone of these two communications is very different. The Archbishop is explicit, the Cardinal is vague and general, but I do not think one can argue from this that the Englishman's heart was the warmer. It is the difference between the leader of a more or less homogeneous body and the head of a worldwide and heterogeneous community of believers. The Pope had followers in every land, all the Archbishop's were in one. Our disappointment in Pius XII springs from the delusive hopes that have been placed in universalism, in ecumenism. Now we know that if Christendom were ever to speak with one official voice, it would be a mouse's squeak. There would be so many conflicting sympathies to reconcile that in the end silence might seem best.

Catholics claim the Pope was impotent and I believe that was so. For example it was said that the Pope saved 400,000 Jews in Hungary. But these Jews owed their lives principally to the fact that Roosevelt had followed up an ultimatum about the deportations with a tremendous bombardment of Budapest on 2nd July 1944.

As it happens, we were all wrong about the 400,000. It emerged at the Eichmann trial that he had defied all the neutral nations, Roosevelt and the Pope, and deported 1500 Hungarian Jews in mid-July, and in October the shortage of labour in Germany was so great that they asked for a further 100,000. Since trains were no longer running, they were obliged to walk. Of 800,000 Hungarian Jews, some 100,000 survived.

Some are surprised that people are not more impressed by the compliments paid to the Vatican by the Jewish leaders and the fact that the Rabbi of Rome even gave up his Jewish faith. But are the few who are dragged ashore entitled to give thanks on behalf of the millions who drowned? And is it not easy to undervalue the formidable social power of the community? The Jews were penniless refugees in foreign lands. Would many countries (Ireland for example) have accepted them readily if they had publicly claimed that the Pope or the Church had failed them in their hour of need? The Austrians who came to Ireland never even blamed Cardinal Innitzer, the Austrian Primate, who ordered all the church-bells in Austria to be rung when Hitler entered Austria to forestall the plebiscite. In reply to Cardinal Pacelli's cautious telegram, they themselves sent a very grateful one from Ireland to Rome. The Jews have reason to be apprehensive, even when a non-Jew like Hochhuth criticizes the Pope on their behalf. When *The Representative* was played in Paris, demonstrators leapt into the auditorium crying 'A bas les Juifs!'

It is clear that in times of stress parliaments and Churches are peculiarly subject to mass-pressure and one cannot expect too much from them. Nobody, whatever his faith, who had read the fulsome greeting from the leaders of the Evangelical Church in Austria to Hitler, 'the Tool in the hands of the Almighty' and 'the Fulfiller of the Divine Will for the Salvation of our People', could be confident that his own Church would have shown greater courage or foresight.

In the twentieth, as in the first century, we find the burden of Christianity borne by solitary and often anonymous individuals.

[1988]

THE INVADER WORE SLIPPERS

During the war, we in Ireland heard much of the jackboot and how we should be trampled beneath it, if Britain's protection failed us. We thought we could meet this challenge as well as any other small nation, and looking into the future, our imagination, fed on the daily press, showed us a technicolour picture of barbarity and heroism.

It never occurred to us that for ninety per cent of the population the moral problems of an occupation would be small and squalid. Acting under pressure we should often have to choose between two courses of action, both inglorious. And, if there was moral integrity about our choice, it certainly would not get into the headlines.

We did not ask ourselves: 'Supposing the invader wears not jackboots, but carpet slippers or patent leather pumps, how will I behave, and the respectable Xs, the patriotic Ys and the pious Zs?' How could we? The newspapers only told us about the jackboots.

The newspapers have by this time worked the subject of resistance to the Nazis to death. They have passed on to livelier issues, so it is possible to anatomize this now desiccated topic in a quite callous way. We can forget about the heroic or villainous minority or those other irreconcilables who adhered to some uncompromising political or religious creed. We can look at the ordinary people, the Xs, the Ys and the Zs, about whom there is a mass of documentation. By a little careful analogy and substitution we can see ourselves, and a picture of our home under occupation emerges with moderate clarity. It is more like an X-ray photo than a war film. It is quite unglamorous and perhaps it is only by the trained mind that the darker shadows can be interpreted.

In totalitarian war human nature is reduced to its simplest terms and a skilled invader can predict with fair accuracy the behaviour of the respectable Xs, the patriotic Ys, the pious Zs. Of course there are innumerable divagations but in an avalanche it is the valleys and the riverbeds that count, the hundred thousand cart tracks can be disregarded.

I know that we Irish were not more complex than anyone else and that our percentages of Xs, Ys, and Zs were about average and known to every likely invader. And I dismissed as inapplicable to us the propaganda stories of the jackboot with which the allies tried to shake our neutrality. We did not, I thought, like most of the Slav regions, belong to the area of German colonization in which extermination and spiritual enslavement would be practised. And it seemed to me that the respectable Xs who told us the reverse were speaking either without reflection or with concealed motives. It was surprising when the inevitable volte-face came after the war. The people who had been threatening us with the jackboot in places where no sensible invader would dream of using it, began to applaud his restraint. Indulgent things were said of generals, even jackbooted ones like von Manstein, 'who simply did their duty', and Rommel's biography was widely read in those pleasant Dublin suburbs where the Xs live.

It seems to me that we civilian Irish, finding indulgence where we had been led to expect violence, might easily have been tricked into easy-going collaboration. Yet small peoples should become specialists in the art of non-cooperation with tyranny. It is the only role we can play when the great powers clash, and we are hopelessly untrained in it.

Careful observation of precedent and analogy is the first need. This can be done best in small circumscribed regions, whose characters are fairly homogeneous. I found three such occupied zones within my reach, where the tactics of the invader with the Xs, Ys and Zs severally were displayed as on a small diagram which could be indefinitely enlarged. There were the Channel Islands where the respectable Xs were in the majority, Brittany, where the influence of the romantically patriotic Ys was strong, Croatia, where the Ys were reinforced by the fervently pious Zs.

The policy of the invader in all these places, and the response it met, is best studied in the newspapers of the occupation. Reminiscences of course are helpful but they are usually written by men who are exceptional either for their independence of mind or their complacency. They are edited to flatter the vanity of their compatriots, seldom to chasten it. But the newspapers show the invader at his highly skilled task of manipulating the Xs and Ys and Zs. Reading between the lines you can judge of his success.

I think it was only in Zagreb that I found easy access to the files, though even there I was met with some suspicion and surprise. The reason was that in Zagreb a revolution had taken place which had, temporarily at least, undermined the natural desire of every nation to conceal its weaknesses from itself, or in the smooth phraseology of self-deception, to 'let bygones be bygones'. Somebody before me had been over the files in the university library with faint pencil marks and an incriminating collection of the acta and dicta of the Xs, Ys and Zs had been published.

This had certainly not been done in Rennes, the capital of Brittany. In Jersey there is an excellent museum of the occupation but it deals with the behaviour of the Germans and not with that of the Jersey people themselves. And in the newspaper room of the British Museum I searched in vain for the Jersey newspapers which were published all through the war, and had to be content with the incomplete Guernsey file, the personal gift of a Guernsey man. This indifference of the British archivist to the history of the Channel Islands under occupation struck me as curious and significant. Has the national mind, like its individual proto-type, some Freudian censor, which automatically suppresses what is shameful or embarrassing?

The public does not want a truthful account of occupation. It prefers to switch over from extremes of reprobation to extremes of condonation. You will see what I mean if you read the most authoritative book on the occupation of Jersey by R. C. Maugham. The publisher appears to be about four years behind the author. On the dust-cover the title, 'Jersey under the Jackboot', is illustrated by a big cruel boot crashing down on a helpless little green island and the blurb talks of the 'courage and fortitude of the islanders' and 'the misery, ignominy and privations that marked the trail of the Nazi hordes across the face of Europe'. But the author makes it plain that the islanders were subjected to a more subtle instru-ment of pressure than the jackboot. They were very liberally treated indeed. The small island parliaments and courts continued to function, provided all their measures were submitted to German sanction. It was by an ordinance of the Guernsey Royal Court that all talk against the Germans was made punishable; thus when the manager of the Rich's stores was cheeky to a German customer, it was before the Guernsey Court that he appeared. He got off by explaining that it was all a mistake, that the German officers had all been charming and his son-in-law was taking German lessons. Divine service with prayers for the Royal family and the Empire were permitted. So were cinemas and newspapers.

In an organized society our dependence on the newspapers is abject. The readers of the *Guernsey Evening Post* were shocked and repelled no doubt to see articles by Goebbels and Lord Haw-Haw, but not to the pitch of stopping their subscriptions. How else could they advertise their cocker spaniels and their lawn mowers or learn about the cricket results? Ultimately Haw-Haw became an accepted feature like the testimonials for digestive pills, and an edge of horror and revulsion was blunted. Here is the printed summary of events for an October day in the first year of the occupation.

'Dog-biscuits made locally. Table-tennis League of Six Teams formed. German orders relating to measures against Jews published. Silver Wedding anniversary of Mr and Mrs W. J. Bird.' The news of the deportation and torture of the local shopkeepers is made more palatable by being sandwiched between sport and domestic pets and society gossip. 'Lady Ozanne had passed a fairly good night.' 'Mr Stephen Candon is as comfortable as can be expected.' There was Roller Skating at St George's Hall and 'Laugh it Off' was still retained at The Regal and 'the bride looked charming in a white georgette frock'. Lubricated by familiar trivialities, the mind glided over what was barbarous and terrible.

The *Herrenvolk* philosophy judiciously applied, as it was in the Channel Islands, can be swallowed easily enough if you have not too sensitive a digestion and belong to a ruling race yourself. Flowerbeds were trampled, housemaids whistled to, garden tools unceremoniously borrowed, but formal apologies, printed receipts were often forthcoming if applied for. 'I must record,' wrote Mr Maugham, of the German soldiers in his garage, 'they did their best to give us as little trouble as possible, were perfectly polite and grateful for any slight help which they received from us,' and the Procurator of Guernsey officially declared: 'The Germans behaved as good soldiers, sans peur et sans reproche.'

Such behaviour is plainly more formidable than the jackboot, we are hypnotized by the correctness of the invader into accepting invasion itself as correct. The solidarity of our resistance is undermined by carefully graded civilities, our social and racial hierarchies are respected. For example in Jersey there were Irish tomato pickers and Russian prisoners at whose expense German prestige was adroitly raised in British eyes. When wireless sets were confiscated the Irish, with disdainful correctness, were paid for theirs as they were neutrals. This punctiliousness was more repaying than jackboots since it drove a wedge of jealousy between English and Irish. When later on a feud broke out between the 'correct' occupation troops and some 'incorrect' naval ratings who daubed the shop fronts of St Helier with swastikas, the authorities blamed this breach of etiquette upon the Irish, and there were some gentlemanly headshakings between the German and English officials over these vulgar antics of an inferior breed.

I don't think the Germans on the island had a difficult task in making the Russians in Jersey detested. Some of the Russians, who were employed in the fortification of the island, were convicts liberated from prison in the German advance into Russia. They were worked hard, fed little and flogged. A whip that was used on them can be seen in the Jersey Museum. They were inadequately guarded. Almost mad with hunger, they broke loose and pillaged the neat holdings of the Jersey farmers, taking hens, pigs, cabbages, clothes from the line. These raids began through the carelessness of the guards, continued through their connivance and finally had their active encouragement. The guards indicated the eligible premises and exacted a huge percentage of the plunder. When the Jersey people asked for protection they were met with a humorous shrug from the officials. 'Well, they are your allies. Must *we* protect you from them?'

It is hard for the Xs to keep a balanced judgment in such circumstances. Other problems too arise. Should they acknowledge the salute of the amiable Rittmeister, who had known their cousins at Weybridge? Should they turn the other cheek when a degenerate Mongol ally robs the hen-roost? These problems are more disintegrating to the resistance of the Xs than bombs or jackboots, and a competent invader will make them inescapable.

In a Zagreb newspaper of 1942, *Deutsche Zeitung in Kroatien*, I read that Ireland, with Croatia and Slovakia, was to be one of the three model 'allied' states in German Europe. In other papers too there was much of flattering intent about the common loyalty of Croats and Irish to Faith and Fatherland, our similar histories, romantic temperaments and literary gifts. Irish plays continued to be played in Zagreb, when English were tabu.

All the same I think that Brittany under the Nazis offers more profitable analogies for us in Ireland than does Croatia. In Brittany the German attempt to exploit the patriotism of the Ys and the piety of the Zs, which in Croatia had been triumphantly successful, was only half-hearted. The Nazis had no doubt of the need to disintegrate Yugoslavia, they were undecided about France. Perhaps, after defeat, France might be won over more easily if her unity was not impaired, perhaps a separatist and Celtic Brittany might slip out of German influence and look westward to Celtic Wales. Also in Brittany the Catholic Church did not support the separatist movement, as it did in Croatia. There was no wide-scale convergence of patriotism and piety. By conciliating the patriotic Ys, the Germans might risk offending the pious Zs.

For all these reasons Nazi policy in Brittany was very inconsistent.

The Germans sheltered the Breton rebel leaders, Mordrel and Debauvais, as they had once sheltered Roger Casement and they too were invited to recruit a rebel army to fight for independence among the prisoners of war. The Breton prisoners responded in the same half-hearted way as the Irish had once done. The Germans, however, continued to support the Breton movement till France had been brought to her knees. Then they made terms with Vichy, withdrew all aid from the Breton separatists and allowed them to operate only against the Maquis. They led the Bretons the sort of dance that cannot be done in jackboots.

I think the Nazi policy in regard to Ireland would have been equally agile and ambiguous. The Celtic nationalist would, as in Brittany, have been regarded as a valuable tool for undermining a non-German hegemony, but of decidedly less value for the reconstruction of a German one. The nationalist would have been manoeuvred, not kicked, out of his privileged position.

Judging by the Breton analogy, I think the first impact of the changed policy might have been borne by the handful of single-minded German Celtophiles, who would have been entrusted with the early stages of the programme. A successfully double-faced policy requires at the start the complicity of many single-minded idealists, native and foreign.

I think when the success of the invasion had been assured, it would have emerged that the respectable Xs, the Anglo-Irish *Herrenvolk* of Ulster and the Dublin suburbs, would prove the more satisfactory accomplices in establishing the German hegemony. The Jersey treatment would have been applied to them, insofar as they were civilians. There would have been a dazzling display of 'correctness'. It is probable that at Greystones and Newtownards, as at St Helier and at Peterport, divine service with prayers for the King and the British Empire would continue to be permitted in the Protestant churches. Certainly the inevitable bias of German correctness would have been towards the Anglo-Saxon, towards bridge and fox hunting, and away from the Irish, from ceilidhes and hurley matches and language festivals. A master race will be at times indulgent to these regional enthusiasms but will not participate in them. Ultimately this bias would have led to a complete reversal of policy, more in keeping with the *Herrenvolk* philosophy. Lord Haw-Haw, an Irishman himself, seems to have been in closer sympathy with the Mosleyites than with the Irish republicans. The British Naziphiles were romantic, traditional, imperialist. Irish separatism would have been incompatible with their Kiplingesque ideal of a merry, beer-drinking 'old' England, allied with Germany, grasping once more in her strong right hand the reins of empire and dealing out firm justice to the lesser breeds. I do not see how the Irish could have raised themselves permanently into the *Herrenvolk* class from which Czechs and Poles had been excluded. Of course the Croats had arrived there. But they must have felt their position precarious, because two well-known Croatian scholars, Father Shegitch and Professor Butch, developed the theory that the Croats were really Goths who had slipped into a Slav language by some accident. Pavelitch, the 'Leader' of Croatia, who had a private passion for philology, favoured the theory and brought out a Croat lexicon in which all words of Serbian origin were eliminated, a work of great ingenuity because the Serbian and Croatian languages are all but identical. We Irish would inevitably have felt uneasy. There had been in Ireland eminent German Celtic scholars who had not managed to conceal their contempt for the modern representatives of those Celtic peoples whose early history enthralled them. Nazi philosophy was permeated with race snobbery and we are outwardly a rustic and unpretentious people. When a Nazi leader, Ribbentrop, visited Ireland, it was with a Unionist leader, Lord Londonderry, at Newtownards that he stayed. In the Nazi hierarchy of races the Irish would not I think have ranked high.

It is likely that ultimately more attention would have been paid to our piety than to our patriotism. Its pattern is universal and familiar and so more easily faked, whereas patriotism has so many regional variations that no ready-made formula could be devised to fit them all. Many of the pious Zs would have responded to skilful handling. The other day I read in an Irish newspaper the sermon of a well-known preacher. 'The world', he said, 'may one day come to be grateful to Hitler.' He was thinking, of course, of Communism and it was the constant preoccupation of the Nazis that the minds of the pious should always be inflamed with the fear of it. In that way charity and humanity, where they were only superficial, could be skinned away like paint under a blow-lamp. But in the technique of perverting piety it was in the Independent State of Croatia that the Nazis first showed their consummate skill. Pavelitch's Croatia deserves the closest study.

When an incendiary sets a match to respectability, it smoulders malodorously, but piety, like patriotism, goes off like a rocket. The jackboot was worn by the Croats themselves and used so vigorously against the schismatic Serbs that the Germans and the Italians, who had established the little state, were amazed. Pavelitch, the regicide ruler of Croatia, was himself the epitome, the personification, of the extraordinary alliance of religion and crime, which for four years made Croatia the model for all satellite states in German Europe. He was extremely devout, attending

Mass every morning with his family in a private chapel built onto his house. He received expressions of devoted loyalty from the leaders of the Churches, including the Orthodox, whose murdered metropolitan had been replaced by a subservient nominee. He gave them medals and enriched their parishes with the plundered property of the schismatics, and he applied the simple creed of One Faith, One Fatherland, with a literalness that makes the heart stand still. It was an equation which had to be solved in blood. Nearly two million Orthodox were offered the alternatives of death or conversion to the faith of the majority. The protests of the Xs, Ys and Zs were scarcely audible.

Yet, as I read the newspaper files in Zagreb, I felt that it was not the human disaster but the damage done to honoured words and thoughts that was most irreparable. The letter and the spirit had been wrested violently apart and a whole vocabulary of Christian goodness had blown inside out like an umbrella in a thunderstorm.

It is easy to illustrate this from the newspapers of a single week in spring 1941. In one Zagreb paper, for example, the king's speech on the bombing of Belgrade was published with appropriate comments on April 10.

'On the morning of Palm Sunday,' he said, 'while children slept their innocent sleep and the church bells were ringing for prayer to God, the German aeroplanes without warning let fall a rain of bombs on this historic town...' and the king went on to describe the terror of the women and children, who were machine-gunned as they fled from their homes, by low-flying planes.

The following day the Germans in Panzer divisions arrived in Zagreb. Flags were out in the streets to welcome them and the same paper wrote in solemn phrases: 'God's providence in concord with the resolve of our allies has brought it about that today on the eve of the resurrection of the Son of God our Independent Croatian State is also resurrected... all that is right and true in Christianity stands on the side of the Germans'!

When Pavelitch fell, the Zs had to take a third somersault. Words had by then lost all relation to fact and thereafter there was something schizophrenic about the exaggerations of the Croatian Zs and their sympathizers. Rather than admit their horrible inadequacy, they plunged about in contrary directions, sometimes whitewashing Pavelitch, sometimes making him blacker than life.

Many were able to turn head over heels in a quiet, gentlemanly way. For example the Bishop of Djakovo, Dr Akshamovitch, who received the Delegation from the National Peace Council, of which I was a member, in a very friendly way, was a kind old man of whom we already knew a little. Under Pavelitch circulars flowed from his diocesan printing press headed 'Friendly Advice', reminding the Serbs that Jesus had said there was to be one flock and one shepherd and that, as Catholics, they could stay in their homes, improve their properties and educate their children.

When Tito came to power the bishop is said to have invited the Central Committee of the Croatian Communist Party to lunch. He certainly attended a Peace Meeting in Belgrade. His photograph was printed in the press, as was his speech, in which warm praise was given to Tito. Should one charge him with opportunism? At this range one cannot judge him, but what is clear is that both governments valued his support and profited by it.

In future wars, if there are any, the formulae of corruption will be a little different but the principle will be the same. It may be said that the respectable Xs will only be wooed by the invader if he comes from a capitalist country, but that, if he is Communist, no dangerous flirtations need be feared. I am not so sure. Acquisitive, tenacious, timidly orthodox people are not confined to any class or creed. It is a matter of temperament rather than of social standing or of politics. They have the force of inertia, which all invaders will wish to have on their side. As for piety and patriotism, whether they are deep or superficial, they are ineradicable from the human race. In the long run the modern state, east or west, will try to assimilate the Xs, Ys and Zs, not to exterminate them.

Horace once wrote that the honest man, innocent of crime, could protect himself without Moorish javelins, without his bow or his quiver full of poisoned arrows. But is ordinary innocence enough nowadays or must he cultivate the unseeing eye? Must he not 'mind his own business' like the professional man, or 'simply do his duty and carry out orders' like the soldier, or like the tradesman 'just get on with the job'? (The Channel Island papers are full of cheery synonyms for connivance!) Are we really obliged to admire the armour-plated innocence and respectability of General Rommel, that 'preux chevalier' of the sub-scription libraries? He concentrated so fiercely on his professional duties that ten years after Hitler came to power he was still able to be ignorant of, and shocked by, the Jewish extermination policy, by gas-chambers and the destruction of Warsaw. I don't think these questions can be answered unless we isolate them and study them in a small more or less homogeneous area. It is clear that small peoples are used as guinea pigs by the great powers. Experiments are tried out on them which are later applied on a wider scale. Their suffering and their reaction to suffering are studied but only for selfish, imperialistic ends. Should not the results of these experiments be recorded now while the memory is still fresh and accuracy and candour are available? For though such knowledge will not of itself bring us the will or the courage to resist tyranny, it will prevent us from dispersing our strength in fighting against shadows. By learning from which direction the most insidious attacks are likely to come, we may acquire the skill to forestall them.

[1950]

THE CHILDREN OF DRANCY

Lately I was comparing three versions of the story of the Children of Drancy and it occurred to me that we mostly have more detailed information, more curiosity, about remote and now irrelevant events like the murder of the two little Princes in the Tower in the summer of 1483 or the death of 123 English people in the Black Hole of Calcutta on 19 June 1756. Two of the writers I consulted said it was in July, a third said it was in August 1942 that the 4051 children were sent off to be killed in Poland from the transit camp at Drancy north of Paris. Were they French Jews or foreigners? Were they girls or boys? It is usually said boys, but suburban residents on the outskirts of Paris who heard them wailing at night say they were little girls, and there is a story of a bleeding ear torn by a harried police inspector as he removed an earring.

They spent four days without food at the Vélodrôme d'Hiver (the winter cycle-racing stadium) before their mothers were taken from them, then they were loaded three or four hundred at a time into cattle trains at the Gare d'Austerlitz and taken to Auschwitz. It was related at Nuremberg that an order came from Berlin that deportees from Vichy, France should be mingled discreetly with the children to make them look like family groups. Was this done? It is not as though dubious legend has grown up around these children as it has around King Herod's far smaller enterprise in Bethlehem. The facts are bleak and few. It should not be hard to find more and to iron out discrepancies. But no one seems interested.

I believe we are bored because the scale is so large that the children seem to belong to sociology and statistics. We cannot visualize them reading Babar books, having their teeth straightened, arranging dolls' tea parties. Their sufferings are too great and protracted to be imagined, and the range of human sympathy is narrowly restricted.

Had four or five children only been killed and burnt, and had it happened outside the booking office at the Gare d'Austerlitz, we would have responded emotionally and probably their names and their fate would have been carved on a marble tablet like that which commemorates the victims of the Black Hole outside the Post Office in Calcutta. And the names of their murderers would be remembered for ever. But to kill and burn 4051 children after transporting them to Poland was a huge co-operative endeavour, in which thousands of French and German policemen, typists, railway officials, gas-fitters and electricians were engaged. It was composite villainy, and when you try to break it down there are no villains, just functionaries as neutral and characterless as the clusters of ink blobs of which a press photograph is composed. The officials who handled the children were, we are told, deeply affected. Even the Vichy Commissioner for Jewish Affairs, Louis Darquier, who deported Jews in their thousands from France, had suggested that the children be transferred to a French orphanage, but he did nothing about it. Though Pierre Laval, the French Premier, was enthusiastic about the deportation of all foreign Jews, even those under sixteen, neither he nor Pétain realized that they were not going to be 'settled' in the East but killed there.

Even at the peak of the organizational pyramid one finds duty, routine, idealism of a kind more often than sadism as the motive power; in the interests of a more glorious future the tender impulses had to be suppressed. At the Jerusalem trial even the most hostile witnesses failed to prove that Eichmann, an exemplary husband and father, had ever been guilty of wanton cruelty. These people were really what they claimed to be, idealists, whose seedy ideals would never have germinated and pullulated in any other century but ours.

However confident we may be of the facts, there are irreconcilable divergences when we come to their interpretation. 'Too much science,' say some. 'Too much literary scorn for science,' say others. François Mauriac, who was in Paris at the time, wrote some twenty years later:

Nothing I had seen during those sombre years of the Occupation had left so deep a mark on me as those trainloads of Jewish children standing at the Gare d'Austerlitz. Yet I did not even see them myself. My wife described them to me, her voice still filled with horror. At that time we knew nothing of Nazi methods of extermination. And who could have imagined them? Yet the way these lambs had been torn from their mothers in itself exceeded anything we had so far thought possible. I believe that on that day I touched upon the mystery of iniquity whose revelation was to mark the end of one era and the beginning of another. The dream which Western man conceived in the eighteenth century, whose dawn he thought he saw in 1789, and which, until 2 August 1914, had

grown stronger with the process of enlightenment and the discoveries of science –
this dream vanished finally for me before those trainloads of little children. And
yet I was still thousands of miles away from thinking that they were to be fuel
for the gas chamber and crematorium.

Yet even at the time few thought like that. It is easier to forget about
the Children of Drancy than to liberate ourselves from the increasing
control that science has over our lives. The year after Mauriac wrote
what I have quoted, Charles Snow delivered at Cambridge his famous
lecture on 'The Two Cultures' in which he claimed the traditional
culture of the past, and science, the culture of the future, should make
peace with one another. Charles Snow, a novelist himself, addressed his
lecture mainly to the 'traditional' man of letters, scolding him for being
ignorant of elementary scientific knowledge like molecular biology and
the Second Law of Thermodynamics.

He quoted with approval someone he referred to as 'a distinguished
scientist':

Why do most writers take on social opinions which would have been thought
uncivilized at the time of the Plantagenets? Wasn't that true of most of the
famous writers of the twentieth century – Yeats, Pound, Wyndham Lewis –
nine out of ten of those who have dominated literary sensitivity in our time?
Weren't they not only politically silly, but politically wicked? Didn't the
influence of all they represent bring Auschwitz that much nearer?

Snow scolds Ruskin, William Morris, Thoreau, Emerson and D.H.
Lawrence for their rebellion against the Age of Science: 'They tried
various fancies, which were not in effect more than screams of horror.'

I dislike quoting Snow when he talks nonsense or endorses other
people's nonsense (when I was younger I enjoyed his novels and in 1941
wrote a rave review of *The Masters* in *The Bell*). As an Irishman, who
knew Yeats, I can only gasp when the great Irish poet is linked with
Auschwitz.

Snow's lecture caused tremendous interest. It was published and many
times reprinted. There was a three-week long correspondence in *The
Spectator*, most of it favourable to Snow. He was thinking on popular
lines. When he wrote his novels he was Charles Snow, then he became
Sir Charles, and finally Lord Snow.

Only F.R. Leavis, Professor of English Literature at Cambridge,
reacted violently. He delivered and later printed a lecture furiously
attacking Snow, denouncing him as few leading writers have been
denounced before. He too was printed in *The Spectator* and there was
much comment, most of it hostile.

Snow [writes Leavis] takes inertly the characteristic and disastrous confusion of
the civilization he is trying to instruct.

He is intellectually as undistinguished as it is possible to be.

He thinks he has literary culture and scientific culture. In fact he has neither.

He rides on an advancing swell of cliché without a glimmer of what creative
literature is or what it signifies.

Who will assert that the average member of a modern society is more fully
human or alive than an Indian peasant?

As a novelist he doesn't exist. He can't be said to know what a novel is.

Leavis is an ardent champion of D.H. Lawrence, and, possibly, compared to Lawrence, Snow as a novelist is negligible.

Leavis mentions the Indian because Snow had a detailed plan for
rescuing the poorer peoples of the world by means of a scientific revolution. He thought, for instance, that the USA and Britain should educate
ten or twenty-thousand scientific specialists 'to the level of Part 1 Natural
Science or Mechanized Science Tripos' and send them to India, Africa
and South-East Asia to help industrialize the inhabitants and lever them
out of their pre-scientific stagnation.

How could Snow fail to see that the transportation of six million Jews
to the camps was, like the atom bomb, among the most sensational of
science's achievements and that, in the international field, science is more
often used as an instrument of hatred than of neighbourly love. Think
of the export of arms to Iran and the Contras in Nicaragua, and indeed
of the great build-up of armaments all over the globe.

He was surely driven to entertain these visions, more fantastic than
the dreams of William Morris, by his knowledge that science was in fact
irresistible and had enormous potentialities for good and evil, which
only men of traditional culture, if they accepted it and understood it a
little, might be able to control. If they know a little about genetics,
for example, they might be able to monitor and arrest the appalling
experiments of the geneticists, which now only religious leaders with
the wisdom and authority of the pre-scientific centuries behind them
can forbid. They might have persuaded the Americans to industrialize
Vietnam (if the Vietnamese wanted to be industrialized) rather than
devastate it. But at present the average man of letters knows nothing of
science and most scientists are culturally illiterate. Snow says that the
average scientist, when one tries to probe what books he'd read, would
modestly confess, 'Well, I've tried a bit of Dickens.' Snow himself must
have guessed that the gulf between the Two Cultures is unbridgeable.

Has any decade seen so much sophisticated science-promoted violence
as the Eighties? All over the world, in small countries and large ones,

men who could not invent a pop-gun themselves have access to the newest and most lethal weapons. In Ireland the IRA get their arms from Libya and pay for them by kidnapping the owners of supermarkets (the ransom is always paid and then lied about). Where do the Libyans get their arms from? Who knows? A brisk trade goes on all round the world and the great powers are helpless to end it.

For Mauriac, the eighteenth-century dream of a future enlightened by the discoveries of science had died at Drancy. In England Aldous Huxley and George Orwell had earlier predicted all sorts of horrors. In his book *The Revolt of the Masses* (1932) the Spaniard Ortega y Gasset had analyzed what was happening much more accurately: 'Technicism, in combination with liberal democracy, had engendered the Mass Man. . . Modern science has handed over the command of public life to the intellectually commonplace.' Observe the calibre of the world leaders of 1987.

Snow would have none of this. 'The scientific edifice of the physical world is in its intellectual depth, complexity and articulation the most beautiful and wonderful work of the mind of man.' In fact beauty is in the eye of the beholder. A primrose by the river's brim is just as likely to dazzle it as the structure of the haemoglobin molecule. All nature can be seen as beautiful.

According to Snow let the Two Cultures but unite and educate those twenty-thousand Mechanical Science Tripos men and the gap between the rich and the poor will be bridged, overpopulation checked and the atomic war averted.

Most thinking men stand midway between the despair of Orwell and Mauriac from which only the grace of God can rescue us and the twenty-thousand Tripos men, but believe that God and the Tripos men are slowly converging. Though they might express themselves differently, they would concur with the prayer which Major Cooper, the heroic astronaut, composed on his seventeenth orbit round the earth; it ends:

Help us in future space endeavours to show the world that democracy really can compete and still is able to do things in a big way and is able to do research development and conduct new scientific and technical programmes.

Be with all our families. Give us guidance and encouragement and let them know that everything will be okay. We ask in Thy name. Amen.

Though the joint session of Congress to which this prayer was read approved of it, a Hindu about to be industrialized might complain that life is more complex than Major Cooper and Charles Snow believed. A certain intellectual simplicity is the price that has to be paid for irrigation and tractors and freedom from famine and disease. An idea that has to travel far by modern means and circulate freely among alien people must, like an air passenger's luggage, be very meagre indeed.

In spite of that, most men would sooner believe in the healing powers of scientific research and technology than accept François Mauriac's counsel of despair.

But the true answer of the scientific optimist to Mauriac will not, I think, be found by Major Cooper in outer space or by those twenty-thousand Tripos men. Should one not consider the question of size and whether we really have 'to do things in a big way'?

Anti-Semitism, the idea which killed the Children of Drancy, was small and old and had existed for centuries in small pockets all over Europe. If humane ideals had been cultivated as assiduously as technical ones it would long ago have died without issue in some Lithuanian village. But science gave it wings and swept it by aeroplane and wireless and octuple rotary machines all over Europe and even lodged it in Paris, the cultural capital.

No one likes thinking on these lines. Yet observe how even pity can become helpless and sometimes destructive when it is divorced from deep personal concern and becomes a public matter. Public pity forms committees, sends tinned meat, secures entry visas, but the beating of its collective heart can be heard from miles away and it is easily eluded. Those in charge of the children eluded it by taking them to Auschwitz. It was to dodge public pity that the children were torn from their mothers and travelled alone or with doomed strangers. The mothers, when their future first became known, preferring death for their children to the lonely fate they foresaw for them, had started to throw them down from the tops of buildings. They would have continued to do this from the railway carriage windows and the dead or dying bodies might have roused some dormant committee into action in France or Germany or Poland.

Something similar was happening in Free Europe. As the funds of the refugee committees swelled, the price of liberty for a Jew went higher and higher. The compassion of the Allies, turned into cash, could be used against them. In 1944 Allied pity could have saved a million Jews in return for 100,000 trucks, but the trucks would have been used against Russia and so divided the Allies and resuscitated the latent anti-Semitism of the Russians. Looking at the matter in the large way it was better even for Jewry as a whole that a further million Jews should die.

Because of these complexities the Children of Drancy will always remain shadowy figures, and as nursery symbols of the vast cruelty of the world we shall go on using Herod and the little princes and the Black Hole. These stories are educative because they are about wicked men who can be punished or at least reviled, and not about that Faceless and Mysterious Collective Iniquity against which we are powerless. It is not a satisfactory choice, all the same, because historians now think that Herod never massacred the Innocents and that Richard Crookback never smothered the princes and that Suraja Dowlah thought the Black Hole was properly ventilated, whereas no one denies what happened to the Children of Drancy.

It is because we do things in the big way that the Wicked Man has now become so elusive and almost an abstraction. The chain of responsibility lengthens every day; we can think of it as an immense row of Part 1 Science Tripos graduates holding hands across the earth and linking together the triumphs of civilization to a depth of savage misery which the Aztecs, because they never discovered the wheel, could not inflict upon their victims. Snow mentions with approval a prototype of these Tripos men, a Prussian called Siemens, a pioneer in electrical engineering over a hundred years ago. I prepared this paper by the light of electricity that was brought from the great dam at Ardnacrusha on the river Shannon by Messrs Siemens a generation ago; each bulb had 'Siemens, made in Germany' printed on it. In this way Siemens helped to modernize Ireland, but Ireland was only one link in a long chain. In November 1932 Karl von Siemens used his wealth and influence to bring Hitler to power and later his firm installed the electricity at Auschwitz, where of course it was not used just for reading lamps and making toast. There too, as at Lublin, Siemens set up factories for the employment of slave labour, while for their factory at Berlin Haselhaorst they bought seven hundred women from the SS at Ravensbruck at four to six marks a head. The directors of Siemens were on the American list of German industrialists to be prosecuted at Nuremberg, but probably they were all humane and agreeable men belonging to the upper, beneficent end of the long chain; anyway, the charges against them were dropped. On the other hand, Ezra Pound, who had, on his own responsibility and not as a link in a chain, given much foolish praise to the Fascists, was punished and arraigned. Yet he had never killed or enslaved anybody.

It will always be so. A mischievous poet is like a thorn in the finger. He can be pulled out. But the mischief that results from a concentration of Tripos men is like disseminated sclerosis. And that is another reason why we talk so little about the Children of Drancy.

Charles Snow was surely right when he said that most literary intellectuals are 'natural Luddites'. I think he meant that they continue to worry when worry is useless. Ruskin, Morris, Thoreau, Lawrence, all repudiated the new world to which engineer Siemens was devoting his genius, but even a century ago it was hard already to contract out while now it is all but impossible. Should I read by candlelight because the firm that gave me electricity illuminated also the last agony of the Children of Drancy? I don't think so. I am less frightened of science than I am of that doctrine of the Mystery of Iniquity, which is to many the only consolation left now that there is no traffic on the road to Brook Farm, and New Harmony is sealed off. The Mystery of Iniquity has its roots in despair, but wickedness would no longer be mysterious if the chains of responsibility were shorter and science, which lengthened those chains, must be forced to go into reverse and shorten them.

Fortunately there are still small communities where the Wicked Man is not yet woven so scientifically into the fabric of society that he cannot be extracted without stopping the trains and fusing the electric light. It is not a coincidence that two small countries, Denmark and Bulgaria, stemmed the flow to Auschwitz better than any of their more powerful neighbours on the continent. Apart from size the two countries have nothing in common. The Bulgars are primitive, the Danes a highly sophisticated people. They are no doubt individually as wicked as the rest of us, but wickedness still has a name and an address and a face. When the rumour, a false one, went round Sofia that the government intended to deport its Jews, the citizens demonstrated outside the Palace and blocked the roads to the railway station. In Denmark on the night of 1 October 1943, when the Jews heard they were to be rounded up, each family knew which Danish family was prepared to hide them. Very few were caught. At the Gare d'Austerlitz the Children of Drancy were surrounded by the most civilized and humane people in Europe, but they were scarcely less isolated and abandoned than when they queued up naked for their 'shower-bath' in the Polish forest.

But I must answer the charge made by Snow's scientist that W. B. Yeats 'brought Auschwitz nearer', because by focussing his mind on distant horizons Snow failed to see what was under his nose. Yeats deliberately chose the small community, moving his heart and his body and as much as he could of his mind from London to Ireland, his birthplace. For him and a dozen other well-known Irish writers Ireland had been a larger Brook Farm, a refuge whose walls were built not by some transcendental theory but by history and geography. For a few years our most parochial period became also our most creative. If there was in Yeats a Fascist streak it derived from his disillusionment with the drab unheroic Ireland in which the dreams of the visionaries of 1916 had ended. He complained that 'men of letters lived like outlaws in their own country'. When he saw that Irish Fascism promised to be as drab and demagogic as Irish democracy, he rapidly back-pedalled and rewrote the song he had composed for the Blue Shirts, making it so fantastic that no political party could sing it. He led the campaign against the Irish censorship and in everything he did and said he was a champion of intellectual and moral and social freedom.

In all this he was an isolated figure and even in Ireland the range of his influence was very small. But in my opinion personal and parochial efforts like his did form a real obstruction on the road to Auschwitz, whereas its traffic was never once interrupted by conventional weapons.

The courage of the astronauts, the talents of the twenty-thousand Tripos men are needed, but they must break down, link by link, those long chains of atomized guilt with which the Children of Drancy were strangled.

POSTSCRIPT

The Children of Drancy were not totally forgotten in France. On 5 November 1978 a programme on the last days of Marshal Pétain was to be screened. It was abruptly withdrawn and a film on the Renaissance Pope Clement VII was substituted. The reason was that there had been a remarkable national re-examination of conscience in France due to an interview published in L'Express with the eighty-year-old Darquier, the Vichy Government's Commissioner for Jewish Affairs, whom I have mentioned already. Despite the kindly intentions towards the Children of Drancy with which he has been credited, he had deported 75,721 French Jews to German concentration camps, including the Children. He was so virulent an anti-Semite that even the Germans were surprised by his zeal. He escaped to Spain and was condemned to death in his absence but this was soon forgotten. After a pause he changed his name to d'Arquier de Pellepoix[1] and, an elegant figure with a monocle, he became a welcome guest in the cocktail circles of Franco's Spain. It was here that the enterprising correspondent of L'Express contacted him thirty-three years after the war was over. He was a sick man crippled by hardening of the arteries, but he still enjoyed the protection of many leading figures, military and political, and he met the correspondent's enquiries with amused condescension. The six million concentration camp deaths, he declared, were a Jewish invention. 'They were all of them exported to new homes in Central Europe,' he said. 'The only victims of the Auschwitz gas-ovens', he added, 'were fleas.' (I suppose he meant that their clothes were fumigated in preparation for their new life.) He refused to look at the photographs of the piles of gas-chamber victims. 'Jewish fakes!' he exclaimed.

The whole of France was moved by the new revelations. President Giscard d'Estaing and Prime Minister Barre warned about the treatment of their Nazi past on the television screen and the press. Simone Veil, the Minister of Health, was profoundly stirred. She had been deported to Auschwitz with her family at the age of fourteen.

'It is the first time since the war,' she said in the National Assembly, 'that anyone has dared to go so far.' There were pictures of Auschwitz and the other death camps shown on television and in the press. There was a clamour to have Darquier extradited. There was much indignation that French television refused to acquire the American series 'Holocaust'. 'Too expensive,' one network said, and an artist, Marek Halter, opened a fund for private donations to contribute to the cost.

Then the public prosecutor, acting on orders from the Minister of Justice, opened a new case against Darquier for 'defence of war-crimes and incitement to racial hatred'. But Spain has never extradited political offenders to France and time had run out under the twenty-year Statute of Limitations.

[1968/78]

1. He did not have to do even this much. Max Ophuls's documentary film *Le Chagrin et la Pitié* shows him in 1940, proudly greeting Streicher under his full name.

THE SUB-PREFECT SHOULD HAVE
HELD HIS TONGUE

In countries where the old beliefs are dying it is the custom for educated people to handle them with nostalgic reverence. It is thought crude and undignified for a sophisticated man to take sides in a religious squabble, and it often happens that, the less he believes in himself, the more indulgent he is to the time-honoured beliefs of others. I have been reproached several times by sincere and civilized unbelievers for my efforts to find out the details of the vast campaign in Croatia in 1941 to convert two and a half million Orthodox to Catholicism.[1] 'Why not let bygones be bygones?' they say. 'If we rake these things up we'll merely start trouble at home and play into the hands of the Communists. And anyway, they are always killing each other in the Balkans.' I once heard an ambassador in Belgrade argue like that, and indeed I have never heard a British or American official abroad argue in any other way. When in 1946 I went to Zagreb and looked up the files of the war-time newspapers of Croatia in which the whole story was to be read, it was obvious that no foreign inquirer had handled them before, and the library clerks regarded me with wonder and suspicion.

Yet it seemed to me that for a man as for a community too high a price can be paid for tranquillity. If you suppress a fact because it is awkward, you will next be asked to contradict it. And so it happened to me when I got back to Ireland, and gave a talk about Yugoslavia, the country and its people, on Radio Éireann. I did not mention the Communist war on the Church, or Archbishop Stepinac, who had just been sentenced to imprisonment for collaboration with Pavelitch, the Quisling ruler of Croatia, and for conniving at the forced conversion campaign. I could not refer to the Communist persecution of religion without mentioning the more terrible Catholic persecution which had preceded it, so I thought silence was best. But silence did not help me. In the following week our leading Roman Catholic weekly,

The Standard, published a long editorial diatribe against myself and against Radio Éireann. I had not, it declared, said a word about the sufferings of the Church and its ministers under Tito and, by sponsoring me, Radio Éireann had connived at a vile piece of subversive propaganda. The officials of Radio Éireann, knowing I was no Communist, supported me, and finally *The Standard*, under pressure from my solicitor, agreed to print a long reply from me. I received the proof-sheets, corrected and returned them, but the reply never appeared. Months later, a muddled, amiable explanation reached me, and my friends said 'let bygones be bygones'. I did. That is the way things happen in Ireland.

But it became increasingly difficult to be silent. The foreign editor of *The Standard*, Count O'Brien of Thomond, published a little book called *Archbishop Stepinac, The Man and his Case*. It had an introduction by the Archbishop of Dublin, and commendation on the dust-cover from a couple of cardinals, Canadian and English, and half a dozen bishops and archbishops. Cardinal Spellman laid a copy of the book on the foundation stone of the new Stepinac Institute in New York, USA, and told 1700 schoolgirls, drawn up on a polo-ground in the form of a rosary, what they were to think about Croatian ecclesiastical history. Yet it seemed to me that there was a major error of fact or of interpretation, or a significant omission, on almost every page of this book. Meanwhile all the county councils and corporations in Ireland met and passed resolutions. Extracts from Count O'Brien's book were hurled about, and fiery telegrams despatched to parliaments and ambassadors.* But the climax of my discomfort was reached when our Minister for Agriculture, Mr Dillon, addressing some law students, advised them to model themselves on Mindzenty, Stepinac and Pavelitch, who had 'so gallantly defended freedom of thought and freedom of conscience'. Those who knew Yugoslavia were aghast, for Pavelitch, one of the major war criminals, was the Yugoslav counterpart of Himmler, and it was under his rule that the gas chamber and the concentration camp were introduced into Yugoslavia and the forced conversion campaign initiated. Clearly Mr Dillon was speaking in ignorance, not in bigotry, but ignorance rampaging with such assurance and harnessed to religious enthusiasm is like a runaway horse and cart. It must be stopped before serious mischief results.

I felt that the honour of the small Protestant community in Southern

---

* In my own county town, Kilkenny, a muddled but enthusiastic alderman insisted that Tito was in Dublin in the capacity of Yugoslav ambassador, and proposed at the Corporation meeting that he should be told 'Get out, Tito!'

Ireland would be compromised if those of us who had investigated the facts remained silent about what we had discovered. In many Roman Catholic pulpits the sufferings of the Catholics under Tito were being compared to the long martyrdom of Catholic Ireland under Protestant rule. 'Yesterday and today Herod abides.' If we agree that history should be falsified in Croatia in the interests of Catholic piety, how could we protest when our own history was similarly distorted?

In letters to the newspapers I had replied to Mr Dillon and many others who had expressed similar opinions. A well known Irish Jesuit, Father Devane, assuming a Slav name, Mihajlo Dvornik, to lend force to his accuracy, solemnly declared that there had been no forced religious conversions in Croatia, but I could find no one ready to argue the details. Mostly they quoted at me passages from Count O'Brien, or, on *a priori* grounds, accused me of vile slander. 'The Catholic Church had always insisted that conversion must be from the heart. *Ad amplexandam fidem Catholicam nemo invitus cogatur.*' I was alleging the impossible.

Soon afterwards it was announced that Tito was to visit London, and in Ireland, as in England, various anti-Yugoslav demonstrations were arranged. My friend, Owen Sheehy-Skeffington, a lecturer in Trinity College and now a member of the Irish Senate, invited me to a meeting of the Foreign Affairs Association, at which the editor of *The Standard* was to read a paper on 'Yugoslavia – the Pattern of Persecution'. The Association had been modelled on Chatham House as an international fact-finding society and Arnold Toynbee himself had come over to give his blessing to the first meeting. In the *Survey of International Affairs* of 1955 he was later to express himself as strongly as I had about the persecution of the Orthodox. This is an undenominational society with a tradition of free speech. The lecturer had never been to Yugoslavia, and I believe that all the others on the platform were in the same position, though one of them said that on a cruise down the Dalmatian coast he had met members of a Yugoslav football team. I decided that at the end of his paper I would try to make those points which he had failed, despite his promise, to publish for me. I would try to show how variegated was the pattern of persecution in Yugoslavia, and how misleading our crude simplifications would be. What followed has been told by Paul Blanshard, whom I met for the first time that evening, in his book *The Irish and Catholic Power*. It is enough to say here that the Chairman's attempt to close the meeting at the end of the paper was ruled out, on a vote, as unconstitutional. I got up, holding in my hand *The Martyrdom of the Serbs*, a book published by the exiled Serbian Orthodox Church in Chicago, in case anything I said required authoritative corroboration. It had been given me by archpriest Nicolitch, the head of the Serbian Orthodox Church in England. But I had spoken only a few sentences when a stately figure rose from among the audience and walked out. It was the Papal Nuncio, of whose presence I had been unaware. The Chairman instantly closed the meeting, and there was an appalled silence, followed by a rush of reporters in my direction. They had understood nothing in the confusion. There was, consequently, some lively reporting, and two leading dailies quoted me as saying that the Orthodox Church, not the Communists, had initiated the persecution of the Catholics in Yugoslavia. In gigantic letters in the *Sunday Express* (Irish edition) I read: 'Pope's Envoy Walks Out. Government to Discuss Insult to Nuncio.'

Blanshard has described the measures taken against Skeffington in Dublin and myself in Kilkenny. The persecution was of a familiar pattern, and I try to see in it not a personal hard-luck story, but material for a study in the modern indifference to evidence, but I think both of us knew that had we been less fortunate in our backgrounds we would have been ruined. Skeffington, the son of a father executed by the British in 1916 – or, to be more accurate, murdered at the orders of a hysterical British officer – is at his happiest when he is fighting, and shortly afterwards he had fought his way into the Irish Senate. For myself, I am grateful for the few inherited acres which have helped me to survive the disapproval of my neighbours. All the local government bodies of the city and county held special meetings to condemn 'the Insult'. There were speeches from mayors, ex-mayors, aldermen, creamery managers. The County Council expelled me from one of its sub-committees, and I was obliged to resign from another committee. Although my friends put up a fight, I was forced to give up the honorary secretaryship of an archaeological society which I had myself founded and guided through seven difficult years. My opponents hoped that my liquidation would be decorous and quickly forgotten, but my friends and myself were little inclined to oblige them, and for a time our small society enjoyed in the metropolitan press a blaze of publicity which its archaeological activities had never won for it.

I decided that before I resigned I would tell our two or three hundred members something about the forced conversion campaign in Yugoslavia. Much of the evidence, including the utterances of the Orthodox Church and its bishops, and Archbishop Sharitch's 'Ode to Pavelitch', with its sonorous denunciations of Serbs and Jews, I put aside, because I was certain that it would not be believed. Finally, I decided to publish the long letter written by Stepinac to Pavelitch on the subject of the forced conversions. I had translated it from a typescript in Zagreb in 1946, and it seems to me a document of vast importance which deserves a prominent place in the annals of religious history. Its reception was disappointing. Many were confused by the outlandish names and inextricably complicated series of events, and I was taken aback when one friendly disposed reader congratulated me on 'my interesting article on Czechoslavia'.

There is in Ireland a historic loathing of proselytism. The well-meaning Protestants who plied the starving peasants of the west with soup and Bibles after the famine of 1846 had never been forgiven. Religious apprehensions as strong as these survive in Yugoslavia, and I had hoped that some of my neighbours would be capable of the necessary mental adjustment and would see the parallel. Surely it would be obvious to them from the Stepinac letter that the Croatian bishops, while denouncing the use of force, were delighted with the opportunities for mass conversion which the chaos and defeat of Yugoslavia afforded them. There was, for example, Dr Mishitch, the Bishop of Mostar and the kindliest of mortals, whom even the Communists have praised for his clemency. He too had made quite plain the hopes which he had entertained at the beginning of Pavelitch's régime:

By the mercy of God [he wrote] there was never such a good occasion as now for us to help Croatia to save the countless souls, people of good will, well-disposed peasants, who live side by side with Catholics... Conversion would be appropriate and easy. Unfortunately the authorities in their narrow views are involuntarily hindering the Croatian and Catholic cause. In many parishes of (my) diocese... very honest peasants of the Orthodox faith have registered in the Catholic Church... But then outsiders take things in hand. While the newly-converted are at Mass they seize them, old and young, men and women, and hunt them like slaves. From Mostar and Chapljina the railway carried six waggons full of mothers, girls, and children under eight to the station of Surmanci, where they were taken out of the waggons, brought into the hills and thrown alive, mothers and children, into deep ravines. In the parish of Klepca seven hundred schismatics from the neighbouring villages were slaughtered. The Sub-Prefect of Mostar, Mr Bajitch, a Moslem, publicly declared (as a state employé he should have held his tongue) that in Ljubina alone 700 schismatics have been thrown into one pit.

Elsewhere in his letter the Bishop wrote:

At one time there was a likelihood that a great number of schismatics would be united to the Catholic Church. If God had given to those in authority the understanding and the good sense to deal effectively with conversion, so that it could have been carried through more ably, more smoothly and by degrees, the number of Catholics might have been increased by at least five or six hundred thousand. Such a number is required in Bosnia and Herzegovina, if there is to be an increase from 700,000 to 1,300,000.

The other three bishops, whose letters Stepinac quoted, all took the normal human view that it is inadvisable in the name of religion to throw waggon-loads of schismatics over cliffs; they were critical of the conversion campaign, but they did not find the occasion for it un-seasonable. Had there been no cruelty, and if possible a little soup, they would have welcomed it. But compared with Mgr Mishitch's letters theirs are cold, calculating and self-righteous. Archbishop Sharitch opined that the town council of Sarajevo was imposing too high a tax on the Bosnian Orthodox for their change of religion. The Bishop of Kotor, Dr Butorac, declared that the missionaries to the Serbs must be wisely selected. 'We must not entrust the problem,' he wrote, 'to monks or priests who have no tact at all and who would be much better suited to carry a revolver in their hands than a cross.' And he expressed the fear that if the Serbs were driven too hard they might, out of defiance, pass over in a body to Islam.

I must confess that I find Mgr Stepinac's comments on these letters and the situation that provoked them curiously narrow and thin-lipped. He scolds the miserable, hunted Orthodox for their terrible errors, deriving, he declares, from 'hatred and schism', and he blames them for the Russian Revolution, just as he blames the crimes of Pavelitch and his gang on the Chetniks – that is, the followers of Mihailovitch – the Communists, and the Royal Yugoslav Government. He considers that the best way to convert the Orthodox might often be found through the medium of the Greek Catholic Church, which recognizes the authority of the Pope while preserving its Orthodox ritual. He ends his letter, as he began it, by exonerating Pavelitch from all blame in the crimes that had been committed.

Yet Count O'Brien tells us in his little book that at this time, in defence of the Orthodox, the Archbishop had swept into Pavelitch's office. '"It is God's command!" he said, "Thou shalt not kill!" and without another word he left the Quisling's palace.'

Stepinac's long and respectful letter to Pavelitch at this date proves the anecdote to be a hagiographical fabrication. Yet it was quoted at me several times in the press of Kilkenny and Dublin. The letter was obviously the longest and most important that Stepinac had ever written, and it struck me as odd that though I had published it twice in Ireland – for my critics in Kilkenny and also in *The Church of Ireland Gazette* –

nobody in the British Isles, at a time when so much was written and said about the imprisoned Archbishop, ever commented on it, quoted from it, or wrote to me to enquire how I had secured it. Three years later, however, Richard Pattee published in America a lengthy book in defence of Stepinac, and among his documents the letter belatedly appeared. Yet I believe that my translation is the more accurate of the two. Mr Pattee has thought it best to omit a sentence or two here and there. He leaves out, for instance, Mgr Mishitch's calculations of the number of conversions required in Bosnia and Herzegovina. Again, wherever the word 'conversion' appears in the text Mr Pattee reads it as 'legitimate conversion', thus adding a epithet which I could not trace in the original. Stepinac's admiring description of the Bishop of Banja Luka as 'that old Croatian warrior' likewise disappears, presumably because Mr Pattee does not wish his readers to infer that the bishops were Croatian separatists trying to ingratiate themselves with Pavelitch.

About the same time Mr Michael Derrick published in *The Tablet* a paragraph or two from Mishitch's letter, but he attributed it to Stepinac, and he omitted the extraordinary parenthesis about the Sub-Prefect who told of the barbarities inflicted upon the Orthodox, and the bishop's comment that 'as a state employé he should have held his tongue'. In the succeeding issue of *The Sword*, Mr Derrick published my translation of Stepinac's *The Regulations for Conversion* without acknowledgment! Anybody who read these regulations with an open mind, and particularly an Irish Catholic with his inherited horror of 'souperism', would have to admit that they bore every trace, except soup, of *illegitimate* conversion. For instance, Clause XI, an appeal that the Orthodox be granted full civic rights, has been much applauded, but it begins, 'A psychological basis for conversion must be created among the Greek Orthodox inhabitants.' If still in doubt as to the bearing of these regulations one would have only to read the manifesto of Dr Shimrak, editor of the leading Catholic daily, and chosen by Stepinac as one of his two colleagues in the supervision of conversion:

Every priest must have before his eyes that historic days have come for our mission. Now we must put into practice that which we have spoken of in theory throughout the centuries. In the matter of conversion we have done very little up to this, simply because we were irresolute and dreaded the small reproaches and censure of men. Every great task has its opponents, but we must not be downcast on that account, because it is a question of a holy union, the salvation of souls and the eternal glory of the Lord Christ. Our work is legal in the light of the ruling of the Holy See... also in the light of the ruling of the Holy Congregation of Cardinals for the Eastern Church... and finally in the light of the circular sent by the Government of Independent Croatia, July 30, 1941, whose intention it is that the Orthodox should be converted to the Catholic faith (*Diocesan Magazine of Krizhevtsi*, No. 2 [1942], pp. 10–11).

Count O'Brien, an Austrian of Irish descent, had been until he came to Ireland after the war the editor of an important Viennese paper, and he claims in his book to have known Shimrak intimately for twenty years. He also writes that all the Croat bishops had opposed Pavelitch's 'evil plan' for the forced conversion of the Orthodox. This seemed in such strong conflict with Shimrak's declaration that long before the 'Insult' I had visited Count O'Brien to ask for an explanation. An explanation was forthcoming. The Count replied at once that Shimrak had not been a bishop at the time, but only an administrator. It appeared from his reply that it was actually after he had proved himself in sympathy with Pavelitch's plan that Shimrak was appointed to the bishopric and to Stepinac's committee for regulating conversion. I then asked how it came about that, if all the bishops were hostile to Pavelitch and his plans, Archbishop Sharitch of Bosnia, one of the greatest of them, had been able to print his *Ode to Pavelitch* in the ecclesiastical papers of his own archdiocese and that of Zagreb. I had made a translation of his ode in twenty-six verses, describing his meeting with Pavelitch at St Peter's in Rome, and I now ventured to remind Count O'Brien of a few lines:

> Embracing thee was precious to the poet
> as embracing our beloved Homeland.
> For God himself was at thy side, thou good and strong one,
> so that thou mightest perform thy deeds for the Homeland...
> And against the Jews, who had all the money,
> who wanted to sell our souls,
> who built a prison round our name,
> the miserable traitors...
> Dr Ante Pavelić! the dear name!
> Croatia has therein a treasure from Heaven.
> May the King of Heaven accompany thee, our Golden Leader!

Count O'Brien had an explanation for that, too. He said: 'The Archbishop was an abnormal man, very emotional. He was always embracing people. Whenever we met, he used to kiss me on both cheeks. He can't be taken seriously.'

These replies made me feel very helpless, since they could not have been made if venal indifference had not reigned around us. When I went home I was feeling as emotional as the Archbishop, and I remember that I wrote a poem myself on the Massacre of the Orthodox, though I must admit that it was the massacre of the truth that really outraged me.

> Milton, if you were living at this hour,
> they'd make you trim your sonnet to appease
> the triple tyrant and the Piedmontese.
> 'Why for some peasants vex a friendly power?
> We'd like to print it, but Sir Tottenham Bauer
> and half the Board would blame us. Colleen Cheese
> would stop its full-page ad. They're strong RCs.
> It's old stuff now, and truth, deferred, goes sour.
> So cut those lines about "the stocks and stones"
> and "slaughtered saints", or keep for private ears
> that fell crusade, for even in undertones,
> it breeds disunion and the Kremlin hears.
> Say nothing rash or rude, for it is right
> that all the godly (west of Kiel), unite!'

I thought my poem almost as good as the Archbishop's, but I had some difficulty in getting it published. In the end it appeared in a pacifist weekly, but very inconspicuously and in very small print. The Archbishop had been luckier. His had appeared in *Katolicki Tjednik (The Catholic Weekly)* on Christmas Day, with a signed portrait of Pavelitch and a decorative border of Christmas tree candles and little silver bells.

I suppose that the small community in which I live has about the same significance for the world as the community of Mr Bjitch, who as a state employé 'should have held his tongue' about the massacres, so I need not apologize for returning to it. My friends and neighbours were memorably kind and supporting; for they knew that I had not intended to insult anybody. But others were puzzled. I was not, like Mr Bjitch, a state employé, and some found it difficult to make their disapproval materially felt. This problem would not have baffled them for long had it not been for the courtesy and good sense of the local Catholic clergy. I was most vulnerable through the Kilkenny Archaeological Society. This had been a famous Victorian institution, with the Prince Consort as patron and the Marquess of Ormond as President, but it has shifted to Dublin as an All-Ireland Society, and when I revived it in Kilkenny in 1944 it had been dead there for half a century. In a couple of years the new Society became a real bridge between Protestant and Catholic, Anglo-Irishman and Celt. The friendliness which it created was perhaps our main achievement, but we did other things, too. Mr O. G. S. Crawford made for us a photographic survey of old Kilkenny such as no other Irish provincial town possesses; Dr Bersu, the Director of the Institute of Frankfurt, made his principal Irish excavation on a hill fort outside Kilkenny and reported it in our journal; we had a centenary celebration of the old society in Kilkenny Castle; and the National Museum co-operated in a very successful Kilkenny Exhibition. But I think I was proudest of having organized a week's visit from the principal archaeological society in Northern Ireland; for cultural fraternizations between North and South are as rare as they are valuable. I feared that all this work would be wasted, so I decided to appeal to a certain Stephen Brown, a Jesuit, who had attended meetings of our Society. He had escorted the Nuncio to the fateful meeting, and afterwards in the *Irish Independent* had defended the Croatian hierarchy against the charges of illegitimate proselytism, with copious quotations from Count O'Brien but, as it seemed to me, with a total ignorance of Yugoslav conditions. Father Brown received me warmly. He said he was satisfied that I had not intended to insult the Nuncio, that he strongly disapproved the introduction of the incident into the affairs of an archaeological society, and that in any case the Nuncio had visited the meeting by mistake under the impression that he was bound for a meeting of a Catholic society with a similar name. Father Brown said that he would send me a letter making these three points, and that I might publish it in any paper I chose. The letter never arrived. It seemed, however, that a compromise had been reached in the matter, for a few days later a paragraph appeared in *The Standard* under the heading 'Mr Butler rebuked'. After commending all the denunciations by public bodies, the passage ended:

It is well that such repudiation should be known. But we doubt if any good purpose would have been served by the proposed step by which Mr Butler would have been deprived of office in, say, the Kilkenny Archaeological Society, of which he is presumably an efficient functionary, and into which he can scarcely introduce sectarian issues. If he has any regard for public opinion he must know by now that his action met with not alone local but national disapproval. That is sufficient.

It was difficult for me to return as a presumably efficient functionary to a Society which I had myself founded, so I never after attended a meeting, but my friends, both Catholic and Protestant, still support the Society and I am glad today that it continues.

I hope I have not appeared to diagnose in my Catholic countrymen a unique susceptibility to a disease with which we are all of us more or less infected. Speed of communications has increased, and we are expected to have strong feelings about an infinite series of remote events. But our powers of understanding and sympathy have not correspondingly increased. In an atmosphere of artificially heated emotionalism truth simply dissolves into expediency. This shifting current of expediency may be illustrated by a chronicle of the changing attitudes to Pavelitch in the past ten years. In Croatia, upheld by the victorious Germans, he had for four years been regarded as a great Christian gentleman and patriot. All the Catholic bishops and the Evangelical bishops were among his panegyrists and had received decorations from him. Then the Nazis collapsed, and Pavelitch was regarded by the outer world as one of the basest of war criminals, while in Croatia all the dignitaries hastened to disavow the compliments they had paid him. A former Italian Fascist, Malaparte, in his book, *Kaputt*, has described how, as correspondent of *Corriere Della Sera*, he visited Pavelitch in his office in 1942 and saw behind him what appeared to be a basket of shelled oysters. 'Are these Dalmatian oysters?' Malaparte asked. 'No,' Pavelitch replied, 'that's forty pounds of human eyes, a present from my loyal Ustashe in Bosnia' – eyes, that is to say, of the Serbian Orthodox. I am ready to believe that this story is an invention, like Stepinac's visit to 'the Quisling's Palace', and that stories like this were repeated by the ex-Fascists, who thought that if they made the whole world black their own shade of dirty grey would be less conspicuous. But in 1948 no one told Malaparte that he was a liar. Indeed, writing about *Kaputt* in *The Irish Times*, Mr Kees van Hoek, the biographer of the Pope, said that Malaparte was 'the most accurate observer and reliable witness'.

That was the universal western view of Pavelitch seven or eight years ago – a monster of iniquity, an ogre out of a fairy-tale. But since then Pavelitch has become more respectable, and if he was wanted again in a campaign against Communism in the Balkans it is possible that he and his friends would be used. He now lives in South America and two or three papers and journals are published in his interest. Five years ago he issued postage stamps commemorating the tenth anniversary of Independent Croatia, and he has cashed in very effectively on the Stepinac legend, since one of his Ustasha clubs in the Argentine is called after the famous Cardinal. Archbishop Sharitch, the devoted admirer of both Pavelitch and Stepinac, lives in Madrid, but still publishes his odes (rather modified), as well as ecstatic reminiscences of Stepinac, in *Hrvatska Revija*, a Croatian separatist quarterly of Buenos Aires. I once visited Mgr Stepinac in prison and found him a gentle and serious man, who obviously acted as he thought was right. Surely it must be one of the hardest blows that fate has dealt him that both Pavelitch and Sharitch speak well of him?

In one way or another the memory of a terrible crime against humanity is being confused and effaced, so that many people believe that it never happened at all or that it has been monstrously exaggerated. I have seen Pavelitch compared in Irish papers with Roger Casement and Patrick Pearse as a simple-hearted patriot who merely did his best for his country in difficult circumstances. In October 1952 he was interviewed for an Italian picture paper, *Epoca* of Milan. He was photographed basking in the South American sun with his wife and family, stroking a pet dog. He told how he had escaped from Croatia through the Allied lines, how he had paused for weeks at a time in Naples, the Vatican City, and Castel Gandolfo. He was to be considered a romantic fellow, the carefree immunity which he enjoyed no more than his due.

How had all this happened? Three centuries ago Milton gave undying notoriety to the massacre and forced conversion of the Waldenses, and Cromwell sent out emissaries to collect information about the sufferings of this tiny Alpine community. We are mostly now immune from the religious fanaticism which once intensified racial antipathies and to which Cromwell himself was no stranger; why has it become unwise to censure or even to take notice of an explosion of those ancient passions fifty times more devastating than that which Milton observed? There were scarcely ten thousand Waldenses to be persecuted in Piedmont, while the decrees of Pavelitch were launched against more than two million Orthodox, and 240,000 were forcibly converted.

Looking for a reason, I can only conclude that science has enormously extended the sphere of our responsibilities, while our consciences have remained the same size. Parochially minded people neglect their parishes to pronounce ignorantly about the universe, while the universalists are so conscious of the world-wide struggles of opposing philosophies that the rights and wrongs of any regional conflict dwindle to insignificance against a cosmic panorama. They feel that truth is in some way relative to orientation, and falsehood no more than a wrong adjustment, so that they can never say unequivocally 'that is a lie!' Like the needle of a compass at the North Pole, their moral judgment spins round and round, overwhelming them with information, and telling them nothing at all.

[1956]

1. Other relevant essays are 'Yugoslav Papers' and 'Father Chok and Compulsory Conversion' in *Grandmother and Wolfe Tone*.

THE ARTUKOVITCH FILE

I. REFLECTIONS ON A CROATIAN CRUSADE

Some years after I had written 'The Sub-Prefect Should Have Held His Tongue', I was in New York and read how the Yugoslav Government was urging that Artukovitch, Pavelitch's Minister of the Interior, who was living in California, should be extradited. I went to the Yugoslav Consulate to enquire about this and was handed a fat yellow booklet called *Artukovitch, the Himmler of Yugoslavia* by three New Yorkers called Gaffney, Starchevitch and McHugh.

Artukovitch first won notoriety in October 1934. He had gone to England at the time of King Alexander's murder at Marseilles. After his visit to Paris, the king had intended to see his son, Crown Prince Peter, at Sandroyd School, so, in case the Marseilles attempt failed, Artukovitch had been deputed to arrange for the king's assassination in England. It did not fail so Artukovitch waited in Czechoslovakia and Hungary till the Nazi invasion of Yugoslavia. He then returned with them and held various ministerial posts under Pavelitch from 1944 to 1945 in the Independent State of Croatia. Very few people have heard of him, yet if his story were told with remorseless candour, we would have a picture not only of Croatia forty years ago, but of all Christendom in our century. Everything that the New Yorkers relate was already known to me, except for one startling paragraph, an extract from a memoir by Artukovitch himself. After describing how he escaped to Austria and Switzerland in 1945, he goes on:

I stayed in Switzerland until July 1947. Then with the knowledge of the Swiss Ministry of Justice I obtained personal documents for myself and my family, which enabled us to travel to Ireland. Using the name of Anitch, we stayed there until 15th July, 1948. When our Swiss documents expired, the Irish issued new papers and under Irish papers we obtained a visa for entry into the USA.

So evidently we in Ireland had sheltered this notable man for a whole year. He was not, like Eichmann, a humble executive, but himself a maker of history, dedicated to the extermination not of Jews alone, but also of his fellow-Christians, the Serbian Orthodox. He was a member of the government which in the spring of 1941 introduced laws which expelled them from Zagreb, confiscated their property and imposed the death penalty on those who sheltered them. Some twenty concentration camps were established in which they were extermina-ted. Why do we know so little about his sojourn among us? Did he stay in a villa at Foxrock or in lodgings at Bundoran or in some secluded midland cloister? And who looked after him? The Red Cross? And did we cherish him because he presented himself to us as a Christian refugee from godless Communism? That seems to me rather likely.

Nowadays we usually estimate cruelty by statistics and Gaffney and Co. use the figures normally recorded for Croatia by Jewish and Ortho-dox writers, that is to say, 30,000 Jews and 750,000 Orthodox massacred, 240,000 Orthodox forcibly converted to Catholicism. Even if these figures are exaggerated, it was the most bloodthirsty religio-racial crusade in history, far surpassing anything achieved by Cromwell and the Spanish Inquisitors. I am sorry that Gaffney and Co. give so many photographs of headless babies, of disembowelled shopkeepers, of burning beards soaked in kerosene, for Artukovitch was, like Himmler, a 'desk-murderer', who deplored the disorderly and sadistic way in which his instructions were carried out. He was respectable, and it is the correlation of respectability and crime that nowadays has to be so carefully investigated.

The three writers tell Artukovitch's story with much emotion, because, as is plain, they want him to be extradited and hanged. But in itself the story is of the highest importance, for no earlier crusade has been so richly documented. If the abundant material were coolly and carefully studied, how much could we learn about human weakness and hypocrisy! We could observe how adroitly religion can be used in the service of crime. When Pavelitch and Artukovitch and their armies retreated, they were sure that, on the defeat of Germany, England and America would turn upon Russia and they could return to Zagreb. Therefore nothing was destroyed, the state documents were stored in the Archiepiscopal Palace, the gold (dentures, wrist-watches and all) was hidden below the deaf and dumb confessional in the Franciscan mon-astery and cemented over by the friars themselves. The newspapers of the time, secular and ecclesiastical, are still to be seen in the Municipal

Library, but this huge pile of documents, the Rosetta Stone of Christian corruption, has not yet been effectively deciphered.

These terrible Church papers, 1941 to 1945, should destroy forever our faith in those diplomatic prelates, often good and kindly men, who believe that at all costs the ecclesiastical fabric, its schools and rules, its ancient privileges and powers, should be preserved. The clerical editors published the Aryan laws, the accounts of the forced conversions, without protest, the endless photographs of Pavelitch's visits to seminaries and convents and the ecstatic speeches of welcome with which he was greeted. Turn, for example, to *Katolicki Tjednik (The Catholic Weekly)*, Christmas 1941, and read the twenty-six-verse 'Ode to Pavelitch', in which Archbishop Sharitch praises him for his measures against Serbs and Jews. Examine the Protestant papers and you will find the same story. Is it not clear that in times like those the Church doors should be shut, the Church newspapers closed down, and Christians, who believe that we should love our neighbours as ourselves, should go underground and try to build up a new faith in the catacombs?

Why did our professional historians not deal with all this long ago? They seem to wait till history is dead before they dare to touch it. But does a good surgeon only operate on corpses? They have wholly misinterpreted their functions, for it is their duty to expose the liar before his contagion has spread. While Artukovitch was on his way to Ireland, a Dublin publication told us authoritatively that the massacre of the Serbian Orthodox had never happened. In Count O'Brien's book[*] on Mgr Stepinac, to which I have already referred, we read:

They [the Orthodox] were offered by Pavelitch the choice between conversion to the Catholic faith or death... But the Catholic Church as a whole, all her bishops and the overwhelming majority of her priests, led by the Archbishop of Zagreb, made this evil plan impossible.

Some of the correspondence between Artukovitch and Stepinac has been published in English by Richard Pattee[†] and, collating with Gaffney, we see how Stepinac, a brave and merciful though very simple man, was hopelessly compromised by his official connection with the state. It was only his own flock whom he could help, and even them very little. For example, he appealed to Artukovitch on behalf of one of his priests, Father Rihar, who had defied Pavelitch. His failure was absolute, for this is how Artukovitch replied:

[*] A. H. O'Brien, *Archbishop Stepinac, The Man and his Case* (London 1947).
[†] Richard Pattee, *The Case of Cardinal Aloysius Stepinac* (London/Milwaukee 1953).

Zagreb. 17th November, 1942. In connection with your esteemed request of 2nd November, 1942... notice is hereby given that Francis Rihar by the decree of this office of 20th April, 1942, No. 26417/1942, was sentenced to forced detention in the concentration camp at Jasenovac for a period of three years... because as pastor at Gornja Stubica he did not celebrate a solemn high mass on the anniversary of the founding of the Independent State of Croatia... nor did he consent to sing the psalm *Te Deum Laudamus*, saying that it was nowhere prescribed in ecclesiastical usage...

Stepinac appealed again, but Rihar had been already three months at Jasenovac and, therefore, according to the rules of this camp, he was killed.

How, anyway, could Stepinac defend Father Rihar with any authority, since he himself had done what Rihar refused to do? Gaffney and Co., on page 42, reproduced seven photographs of the celebration of Pavelitch's birthday on 15 June 1942, and a letter from the Archbishop exhorting his clergy to hold a *Te Deum* after High Mass the following Sunday, 17 June, because of 'Our Glorious Leader'.

Since Pattee omitted this very relevant letter, it is strange that he printed Stepinac's correspondence with Artukovitch about the Jews, for this makes it clear that in acknowledging the authority of Pavelitch, the Archbishop, for diplomatic reasons, felt obliged to accept the terminology of the anti-semites and their human classifications. For example, on 30 May 1941 he urged Artukovitch 'to separate the Catholic non-Aryans from non-Christian non-Aryans in relation to their social position and in the manner of treating them'.

Much has been written about Communist distortions of history, but only recently has our own inability, as Christians, to report facts honestly been closely investigated. Now, after twenty years, the dam has burst and the truth, a turbid stream, is inundating our self-complacency and irrigating our self-knowledge. Catholic scholars are leading the way. For example, Professor Gordon Zahn has shown how selective is the documentation on which the biographies of Christian heroes of the resistance are based. Their sermons and speeches were pruned of all the compliments they paid to Hitler and his New Order and no row of dots in the text marks the excision of these now-embarrassing ecstasies.

In the long run, remorseless truth-telling is the best basis for ecumenical harmony. Hitler once explained to Hermann Rauschning how he intended to use the Churches as his propagandists. 'Why should we quarrel? They will swallow anything provided they can keep their material advantages.' Yet Hitler never succeeded in corrupting the Churches as effectively as did Pavelitch and Artukovitch, who professed to be Christians. We shall not be able to estimate the extent of their success and how it might have been resisted, while a single fact is diplomatically 'forgotten'. It is well known that those who suppress history have to re-live it.

*

How did Artukovitch (alias Anitch) get to Ireland? I wrote to Yugo-slavia, to America, France, Germany and questioned Yugoslavs in Dublin and London. The Yugoslavs, both Communist and anti-Communist, had no information. A friend in London, who had been to Trinity College, Dublin, remembered someone saying: 'I'd like you to meet a very interesting chap called Anitch', but the meeting had never happened. In the end Branko Miljus, a former minister of the pre-war government in Belgrade, who now lives in Paris, got some news for me from a friend in Switzerland. If I seem to give too many names and details, it is so that his story can be checked and completed.

The first stage of the journey is fairly well known. Pavelitch and Artukovitch had escaped to Austria when the Croatian state collapsed. They seem to have been arrested by the British in Salzburg and, after 'a mysterious intervention', released and there was an interval of hiding in monasteries at Sankt Gilgen and Bad Ischl. The Yugoslavs were in hot pursuit, so Pavelitch fled to Rome, disguised as a Spanish priest called Gomez. Artukovitch stayed on till November 1946, when he met the learned Dr Draganovitch, Professor of Theology at Zagreb, who was touring the internment camps with a Vatican passport. He had secured the release of many hundreds of Croat priests who had fled with Pavel-itch. Now he obtained for Artukovitch papers under the name Alowz Anitch and put some money for him in a Swiss bank. Two other priests, Fathers Manditch and Juretitch, also came to his aid. The former, the treasurer to the Franciscan order, controlled a printing press at the Italian camp of Fermo and assisted the Ustashe (Croatian nationalist) refugees with funds and propaganda. Juretitch had been sent on a mission to Fribourg by Archbishop Stepinac, so he and Manditch, both former students of Fribourg University, were able to secure a welcome there for Artukovitch. Archbishop Sharitch, Pavelitch's poet-champion, had got there ahead of him. Both Draganovitch and Juretitch had been appointed by Mgr Stepinac to the Commission of Five for the Conversion of the Orthodox in November 1941. These three were important people to have as sponsors. The ecclesiastics of Fribourg must have been impressed. They recommended Artukovitch to the police who got him a *permis de séjour*. There were other difficulties, which, according to report, Artukovitch smoothed out by the gift of a Persian carpet to an influential official.

But meanwhile the Federal Police had learnt that Anitch was the war criminal Artukovitch. They told him he had two weeks in which to leave Switzerland. Once more the Franciscans came to his aid. The prior of the Maison Marianum at Fribourg recommended him to the Irish Consulate at Berne. And so it happened that in July 1947 Artukovitch landed with his family on the Isle of Saints, sponsored by the disciples of that saint, who had prayed:

> Lord, make me an instrument of Thy peace!
> Where there is hatred let me sow love,
> Where there is sadness, joy!

I do not know where Artukovitch spent his Irish year, but one day, as a matter of history, and perhaps of religion, we shall have to know. If Artukovitch had to be carried half-way round the earth on the wings of Christian charity, simply because he favoured the Church, then Christianity is dying. And if now, for ecumenical or other reasons, we are supposed to ask no questions about him, then it is already dead.

On 15 July 1948 Artukovitch with an Irish identity card left Ireland for the USA where he settled as a book-keeper, near his wealthy brother in California, still under the name of Anitch. It was over two years before his true identity was discovered. The Serbian Orthodox were slow to move. Oppressed by the Communists at home, dispersed as refugees abroad, they still managed to publish the facts in books and papers in London, Chicago, Paris. In 1950 Branko Miljus, and two other prominent monarchist politicians in exile, sent a memorandum to the Fifth Assembly of the United Nations urging it to implement its resolution of December 1946, which had branded genocide as a crime against international law. They asked that its member states should take into custody, till a Commission be appointed to try them, some 120 Croat nationals, who had taken refuge among them. On the long list appended, the names of Artukovitch, Archbishop Sharitch, Fathers Draganovitch and Juretitch and many Franciscans were mentioned, and some of the scarcely credible Franciscan story was related. It is stated that a Franciscan had been commandant of Jasenovac, the worst and biggest of the concentration camps for Serbs and Jews (he had personally taken part in murdering the prisoners and Draganovitch, with the rank of Lieut.-Colonel, had been the chaplain). The memorandum relates how the focal centre for the forced conversions and the massacres had been the Franciscan Monastery of Shiroki Brijeg in Herzegovina (Artukovitch had been educated there) and how in 1942 a young man who was a law student at the college and a member of the Catholic organization, The Crusaders, had won a prize in a competition for the slaughter of the Orthodox by cutting the throats of 1360 Serbs with a special knife. The prize had been a gold watch, a silver service, a roast sucking pig and some wine.

How can this be true? One recalls that great hero of Auschwitz, the Polish Franciscan Father Kolbe. But it *was* true and rumours of it had reached Rome. Rushinovitch, Pavelitch's representative at the Vatican, had reported to his Foreign Minister in Zagreb the remarks of Cardinal Tisserant, with whom he had an audience on 5 March 1942:

I know for sure that even the Franciscans of Bosnia-Herzegovina behaved atrociously. Father Shimitch, with a revolver in his hand, led an armed gang and destroyed Orthodox Churches. No civilized and cultured man, let alone a priest, can behave like that.

Tisserant had probably got some of his information from the Italian general of the Sassari division at Knin, who had reported that Shimitch had come to him as local representative of the Croatian Government and had told him that he had orders to kill all the Serbs. The general had had instructions not to interfere in local politics, so he could only protest. The killing, under Franciscan leadership, had begun. The following year the Superior of the Franciscan Monastery in Knin was decorated by Pavelitch for his military activities with the order of King Zvonimir III.

The Croat bishops themselves were aware of what was happening. The Bishop of Kotor, Dr Butorac, while agreeing that the moment was propitious for mass conversion, wrote to Mgr Stepinac (4 November 1941) that the wrong type of missionaries were being sent – 'priests in whose hands revolvers might better be placed than a crucifix'.

In parenthesis, I should say, how fascinating are Rushinovitch's accounts of his audiences in Rome with Pius XII, with Cardinals Tardini, Maglione, Sigismondi and Spellman. Only Tisserant, and to a lesser extent Mgr Montini, the present Pope, appear to have fully grasped what was happening in Croatia. In Cardinal Ruffini the Ustashe had a firm supporter.

The memorandum had made little impression on the United Nations, since it had no member state behind it. It had accused Tito's Government, which *was* a member state, of sheltering many Croat criminals and using them to break down the anti-Communist resistance of the Serbs. However, in 1952 Tito appealed to the USA for the extradition of Artukovitch. The California Courts to whom the case was referred argued that the extradition treaty of 1901 between USA and Serbia had never been renewed and that therefore Artukovitch could not be handed over to Yugoslavia. Six years later the Supreme Court rejected this view (by 7 to 1) and decreed that the case must be tried again in California. In the meantime Artukovitch had become a member of the Knights of Columbus and a much-respected figure who gave lectures to institutes and interviews on TV. When he was arrested again 50,000 Knights sent petitions on his behalf to Congress, and the West Pennsylvania Lodges of the Croatian Catholic Union forwarded a resolution that 'his only crime is his ceaseless fight against Communism' and that he was a champion of the rights and freedoms of all the peoples of the world.

That was the way his counsel, O'Connors and Reynolds, presented him, too, and Father Manditch, who had helped him in Switzerland, was once more by his side, in charge of another printing press and now Superior of the Franciscan Monastery in Drexel Boulevard, Chicago. His papers *Nasha Nada* and *Danica (Our Hope* and *Morning Star)* not only supported him but in their issues of 7 May 1958 urged their readers to send subscriptions for the Ustashe refugee fund to Artukovitch at his address in Surfside, California.

Another very useful ally was Cardinal Stepinac's secretary, Father Lackovitch, who had sought asylum at Youngstown, Ohio. In Europe Stepinac had been almost beatified for his implacable hostility to Pavelitch and Artukovitch, but now *The Mirror News* of Los Angeles (24 January 1958) reported Lackovitch as saying that he had seen Artukovitch almost daily and that he had been 'the leading Catholic layman of Croatia and the lay spokesman of Cardinal Stepinac and had consulted him on the moral aspect of every action he took'. The murderers of the Old World had become the martyrs of the New.

The American public was so ill-informed that it was possible to get away with almost anything. Pattee prints a statement that 200,000 of the converts from Orthodoxy were returning 'with a right intention' to a Church, which 'for political reasons' they had been forced to abandon. In fact, of course, the Serbian Orthodox had been in schism for some three centuries before the Protestant Reformation. Cardinal Tisserant, who had a rare tolerance of disagreeable truths, denounced Rushinovitch vigorously when he tried out this argument on him:

I am well acquainted with the history of Christianity and to my knowledge Catholics of Roman rite never became Orthodox... The Germans helped you kill all the priests and you got rid of 350,000 Serbs, before you set up the Croatian Orthodox Church. What right have you to accuse others and keep on telling us that you are guardians of culture and the faith? In the war with the Turks the Serbs did just as much for Catholicism as you did and perhaps more. But it was the Croats, all the same, who got the title of *Antemurale Christianitatis*.

When I was in California, I sent to see Father Mrvicin of the Serbian Orthodox Church at West Garvey, near Los Angeles, and asked him why the Orthodox and the Jews of California had tolerated so many lies. He told me that at the time of the extradition trial he had circularized close on a thousand Serbs, who must have known well about Artukovitch, urging them to give evidence, but very few had replied. Life in USA was hard for them as refugees, they did not want to affront a powerful community, McCarthyism was not yet dead and they were shy of associating themselves with an appeal that came from a Communist country. A naturalized American, who took the matter up, died violently and mysteriously.

As for the Jews, though 30,000 with their 47 rabbis had been murdered in Croatia, Croatia was far away, and many who had escaped to USA had owed their safety to holding their tongues. Even so, the Jewish War Veterans of California, *The Valley Jewish News* and some Gentile papers like *The Daily Signal* of California came out against Artukovitch. But most Americans felt for the unknown refugee and his five children the easy charity of indifference. Finally the Yugoslav Government did some profitable deals with the USA and became indifferent, too. It is now interested only in proving that Artukovitch was a helpless stooge of the Nazis and that therefore the Bonn Government should pay compensation to Yugoslavia for the damage that he and the Ustashe had done.

The other day I came across a *History of Croatia*, published by the New York Philosophical Library. The author, Mr Preveden, acknowledges various 'inspiring messages of commendation and encouragement'. One of them comes from 'Dr Andrija Artukovitch of Los Angeles'. He is quite a public figure. He may have changed his address but his telephone number used to be Plymouth 5–1147.

Now many people want him hanged but there would not be much point in it. He was an insignificant man, who got his chance because there had been a great breakdown in the machinery of Christianity and he was able to pose as its protector. Why did this breakdown occur? Can it be repaired and, if so, how? So long as we are obliged to pretend that the breakdown did not happen, we shall never find out.

[1970]

Postscript 1971
There has since been an easing of tension between Communism and Christianity, most notably in Yugoslavia, where diplomatic relations with the Vatican have been resumed and there has been friendship between Catholic and Orthodox. For example, in a Christmas message, Bishop Pichler begged forgiveness of the Orthodox Church and their

Serbian brothers for all the wrongs done to them and funds have been raised by Catholics to restore the destroyed Orthodox churches.

Some of the leading Orthodox are not wholly happy about all this. Is it spontaneous or Government inspired? Is it possible that Tito fears the deep-rooted and passionate nationalism of the Orthodox more than Catholic universalism, which can be manipulated by external arrangements? Under the amnesty to political offenders, many Ustashe have returned home, notably Father Draganovitch, one of the five 'regulators' of the Forced Conversions, who escorted Pavelitch and Artukovitch to safety. He is in a monastery near Sarajevo editing the Schematismus, a sort of ecclesiastical year-book, whose publication has been suspended since 1939. Some of his returned colleagues are more active politically.

There is, of course, everything to be said for peace and conciliation, but the brotherly love that is brought about by diplomatic manoeuvres is often a little suspect.

II. IN SEARCH OF A PROFESSOR OF HISTORY

I could not get it out of my head that eighteen years before, Artukovitch had stayed for a year in Ireland. How had he come here? Who had sheltered him and where? In the spring of 1966 I was in Dublin for a week and I decided to find out. I was convinced that only some highly organized international body could have brought a wanted man so secretly and efficiently across Europe and, since the Franciscans had been so closely associated with the Ustashe in Croatia and had many international links I was confident that it was they who had brought him. I have never heard anything but good of Irish Franciscans but they were an institutionalized body and as such able and anxious to protect their members who get into trouble abroad.

There were a dozen Franciscan Houses in Ireland and I wrote to the Provincial in Merchant's Quay, Dublin, and also to four or five other houses, which, because of their remoteness, I thought were likely. Most of them answered with polite negative replies. The Provincial told me that there had been a Croat Franciscan at their Galway house for some time but his name, Brother Ivanditch, was on the list of their Order and they had no doubt of his identity.

It was not until Branko Miljus sent me his copy of *The Mirror News* of Los Angeles that I made any progress. Artukovitch had been interviewed by the reporter, Henry Frank, who for the photograph had arranged him at a piano, grouping his wife and five handsome children round him. The Rev. Robert Ross of the Blessed Sacrament Church was there too as a friend and advocate. He told Frank how, as Minister of the Interior, Artukovitch had helped the Jews and been a formidable foe to the Communists.

'Artukovitch listened gravely and said with quiet dignity, "I put my faith in God".'

Frank spoke of Artukovitch's 'strong, seamed face' and his 'modest well lived-in living-room'. He told how his daughter, Zorica, had won an essay competition in Orange County High School and his nine-year-old son, Radoslav, had been born in Ireland.

Here was a clue. The children had been exploited sentimentally to mask the truth, so they could be used to rediscover it. I went to the Customs House and after prolonged search I found Radoslav Anitch's birth certificate (A.164, No. 75). He was born on 1 June 1948 at the Prague House Nursing Home, 28 Terenure Road East; he was the son of Alois Anitch, Professor of History, of 6 Zion Road, Rathgar.

On the strength of this discovery, I sent a letter to all the Dublin dailies, explaining that I was writing an account of the Independent State of Croatia (1941–45) and that I wished information about the former Minister of the Interior, Andrija Artukovitch, (alias Alois Anitch) who had lived at 6 Zion Road, Rathgar, in 1947. Only *The Irish Times* printed my letter, turning him into a lady called Audrey.

In the meantime I visited the two houses, which were close to each other. No. 6 Zion Road is a two-storied house of red brick with an ivy-tangled sycamore and an overgrown privet hedge, but it had changed hands so often that it told me nothing about Artukovitch's Irish sponsors.

No. 28 Terenure Road, a tall building of red and white brick with much ornamental ironwork, has ceased for some years to be a nursing home. Nobody knew where the former owner had gone and it was not till I paid two visits to the Guards Barracks at Terenure that one of them recalled where she now lived. It was not far off at 7 Greenmount Road and I went there immediately. The matron was a charming and intelligent woman and after eighteen years she remembered the Anitches perfectly. She had found them a pleasant and pathetic couple. He had spoken little English, Mrs Anitch had spoken fluently and, because of that, she had asked that he should have lunch with her in the Nursing Home. 'He is my baby,' Mrs Anitch had said, 'he wouldn't know how to get lunch without me.' They had two little girls who were at the Sacred Heart Convent, in Drumcondra Road, and now they wanted a boy. 'If it's a girl,' said Mrs Anitch, 'don't call him till the evening.' But when on the morning of 1 June Radoslav had been born, she was so delighted that she said her husband must be called at once. Anitch came and in his joy he had embraced the matron, much to her embarrassment.

The Anitches had behaved nicely, paying all their debts with money from America. After they had gone some months Mrs Anitch had written a grateful letter, which the matron showed me.

Only one person besides her husband had visited Mrs Anitch in the Nursing Home. He was a Franciscan who had been in Croatia, but the matron was not clear whether or not he was a foreigner. The Anitches had told her that the Communists had been particularly vindictive against the Franciscans.

My anticipations that the Franciscans had helped Artukovitch in Ireland had now been confirmed so I went to see the Provincial at Merchant's Quay. This time he agreed with me that the friar at the Nursing Home must have been the Croat at the Galway House. His name, he said, was Ivanditch. He was a supporter of Pavelitch and had often gone from Galway to Dublin.

Yet a Croat friar could not have made all these arrangements without powerful Irish assistance. Where had it come from?

The process by which a great persecutor is turned into a martyr is surely an interesting one that needs the closest investigation. I had only four days left in Dublin, so I could not follow up all the clues, but I made some progress.

First I went to the Sacred Heart Convent, 40 Drumcondra Road, a big red building on the left hand side of the street. I was shown into a little waiting-room and was received by a charming and friendly nun. I told her I was trying to trace the family of two little girls called Zorica and Vishnya Anitch, who had been at the convent in 1947 when they were four and five years old. She went away to look them up in her register and I sat for a very long time contemplating the plate of wax fruit and the little figurine of St Anthony. Then the nun returned and told me that the two little girls (but they were called Katherina and Aurea Anitch) had been admitted on 9 August 1947. Their parents had lived at 7 Tower Avenue, Rathgar and had taken the children to USA on 15 July 1948. She did not recall them herself but suggested that I ring up an older nun, Sister Agnes, who would certainly remember them. She was at St Vincent's Convent, North William Street. I rang Sister Agnes, who remembered them all vividly. The little girls were sweet and she had found the two parents 'a lovely pair' and Dr Anitch was 'a marvellous musician'. She did not remember that anybody came to visit the children except their parents, but a Franciscan monk, a nephew of Dr Anitch's, who had escaped with them from Croatia, was with them and had helped them to find lodgings.

Next I visited 7 Tower Avenue and was directed to a previous tenant, who worked in an ironmongery in D'Olier Street. He said he did remember having a lodger with a name like Anitch. He added, 'He was black, you know.' I tried other houses in Tower Avenue. Everybody was helpful and interested but I got no further clues.

After this I returned to Mrs O'Donoghue in Greenmount Road and found she had been keenly interested in what I had told her and herself had been trying to find out who had been the landlord in 6 Zion Road when the Anitches had lived there. She said I should get in touch with Patrick Lawlor, 32 Hazelbrook Road, who had sold the house to some woman in 1947.

I wrote to him and the next day he rang me up. He said it was so long ago that he could not remember the woman's name, but the auctioneer might know. After that I made some dozen visits and twenty telephone calls. They would be boring to relate but I found them exhilarating, as each clue led to another clue. I telephoned the doctor who had delivered Radoslav and examined the parish registers in Terenure and Rathgar for christenings. I went to the Valuation Office and telephoned the Voters Register, the Irish Red Cross, the Aliens Office and the International Office of Refugees. I enquired at the City Hall about Corporation Rates. In the end I got onto the solicitor who had acted both for Mr Lawlor and for the woman to whom he had sold 6 Zion Road. His clerk made an unsuccessful search for her name and then suggested, 'Why not call on Thom's Directory?'

I went there the next day and the secretary took down from a shelf the directories for 1947 and 1948 and found Patrick Lawlor's name in both. 'But that's impossible,' I protested. 'He sold the house to a woman in 1947.' 'Yes, but there might have been a delay in publishing after we collected the information.' She took down the directory for 1949. 'The woman's name was Kathleen Murphy,' she said. I was off like a shot to a telephone-box.

There were three Miss K. Murphys in the directory and five Mrs Kathleen Murphys and several K. Murphys, who might be either male or female. It was a lengthy business for some were out and I was asked to ring later and some were testy at being catechised by a stranger. The fifth answered very suspiciously. 'Who are you? Why do you want to know? Yes, I was at 6 Zion Road, but if you want to know more you must come down. I remember the Anitches and, if you're friends of theirs I'd be glad to see you. Do you know them?' I said I did not but that a friend of mine in Paris, M. Miljus, would like to get in touch with them.

So we drove down to 6 Barnhill Road, Dalkey, a fine broad street with handsome villas. My wife waited outside in the car writing letters, while Mrs Murphy, a friendly middle-aged woman, talked to me in her drawing-room. A friend of hers was just leaving when I came in, an Ulsterwoman with a nice downright manner, whose husband had been a bank manager in Kilkenny. She remembered us straight off when I said my name. 'Yes, I know who you are. I read your letters and articles in *The Irish Times*. I remember you got into a row with the Nuncio, Dr O'Hara, and it was on the head of you he got the boot!' She and Peggy talked together while I was with Mrs Murphy, who I could see had a powerful affection for this foreign family who had lodged with her. In particular she admired 'Dr Anish', whom she connected with 'Czechoslavia'. This confusion is not very surprising. Artukovitch would not have mentioned Yugoslavia, which did not exist for him, and not much was known in Ireland of Croatia, though one of those who were kind to him in Dublin said he came from Craishe. In general he was befriended as a foreign refugee from Communism and hitherto I have found no trace of sinister international intrigue among those who gave him hospitality.

Mrs Murphy reproached herself repeatedly for not having kept in touch with the 'Anishes' in California. Several times they had written charming letters. What a delightful family they were! 'They made a wonderful impression all round,' she said. 'I'd like to show you some snaps I have of them.' Mrs Murphy took down a photograph album with a large bundle of snaps in the middle. She rummaged through them all the time we were talking but never found what she was looking for. I explained to her that some time after Dr Anitch had got to California he had been the subject of bitter controversy and I showed her the picture of the family in *The Mirror News*. 'Ah, how old he has got to look, poor man! And that big girl must be Katerina and that one Aurea. And goodness me that young chap must be Radoslav! How time flies!' When I told her what his enemies were saying she shook her head indignantly. 'People will say anything! I don't think he thought of politics at all. All he cared about was his family. He was a wonderful father and husband! He was a very good man you know. He was rather like President Kennedy. He wanted justice for everybody. And he loved the Church. They were daily communicants.' Then I asked her how she had met him in the first place and she said she thought it had been at some party. Maybe some priest had introduced them. She became a little vague on the whole in this pregnant conversation. I was being the sly one, she the candid one. I asked did she meet a Franciscan with him and she said, 'Oh, yes, there was one came to lunch a couple of times. But the Anishes lived very quietly. They hardly saw anyone. You see he was a very retiring scholarly man. He once or twice gave a lecture at UCD, but otherwise they just thought of the children.' I subsequently made enquiries about those lectures at UCD but with no success.

Then I told her what remorseless enemies he had and explained something of the collapse of Yugoslavia. I showed her *Artukovitch, the Himmler of Yugoslavia*, turning the pages rapidly so as to reach some not too emotive pictures of him in the days of his glory. There he was giving the Nazi salute to a German general and there again greeting Hitler's envoy at the head of his Security Police, and there with his wife at a cocktail party in the Hungarian Embassy. I skipped some horror pages, headed with heavy irony ANDRIJA ARTUKOVITCH'S HEROIC DEEDS and including a picture of a soldier scissoring off the head of a seated peasant with some shears. Except for their attribution, such photographs are probably genuine. As I have said, Artukovitch was probably a desk murderer only. Mrs Murphy must have caught a glimpse of the scissored head for she stiffened and started to fumble again in her album for her friendly snapshots.

'Everybody in Dublin seems to have liked him,' I said, 'but why did he come here with a false name?'

'Probably he was forced to. Lots of people are. He couldn't have been a Nazi, though he may have been forced to take that side. I'm a good judge of character. I've travelled in sixteen countries and know a good man when I see one.'

'But he signed all those laws against the Jews' (I thought it would be too complicated to talk about the Orthodox; she might not know who they were).

'Well, look what the Jews are doing to other people!' (I suppose she was thinking of the Arabs.)

Then we said good bye. As I left she repeated; 'They just lived for their children. They thought the world of them.'

The next place I had to visit was the Franciscan House in Galway from which Dr Anitch's nephew, Brother Ivanditch, paid visits to Dublin to see him.

When we reached Galway I went round to the Franciscan House, which is a few streets away from Eyre Square. Beside the big church I saw a small private door through which some travelling clerics with suit-cases were being hospitably ushered. I waited till they had all been welcomed before I went in, and after a few moments, the Father Superior appeared. Though he was preoccupied with his visitors he received me kindly. Seeing my attaché case he thought I was a commercial traveller, but when I explained I had come as a historian interested to find out about a Croat friar called Ivanditch, who was in Galway in 1947, he said, 'I'm afraid I don't know the good man. I'm only here three years, but, if you come tomorrow, when we've a bit more time, I'll get Brother Bede onto you. He was here in 1947.'

The following day I went round to the Franciscan House at 11.30 and Brother Bede received me. Yes. He remembered Brother Ivanditch well and had looked him up in the 'Schematismus' of the Order. He was from the province of Bosnia, near Sarajevo. He was a very striking looking chap and must have been over six foot. He was born in 1913. 'He wasn't here but at our hostel, St Anthony's College along the Moycullen Road, so I didn't see much of him. But they say he spent all his time at the wireless listening to the news in German, French, Italian, Spanish; he was a very intelligent fellow, learnt English quickly. But he was broody, reserved and melancholy. All soul, you might say.'

Brother Bede had spent the war years in Rome. In the Franciscan headquarters the Croats had been more prominent than any other Slav group. Apart from Father Manditch, the treasurer of the Order, there was Father Jelachitch, a great canon-lawyer, and Brother Balitch, an eminent palaeographer who had written about Duns Scotus. 'You've no idea what confusion there was in Rome at that time. As for us, we put all the Slavs in one basket, a terribly passionate lot. We couldn't unscramble them.'

'Who sent him here? Oh, I suppose it was the General of our Order in Rome. I think it was Schaaf at that time, but I could look that one up. It was a question of obedience, you know.'

I told him that the Ustashe ambassador to Rome, Rushinovitch, had been given audiences by many cardinals and had sent his impressions of them back to Zagreb. It was obvious that not only the Irish but all the clerics at Rome had been highly confused by what was happening in Croatia. Only Cardinal Tisserant, I said, had a clear idea. On the other hand Cardinal Ruffini was a vigorous supporter and protector of the Ustashe!

'Ruffini!' Brother Bede laughed. 'Yes, indeed. He was a Sicilian, a great nationalist! They are as excitable as the Slavs. We took everything they said with a pinch of salt.'

As for Ivanditch, he had stayed for about a year in Galway and then gone to Canada. But there was a rumour that he was in Valencia, Spain, now. He was still alive or he wouldn't be in the Schematismus.

Brother Bede did not think I would get much more information from St Anthony's College as they were always changing their staff there, but there was a Brother David who might remember him. 'Worth trying anyway. Cross the salmon-weir bridge and along the Moycullen Road till you come to a long grey building on the left.'

They were widening the road and the surface was terrible so it must

have been very close to the Brothers' dinner-time when I got to St
Anthony's. The most pleasant thing about the building was the fine
stone wall, a new one, that surrounded it. Most of the Galway walls are
still excellently built and of stone, as unlike as possible to the new walls
of the midlands, which, maybe because of the rich stoneless soil, are built
of concrete, which submits itself readily to many vulgar and modish
fancies.

I waited in a very clean and polished parlour under a picture of Jesus
meditating on the Mount of Olives, till Brother David came along. He
and his colleague, Brother Edmond, remembered Ivanditch well, and
Brother David showed me a photograph of himself and Brother Ivanditch and a Galway lady, Mrs O'Halloran. They were a handsome
group. Ivanditch, whose religious name was Brother Louis (Croatian
Luji), was dark, clean-shaven, spectacled. A pleasant serious person he
looked in his long brown habit with its white cord.

'But he was very hysterical,' Brother David said. 'He'd been sentenced
to death by the Communists and he spent all his time listening to the
ups and downs of Communism on the wireless. He was with us about
a year, sent here by the General at Rome, waiting for instructions where
to go. He was a professor of Dogmatic Theology. According to what
he said, he was second-in-command to the Provincial at Zagreb. He had
been given the seal of the Province of Croatia – he had it with him
here – when the Provincial was imprisoned.'

I asked him if Artukovitch (Anitch) had ever been to visit him. 'No,
he had no visitors at all though once or twice he went to Dublin.'

'He brooded the whole time. He said the only hope for us was to
have a third world war immediately. He thought us a very weak lot.
There was a milk strike in Galway at the time and he could not
understand why we did not settle it straight away by shooting the
milkmen. And we should invade the six counties and settle that matter
too *immediately*.'

'What amazed us about him,' Brother Edmond said, 'was the way he
ate jam for breakfast. . . sometimes nearly a whole pot, and without any
bread, just with a spoon. And though he got to know English very well,
he used some very funny expressions. When we used to ask him if he
would like another helping of anything, he would say, "Thank you, no,
I am fed up!" But he made a great friend in the town who could tell
you more about him than I can, Joe O'Halloran of the Corrib Printing
Works. He was working in O'Gorman's book shop in those days and
he and Brother Louis used to see a lot of each other. Joe is the son of
Mrs O'Halloran you saw in the snap shot.'

It was difficult to believe that the Galway Brothers belonged to the same order as the Ustashe Franciscans. What was nearest to Brother Edmond's heart was a scheme for building houses for the homeless by voluntary groups. He had been considering this idea, while he was with the Order in Louvain.

Joe O'Halloran was in a white coat working at the Corrib Printers when I called. He asked for a few moments to change and then he joined me at the Imperial Hotel and we had vodka and orange together. He had only been eighteen when Brother Ivanditch was in Galway, and he had been hugely impressed by this glamorous and passionate foreigner who had fled from his country under sentence of death, who had seen his Provincial sentenced to five years' penal servitude and his Primate, a world famous cardinal, condemned to sixteen years imprisonment by a Communist government. They had spent every Sunday together and Joe's parents had been equally captivated by this engaging person, who bore with him the seals of the Franciscan Order in Croatia and the responsibility to make its sorrows known to the world. It was his dream to establish a Croatian Seminary in Dublin. Ireland must know what Croatia had suffered and was still suffering in the name of Christ. She must know that the fate that had befallen Croatia awaited all Europe. They must be prepared.

Brother Luji counted on Joe O'Halloran's support in this sacred cause. But after a year the orders came from Rome for him to cross the Atlantic. He sailed from Liverpool to Montreal and Joe O'Halloran saw him off in Dublin. But though he had left Joe in charge of a sort of crusade, he had not replied at all regularly to his letters and slowly they had lost touch with each other. Joe learnt, though, that Brother Luji had been appointed chaplain to the Croat workers at Windsor, which is on the Canadian side of the Detroit river. They worked in the Ford factory at Dearborn and Brother Luji built for them the Chapel of St Joseph. Later on he had heard that he had been secularized and had left the Franciscan Order and it now occurred to Joe O'Halloran that this might have been because the French-Canadian Franciscans did not like Ivanditch's Croatian politics, which a few years later resulted in the murder of the Yugoslav consul in Stockholm and a curious entente with the Communists.

I asked about Artukovitch-Anitch and also about Count O'Brien, but Joe knew nothing of them. The only layman in Galway that Ivanditch saw was Mr O'Flynn, the County Manager, who invited him to tea, because his niece had once taught in Zagreb. Ivanditch had however told Joe that he had an uncle in Dublin who had been a Minister in the government of Croatia. Joe O'Halloran stressed that Ivanditch had totally failed to inflame the Franciscans in Galway and was very much

disappointed in the Irish. He had been in Galway when the Republic
was proclaimed in Eyre Square, and he was amazed that the Government
had tolerated an opposition for so long. Why had not they just shot
them?

In the past eighteen years Joe had changed. Ivanditch, were he to
return, would no longer have the intoxicating effect which he had had
on him as a very young man. In those days he had been puzzled that his
elders should be so apathetic. For example, Father Felim O'Brien, a well-
known Franciscan, had been lecturing in Galway and had treated very
coolly Ivanditch's passionate appeals for a crusade. O'Brien was known
all over Ireland for his dislike of 'liberalism'. Two or three years later,
in 1950, he engaged Owen Sheehy-Skeffington in a long controversy in
The Irish Times later published as a pamphlet, on *The Liberal Ethic*. I had
contributed to this controversy so I have kept some records of it. O'Brien
had maintained that in Ireland we owe our freedom of expression more
to the clerics than to the liberal doctrine of tolerance, and that in Europe
the Catholic clergy are the chief champions of liberty.

We got back late from Galway and it was a day before I was able to
look up Ivanditch in my books. I found only one reference to him. He
was referred to on page 20 in the report of the Stepinac Trial, *Sudenje
Lisaku, Stepincu, Salicu I Druzini*, in connection with the trial of the
Provincial of the Franciscan Order, Father Modesto Martinchitch. The
Provincial is said to have given Brother Luji (Ivanditch), an Ustashe, a
large sum of money to enable him to escape abroad. Brother Luji was
not one of the five friars who helped the Provincial bury the thirty-four
trunks of Ustasha treasure under the confessional in the Franciscan
Church in May 1945, and I find no record of any activities that in
Communist eyes were criminal. I think that when he claimed to have
been sentenced to death by the Communists, Ivanditch was trying to
make himself more glamorous. He seems to have escaped early on with
an ample travel allowance and the seals of the province. Whether or not
Artukovitch was really his uncle, it may have been his task to escort him
abroad in safety.

Since Brother Bede had mentioned Dr Balitch, the eminent palaeographer, at the Vatican, I looked him up in the vast book *Magnum
Crimen* by Professor Victor Novak of Belgrade, not expecting to find
anyone so scholarly and remote in this record of horror. But there he was
on page 900. 'Brother Doctor Karlo Balitch, Professor at the Franciscan
University at Rome.' His offence seems to have been slight but significant. When Marshal Kvaternik, the Commander of the Ustashe
Forces, had arrived in Rome and visited the Institute of St Jerome in

February 1942, Professor Balitch had been there to receive him, together with several other distinguished Croatian clerics and the whole staff of the Institute. Dr Balitch seems to have listened appreciatively while Dr Madjerec, the Rector, praised Kvaternik and the leader Pavelitch for their illustrious deeds in the cause of Christ.

The St Jerome Society was a very old and established Croat Institution with headquarters at Rome. Every year, even when Novak published his book in 1948, there were celebrations there in honour of Pavelitch's birthday, attended by Croat Jesuits, Dominicans, Capuchins, Benedictines. When Marshal Kvaternik addressed the Institute praising its work for the Ustashe there was loud and prolonged applause. This was in Rome, yet we have been told repeatedly that it was only under the strongest pressure that in Croatia itself the hierarchy lent their support to Pavelitch.

After the St Jerome Society had been suppressed in Croatia by Tito, Mgr Stepinac declared in his speech of defence: 'The St Jerome Society has ceased to exist. Its suppression is a grave offence against the whole people.' But surely it was rightly suppressed.

In an authoritarian community, when there is hypocrisy and connivance at the centre, the ripples from them spread outwards to the remote circumference: 'In vain do they worship me, teaching as their doctrines the precepts of men.'

In 1985 there is news of Dr Draganovitch, who helped Artukovitch to escape. I have been reading Tom Bower's story of Barbie, 'the Butcher of Lyons' who eluded French justice after the war in 1951 by the 'Rat Line', an escape-route which the Americans set up for people who were valuable to the CIA. They were equipped with fake passports and identity cards, but a contact was needed in Genoa, the port of embarkation, to supply the Rats with immigration papers for South America. Draganovitch, who had helped so many Ustashe escape to the Argentine, was obviously the man for the job. His fees for the Rat Line, according to Tom Bower, were $1000 for adults, half-price for children and $1400 for VIP treatment.

Surprisingly, though his services to the escaping Ustashe were well-known and though he had been on the infamous Committee of Five for the conversion of the Orthodox, he was permitted legally to return to Yugoslavia.

Is it possible that just as Barbie had useful information to give the Americans about the Communists, so Draganovitch had useful information to give the Communists about the Americans?

Artukovitch himself is still in California and, as I have related, some-time in the sixties the Yugoslav Government tired of asking for his extradition. Among other reasons, maybe, they thought that a sensational state trial in Zagreb might revive animosities between Serb and Croat.

However, in July 1981, the Board of Immigration Appeals in the USA, in view of a 1979 ruling of Congress, ordered that Artukovitch be deported. This was followed by further legal proceedings, appeals, counter-appeals, hearings and re-hearings.

In spring 1984 a civil suit against Artukovitch was filed in Los Angeles by relatives of twelve Yugoslav Jews murdered 'in the death camps'. An *Irish Times* report (2 April 1984) said, 'US officials familiar with the case always expressed puzzlement at how Artukovitch obtained sanctuary in Ireland and then received a visa to visit the US where his brother, a contractor, lived.' How much of the puzzle have I solved?

The US Justice Department acted on a legal reform excluding 'Nazi collaborators' from seeking refuge and on 14 November 1984 'three carloads of federal marshals, guns drawn,' burst into Artukovitch's house at Seal Beach and took him into custody (*The Sunday Times*, 12 January 1985). He is now eighty-five and, according to his Dublin-born son Radoslav, he has Parkinson's Disease, a congestive heart condition, and is also blind and suffering from delusional paranoia. It is uncertain whether he will be competent to take part in an extradition hearing and its sequel, deportation to Yugoslavia and a show-trial at Zagreb.[1]

[1985]

1. Artukovitch was finally extradited to Yugoslavia in February 1986, tried, and sentenced to death by firing squad in May 1986. Now very infirm, he stayed in prison until his death in January 1988. During the trial a special law was hastily passed whereby anyone who had been accused of genocide was forbidden burial in consecrated ground, for fear that Artukovitch might die before sentence was passed and become the focus of a martyr's cult.

THE LAST IZMERENJE

For three days the rain had fallen steadily. When we arrived in Kotor, the top of Lovcen was invisible, and festoons of moist cloud swam across the mountains behind us. Nonetheless, there was a band to meet the boat and a great crowd, and on an iron mooring post a youth was arranging salvoes of welcome. Every now and then there was an enormous bang, and he disappeared in thick white smoke, for explosions are the Dalmatians' favourite way of celebrating great occasions, and today was a feast day in both the Catholic and Greek Churches. It was Easter Day [1937] for the Orthodox, while for the Catholics it was the feast of St Hosanna, a nun whose mummified body lies below an altar in one of the Kotor churches.

I pushed my way through the crowd, and asked the first likely person I met where the monastery of Grbalj was, and what time the 'izmerenje' was to be. Nobody knew, though I had heard in Belgrade about it three hundred miles away, while here it was only half-an-hour's drive by car. It was not till I had searched the town for information that I found, at last, that I was a day too early. I was rather relieved; perhaps the next day the rain–clouds would have lifted.

In the afternoon, with two others, I made a half–hearted attempt to drive to Cetinje, but soon after we had passed the old Austrian customs house, at the frontier of Dalmatia and Montenegro, we were in dense fog and the whole panorama of Kotor Bay, which must be one of the loveliest in the world, had disappeared, and we were shivering with cold and damp. We went back; and that evening, when I was having tea in one of the old houses at Dobrota, I was told the story of the Montenegrin blood feud by a lady who had studied law and had attended the trial of Stevo Orlovich in an official capacity.

The Orlovichs and the Bauks were two families living some fifteen miles from Kotor, not in Montenegro itself, but observing the old

Montenegrin customs. Two years ago the Orlovichs had made enquiries
and learnt that Stjepo Bauk, whose father was dead, would let his sister
accept a proposal from Stevo Orlovich. Stevo, thereupon, set out with
a group of his relations to make a formal offer, carrying firearms, as was
the custom, so as to celebrate the betrothal with the usual explosions.
When they reached the Bauks' house, they were told that the offer was
refused.

It appeared that an old uncle of the Bauks had been greatly insulted
that his permission had not been asked. He had made a row, and Stjepo
had given in to him. Stevo Orlovich was outraged and indignant, and
whipping out his gun he fired at Stjepo Bauk and hit him in the leg.
Bauk fired back and injured Orlovich – there was a scuffle and the
Orlovichs took to their heels. A few days later, Stjepo Bauk's leg had
to be amputated, and he died. The case was tried in the courts, and Stevo
Orlovich was sentenced to three years' imprisonment.

But the Bauks were not in the least pacified by this; they held to the
old Montenegrin tradition that blood should be avenged by blood, and
the Orlovichs continued to feel uneasy. Near Podgorica, in Montenegro,
just such a murder had taken place in 1930, and since then thirty murders
have followed it in alternate families, the last one six months ago. It has
been impossible for the courts to collect satisfactory evidence; though
the relations of the victim in most cases knew the murderer, they would
scorn to hand him over to justice. Revenge is a private, not a public,
responsibility. But there was a way out, and this the Orlovichs took.

Some ten months ago, when Stevo Orlovich had had the rest of his
sentence remitted for good behaviour, twenty-four 'good men' of the
Orlovichs called on the Bauks, and asked them to agree to the izmerenje
ceremony. The Bauks refused. Five months later, the Orlovichs appealed
again, and this time they were granted a day's armistice for every
member of the deputation, that is to say, twenty-four. After that they
came a third time, and at last the Bauks granted their request. It would
be the first izmerenje celebrated in the neighbourhood for more than a
generation, and it was this ceremony that I had come to Kotor to see.

'Of course,' my friend said, 'it won't be nearly as elaborate an affair
as it used to be. In the old days the murderer had to crawl on his hands
and knees and beg forgiveness; and then he must give a gun to the head
of the other family as a token. And then there were the babies at the
breast. Seven women of the murderer's family had to come with their
seven babies in cradles, and ask the head of the family of the murdered
man to be the "kum" or godfather, and he was obliged to accept.

'That shows what size the families were,' she added. 'Today, in all

Dobrota, you couldn't find seven babies at the breast, far less in one family.'

The birds were singing next morning at six o'clock, and the fog seemed to have lifted completely from Lovcen. It looked as if the day was to be fine. I was told to be ready on the quay at 7 a.m., and was to share a car with the two judges who had sentenced Orlovich, two local correspondents of a Belgrade paper, and one of the hundred guests invited by Orlovich. This guest was so confident that the ceremony would wait for him that we were an hour late in starting. To get to the monastery of Grbalj you must climb up the slope of Lovcen out of the Boka, and then down again towards Budva on the open sea. Most of the district is a 'polje' or flat space between the mountains, and relatively fertile; the peasant houses are placed for the most part on the rocky, barren slopes, where nothing grows except scrub or wild pomegranates and stunted oak; their farms lie below them in the polje, full of vines, fig-trees, beans and potatoes, market crops that they can sell in Kotor.

The people of Grbalj were always an enterprising community from the time of the great medieval Tsar of Serbia, Dushan; they had their own laws, and the Venetians, when they occupied the Boka and its surroundings, respected the Grbalj Statute, which was only abolished when Dalmatia was seized by Austria after the Napoleonic wars.

We soon saw the monastery perched on a hill on the left – an unexpectedly small, insignificant building, its courtyard black with moving people. The larger half was completely new.

'The old building was raided and burnt by the Montenegrins themselves during the war,' the judge told me. 'They say the Austrians were using it as a store for ammunition. It was rebuilt, and they opened it again last year. There are some twelfth-century frescoes in the end of the chapel, but they're badly damaged by damp, as it was roofless for so long.'

Behind us, a mile or two away, but plainly visible as it lay open on the rocky face of the mountain over against the monastery, was the cluster of houses where the Bauks and the Orlovichs lived. They were large red-tiled farmhouses two or three storeys high, with big windows and several annexes. The Bauks' house was the bigger of the two.

'The Bauks have a dozen families scattered over the place,' said the judge, 'but the Orlovichs only have two, so I don't know how they'll pay for the dinner; you see, they must bring a hundred of their supporters and the Bauks must bring a hundred of theirs: the Bauks will be the hosts, but the Orlovichs must pay for it all. It may run them into a couple of thousand dinars [about £8]. If either side brings more or less than a hundred, it's a gross insult, and they'll have to start the whole business over again.'

The hundred Orlovich guests were already there when we arrived; outside the wall of the churchyard a group of women and neighbours, whom neither side had invited, were leaning watching. The women, in Montenegrin fashion, had their thick black hair wound across their foreheads in heavy plaits, a black lace veil fell from behind to their shoulders.

There were two long tables stretched out in the courtyard covered with brown paper, but the Orlovichs were most of them sitting upon the wall. The six 'good men' who headed the Orlovich deputation were in the vestry when we arrived, drinking Turkish coffee. One was a fat, pleasant-looking priest in a grey soutane from a neighbouring parish. Two seemed prosperous town relations in smart overcoats, clean-shaven, with gold teeth and Homburg hats; two were well-to-do farmers in full Montenegrin dress, round caps with red crowns embroidered in gold and the black bands that all Montenegrins wear in mourning for the battle of Kossovo, when the Serbians were defeated by the Turks in 1399. They had red waistcoats with heavy gold embroidery, orange sashes and blue breeches with thick white woollen stockings and string shoes. The other ninety-four Orlovichs had compromised about their clothes; they nearly all had the caps and some had either the breeches or the waistcoat, but they mostly had an ordinary Sunday coat on top of it. They all had black moustaches, and held either a heavy stick or an umbrella in their hands. I saw one or two men who had both.

One of the journalists from Kotor beckoned me into the church, and introduced me to the priest and a small dark man with terrified eyes who stood beside him.

'That's the murderer,' he told me. 'You are the murderer, Stevo Orlovich, aren't you?' he asked to make certain.

'Yes' – and we shook hands.

We shook hands with his brother, too, an older, solid-looking man. He, too, had received a bullet wound in the leg as he was running away from the Bauks' house. Stevo Orlovich shrank away behind the chapel walls as soon as he could; he was very slightly built, and had black bristly hair and a small Charlie Chaplin moustache; he wore a neat but worn black suit, with a fountain pen clipped in the breast pocket. He was evidently in an agony of shame and embarrassment about the ceremony he was going to have to go through. But he was sufficiently collected to make it clear that he wasn't pleased to see us.

All at once a boy began to toll the three small bells of the chapel, and five or six people went in to hear the priest celebrate the short Easter Mass according to the Greek rite. I saw the correspondent of the Belgrade *Politika* standing beside them leading the responses in a booming voice.

'Christ is risen!'

'Lord, have mercy on us!'

The priest was swinging a censer vigorously, and the whole courtyard was filled with sound and the smell of incense.

It lasted a quarter of an hour. When I came out of the church one of the Orlovichs who was sitting on the seat, cried out, 'Hello, boy!' and I went and sat down beside him. He had been at the copper mines in Butte, Montana, and said that at least ten others present had been there, too. I complimented him on his gorgeous embroidered waistcoat, but he said it was nothing to what they used to have. Times were bad...

'Montenegrin mans should do like Irishmans,' he said, 'raise hell, holler!'

Evidently, a good deal of information about Ireland had filtered via Butte, Montana, to Grbalj, because he had a muttered conversation with his neighbour about de Valera and the Lord Mayor who had died after a seventy day hunger-strike.

'I was telling him about the Liberty Irish State,' he said.

The six good men walked out of the churchyard and he said:

'You see that bunch? They go to fetch the otha bunch!'

But the six Orlovichs returned alone and another hour passed before down the mountain slope the procession of the Bauks, a long black line like a school crocodile, issued slowly from behind a little wood. They were a long way off still. From the terrace of the priest's house I watched them going down a small lane through an olive grove into the main road, crossing the wooden bridge over a very swift stream then climbing up the hill towards the monastery.

A man came out of the monastery with a big basket of bread and he was followed surprisingly by a sailor with some paper table napkins. Carafes of rakkia were planted at intervals along the table... The Orlovichs got up and walked leisurely towards one side of the churchyard; they formed themselves in a long row, fifty abreast, two deep. In the back row towards the end I saw the murderer flatten himself against the wall. He was fingering his fountain pen nervously. His brother was beside him.

The little priest in the grey soutane came bustling out of the church.

'Take off your hats,' he said, and we all did so.

Then the Bauks came in, headed by two handsome elderly priests with black beards, then four other good men.

They lined themselves opposite the Orlovichs, exactly a hundred, with their hats still firmly on, facing a hundred with bare heads. It was like Sir Roger de Coverley.

There was a long silence and then one of the Bauk 'good men', a professor from Kotor, came out into the middle and in a loud voice read the sentence. This is a slightly abbreviated version of what he read:

In the name of Christ the Saviour Who is eternal peace between men.

Today, when the Ascension is near at hand, in the year of Our Lord 1937 in the monastery of the Blessed Virgin of Grbalj good men have met together and pleaded with the families of Bauk and Orlovich to lay aside their blood feud which arose in the month of February 1935.

In the name of God from Whom all true justice proceeds and after long cognition, they pronounced this sentence which shall be executed on the third day of Easter, 1937, in the monastery of the Blessed Virgin of Grbalj.

Seeing that God's justice fell upon the wounds of Stjepo Bauk, the son of Vuk and Stevo Orlovich the son of Lazo, who remained alive after wounds received, and seeing that Mirko Bauk valiantly forgave the murder of his brother Stjepo and reconciled himself through God and St John with the Orlovichs, we declare this sentence:

1. That the brothers Orlovich wait with a hundred of their people on the Bauks with a hundred of theirs.

2. That the Orlovichs humbly, according to custom (but not carrying firearms), shall approach the Bauks who shall embrace them in this order.

Mirko Bauk, the son of Vuk, shall kiss Stevo Orlovich, the son of Lazo.

Vaso Bauk, the son of Rado, shall kiss Ilya Orlovich, the son of Lazo.

3. That at the first baptism of a child of theirs the Orlovichs shall ask Bauk to be godfather and he shall accept.

4. That from this reconciliation everlasting friendship and mutual respect for their mutual honour in word and deed shall proceed and that this blood feud shall be ended for all time.

Each family must receive a copy of this sentence and one must be preserved in the archives of the monastery where this reconciliation was made.

Drawn up by the undersigned: [Here follow the signatures of the six good men of the Bauks and the six good men of the Orlovichs.]

The professor stepped back into the Bauk ranks and put the sentence back into his leather portfolio.

Then one of the Orlovich good men cried out in a voice breaking with emotion:

'Stevo Orlovich!'

The murderer folded his arms across his breast and bending down from the waist he darted forward from the wall. He was like someone in a trance. He did not see where he was going and butted his bowed head into a man in front. It was a second before he had disentangled himself from the overcoat and was heading once more for the Bauks. Mirko Bauk, a fat young man with fair hair and moustache, all in black except for the red crown of his Montenegrin cap, stepped out and raised him up.

'Forgive me!' said Orlovich.

'I forgive you my brother's blood,' Bauk answered and they kissed each other on both cheeks. I heard people sobbing behind me. Then Vaso Bauk, who was small and puny, embraced Ilya Orlovich and finally all the hundred Bauks stepped forward and shook hands and greeted the hundred Orlovichs. Then they all took their seats at the table, the Orlovichs sitting at one table, the Bauks at another. Stevo Orlovich did not appear but stayed in the monastery with his brother.

I and the four men from Kotor were preparing to go home but the Bauk professor pressed us to stay.

'The Orlovichs would like to ask you,' he said, 'but they have to be so humble today – it isn't the custom – so we invite you.'

A table was brought out from the vestry and a red table cloth and we sat by ourselves in the other side of the courtyard.

Before we started to feed, the Bauk priest got up and began an Easter hymn... and once more the journalist's big voice filled the courtyard.

A lot of forks arrived and a platter heaped with boiled beef. Someone else explained to me that when the monastery had been rededicated last year, there had been six hundred guests and each had a knife for himself and also a tumbler; but today it was different – it was custom. So there were no tumblers and we pushed round from mouth to mouth, first a big bottle of rakkia, then a big flask of an excellent red wine.

'Please you thank you, Mister!' the journalist with the big voice said every time he gave the flask a shove in my direction.

He then muttered very rapidly into my ear a couple of verses of a poem beginning:

> My 'ome iz zy ocean
> My 'arth iz ze ship!'

The meal was quite good and the platters were constantly replenished by the sailor and two men running backward and forward with white napkins held in their teeth. After the beef came boiled ham. Except at our table nobody talked very much. There seemed to be no fraternization between the Bauks and the Orlovichs. First came forgiveness, a little later, perhaps, friendship would follow.

They must have had an extraordinary capacity for keeping the practical and the emotional side of their lives distant for on the slope of the hill their two houses seemed only a few hundred yards apart. Their sheep must graze the same mountains, they must use the same tracks. How had they managed to pass two years so close without lending things and without borrowing things?

There could be no doubt, anyway, that the quarrel had at last been settled. The sentences of the law courts usually leave bitterness and dissatisfaction behind but the ceremony at Grbalj, so impressive and deeply moving, aimed at something far higher. Did it achieve it? I thought so, but couldn't be sure. Did Mirko perhaps look a bit too self-righteous? Does one ever feel very friendly towards people who force on one too abject an apology or towards one's relations who watch it? I think Stevo may go to Butte, Montana.

Most European law is based on compensation and punishment; justice is important, but it is also impersonal. Montenegrin custom on the other hand takes into account forgiveness which English justice ignores, and because of that, when 'izmerenje' passes away, as pass it must, an important element of justice will have gone with it.

The journalist borrowed the copy of the sentence from the monastery archives.

'Meet me in the Café at Kotor,' he said to me, 'and I'll let you have a read of it.'

And we crammed in eleven of us, for some of the Orlovich friends came too, into the car... There was some angry tooting behind us and a lemon-coloured sports car thrust past, containing the professor and two of the Bauk 'good men'.

A moment later we were on the main highway to Cetinje, negotiating the hair-pin bends of that incredible road. Every now and then we passed policemen with fixed bayonets and we dodged a charabanc full of German tourists. Below us at Kotor a yacht lay at anchor by the quays, a procession of soldiers was marching through the streets which were green with acacia trees. The grimness of the mountains lay behind us and we were in the twentieth century again.

'It's beautiful,' I said to one of the judges.

'Yes,' he replied, 'but you should have seen it when the King and Mrs Simpson were here. The evening they arrived all the bay from Tivat to Kotor was illuminated – bonfires and petrol. It was wonderful. One of the bonfires set alight to some dry grass where there were some young trees. Not much damage done, but it made a wonderful blaze!'

By the time our car had drawn up at the Town Kafana, the izmerenje at Grbalj was like something that happened in a dream. Will there ever be another one in Montenegro? I can hardly believe it. The 'good men' in the Homburg hats were getting self-conscious about it and I am convinced I heard the murderer and his brother grumbling about the journalists behind the chapel wall. I was glad he didn't know that someone had suggested bringing a film apparatus. Nowadays, too, one can always interrupt blood feuds by going to Butte, Montana.

[1947]

AMERICAN IMPRESSIONS

IN SALT LAKE CITY

The plane plunged down through the clouds and scattered the last wisps of fog that protected the burnished platter of the Great Salt Lake. It is ribbed north and south like smoothest corduroy and around its shores the salty tide has mapped out its ebb and flow in many-coloured Paisley spirals. Is one looking at water or rock or mud or salt or powdered ice? A shift in the light can turn any of these grotesque cones and curves to rose-pink or opal. The mountains that surround Salt Lake City have often been televised. There is an abundance of picture postcards and brochures about its canyons and copper mines, its glaciers and limestone caves, but the apocalyptic landscape has not yet been tamed. You can see how it must have appeared to Brigham Young and his followers as a final refuge, a sanctuary so inhospitable that no one would wish to violate it.

In a different way the city is equally arresting. After reading the fantastic history of the Mormons and their bloody progress across the continent, founding cities and then having to abandon them, one is surprised to find how demurely Brigham Young and his followers settled down in their Utah wilderness, having been driven successfully from foundations in New England, Ohio and Illinois, with great brutality. His mansion, the Beehive House, is as appropriate for a Founding Father as Mount Vernon or Monticello; it is both homely and dignified and he had Jefferson's passion for experiment and ingenious contraptions. He lived there with his principal wife and her seven children and many up-to-date conveniences, a sewing machine, a 'Lady Franklin' stove, a rocking-horse, and much evidence that his daughters sketched and embroidered.

There is a possibility that the next President of the United States will be a distinguished leader of the Mormon community. George Romney is the president of a state, ranking with a bishop of the Episcopalian Church, and at one time an active missionary in Britain. A great figure in the automobile industry, he is standing for the governorship of Michigan and, if he succeeds, has equal chances with Nixon and Rockefeller of being the Republican nominee for the Presidency. Conservative Americans of all creeds agree that he would make an honourable and dependable leader. On religious grounds only the negroes and their integrationist allies are disturbed, for the Mormons believe, like other Fundamentalists, that Noah cursed the descendants of Ham and that a dark skin is a token of God's displeasure. Mr Romney has dealt with this problem in a statesmanlike way, being conciliatory to the negroes without disrespect to Noah.

Esteemed physicists, bank directors, congressmen, adhere loyally to the beliefs which the Angel Moroni communicated to Joseph Smith in 1833 and the Angel's golden figure crowning the Mormon Temple in 16th Street is one of the landmarks of Washington. In the Book of Mormon, which ranks with the Bible as a source of truth, Moroni told how in 600 BC colonists from Jerusalem landed in Chile and like an earlier emigration from the Tower of Babel fell into sin and strife, so that God condemned the wicked portion of them to wear dark skins and, as Lamanites, to become the ancestors of the Red Indians. Finally these unworthy people at the great battle of Cumorah slaughtered their white brethren and only Moroni survived to tell their story, in many complicated and exciting chapters.

By later revelation Smith was told that mankind was permitted to be polygamous like the patriarchs of Israel. The Mormons maintain though that only 3 per cent of them ever accepted this privilege, for it was stipulated that the first wife must always give her consent and the husband had to convince his Church that he was capable of maintaining more than one family. So practised, they contend that plural marriage brought comfort rather than discord, for few women lacked a protector and society was closely knit by family kinship. It is only in deference to worldly laws that they abandoned polygamy.

Certainly today Salt Lake City seems happy and harmonious. The citizens are well-dressed, polite and competent. There are few beggars or unemployed and the statisticians say that in proportion to its population Utah has more scientists than any other state in the union, 11.7 per 10,000 to be precise. Possibly applied science will flourish in a soil that is too arid to nourish more delicate forms of art or speculation, since

I have heard Utah described as an intellectual desert. Praise or blame belongs to the Mormons who still dominate Salt Lake City in a way that Quakers and Moravians have long since ceased to dominate Philadelphia and Bethlehem, their cities of refuge. I am sure that the Mormons owe most to the enforced harmony that comes to proud, ignorant people who are persecuted for their convictions. After George Romney's candidature was announced, there were photographs published of him and his son speaking to jeering crowds in Edinburgh and at the Marble Arch.

They are, of course, immensely conservative, believing in the separation of Church and State on the federal level, because their own state is almost a Church in itself. The Church cares for the indigent, the old, the adolescents. The bishops collect tithes in food and factory products from the farmers and manufacturers and store them in great produce barns in every county. There is no need for federal officials to intervene.

Obviously there are rebels and backsliders, but the three or four whom I met were apathetic rather than sceptical. A taxi-driver said to me: 'My dad went on about it so, I got kinda bored.' But observing that I was a heretic, he swiftly went on the defensive and told me that long before the ancient Maya cities of Central America had been discovered they had been mentioned in the Book of Mormon and that geologists working in the copper mines had confirmed the truth of Moroni's revelations. More sophisticated Mormons do not, I think, concern themselves much with these scientific corroborations. When the angels intervene in human history, they are surely capable of covering up their traces, if they wish.

In the Temple precincts there is an excellent but matter-of-fact ethnological museum, in which there is no reminder that the Ute Indians, whose remains are admirably displayed, were descendants of the Lamanites, who came from Jerusalem. I could nowhere detect any trace of those symbolic or existentialist interpretations which have brought comfort to the sceptics of other confessions. About this I questioned a distinguished Mormon who had been in his time Elder, Bishop, High Priest and Patriarch, and he said, 'If what we believe is not true, then our religion is one of the biggest frauds in history.'

A friend took me to a service in a suburban temple (judging by the telephone directory, there are several hundred temples in SLC), a fine building with many offices and rooms for basketball, reading, science, gymnastics and hobbies. There were many children as well as adults, and as the service proceeded some sixteen-year-old boys began to slice up bread into small portions, while smaller boys of eleven or twelve filled up little silver cups with water. A big boy blessed them. The big boys were priests, the little boys, who then carried the bread and water round the pews, were deacons. Informality and reverence were gracefully blended. Even the babies took the consecrated bread and drank from the silver cups. Two small girls beside me, who had been quietly decorating a book called *Fun with Crayons*, put their chalks aside for a moment to take some bread and water. A young man stepped forward beside the bishop to report on his recent mission to Liverpool. He veiled his adventures in theological imagery, 'The Vineyard of the Lord and its pruning,' etc. Yet, little more than a child himself, he appeared to have converted some English children to the faith of the Latter Day Saints. These pilgrimages plainly affect the missionary more than the mission field, the Vinedresser more than the Vineyard. The missionaries seem to bring back to Salt Lake City a replenishment of that blended innocence and worldly wisdom which make it one of the most fascinating cities in the US.

[1962]

THE BOB JONES UNIVERSITY

I constantly see in the newspapers contemptuous little gibes at the Bob Jones University. Since I must be one of the few Irishmen actually to have been there, I would like to add to the picture. Mr Tom Luby writes that it is 'bogus' and suggests that a book about Orange Ulster, *America's Debt to Ulster*, which emanated from it must be nonsense. Well, I found it an awful place, but then I dislike all modern universities and modernized ancient ones. Built like airports, they function like factories for processing lively children into civil servants and narrow 'experts'. By those standards, BJU is perfectly normal.

I saw it by accident. I was staying with a friend in the large and hideous industrial town of Greenville, South Carolina, when one of her after-dinner guests said to me, 'The President of Ulster was in Greenville last month and Bob Jones [the Third] is going to preach the Easter sermon for him in Belfast.' I sorted that one out and asked her to show me BJU before I left. My hostess and her friends were Episcopalians but they regarded BJU as an adornment to the town. It is a mark of distinction to have a university, and leading citizens had seduced Bob Jones from Tennessee by offering 200 acres of land in an important location. They told me of the huge 'amphitorium' which houses 7000, what an 'aristocratic' figure Miss Jones presented at the numerous civic functions she graced, and how well-behaved the students all were:

They are clean-living, they never have scruffy long hair or take drugs or drink; student riots would be unthinkable and . . . [a pause to think of a telling indication of their quality] they always wear ties at symphony concerts. They have very dogmatic views, of course, but then in these days of laxity and permissiveness. . .

On the way to the station I made a brief tour of the university. The 'amphitorium' was as monstrous as I had been told, and there were acres of lawn, fountains, begonias, laboratories and other academic appurtenances. It did not seem to me any more or less frightful than other modern academies, but my train was soon due and the rest of this account stems from the *Bob Jones University Bulletin* of 255 closely printed pages.

One of the arguments for calling it 'bogus' is that it does not belong to 'any educational association, regional or national'. On page 8 Bob Jones III takes a header in to this rather stagnant pond and comes up composed: 'It is our sincere conviction that BJU can do more for the cause of the Lord Jesus Christ by not holding organic membership in any such association, though our finances, our equipment, our academic standards would fully qualify us.'

A brief inspection of the university and a long perusal of the *Bulletin* convinced me that it is rich and well equipped. What about academic standards? These are harder to assess. A little over a thousand courses are listed, including 'Advanced Hebrew Grammar', 'Botanical Taxonomy', 'Coaching Soccer', 'Elementary Sumero-Akkadian', 'Parasitology' and 'Papyrology'. There are also many European History courses, so I doubt whether *America's Debt to Ulster*, which Bob Jones it seems has written with Ian Paisley, can be as inaccurate as Mr Luby claims. He is annoyed with the authors for saying that 'Orangemen' played a leading part in the American Revolution of 1776, 'because the Orange Order was not set up for another twenty years'. This is a quibble. July the Twelfth and the Relief of Londonderry had been annually celebrated before 1795 and, whatever they called themselves, Ulstermen played a prodigious part in the creation of the United States and in building into the Constitution Orange William's civil and religious liberties. Ulstermen have a right to be proud.

To quote further from the prospectus, they have '42 flourishing literary societies', a library of 150,000 books, a 'collection of Sacred Art' containing pictures by Tintoretto, Titian, Rembrandt, Rubens and Van Dyck, a museum in which thousands of visitors are given guided tours each year, a radio station 'for the winning of souls round the globe', a printing press and a film studio for roughly the same purpose, and an abundance of athletical playgrounds, gymnasia, pavilions. Unless the religion which informs these activities is 'bogus', all the rest seems (to me depressingly) normal. The religion is shared by the majority of Christians, black and white, in the Southern States, for it is Fundamentalist and the Southern Baptist Church is the citadel of biblical Fundamentalism.

So why all this chatter about Paisley's bogus doctorate? The university draws its pupils from 80 of the 243 American Protestant sects, each of which, like Paisleyism, started as a breakaway from some parent Church, which at first angrily repudiated and then finally accepted it. The sects later seldom quarrel; the 19 distinct sects of the Baptists, who are particularly prone to schism, live together now in perfect amity, and many of them get their ministers from BJU, where, according to the prospectus, approximately a thousand students study for the Church or some other religious post every year.

Dean Sperry of Harvard, who wrote the classic book on religion in America, deplores the anti-intellectualism of the Fundamentalist ministers and their mistrust of biblical criticism. 'The inspiration of the Holy Spirit', he writes, 'is invoked to do duty for book-learning.' That of course is the level on which Paisleyism should be attacked, but it never is, for here in the Republic there is an equal mistrust of intellectualism and biblical criticism. Insults and bombs are much easier to handle.

My friends in Greenville praised the Fundamentalists for their nice behaviour; they often have a simple goodness and piety that shames one (everyone ought to read Thornton Wilder's novel *Heaven's My Destination*). Most important of all, they pay for their own doctrines, for the amphitorium, for the global winning of souls. Like most American Protestants they are staunch supporters of the separation of Church and State, which derives from Jefferson's Statute of Religious Freedom in Virginia. They ask no one else to pay for the inculcation of what they believe.

The Fundamentalists are old-fashioned, very resolute people, but no more bogus than anyone else whose views we do not share. Their record of resistance to Hitler, Stalin and Franco is better than that of any of the established Churches (consider also, for example, the Russian Baptists and the Jehovah's Witnesses in Nazi concentration camps). It would be wrong for us to underestimate their strength, their sincerity, or their iron determination on either side of the Atlantic.

[1977]

A Visit to Oneida

I was in luck. It was Thanksgiving Day in upstate New York and, though this meant that the factory was closed and the official guide was away and the stall of Oneida silverware from which tourists were expected to select souvenirs was closed, some of the leaders of the community were taking the day off in the Mansion House and could show me round. Many of their names were familiar, that of Mr Inslee, for example, who took charge of me, for I had read of their fathers and grandfathers in Pierrepoint Noyes' books. In an age of conformity, the Mansion House has kept its continuity with the America of revolution and experiment surprisingly well, better perhaps than more distinguished shrines like Mount Vernon or Monticello, or Brigham Young's house at Salt Lake City. I suppose this is because it was never just the family home of a revolutionary. It was itself built as the workshop in which a revolution was planned and carried out. Then it became a besieged fortress, which surrendered more or less, but was never quite abandoned or assimilated to ordinariness. It still has an air of not impolite dis-engagement. The big trees and the lawns which the community laid out still make a small but perceptible psychological barrier against the encroachments of its post-revolutionary prosperity, the factory workers' ranch-type and colonial villas and the social annexes to the factory. There is a charming library where the books on the shelves and periodicals that lie on the table are serious, adventurous, unprejudiced. There is a big saloon at the back where some of the staff from the silver factory were playing cards, talking or reading and I recognized over the big fire-place a portrait of Pierrepoint Noyes. While I was looking at it, his son, a director of the firm and Dr Noyes' grandson detached himself from his card game and, learning that I was Irish, told me that the Oneida firm was about to start a branch in Belfast. I followed Mr Inslee to the music room with its big gallery and to the council room where the community

had its meetings to discuss the future and to listen to addresses from the
founder. On the staircase there are framed daguerrotypes of the
community, sitting or standing in rows like rather relaxed college
groups. The men all have beards or side burns and the women have
rather odd but reasonably feminine garments of a Victorian cut. Walking
on beyond them I saw through a big window a magnolia tree shedding
its petals onto a demure well-kept courtyard. Some decades ago H. G.
Wells visited Oneida and was struck by the contrast between these
prim photographs in their quietly prosperous setting and the wildly
adventurous social experiment which had drawn them together and
resulted in the Mansion House. And indeed I do not know of any Utopia
which dissolved into such elegant and agreeable ruins, for, of course,
from the standpoint of Utopia, the large efficient factory and its branches
spreading as far as Belfast, and the village that has grown up around the
Mansion House and Mr Inslee and Mr Noyes and their pleasant and
contented-looking companions, are all of them ruinous symbols of
defeat, pitiful distortions of the intentions of their progenitors. For
the silverware factory is run on what are roughly speaking ordinary
commercial lines, though in a very enlightened way, and the group that
lives in the Mansion House is married or celibate according to the normal
pattern. Yet there has been no express repudiation or recantation. In the
library I felt an air of patient expectation as though the final report on
the great adventure had not yet been published, and as though somewhere there was a great chest of psychological exhibits still to be ticketed
and displayed and nuggets of social experience which had, if anything,
appreciated in value as the years passed by.

I think that the caretakers of all this still thought of their grandparents
as famous explorers. That is how they appeared to Pierrepoint Noyes,
one of the planned children of the second generation round whom the
experimental society in which he had been born and reared had
crumbled. He was deeply proud of his origins: 'We had made a raid
into an unknown country, charted it and returned without the loss of
man, woman or child.'

While I was still in the library waiting till my bus back to Albany
was due, I heard a group walking towards me down the passage very
ponderously and slowly. The door opened and a very old man – he
must have been ninety – came into the room led by a young girl. 'This
is Mr Leonard,' Mr Inslee who accompanied them explained to me, 'the
last surviving planned baby.' Mr Leonard was too old to make any
articulate comment, but, as the conversation moved round him, he
contributed some proud and smiling acknowledgments. Then after a

few minutes he was led away again by the girl. His name, like most of
the other names I had heard in the saloon, was familiar to me, since a
century before it had been borne by one of the pioneers. But only when
I got back to New York was I able to collate what I had heard and seen
in the Mansion House with what I had read.

How had it happened that Noyes, despite his failure, had at least left
behind some proud memories and a flourishing business community,
while Joyce and Lawrence and their numerous imitators had achieved
so little? Lawrence had aimed at being a sexual reformer in a bigger way
and Joyce, engaged on his cold, private conjuring trick, had tried to see
how many obscene words he could balance chastely on his towering
literary integrity. What had been the result? They had liberated a few
condemned words, but the ideas and images which they released loiter
uselessly in the mind like an audience reluctant to believe that the show
to which they have been summoned has been postponed. And ideas that
loiter, disengaged from reality however fine in intention, are specially
corruptible. Despite all the serious criticism, the Ph.D. theses and the
championship of the high-minded, they have as paperbacks found appalling companions on the bus-terminal book stall.

As a pioneer Noyes had two obvious advantages over Lawrence.
Firstly he was a God-believer in a God-believing society, and like other
religious leaders could call on divine authority to strengthen his own
convictions and to bind his followers to him. Secondly he lived before
buses and telegrams could publicize or vulgarize an adventure whose
development depended on patience and privacy.

Pioneers who find causes by examining their hearts inevitably assume
that what they find there comes from some source that transcends reason.
And in Noyes' day the common name for such a source was 'God'. And
religion was a bridge between the consciousness of divine purpose and
the obligation to assist others to understand and acquiesce. That is to say
one might at any moment become the authorized interpreter of God's
will to others. New England had for half a century produced a succession
of leaders to whom some truth had been revealed. Ever since the Puritan
revolt against popes and bishops and the whole hierarchy of interpreters
of God's will, it had been easier for an unofficial mediator between God
and Man to sway the minds of men who had thrown off ecclesiastical
tyranny yet retained the habit of obedience. Then too there was still the
Bible, a great bran-pie of intoxicating poetry, of stern exhortations and
luminous phrases, on which a man could draw to explain and justify and
enforce the revelation which he had received.

Can one assess the value of one man's revelation of the divine as against another's? Not easily. One man with a command of words may describe some not very startling spiritual adventure so luminously that we follow him. Another man, who is ignorant and reared in platitudes, may be able to express only in nonsense words and a discredited mythology some great spiritual disentanglement from our worldly prejudices and preoccupations. Perhaps indeed Joseph Smith of the Mormons did have some dazzling revelation of the divine such as was never vouched to more sober prophets like John Wesley. Truth against which the study and the drawing-room windows are barred is obliged to force its way through the basement.

Noyes could never have embarked on his revolutionary programme or acquired any converts if he had not felt the hand of God guiding him and been able to justify his revolutionary ethic from the scriptures. I do not think he indulged in any more self-deception than is natural to the human condition. One of his biographers called him 'a divine madman' and we shall have been fair to him if we add to this that like so many of America's great spiritual prophets, Brigham Young and the leaders of the Mennonites and Moravians, he was extremely practical and domesticated, an expert at turning lathes and water-pumps and pig-mash, with informed views about pedagogy and medicine. Giving to God the credit for all his ideas, he was able to propagate them more vigorously than if he claimed them as his own. And in his immense unconcern for public opinion there was indeed some of that superhuman detachment to which our ancestors gave the name 'divine'. By degrees the elaborate pattern of Oneida evolved. Little groups of explorers in the domain of love, human and divine, approaching each other, were sometimes attracted, sometimes repelled. Public pressure moved the gathering communities from one New England village to another. They converged with the slow uncertainty of a swarm of bees that scatters and swirls and first appears to coagulate on one twig and then on another. Finally, around the caprice or the instinct of a single bee, the firm decision of the multitude takes shape. They settle in a large symmetrical bag and a new stage of consolidation and differentiation begins. At first the scandalized neighbours observed only a random patchwork of adulteries, but as the families gathered and merged, it was seen that on chaos and confusion a master hand was imposing an orderly design. On territory which the Oneida Indians, recently moved to Wisconsin, had evacuated, the Mansion House was rising by degrees, the religious basis of the community had been secured and Noyes established as their God-given leader.

Noyes preached that monogamic marriage was founded on selfishness but that unselfishness is the fundamental principle of the heavenly state. All sins come from selfishness, and true love alone excludes it. In the New Testament there is a problem which we must resolve for ourselves. When the Jews asked Jesus, 'If a man marries seven times, whose husband shall he be at the resurrection?', and when Jesus replied 'In the resurrection they neither marry nor are given in marriage but are as the angels', what did this mean? Noyes maintained that the angels were not celibate but that in some etherealized form, far above the crude possessive monopolies of this world, 'sex intercourse did take place in Heaven'.

This was the gospel which was preached and elaborated in the meeting hall at Oneida and published in *The Oneida Circular*. Writing about the community in 1900 Allan Eastlake has described it as 'the most extraordinary and the most valuable enterprise which has ever been undertaken since the foundation of Christianity, one which hints at the direction in which the world at large should gradually move'.

This was not how it appeared to the Methodist Meeting which gathered to consider it at Perryville in 1873. They named it 'the hideous thing that hides itself away from the light of day and revels in debauchery and shame, corrupting the very fountains of social and domestic virtue'.

The best account of Oneida comes from Pierrepoint Noyes' books. He was one of the nine children whom Noyes fathered from different mothers when he was in his sixties. Some years after the community had dissolved under the threat of a legal prosecution, Pierrepoint had reassembled as many as he could of the fifty-eight 'planned babies', his cousins and kinsmen, who had been born in the Mansion House, and together they revived the lapsing industries of the community and forged a new solidarity, strictly in accord with the laws and the proprieties, on the foundation of the scandalous one which had collapsed. Pierrepoint had even before his birth been carefully planned to fit into an imaginary society different in every detail from that in which he was to prosper as an adult; everything had been done to make him 'maladjusted' and yet he felt immediately at ease in the great world into which he was so suddenly plunged. He had his first glimpse of it on a visit to Niagara Falls; it was already organized for the American tourist and coming from the complex society of Oneida it struck him as amazingly simple. He was filled with 'confidence of his ability to compete in such a world of sham and futility'. He had no grievance then or later against his father or his upbringing. He had not disliked the communism in which he had been reared and he claimed, from his own experience, that 'the desire for exclusive ownership of things is not a primal human instinct'. He had not, for instance, resented the communal best suit which he and other boys of his age would take out in turn when they paid visits away from the community. Looking back on the Oneida discipline with its odd blend of rigours and laxities, he recalled with contentment 'the pleasant aroma of spirituality so humanized as to be inoffensive to a boy'.

For the first twenty years of the Oneida community only two babies had been born every year because a form of contraception was in use, the result of long and careful training. It depended on the indefinite postponement of the orgasm, a difficult feat in which the young men trained themselves through intercourse with elder women beyond the age of child-bearing. Noyes believed that 'the normal man loved the normal woman and only exclusiveness is abnormal', and he added, surprisingly, that exclusiveness was 'fatal to the highest type of romantic love'. This last seems contrary to the usual opinion. Desmond MacCarthy, for instance, once wrote that if men ever lived and loved as Lawrence had preached, two things would disappear from the earth, the smoking-room story and the love-lyric. There were certainly no smoking-room stories in the Mansion House, but were there love-lyrics? Noyes seems to have firmly blocked all the normal channels of romance and to have scrutinized carefully the sources of pleasure. The community was not in the habit of expressing affection openly. Like the Chinese, they did not kiss much – nor did they shake hands. Noyes distinguished the Oneida system sharply from Free Love which was only for 'irresponsible pleasure-seekers'. Men were not entitled to pleasures 'beyond the freedoms licensed by their degree of perfection'. What did Noyes mean by perfection? Just as the Mormons considered themselves saints redeemed from sin, the Oneida community did in fact believe that in some respects the Kingdom of Heaven had arrived and that their love affairs were as innocent as those of the angels. They did not claim 'perfection in externals', but they claimed to have attained 'purity of heart' and 'salvation from sin'. Perhaps this meant that if all those sins which derive from encroachment upon the conjugal rights of others (and that means perhaps the majority of the traditional sins of sex) had been abolished and women were freed from the obligation to respond to demands which they did not desire, sin could only survive where love was tainted with the old egoisms. It survived where men introduced sexual thoughts disharmoniously or soiled the expression of love by the furtiveness or the calculations of the everyday world. As one advanced towards perfect understanding, the temptations to such sins became fewer and a more exquisite, because a more refined, pleasure came within reach. Was that what Noyes meant? Was that where the love-lyrics began? One might get contradictory replies from the community; they were explorers in an unknown land and it might not be easy to harmonize completely the reports, the explanations, of the different travellers.

Noyes believed that righteousness would ultimately triumph and that glimpses of the predestined paradise appear to us from time to time to strengthen our courage and illuminate our path. I cannot quite reconcile this with his statement that on 1 June 1846 the Kingdom of Heaven had actually come. This perhaps is one of those inner circle observations which an outsider finds it hard to interpret, especially as at this time he was deeply engaged in launching his small industries and had started to play golf.

Noyes believed that the pioneers must prove themselves more conservative than the clergy, that is to say that they must strictly observe the rules which they had made for themselves by breaking through the apathy and laziness on which conventional morality depends. The rule against exclusiveness in love was rigorously applied and after a time the community adapted itself to it and ceased to consider it onerous. Pierrepoint Noyes relates how one day his mother was playing with him very affectionately, when his father came in. 'Harriet!' he said firmly, 'this is idolatry!', and took the little boy away. Pierrepoint says that he thinks his mother grieved at this restriction on their intimacy (they were only allowed to meet at fixed intervals every week), but he himself did not, though he was a devoted son who looked after his mother when the community dissolved. He was happy in the shared affection of forty or fifty kind and varied aunts and uncles. For the young adults often there were very hard decisions to be made. For instance Charles C. became attached to Miss B. with a love that transgressed the law against exclusiveness. But he overcame it. One day he found another member of the community making love to Miss B. while his baby lay in a cradle beside them, making some demand. He walked gently into the room and removed the baby which was disturbing them to comfort it himself.

In March 1843 the community numbered twenty-eight adults and nine children; they had originally developed out of small converging groups but once established, they attracted miscellaneous outsiders. Mr Herrick came, a New York episcopal clergyman, and Mr E. Hamilton, an architect. The cook at Oneida had been a lawyer and other professional men took up work with them such as stokers, lamp-cleaners, farmhands, proof-readers, laundrymen. They had a severe critic in one of the governors of the New York YMCA, a man who had brought life into that institution and been active in the Ragged Schools. He was converted to Oneida and taken on a five years' probation, which was described in this way: 'He was stood on his head and allowed to drain till all self-righteousness had dripped away.'

Another converted enemy was E. P. Freeman, a journalist, who attacked Oneida fiercely in *The Schenectady News*. His son joined Oneida and the journalist in his old age was supported by the community. And of course many distressed people joined. Though they were careful in their acceptance of new recruits, they laid themselves open inevitably to the exploitation of charlatans.

In its early days the community had sold vegetables and fruit and other country produce and then had branched out into a factory for animal traps and another one for tea-spoons. In the evenings the women made artificial flowers out of shells, fish scales and silver thread, as well as other ornaments and toys. They had no regular meals except breakfast; for the rest of the day they helped themselves off shelves in the pantry.

Later on the community was helped by the fact that its land adjoined the newly built Midland Railway and by degrees they got the reputation of having the best farm and grazing land in the state. They won prizes at the Lennox Fair and farther afield for their thoroughbred Ayrshires, their Aylesbury ducks and Leghorn poultry. Though they had suffered bitter reverses and were often near starvation, they made progress. Between 1860 and 1869 they earned 200,000 dollars profit. In the year 1880 they bred the third-finest Holstein in the state. They started canning on a vast commercial scale, paying to those outside the community 25,000 dollars in salaries. They co-operated with Wrigley's Chewing Gum and popularized their spoons by giving away a spoon with each 5 cent cake of soap. According to Pierrepoint Noyes, who was the most objective of chroniclers, these spoons had the reputation of being the worst silverware in the country. From their animal-trap factory they supplied four southern states with twenty-foot tie-out chains.

At last after twenty years a great decision was made. It was decided that to secure the continuity of the community and in the interests of science and religion, children must be born to Oneida. This was the beginning of Oneida's great experiment of Stirpiculture. It was the practical fulfilment, Noyes believed, of Galton's theories of heredity. 'The law of God', he wrote, 'urges us on; the law of society holds us back. When Galton comes to the point where it is necessary to look beyond his theory to the duties it suggests, he subsides into the meekest conservatism.' The community considered, rather like the eighteenth-century aristocracy, that the business of love was too serious to be left in the hands of the young people themselves with their immature and unreasoning passions. They believed that one day when communal life prevailed the regulations which they proposed would be universally adopted: 'Through propagation by wise selection, higher spiritual traits would be transmitted.' For unlike the aristocrats they were not concerned to preserve property and power by their organized alliances, but to maintain and increase virtue, wisdom, strength and unselfishness. In just a way nature and providence were wont to offer compensation for the blunders of man. 'Who can say how much the present race of men in Connecticut owes to the numberless adulteries and fornications of Pierrepoint Edwards. Corrupt as he was, he must have distributed a good deal of the good blood of his noble father, Jonathan Edwards.' Maybe even from the wicked practice of *Jus primae noctis* the human breed had been improved, but we must not leave such arrangement to chance and to ignorant and violent men. We must intervene ourselves. The community appointed a stirpicultural committee on which there were two graduates of Yale Medical School. Fifty-three young women signed a declaration: 'We do not belong to ourselves in any respect but first to God and secondly to Mr Noyes, as God's true representative... We offer ourselves as living sacrifices to God and to true communism.' The committee claimed that there was no diminution of liberty, even though some were excluded from parenthood. 'It was the free choice of those who love science well enough to make themselves eunuchs for the Kingdom of Heaven.'

Fifty-eight children were born of this experiment and the results must be considered to have been satisfactory. They seem on the whole to have grown up remarkably intelligent and able people. They were healthy as well. In fifty years according to the law of averages forty-five of the fifty-eight would have died, but in fact within that time only five had died. Noyes himself had sired nine of them though in his sixties, and, as I have said, one of these, Pierrepoint, was the leader of the reconstituted family group whose business enterprise still flourishes.

The community developed many practices which have been adopted by later religious or secular fraternities. For example, there was public confession as in Soviet collectives or among the Buchmanites. The competitive spirit seemed the greatest threat to the community and it was in that sphere that tension was greatest. The Oneida orchestra gave difficulties. As it got more skilled the claims of art began to conflict with the claims of perfect brotherhood. Its performances were no longer family occasions, the expression in terms of music of their fraternal solidarity. They became famous and attracted audiences and discriminating critics from far afield. The seniors feared that it was ending in 'professional sterility' because it had never been communized properly. The juniors suspected them of Philistinism. Carry had been asked to play the accompaniments only because Edith was ill, but what was to be done when Edith recovered and it appeared that Carry played better? Clearly in art as in stirpiculture the inferior had to make way for his betters, but how hard it was to do this without injuring the harmony of the group. The community tried to solve this by their criticism committees and their practice of openness, and candour among themselves. Lily, for example, admitted to the community that she hated Marion because Marion sang better. Marion had to decide for herself whether the applause of the outer world mattered more to her than the unity of the little inner world to which she had devoted herself. It was by meeting and overcoming or perhaps simply evading such crises that the community developed.

It appeared to the community that illness as well as jealousy could be alleviated by criticism. Did they think that illness was 'error' as the Christian Scientists think, or 'sin' as the inhabitants of Erewhon thought it? When one of the community fell ill a group of his colleagues would gather round and discuss his moral failings and, like the faith healers of all creeds, they had startling triumphs to record. A pedestrian explanation of some of these cures was given by one of the members. He said that the patient was often so appalled by the earnest, perspicacious and unanswerable criticism' of the friends gathered round his bedside that he broke into a sweat as though he had swallowed half a dozen aspirins and the fever left him. And the healthy too were criticized on regular occasions, and sometimes criticism took a highly original form. John Skinner, for example, was told he was too fond of his food to be sufficiently amative.

The community had become famous for its agricultural and industrial successes, its musical festivals and its craftsmanship. It had excellent relations with its employees and customers, with the townspeople and local newspapers. Somehow or other the neighbourhood ignored or forgave the unusual tenets and practices which bound the members together. They secured for their sexual innovations a tolerance which the Mormons only won after a slow and bloody retreat westwards as the armed forces of propriety caused them to abandon one stronghold after another.

On one occasion they were visited by a deputation of the New England Shakers. This was an extraordinary event. For the Shakers also had an overruling preoccupation with sex and religion but it had led them in a precisely contrary direction to that followed at Oneida.

They lived male and female together dedicated to absolute chastity. Presumably, though they reacted so differently from the ways of the world, they felt drawn to Oneida because they too repudiated the world utterly and were driven to similar devices to make their isolation bearable.

The community had never concealed its beliefs and its sex problems were openly discussed under the heading 'The Open Secret' in *The Oneida Circular*, which was edited by Pierrepoint Noyes' mother, Harriet. Perhaps in those days of spawning sects men had a more open and experimental approach to the mysteries of God and Man, perhaps too they were less frightened of press publicity. Otherwise it is hard to understand how respectable people could have organized family picnic parties to the Mansion House grounds and should have been shown over its gardens and workshops by the members, and how even Sunday School excursions should have been organized to this pleasant and hospitable abode of sin. Even the travel agencies started tours.

It was, I think, the Sunday School excursions that finally brought into action the Methodists of Perryville and the Reverend Thatcher of the Congregational Church of Hawley, Massachusetts, and the famous Anthony Comstock of the New York Society for the Suppression of Vice, and above all Professor Mears, the Presbyterian Head of Hamilton College, and Bishop Huntington. The time was propitious for the organization of moral indignation and the crusading against vice. In 1873 Congress had enacted a Federal Obscenity Bill. Contraceptive information had been declared lewd, lascivious and obscene. Its mailing was forbidden and a mood of stern censoriousness spread through the countryside. Professor Mears summoned many committee meetings at which 'the organized fanaticism and lust' of the Oneida community was strongly denounced. Was it tolerable that this system of corrupting concubinage should 'luxuriate at ease in the heart of New York State'?

In fact it was strange that this reaction had not come much earlier and that when it did come Noyes should have received as much public support as he did.

If the local papers reflected popular opinion, as they are supposed to do, his neighbours were on his side. The *Fulton Times* praised the community, saying that 'a foul and corrupt fountain cannot send forth a stream so clean, thrifty, respectable and peaceful'. The *Utica Herald* was not prepared to go so far as this but maintained that while one might disapprove of Noyes' theories, one could not disapprove of Noyes himself for it was to him and not to 'the open secret' that the fine qualities and attainments of the community were due. 'You may call it fortune, luck or providence. I call it religion, duty and the help of God.'

The heads of all the sound business houses between Utica and Syracuse, which had dealt with the community, supported them and treated Professor Mears' crusade with icy disapproval. District Attorney Barnett of Oneida County said, 'It is easy enough to reason out that their social habits are wrong, because they don't conform with ours – that is with what we *say* ours are – but if indictments could be procured on the ground of general immorality, who would not be liable?'

My impression is that till sin is formulated and denounced by some prominent and influential person, the average person makes his moral judgments in particular and not in general terms. For as long as it was possible, Professor Mears was ignored.

The community was all the same alarmed at the publicity and it was decreed that 'the open secret' should no longer be discussed in *The Oneida Circular*. It might have weathered the attack from outside if there had not been undermining forces at work within. They had some time before admitted and tried to assimilate a Free-Love community from Cleveland, Ohio, headed by a man called Towner. There had been divergences of ethic and policy and Towner had built up an anti-Noyes faction within the community and tried to usurp his authority. In addition, a real scallywag had been indiscreetly accepted and had had to be violently expelled through a window, and he was threatening prosecution. And finally there were whispers, perhaps fomented by Towner, against Noyes himself. What had he done or allowed to be done? About this the evidence is not clear and his son, so candid about most things, is rather evasive.

Certainly some of the women were complaining that they were being treated like white mice and perhaps there had been some aggression by an older man, which, despite all the promises of obedience which had been signed, was punishable by law, and there was a danger that the law might be invoked. One day in 1876 Noyes went hurriedly away and the community was left leaderless. At this time, when Noyes was in hiding and disgrace, his first cousin Rutherford Hayes moved into the White House as one of America's least distinguished presidents, and the contrast of their destinies became a theme for romantic journalism.

There was another disadvantage. Father Noyes' God was a Bible God and was going out of date. His son and successor, Theodore Noyes, an able physician, was a Darwinian. He did not believe in the angels, so could not maintain as did his father that in their sexual habits they behaved like the Oneida community. And though he accepted 'the open secret' and the community rules, there was a problem about authority.

Noyes had acted as Jehovah's Vice-Regent and had been obeyed but
Theodore, trying to translate the idea of leadership into modern terms,
became a priggish disciplinarian, ruling through reasonable arguments
rather than through divine ordinances. And, though he was a kind
intelligent man, his orders were resented. The woman with whom he
lived as the angels live was a schoolmistressy person and, with her as his
helpmeet, his shyness and uncertainty began to look like aloofness. This
was gently disliked and the deep rifts began to widen.

Rapidly the community dissolved after this. Like the Mormons they
abandoned their practices but not their principles. The ethic of Oneida
was, like Brigham Young's polygamy, postponed for some distant day
when mankind had more of the wisdom and the innocence of the angels.
Marriage was once more to be permitted but the counsel was given that
for those who had once had this brief glimpse of paradise, celebacy was
to be preferred. There were weeks of difficult and tragic manoeuvering
as the community paired itself off into would-be respectable married
couples. Their common property had also to be equitably apportioned
and it was discovered that while collectively they had been rich and
secure, as solitary couples they would be miserably poor and helpless.
Also they would exchange the conviction and confidence of superior
righteousness for tarnished reputations and social ostracism. A handful
stayed on in the all-but-deserted Mansion House; others struggled with
the shattered industries.

This should normally have been the end of a chapter, the unmasking
of illusions, the dissolution of yet another of America's numerous
Utopias. And yet it was not; for the Mansion House is still there and so
are the descendants of its founders, and the wheels of its factories are
turning more vigorously than before. How can one explain this except
by saying that human cohesion on an organized and personal level has
a value quite apart from the principles which bring diverse men and
women together. Even when the principles are rejected the memory of
the cohesion remains and acts as an inspiration to the survivors.

And the cohesion of the Oneida community had been much closer
than that of other Utopias, Robert Owen's for example, for not only
in religious metaphor but also in fact the younger generations were
brothers and sisters or at least kinsmen by birth. The tie of blood was
there to strengthen the weakening bonds of fellowship. Also, genetically
at least, the experiment had succeeded. These young people were vigorous, open-minded and intelligent.

And so it happened that the sons and grandsons of the founder came
together again and built up an economic kingdom on the foundations

of the ruined spiritual one. They make cheap cutlery in greater abundance than ever before. They are not at all embarrassed by their unorthodox past but it is not relevant at present. I visited an Irish branch of the Oneida factory in Belfast and saw men and women tending small machines like church harmoniums and regulating cathodes and anodes in a tank in which sometimes a bowl is being shaped or else an ornamental curlicue is being stamped on a handle. The directors have international problems; once, for instance, the Japanese flooded the market with cheaper spoons stamped with identical curlicues. In regard to love their views are now normal and they make a 'Marriage Gift' set of cutlery. On the lid of its box there is a picture of a bridal pair leaving the church door in wedding clothes. Several of the present Noyes generation, outstanding business men, have sat on Coal Board Commissions and represented America abroad. One or two have written novels. By easy stages they have become like everybody else, only perhaps a little more talented.

Bernard Shaw thought of Noyes as a great pioneer, 'one of those chance attempts at a Superman, which occur from time to time in spite of man's blundering institutions'. There is, of course, today more unregulated sex than Noyes would have approved. Many would agree with him that 'sexual intercourse is an honoured method of innocent and useful communion', but most of those who experiment are attached in one way or another to 'blundering institutions'. The idea of collective experiment has seldom been so successfully fulfilled. It survived the collapse of its principles and retained a measure of its former social cohesion.

Not often expressed, there is still a feeling that sexual power is something like the power of wealth or intellect, which must be exercised with charity. Like money and brains it is not exactly private property. The rich ought to give to the poor. But not only are there no supermen in control but we are all centripetally organized towards some distant focus of authority and small breakaway communities are more short-lived than ever before.

[1962]

LITTLE K

====

PREFACE

I wrote this in 1967 under the impact of a tragedy that was still fresh in my mind. My opinions have not changed and, though more people share them, it has not become easier to express them. I have only once seen my grand-daughter and, as she lives the other side of the Atlantic, I am unlikely to see her again. She has passed from infancy to child-hood, to adolescence, to maturity. Her body has changed but her mental age remains the same. She is one of nature's mistakes and left to herself nature might have taken her away, but though often disastrous exper-iments to improve on nature are made, we seldom trust her to do the best for us.

Yet there seems to have been an unexpected change of policy in the USA. Baby Jane Doe, the three-year-old child of Long Island parents, was born severely retarded with many physical handicaps. Spinal surgery would prolong her life but would not correct her retardation. Her parents, after consulting doctors, clergy and social workers, rejected the operation.

Thereupon a Vermont lawyer, a right-to-life activist, took the child's parents to court to force an operation. The Court of Appeal denounced his suit as offensive and supported Baby Jane's parents.

The Reagan administration then took up the cause but in June 1985 the Supreme Court rejected its appeal. There will be very few parents of such children who will not rejoice at the rebuff to the administration.

A further decision of the Supreme Court invalidated a 1982 Federal Rule which required that hospitals which received Federal money should post up notices urging staff members to report any denial of treatment to handicapped new-born. On behalf of the majority in the Supreme Court, Justice Stevens declared that the reason why new-borns, such as Baby Jane Doe, do not always get special medical treatment is not because hospitals discriminate against them but because their families do not want them to have that treatment. Federal law, he held, does not require hospitals to treat handicapped children without parental consent or require parents to give it.

It was suggested that there should be hospital-based Infant Care Review Committees on which there should be clergy and community representatives as well as legal and medical experts to review such cases. The *New York Times* ended its report succinctly: 'That puts the problem where it belongs: out of Big Brother's hands and into those of concerned committees.'

The Supreme Court has in this way many times proved itself to be the protector of the rights of the citizen against the state, the one against the many. The Reagan administration thrives on broad generalizations. Soviet Russia is an evil empire, Libya a terrorist state, Nicaragua a Communist threat to her neighbours. If we look at a very small map of the Earth and interpret it by the very big headlines in the daily press, this is quite a normal view of the world. But 99 per cent of its inhabitants live out of reach of the headlines; and their deepest feelings, their strongest convictions, are often incommunicable till someone appears like the parents of Baby Jane Doe with the will and the skill to articulate them and present them to the Supreme Court. It has often struck down callous and cruel decisions of the Reagan Justice Department, which, inspired perhaps by the Southern fundamentalists, tried to legislate in the spheres which the Founding Fathers held to be the province of private judgment.

I. LITTLE K

In order to treat this subject objectively I had thought of calling them A, B, C, D and E. C, D and E would be my three grand-daughters, A and B their parents, but I find I cannot reach such heights of detachment and that I must call them by their true initials, J, D, C, S and K.

I do not see them very often for they live in America. C is five years old and rather serious. She does not say very much, preferring to nod for 'Yes' and shake her head for 'No', but the whole time she is remembering and judging. I have an idea that when she grows up she will reject a great deal that most people accept. I feel very close to her and wish I could be beside her when the time comes for her to make decisions. S, who is still only two, is very different. She accepts everything and everybody and flings herself laughing and chattering into the arms of those she knows. C and S both remember K, my youngest grand-daughter, of course, but there is always so much happening that they do not often ask about her. C liked to be photographed holding her but K went away when she was two months old and they will, I think, soon accept her absence as permanent. [So little happens to K that once at least I shall give her her real name, Katherine Synolda, 1987.]

On my way to see K this morning, I walked through the park at Yonkers and tried unsuccessfully to find the Doric temple from which you are supposed to see the broad sweep of the Hudson and the Palisades beyond. The park is laid out so as to make you forget that the largest city in the world stretches all around it. I walked down woodland paths, where wild copses of acacia and fir were choked and bent with their burdens of honeysuckle, and I came at last to a romantically ruined manor house with sagging roof and rotting window frames. The park is a place in which to relax, to tear yourself away from the complex and sophisticated problems of the city, where everything is pulled down before it has time to grow old, and plastic flowers outnumber real ones a hundredfold. So nature is allowed to half-strangle the shrubberies and tear the manor house apart. But, in fact, you cannot walk very far without being reminded of the well-organized sorrows and joys of the city. At one end there is a Cardiac Centre and the jungle slides away from it deferentially towards the river; the rough paths compose them-selves into gentle gradients suitable for wheeled chairs and cautiously shuffling heart cases. There is a smooth lawn with rectangular panels of salvia and petunia as neat and tended as temperature charts.

At the other merrier end of the park, the derelict manor house, embedded in kalmia and rhododendron, has a notice on it, NO WEDDING PHOTOGRAPHS TO BE TAKEN HERE.

If you find relaxation here, it is by withdrawing and pretending; it is that fragile sort of peace which the gravely disturbed find in barbiturates.

East of the park and higher still above the Hudson is the long low white house where K lives. I met D there and together we went to her room. She is with ten other babies and she has her name on her cot. She has a sweet baby mouth and chin and large blue eyes and above it a high domed forehead, which would have been lovely too were it not for the sharp ridge that runs down it from her skull. She has, I am told, agenesis of the corpus callosum. That is to say the central part of her brain has not developed and, therefore, the optic nerve too is defective. The whites of those beautiful eyes are tinged with blue and she is all but blind.

'But look,' said a kind nurse, 'she blinks when I wave my hand. I think she can focus a little too.'

K did indeed blink, but it seemed to me that she just felt the draught of the nurse's hand.

D unclasped her hand, which was folded up like a bud, and showed me the palm.

'That's the Simian line going straight across. You meet it in mongols. But it's not a sure test, as she isn't a mongol. I showed it to an obstetrician and he just held up *his* hand at me. He has the Simian line too. All the other children here are mongols. Look at their lower eyelids! Look at the way their ears are set – very low!'

The nurse leant over and touched a small tin box attached to the cot and a tiny tinkle came from it.

'She loves her little musical box,' she said.

There was a pause while we watched for a sign that K was loving it but none came. The nurse closed it by saying, 'She never cries. She's so good.' (Later D told me that, when K was born, she did not cry, like other babies, but was unnaturally quiet.)

'Will she ever be able to walk?' I asked.

'Oh, why not? Of course!' she replied encouragingly.

'And talk?'

'Oh, I expect so. But you must ask the doctor.' She was embarrassed and broke off to greet a little boy who trotted into the room.

'Hello, Sammy! Back again?' and to us she said, 'Sammy is the brightest of our little mongols.'

I asked to see the older children and she took us into a sunny courtyard, where ten or twelve of them were playing. The swings were soaring up and down and a big ball was rolling about. A tall, almost handsome boy in a jersey with BEATLE printed on it rushed up to us jabbing his left shoulder and shouting something. It sounded like 'Resident! Resident!' 'No, we're not residents here,' D said, 'we're just here on a visit.' 'Resident! Whi How!' the boy bawled on, and we grasped that he was saying that he was the President of the United States. A girl of twenty with a broad blue band round her head, which was flopping from side to side, charged up to us. A swollen tongue stuck out of her mouth and she barked at us something we could not understand.

'Do they ever quarrel?' I asked the nurse.

'Oh, indeed they do!' she smiled at the innocence of my question.

Then we went to the room of the totally unmanageable. 'Don't you come!' I said to D but he insisted on going with me. These children cannot be given toys, because they destroy them. Some were incontinent and some had limbs that were frenetically askew. Television was on non-stop. ('They love their television,' said the nurse.) Many of them had dreary commonplace delusions like the Beatle boy, taken from TV or secondhand from the newspapers. One or two had some droll hallucination which two months ago I would have found touching and even entertaining.

As we went down the passage we passed the open door of a small room and in it I saw a charming-looking woman with greying hair. Her husband was with her and they were talking to a young defective. ('He gets fits,' explained the nurse, 'that's why he has the black eye.') As the mother saw us she turned to the boy with a gay and loving laugh. He looked unresponsively back and I knew that her animation was directed at us rather than at him. She was telling us that she was ready to do her part in trying to lift the great curtain of sadness that hung over us all.

When we reached the hall two merry little girls dashed past us, with their parents behind. 'I know who you've come to see!' said the nurse, bending down to them. 'Yes, Lucy! Lucy!' they shouted and tore ahead. The nurse smiled at us as though to say: 'You see it's not all sadness. Children take it quite as a matter of course.'

But I think it is all sadness, unnecessary sadness, from which the world has piously averted its eyes. The realities are concealed from us by a labyrinth of platitude as specious and unnatural as the honeysuckle jungle at Yonkers. There is not a child in that large establishment whose parents have not at one time thought what they dare not articulate: 'I wish that my child would die!' And many, perhaps most, are still thinking it and secretly praying for it.

II. MME VANDEPUT AND THE NINE CATHOLICS

As we drove home, D told me that one in ten of all the children in the USA is defective. I thought he must be exaggerating but when I got back I turned to the appendix of the book about the trial at Liège of Suzanne Vandeput, who killed her armless 'Thalidomide baby'. The nine gently disapproving Catholic authors of this book, doctors and priests, give statistics of the mental defectives in France. They are about

7 per cent of the population. How many of these, I thought, can be as well cared for as our little K, surrounded from babyhood with toys and paint-boxes and swings, with practised smiles and laughter that is innocent or lovingly simulated?

The nine French Catholics are thinking of that too. Their book is learned, tender, imaginative. Not in one sentence do they denounce Suzanne; she was wrong, of course, they say, but they see her sin against a dark background of callousness, stupidity and smugness, and they recognize that science has transformed the human scene and totally changed the nature of our problems: 'The new drugs', writes Father Roy, 'can be as dangerous as they are salutary. The number of abnormal children is increasing; the doctors are opposing the process of natural selection by allowing beings to exist which are in no way human.'

They are aware that the support that Suzanne Vandeput received from press and public in Liège and beyond was not only sentimental and unreflecting but scholarly as well. Father Roy quotes with bafflement and sadness rather than horror two French doctors, Barrère and Lalou, who present a humanist point of view:

Our age has effected so many transformations on man that the moral problems raised can no longer be answered by the ancient formulae. It is almost a new reality that we must learn to accept and mankind will need many years to construct a new humanism founded on the new man. Euthanasia seems to be one of the keystones of this future edifice.

The fact that this is quoted without horror shows that the nine writers are aware how unresponsive we have mostly become to the ecclesiastical anathemas of the past. With the advent of totalitarian and nuclear war the old Christian tabus on killing have fallen into such confusion that one moral argument has now to support itself with ten practical ones. Most of their arguments are therefore addressed to the humane and far-sighted rather than to the devout.

(1) Only one writer, Father Roy, uses an argument that a sceptic or a Protestant might find offensive, for he links the euthanasia of the defective with divorce as a source of bad examples. Divorce, he says, is not only a disaster for the children of broken marriages but it also influences others to part, who without this way of escape might have 'risen above their selfishness' and 'attained to a richer marital understanding and love'. But a non-Catholic could argue that divorce has brought as much relief as tension, as much joy as sadness, and that this is no argument at all.

(2) Father Beirnaert SJ predicts 'personality disturbances' for the child,

whom Mme Vandeput said she was going to bear in order to replace the armless child that she killed. It is right that we should reflect on such indirect psychological effects, but they are unpredictable. How can we judge their importance? One of the nine, Dr Eck, speaks frankly of the marriages that were broken because of a defective birth, and the jealousy that normal children, brothers and sisters, sometimes feel because of the special love which a good mother will sometimes give to her defective child. All these things may happen. But love and wisdom can sometimes solve these problems, sometimes must recognize that they are insoluble.

(3) Dr de Paillerets asks how can one decide that one malformation will justify infanticide, while another will not? How can we decide who will be unhappy, who not? Healthy people may be miserable and severely handicapped people may be cheerful.

(4) He asks how can we be sure that cures will not be discovered for defects that now seem irremediable?

(5) He says, if doctors, even in exceptional cases, were to become the auxiliaries of death rather than of life, would they not certainly lose the confidence of their patients? 'Without this confidence medicine cannot exist.' And he says that, since the time of Hippocrates in the fifth century BC, this 'unconditional respect for human life' has been obligatory. He quotes the Hippocratic oath, which all doctors are still obliged to swear.

(6) The sixth argument is very odd.

Infanticide [he says] puts a curb on the enthusiasm of those, who through their research contribute to the increase of our knowledge, and on the enthusiasm of those, who, devoting themselves to the care of the unfortunate children, now find that we are equivalently disowning them and regarding their work as unnecessary. Medicine needs support from all of us if it is to keep its essential dynamism.

It is possible that one day some instrument will be invented which will register human sympathy, warmth of feeling. Surely, if it was attached to Dr de Paillerets as he wrote this, it would register zero. How otherwise can he think of a parent's agony in connection with the progress of medicine and the nursing profession? It rouses instantly the suspicion that it may be in the interests of geriatrics and allied studies that men are sometimes forced by doctors to live on beyond their natural span.

(7) The seventh argument also betrays a curious professional egoism, disguised as modesty. Dr de Paillerets dreads the possibility of some kind of medical commission entrusted with the task of selecting infants for

death. 'What a terrible temptation is this for us to accept such a right over the life and death of others.'

But what parents would ever grant to doctors such a right? It is a right that only those who love the child and are close to it could claim and exercise. The doctors' function should be a minor one. It should be little more than that which, under pressure, the Catholic bishops of Nazi Germany permitted when they decreed that Catholic doctors and social workers could report to the authorities those afflicted with ills calling for sterilization, provided they did not at the same time order or authorize sterilization. The operation was performed in scorn rather than love, and permission was granted with casuistry, but it is not impossible to imagine that religious men and doctors could, without casuistry and without scorn, help a parent in a sad decision.

Most of these seven arguments deal with problems that we meet every day and that are solved rightly or wrongly according to our instincts and knowledge. There are stresses and strains in family life which we can palliate but seldom elude. A great sadness will produce other sadness whatever we do. It seems to me that when Dr de Paillerets considers these practical arguments against infanticide he has already despaired of defending the only absolutely compelling argument, which is that all killing is a mortal sin. He may have reflected that public opinion, like war, sometimes has the power to modify the most uncompromising dogma and that there was an absolute and peremptory quality about the support which the people of Liège gave to Mme Vandeput.

Palliatives

In our time there has been so much ecclesiastically condoned and sanctified killing that few clerics would nowadays have the effrontery to bring up again, without diffidence or qualification, that dishonoured and bamboozled old commandment, THOU SHALT NOT KILL. Father Roy condemns the doctor who simply repeats it and concerns himself not at all with the tragic situation of those who must cherish the helpless being which medical science has preserved for them. Left to herself nature would often have borne away the malformed child in a miscarriage or by some ordinary illness like measles to which, without inoculation, the often feeble defective child could have succumbed. The doctors feel a greater responsibility towards their profession than towards their patients. When a friend of mine with a defective child asked that it should not be inoculated he was told that he must not 'tie the hands of the doctor'.

The nine French priests and doctors are fully aware what a burden of responsibility they bear for what is happening. For the doctors save and prolong lives that are useless and unhappy and the priests mount guard over them with moral precepts. They urge upon their colleagues, in recompense, a devotion, a dedicated study, a depth of understanding, which is far beyond the reach of most men.

Dr de Paillerets writes of the meagre, badly supported research which is being done on encephalopaths. In Paris it is often many years before the defective child can even be received into a specialized establishment. 'It is our duty as doctors', he writes, 'to expose this scandal... The Liège Trial has occurred but the real trial is yet to come and, if we do not act in this matter, our place will be in the first row of the accused.'

And Father Roy, stressing the urgency, asks if we are prepared to postpone the laying down of new major roads till the specialized homes are provided. This question carries its own answer with it. No, we are not.

The nine Frenchmen also urge that the parents of the afflicted should form associations to discuss their common problems and share the burden. And Father Roy distinguishes between the 'pity', a negative, egoistic thing which men are ready to show, and the 'compassion' which is demanded of them and which forces them to share the sufferings of the afflicted and to act. He quotes Bernanos: 'Modern man has a hard heart and tender guts.' He weeps for the sufferings of others and winces at the thought of being involved in them.

Is there any likelihood that these generous ideals will ever be fulfilled? The next day, in search of enlightenment, I went uptown to see Dr S, the obstetrician who had delivered K. He confirmed what I had suspected. There is no reality in these dreams of Father Roy. Dr S is a kind and brilliant man but his talents have made him much sought after and there is no likelihood that he will ever desert his other patients in order to show more than perfunctory sympathy with the parents of defective children. Nor, as far as I know, has there been any 'dedicated study', any researches into the origin of K's misfortune, which might be helpful to others.

Then there is the question of parents' association. I learnt from one of the nurses in the home, where K is, that Dr S himself has a mongol child there. Yet he never told J or D about him, though he, as a doctor, frequently handling our problems both in his home and his profession, could have forwarded such an association more than anyone else. About this I do not feel I have any right to reproach him. We are all of us preternaturally sensitive about our defective children. For educated people they may represent a private anguish that is well nigh unshareable.

This intense 'privatization' of our problem (to use an American word) belongs to the Age of Scientific Organization, as does the increase in the number of abnormal children. The bourgeois, for the most part, live in small labour-saving flats and it is usually obvious, if not obligatory, that the defective child should go to an institution where he can receive 'proper care'. Though it may well be that the parents think of their child every hour of the day, they do not have to talk about him or constantly plan for him. Only rarely will talking help them. About this I understand Dr S.

It was very different when I was a child. Our rector had a mongol daughter and the neighbours frequently took charge of her. (Father Roy would say that it was not half frequently enough.) She is looked after by her relations and I still see her sometimes, a woman of fifty. It is possible that our rare gestures of true 'compassion' were largely neutralized by our chattering 'pity'. But even such small efforts as we made would now be difficult and unwanted. The compassion which Father Roy demands is not compatible with professionalism. Doctors, nurses and social workers must take their courses, earn salaries, go where they are told, and so must the clergy. Their lives are too full, too controlled for them to have any time for that total imaginative involvement which is compassion. There is no reality in these dreams of Father Roy. The revolution in men's behaviour which he desires cannot happen in a scientifically organized society. The position which he is trying to defend is based upon moral precepts which have lost their validity. The relief which he promised will never come.

I asked Dr S what he thought of euthanasia and he said that Mme Vandeput was wholly wrong. All life is better than all death. He was coming to believe that only in rare cases was even abortion justifiable.

'Are your objections religious?'

'If you mean am I a Catholic, the answer is no, but I believe in God.'

He was surprised that I should know about his little boy and he told me that he had often longed for him to die but he no longer did so. He had wondered too whether he had been wrong in sending him to an institution.

I did not ask him why he had not told J that he was a fellow-sufferer, as this might have comforted her a little. I now regret my shyness as I believe his answer would have shown that our attitude towards the defective is now one of absolute negation. No trace remains of the old belief that they are in some way the special children of God.* They are

* A friend of mine claims that this is untrue and that here in Ireland the Steiner movement is represented in the village communities at Duffcarrig and Ballaghtobin and other places.

just genetic mistakes which, since we cannot, like the Greeks, extinguish them, we must relegate to some place where they are no nuisance to society.

Dr S's God is different from mine. Churchmen are now ready to admit into their ranks those who reject all historical certainties and see God and his son Christ as constructions of the mind by which the human imagination tries to express its revelation of the divine. This revelation varies from man to man. To me God is the assurance that the world of men is not purposeless or evil and that we can trust ourselves to it and that, when old laws lose their significance, new ones will slowly shape themselves to take their place. As for Christ, he is the assurance that a man can learn when and how to free himself from the power of the law, however strongly it may be reinforced with venerable traditions and popular approval. The show bread may have to be eaten, the sabbath profaned, the prostitute exalted. 'GOD' is the promise that out of this disorder a better order will ultimately ensue.

III. NATURAL LAW AND THE GREEKS

My mention of the Greeks recalls to me that I have not answered one of the arguments (no. 6) used against Mme Vandeput. It is medical rather than religious but seems to suggest, as the clergy do, that there is some sort of Natural Law at issue, which we neglect at our peril.

Dr de Paillerets quotes the Hippocratic oath which doctors have considered binding upon them since the fifth century BC.

I shall not give a homicidal drug to anyone, no matter who may ask me to do so, nor shall I initiate the suggestion that it be given.
... The least exception to the unconditional respect for human life would place the doctor in a position which he could not accept. It would curb the enthusiasm which is the prerequisite of progress in medical knowledge. Furthermore, it

---

I have visited Ballaghtobin, which is in Co. Kilkenny, and know how dedicated men and women have devoted themselves to improving the lives of the handicapped adults. They think of the mentally defective as fellow individual spirits who have slipped sideways on the evolutionary ladder, but who command innate respect, dignity and potential. Some of the villagers among whom they live accept this and conclude that mongols, to whom in particular the movement addresses itself, are in the world to teach their busy 'sane' fellow travellers the true value of brotherhood, love, acceptance. Hence they view them as 'special' and inherit the children-of-God outlook. I appreciate but do not share this sentiment. (*H.B.* 1988)

would destroy the confidence of the patients, without which there can be no Medicine.

But surely the oath is greatly misinterpreted and the historical foundations of medicine strangely misunderstood. The Hippocratic oath mainly concerned the Greek habit of administering poison to those condemned to death. Hippocrates considered it beneath the dignity of a doctor to became a paid executioner. Moreover the world in which Hippocrates practised gave a limited authority to the doctor in the matter of life and death. His duty was to cure those who wished to be cured, but he did not interfere with ancient practices. In his day and for a century or two afterwards, in all the city states except Thebes, deformed or sickly children were exposed. Aristotle, a great admirer and younger contemporary of Hippocrates, thought the custom should be made law, for he writes: 'With respect to the exposing or bringing up of children, let it be a law that nothing imperfect or maimed should be brought up.' Plato gives the same advice to the law-givers in his ideal republic. Is there any evidence that Hippocrates opposed what was a universal custom?

The Greek father could decide whether a child was to live or die, for the infant did not become 'a member of the family' till he was formally presented some days after birth. Infanticide was not eugenic, though Plato and Aristotle would have treated it as such, for the father had a right to eliminate even a healthy infant whom he did not wish to rear, and this was freely exercised in the case of girl infants whose dowry might present a problem. The unwanted infant was placed in a cradle or pot and put in the corner of the marketplace, in the temple or wrestling ground. It might be picked up and reared by a stranger, so sometimes some objects of value were wrapped up with it. But the father had the right later to claim it after it had been reared, so the infant was usually left to die.

Only at Sparta was the absolute right of the parent over his children disputed, for the state would sometimes weed out, for eugenic or military reasons, sickly infants whom the parents had spared.

All this is very shocking to Christians, if Christians have not forfeited their right to be shocked at such things by their connivance at Auschwitz and Hiroshima, but some great classical scholars have shown sympathy. Of Greek infanticide Zimmern writes:

The Athenian had a traditional horror of violence and interfered, when he could, on behalf of the helpless. If he consented to exercise his immemorial right over his own offspring, he did so with regret for the sake of the city and his other children, because it was more merciful in the long run. We have no right to cast stones either at him or his fellows.

And Bernard Bosanquet writes in his *Companion to Plato's Republic*:

The high mortality of young children today suggests that we are superior to the ancients more in theory than in practice... Can any race safely arrest selection? It is quite conceivable that the actual infant mortality on the ancient system might be less than ours at present.

Plato and Aristotle both had the pragmatic, society-centred religion of most modern scientists. They did not see in the eugenic infanticide, which they preached, anything incompatible with orthodoxy. After a sentence or two about infanticide Aristotle returns to the subject of childbirth and urges that for the sake of exercise and the tranquillity of mind, which is favourable to successful parturition, the pregnant woman should walk to the temple every day and offer prayers to the gods who preside over matrimony.

All this has a callous, calculating sound. In our society our leading thinkers are more humane and imaginative, but Greek society itself was less cruel and impersonal and we have discovered new forms of physical agony and lonely introverted misery of mind of which the Greeks were incapable. The gulf between Plato or Aristotle and daily life at Athens was large, but not so large as that between, say, D. H. Lawrence and daily life at Nottingham, or the Bloomsbury group and Bloomsbury (it would be easy to discover some more modern and apposite antithesis), and I do not feel perverse or paradoxical in suggesting that there has been a real deterioration.

What are the principal forces that have drawn us away from the Greeks? First there is 'science', which, looking for conformity in men, tends to impose it. It classifies all living things by their shared characteristics. It pares down those distinctions upon which personality is built and which defy classification. It achieves its best results by treating men as statistical units rather than as individual persons. Such methods are damaging to that flexibility of conduct on which Greek ethic is based.

Secondly there is professionalism, which claims exclusively for itself spheres of authority, fields of investigation and experiment, which were once open to ordinary men, parents, neighbours, friends.

Thirdly there is universal democracy, which aspires to offer to the whole multi-racial, heterogeneous world, laws which all will accept. That means boiling down into a simple code of Do's and Don't's a vast complex of interlocking moralities deriving from very varied traditions and customs.

The Greek moralist or law-giver always had in mind the small community in which public opinion could sometimes enforce the law, sometimes replace it. So occasionally Aristotle, instead of saying, 'Let there be a law that...', says instead, 'Let it be held in utter detestation that...'.

Today public opinion, manipulated by pressmen and politicians, has become so ignoble a thing that we distrust it and put our faith instead in the law. Its chief defect, its inflexibility, becomes in our sad circumstances a merit.

Finally there is Christian theology, which has shaped the law, so that even those who reject its dogma are still bound by it. Bosanquet, for example, argues that our respect for human life has been deepened by religious doctrines, even discredited ones, such as that concerning the fate of unbaptized children in the world to come.

Modern churchmen are evasive about the future world, its penalties and prizes, and tend to judge our actions in accordance with their conformity to something they call 'Natural Law'. But it seems to me that Greek custom was closer to nature than we are and that it is not 'natural' for a doctor to insist on prolonging, by drugs and inoculations, the life of a defective child against the wishes of its parents. Bosanquet is surely justified in writing of the 'immemorial right which a parent has over his own offspring'.

In regard to infanticide I ought to add that the Greek practice had been inherited from primitive times. It can be traced among such primitive peoples as the anthropologists have investigated and it is usually linked with religion or food. The Aruntas of Australia suckle their infant children for several years and a new child whom the mother thinks she will be unable to rear is killed at birth. It is thought that the child's spirit goes back whence it came and can be born again. Twins are thought to be unnatural and are immediately killed.

Among the Todas of South India twins are also regarded with dismay and one of them is killed. New-born female babies are sometimes laid in the mud for buffaloes to trample on. These practices are most prevalent among the priestly caste in the Nilgiri hills where Western influence is weakest. Margaret Mead describes them as 'the desperate expedients to which a simple people have to resort to fit their survival rate to their social structure. These practices are dying out but so are the Todas'. She tells much the same story about the South Seas and the far north, where the Eskimoes practise female infanticide. And there is much in our own social history which is seldom remembered and is never written. An Irish friend of mine, herself the mother of a loved and cherished defective child, remembers as a girl being told how in her country neighbourhood a malformed infant was usually put at the end of the bed and left there unfed and untended till God, in his good time, should take it. I have never heard of this elsewhere or read of it but I believe it to be true.

No sensible person, of course, considers that primitive people can give us directives as to how to behave. We are not qualified to learn much from them or they from us. Yet there is a tendency to argue from 'the natural law' which we are supposed to have inherited from the remote past. There is no such thing. The most that a traditionalist might claim is that in all times, lands, peoples, we can trace, however faintly, one constant passion, the distaste for cruelty, injustice, waste. It is sometimes a minority sentiment but, when held with tenacity, it invariably prevails.

Surely today any deeply concerned parent, grandparent, or friend would agree that we have to retreat from many strongly held convictions which we have inherited from the past, and that 'desperate expedients' may have to be contemplated, if slowly and laboriously a new ethic and a new morality are to be built around our new convictions. How widely are these convictions shared? Am I just dreaming when I think that almost all those who have the same cause for sadness think as I do?

In *Le Dossier Confidentiel de L'Euthanasie*, Barrère and Lalou endorse what I have said about the attitudes of Greeks and Romans with quotations from Epicurus and Seneca. To them a man was the master of his own body and had a right to leave it when it could no longer give shelter and sustenance to his faculties. It was not till St Augustine that suicide and euthanasia became the crimes which Christians hold them to be today. And even in Christian times devout men could think differently. St Thomas More in the Second Book of *Utopia* wrote that when an Utopian was dying in incurable anguish, the priests and the magistrates exhorted him

Either to dispatche himselfe out of that payneful lyffe as out of a prison or a racke of tormente or elles suffer himselfe wyllinglye to be rydde oute of it by other... But they cause none suche to dye agaynste his wyll ... He that killeth himselfe before that the pryestes and the counsel have allowed the cause of his deathe, him an unworthy they caste unburied into some stinkinge marrish.

And Francis Bacon had similar ideas.

As for the present state of the law in various countries I must depend as others have done on R. Raymond Charles's *Peut On Admettre l'Euthanasie?* The laws of Spain, Holland, Hungary, Italy, Poland, Norway, Denmark, Brazil treat with leniency those who kill from pity with the consent of their victim. Peru and Uruguay go further for they permit the judge to grant exemption from all penalty where no selfish motive can be discovered. In Europe the Penal Code of Czechoslovakia arrives more cautiously at the same conclusion.

In the USA and USSR the law has advanced and retreated. In 1906 the State Parliament of Ohio passed the first reading of a law permitting a man who was dying painfully to summon a commission of four to judge his right to end his life. A few months later Iowa voted for a law of still greater latitude, for it embraced defective children and idiots. However, when Congress had to pronounce at Washington, its verdict was wholly hostile.

In the USSR a law of 1922, which abolished the penalty for homicide whose motive was pity, was repealed a few months later because of evidence that it was being abused.

Sometimes the law seems to nourish itself on its own vitals, developing without relation to what happens around it. In Nazi Germany in 1944, when the slaughter at Auschwitz was at its peak, a law was passed which prescribed the full legal penalties for those who from pity kill the incurable and the mentally deficient.

How then does it happen that in France and Britain, countries with long humanist traditions, no special exemption for those who kill from pity is embodied in the law? Is it perhaps that in these sophisticated countries there is an awareness that in human relationships there are zones in which a man may make his own terms with the Source of Law, whether he deems this to be God or the Natural Order, and that such a man needs no intermediary. Certainly in France, at least, euthanasia trials, despite the law, have usually ended with an acquittal or token punishment for those whose integrity is manifest.

IV. CHRISTIANITY AND KILLING

Was there ever before so much mental confusion about the killing of men by men?

Where does human life begin? There is the widest dispute. When does it end? Even that is not so clear as it once was. Granted that a man may kill in self-defence, is he also obliged to? And, if so, how many others is he obliged to defend by killing as well as himself? His family, his friends, his neighbours, his fellow citizens, his nation? And has he to kill on behalf of the friends of his friends and on behalf of the nations, who are allies of his nation? And should he practise preventative killing? Should he in this way defend himself or his friends or his nation when they think they are threatened? Or might be threatened? And has he to kill people in order to bring about justice in the world, in the way that his elected representatives think best?

Wherever his duty may lie, what actually happens is always the same. The individual, till a man rushes at him with knife or gun, can kill nobody, not even himself. The state can force him to kill anybody, though his whole soul rebels against the killing, and the Churches, because for their survival they have made their own pacts with the state, can give him no support in his rebellion. On the contrary they will support the state against him and often bring to bear all their supernatural sanctions against the individual, so it seems to him that he will be damned in the next world as well as in this if he does not kill those whom he neither fears nor dislikes.

Their clergy are kindly sensible men, anxious to preserve the venerable institutions which they serve and whose future is precarious. Therefore almost without exception they have interpreted the commandment THOU SHALT NOT KILL in the way that is most pleasing to secular authority. They have given their blessing to those that kill from fear and hatred, and they have condemned as sinners those who kill from love.

When I was thinking of this, the New York Times came in and I read of a seventeen-year-old boy in Detroit who had tried to kill himself with a stick of dynamite rather than go out to kill people of whom he knew nothing in Vietnam. In the adjoining paragraph I read how 500 Rabbis, American and Canadian, assembled in Toronto, had by a majority vote censured the Vietnamese war and insinuated that its roots were largely commercial. Later on I read how other denominations had also debated the war, and, except for the Orthodox of America, had also by a majority censured it. In fact there can never again be a war whose 'justice' is uncontested by religious men. It is a measure of their helplessness, their cowardice or their confusion of thought that they still continue to sanction war. They will still censure a bewildered boy for killing himself rather than become a killer. Should we censure them? I think not. They are caught, as we are, in a trap from which it is very hard to escape.

Yet the Churches still consider themselves to be the unflinching champions of the rights of the individual and the family, of the sacredness of human life; there is an ostentatious straining at gnats by those who have swallowed camels.

Even the nine Catholic authors, though they write so modestly and perceptively, sometimes appear to picture themselves as representatives of an austere tribunal from whose unbending judgment the timid layman shrinks away. Father Beirnaert SJ, for example, says that a merciful doctor will sometimes in disregard of Christian principles suppress a defective child 'because he finds the morality of the Church too severe'.

On the contrary it is not its severity that is repugnant but its extreme flexibility. The Churches make absolute judgments, but they qualify them for the powerful and only enforce them against the weak.

Father Roy, for example, says: 'The affirmation of respect for human life must therefore be absolute and universal – that is, categorically binding all mankind – if we are not to founder in multiple disasters.'

This covers Mme Vandeput but not Hitler, for conscience obliges Father Roy to add a footnote about the right to kill in war. He makes a distinction between 'human life', which must be absolutely respected, and 'biological life', which we can destroy in self-defence, or in 'a just war'. And he says that the Church, while tolerating killing in war, has 'never given formal approval to it'.

Surely this distinction between 'human life' and 'biological life' is a dishonest one? Does a man's life become biological rather than human when he puts on a uniform? The only true distinction is that between views that it is politic to hold or 'tolerate' and those that are not. Father Roy's Church, a vast multi-racial organization which is unpopular with many, cannot afford to assert unequivocally against everybody the sacredness of life, as it was asserted in the first two centuries of Christianity. In those days there was no conscription and all that the Christian expected from the state was to escape its attention. The distortions and compromises, which we accept as inevitable, had not yet been forced upon him.

Can we still accept them? I think not. There has been a great change. Long after other historic events are forgotten the name Auschwitz will recall the most stupendous crime in history. And, linked to it enduringly is the greatest non-event, the Silence of Pius XII, more terrible now that his apologists have argued that prudence and Christian charity demanded it. For this argument shifts the guilt of impotence from one man to the whole of Christendom and justifies a billion meaner connivances.

The gospels say that a darkness fell upon the earth when Christ was crucified and when a new era began. Surely the Silence of Pius has the same symbolic quality. It was mysterious and ominous, like the silence of woods and fields that precedes a total eclipse of the sun. It must herald some great change, either the final collapse of Christianity or its rebirth in some new and unforeseen shape.

In fact, if there is a rebirth, I believe that the ancient law THOU SHALT NOT KILL will have to be interpreted with greater severity and not less. And, if it is to be qualified at all, those who kill from loving compassion will seem to us far more forgivable that those millions of conscripted killers whom the Churches forgive and even exalt.

The problem of 'unnatural death', that is to say death which is not due to accident or bodily decay, is a unitary one. The hastened death of the defective baby and the incurable adult to whom life is only useless pain is linked to the involuntary death of the criminal and the conscript soldier and allied to all other assaults which we make upon human life, to birth control, sterilization and abortion. We shall never be able to face the problem of the useless, the unwanted, the criminal, the hostile, the unendurable life with courage and understanding, so long as our laws compel the innocent to kill the innocent against his will. So long as the Churches condone it, the taint of expediency must colour everything they say. Nothing can change till the leaders of the Church dare to say once more: 'Those that take the sword shall perish by the sword.'

This would be a lightning flash, dazzling and destructive, that would shake the world. Many venerable establishments would crumble, but the dark unvisited places, which breed ugliness, would be illuminated. All the things that we do or fail to do in the ante-chambers of life or at its exit would be seen in their proper perspective, birth control, sterilization, abortion, euthanasia. Our judgment, no longer clouded and crippled by the great betrayal, the stupendous fallacy, would be free to act. Our little K's life, a frosted bud that will never open and bear fruit, would be allowed to drop.

V. CHURCHES UNDER PRESSURE

The ideal does not become more remote when the real is closely examined. The man who intends to escape must know each stone of his prison walls as though he loved it.

The narrow territory on the verges of life and death, which is now almost all that remains of the once vast spiritual dominion of the Churches, is constantly under dispute. Let us observe how its Christian defenders behave when they are under attack. If most of my information is about Catholics, that is because in recent years they have excelled others in self-scrutiny. Let us watch how they acted when the Nazis tried to interrupt the cycle of man's life at its generation, in its prime and in its decay. We shall see that in general the Churches capitulated to the powerful and compensated themselves for their defeat by tyrannizing over the defenceless.

Maybe this is just a law of life. If you have to draw sound from an instrument whose principal chords are dumb, you must strike those that remain all the harder. As their power to enforce laws that are binding on peoples and governments declines, the Churches enforce them with special vigour in those spheres where men are solitary and amenable to persuasion. In all that concerns child-birth and sex and marrying and the death of relations, we are so much alone as to be almost grateful for public interest and hence ready to be counselled, cajoled and coerced. The warrior, defeated in the field, finds consolation in being a tyrant at home.

In Germany, which sometimes calls itself 'the Heartland of Europe', ideas which are current elsewhere are often acted out so boldly and dramatically that, like the details in an enlarged photograph, we can see universal human behaviour most clearly in a German context.

There were three stages in the attack on the sacredness of human life, and corresponding to them two great ecclesiastical and one partial triumph. The Nazi sterilization laws attacked the unborn; the euthanasia campaign was directed in the first place against life in its decay; genocide, which was an attack on life in all its stages, was little more than an extension of the 'just war' which the Nazis claimed to be waging.

It was to the question of procreation that the Nazis attended first. In May 1933 Hitler laid before the German bishops the draft of a law providing for voluntary sterilization. The Catholic bishops rejected it as a violation of the encyclical *Casti Conubii*, 1930, but the concordat with Hitler was about to be signed and the day after the signing a law for forcible sterilization of the diseased was approved. Catholic resistance was strong but, National Socialism having been accepted, the encyclical had ultimately to be set aside. Finally even in Rome compromises were made, and in 1940 the Sacred Congregation ruled that Catholic nurses in state-run hospitals might under certain circumstances assist at sterilization operations. It was argued that, if a recalcitrant nurse were dismissed, she might be replaced by an anti-religious person who would withhold the sacraments from those in danger of death. And, though it remained sinful for a Catholic physician to apply for the sterilization of any patient, he was allowed to report to the authorities the names of those afflicted with ills calling for sterilization.

The relationship of Church and state followed this familiar pattern of quibble and counter-quibble; when the Church was forced to some shameful capitulation, it invariably tried to make good its losses by some tiny usurpation in the domestic sphere. And thus it was that the German hierarchy forbade the marriage of sterilized persons, since 'by natural law the main purpose of marriage is procreation'. However, in the first three years of the decree 170,000 people had been sterilized and the Catholics among them made a formidable body. So even the Church was forced to retreat and to withdraw its veto.

Then followed the euthanasia campaign and a Church-State war of great significance, for in it the Church proved its power and influence and demonstrated that it was unwilling to use them except when public opinion was favourable. On 1 September 1939 Hitler decreed that all those with incurable diseases should be killed and before the end of the year establishments for the shooting and premises for the gassing of victims were opened in Wurtemberg and Hesse. As soon as rumours of this reached the clergy there were furious protests and after the campaign had lasted two years and 70,000 patients had been killed, there was an abrupt change of policy. The principal credit for this must go to Bishop Galen of Münster, who delivered a famous sermon demanding that those who had done the killing should be prosecuted for murder. He warned them that human life was sacred except in the case of self-defence or a just war, and that invalids and seriously wounded soldiers would be next on the list. Some of the Nazi leaders wanted Galen hanged but they dared not do so, so great was his popularity in Münster and in all Westphalia. Instead, the campaign of euthanasia was called off.

This great Church triumph was significant in several ways. It showed that in our frailty we are strengthened by being able to appeal, beyond our conscience, to infallible dogma. In other words it is easier for us to say: 'That is forbidden by the Encyclical *Casti Conubii*, 1930,' than to protest: 'That revolts me to the bottom of my soul!' But the disadvantage is that if we wait for the august and infallible Voice to proclaim the truth and the Voice is silent, we are more helpless than those who have treated their consciences as primary and not secondary sources of enlightenment. For the testing time for Christians in Germany came not when the government began to kill their crippled and defective kinsmen. It came when the Nazis began to kill their innocent and helpless neighbours the Jews. When the Voice was silent and the priest and the Levite passed by, it was inevitable that the ordinary man should consider it no concern of his and that the cold and cruel heart should be sanctified.

At that time the ecclesiastical opposition to euthanasia, successful as it was, showed that the bishops knew about gas-chambers before the Jews did. They knew that they were built for the elimination of the 'unproductive' and that Jews were officially declared 'unproductive' and that many clergy had endorsed this view. They knew that they had been deported to the east... The bishops were not mentally deficient... and they had heard rumours.

If the purpose of religion is to arouse our conscience and to sharpen our sensibilities to the perception of evil, the Churches had failed disastrously. What they offered was not a stimulant but a drug. In the matter of euthanasia we must turn aside and listen to the voice of our own conscience.

There is abundant evidence that the bishops' minds had been befogged by the theory of the just war and the image that it had printed indelibly on their imaginations of the conscript soldier as a knight errant and even, in the fight against Bolshevism, as a soldier of Christ. In a fog of crusading holiness Auschwitz was hard to distinguish from an air raid, one of those sad events which it is necessary to endure and to inflict if, in our imperfect world, justice is to prevail. In order to preserve morale one must not say too much about specific cruelties and injustices of the war, in fact, better say nothing at all. So that Guenter Lewy in his magnificent book *The Catholic Church and Nazi Germany* writes: 'While thousands of anti-Nazis were beaten to pulp in the concentration camps, the Church talked of supporting the moral renewal brought about by the Hitler government.' And Gordon Zahn in *German Catholics and Hitler's Wars* declares that after exhaustive research he could only find a record of four German Catholics who had openly refused military service. He attributes the 'near unanimity of support' for the war from German Catholics to 'the external pressure exerted by leading Church officials' and the spiritual influence that their words and examples were bound to have on their flock.

For years after the true character of the war had revealed itself the clergy went on proclaiming it a just war and denouncing those brave men who refused to serve. For example, when the Austrian peasant Jägestätter chose to be beheaded rather than to take part in what he deemed an unjust war, his bishop reprimanded him severely for his disloyalty. They were all of them deceiving themselves in the interests of ecclesiastical survival.

Years later the President of Western Germany, Lübke, said in a memorial address: 'No one who was not completely blinded or wholly naive could be completely free of the pressing awareness that this war was not a just war.'

That is to say that much innocent blood was shed, often by innocent men, because of the Church's failure to follow its own teaching. Lewy believes that had the leaders of German Catholicism opposed Hitler from the start, they would have made the home front so unreliable that he 'might not have dared going to war and literally millions of lives would have been saved'. But once a war has started it is not easy to see how the Church, with its intricate relationship with the government of every state, would be able to oppose it. When nations are engaged in combat it is already too late to ask where justice lies and to urge soldiers to desert.

I hope I have shown how vacillating the Christian approach to those problems has been. The encyclical about sterilization was only scrupulously observed so long as observance was not likely to injure the faithful seriously and damage the prestige and authority of the Church and alienate its disciples. The euthanasia of the innocent was only vigorously denounced when it concerned people of the same race as the denouncing ecclesiastics. The problem of the 'just' or 'unjust' war was never seriously considered. I believe that there is not a bishop in Germany or in all Europe and America who would now dare publicly to assert that Hitler's war was a just one. Yet when they were already in full possession of all the facts, thousands of bishops, and not only in Germany, asserted this.

Public and Private Killing

I see only one path through this moral chaos. The Church sometimes claims to be a higher court attending to those spiritual needs of mankind which governments, concerned for its material welfare, must ignore. If that is so, could she not insist that a man is the master of his own life and that he cannot be obliged to offer it or preserve it against his will. The community may try to educate him in the use of this right but cannot deprive him of it. If he should abuse it, no doubt we might suffer 'multiple disasters', but not so many as we suffer through denying that that right exists.

In the matter of killing in self-defence, which the Church tolerates and often commands, this new code of ethics might work more justly and effectively than the old one. Science allied to bureaucracy concentrates power in the hands of the few; a genius in a laboratory conceives an idea and shares it with a governing minority. As a result great cities crumble, army corps collapse, empires capitulate. The only antidote to the captive genius and his captors is the free man's passionate conviction. He normally operates single handed and is trusted by neither Church nor state. All the honours, all the blessings, go to the conscript armies. These armies are composed of a few men who identify themselves with the aims of the government and are prepared to kill for them, a few more who are convinced that it is their duty to suppress all private judgment and to kill as they are ordered, and finally vast hordes of ignorant or innocent or deeply reluctant conscripts. If there is often or ever a clear-cut antithesis of good and evil, the last place to look for it would be in the opposition of rival armies. This is an old story which we have come to accept as inevitable. What we should not accept, what is obscene and intolerable, is that the Churches should bless this arrangement and continue to preach as Father Roy does that 'respect for human life must be absolute and universal and that it must be categorically binding on all mankind'.

Only a Quaker or one of the other pacifist sects can talk like that without the grossest hypocrisy.

Yet if the Quakers are wrong and we have to kill in defence of innocence and justice, how best can it be done? In scientific warfare the innocent and the just who are conscripted and forced to use modern weapons will be as indiscriminatingly murderous as their fellows and must be resisted with the same mechanical ruthlessness. There is only one way in which death can be dealt out selectively and that is by assassination, a form of private enterprise on which the Church has always frowned. Those who took part in the July 20 attack on Hitler are now recognized as great heroes, who, had they succeeded, would have ended the war and preserved the unity of Germany. Yet at the time they received nothing but discouragement from even those of the Church leaders who had opposed the Nazis. Cardinal Faulhaber, for example, when questioned by the Gestapo after the plot had failed, is said to have expressed the most vigorous condemnation of the attempt and to have affirmed his loyalty to Hitler.

Yet it is obvious that assassination, when a man chooses his victim of his own free will and risking his life takes upon himself the complete responsibility for his acts, can have a nobility that must always be lacking in the mass slaughter of conscripts by conscripts. And after the event the successful assassin will certainly get the blessing of the Church. It has been said that Bishop Preising, who had been informed in advance of the July 20 plot, was to have replaced the pro-Nazi Orsenigo as Papal Nuncio to the government of assassins. Whether or not this is true it is certain that Archbishop Stepinac cordially welcomed the government of Pavelitch, whose members had been involved in the assassination of King Alexander. All the Croatian bishops extolled Pavelitch who was himself received in audience by Pope Pius XII.

If the Church were to accept assassination as a form of resistance, which, however deplorable, was preferable to conscript warfare, it might be able to judge it by some subtler criterion than success. In that case it would surely condemn Pavelitch and Stepinac and praise Stauffenberg and Preising.

But could the Church ever show greater indulgence to the assassin than to the soldier? Not as she now is. Being herself a social organization, she is always disposed in a time of crisis to ingratiate herself with the great political aggregations to which she is affiliated. Though she often claims to be the defender of the individual conscience, she usually concedes that when mankind organizes itself into powerful national groupings, it can legitimately dodge the impact of those 'absolute and universal laws' which are 'categorically binding' on the individual. In the matter of killing the Churches will therefore line up with the worst of governments till it is defeated, rather than with the best of assassins before he succeeds.

I have written sympathetically of assassins without recalling any particular one of whom one could unreservedly approve. The German heroes of July 20 seem to have plotted to destroy Hitler principally because he was losing the war. Bonhoeffer, who excites interest and was executed for his complicity, does not seem to have been deeply implicated. Pavelitch was a bloodthirsty fanatic. Perhaps I have most sympathy for Princip and Chubrilovitch, the assassins of Sarajevo, who, as many think (not I), precipitated the First World War. Why are assassins mad or simple or discredited people, or else like Princip have a fatal illness? I think it is because public opinion is conditioned to abhor what they do and only the most desperate conviction and courage will induce a man to risk a healthy life for it. He knows that a conscript who mindlessly kills a hundred other equally harmless conscripts will be criticized by nobody, while a brave and resolute man who rids the world of a tyrant is staking his honour and his reputation as well as his life.

How trivial my problem seems compared to his, yet I have linked them together because law and religion have already done so. I too ask more than orthodoxy could ever concede. I am claiming much more than the right over my own life, which in the long run no one can permanently withhold from me. I believe that love can give us the right of life and death over those who are helpless and dependent on us. And that when circumstances are desperate we must snatch it, as did those parents who flung their children from the trains transporting them to Auschwitz. It is a right that can never be confirmed by any legislature, for the essence of law is impartiality and detachment, and those who are detached cannot judge the depth of love and the urgency of despair.

VI. THE NORMALITY OF LOVE AND THE LAW

It is not healthy to live alone for long periods with dreams which you cannot realize, for it is certain that little K's parents can never claim their rights and it is improbable that I will. But you can obtain relief from a particular problem by generalizing it, observing its impact upon others and preparing for its solution by posterity. So I took the subway downtown to East 57th Street, New York, where the Euthanasia Society of America has its headquarters, and there I came to my senses. The secretary told me that there is no likelihood that in our lifetime euthanasia for defective children will be legalized. 'You see,' she said, 'religion is very powerful in America. Even to work for legalization might be unwise. We have to approach our objective step by step, and the first step concerns the elderly and hopelessly diseased who wish to die.' She showed me an article in *Harper's Magazine* of October 1960, 'The Patient's Right to Die' by Joseph Fletcher, who has a chair in Ethics and Moral Theology at Cambridge, Mass.

This article is very illuminating but confirms what the secretary said. It is the problem of the old who wish to die which occupies the mind of these reformers. He tells the familiar story well. He describes how we have altered the whole pattern of life and death; men live far longer than they used to do and die painfully and slowly as their faculties decay. 'The classical deathbed scene with its loving partings and solemn last words is practically a thing of the past. In its stead is a sedated, comatose, betubed object, manipulated and subconscious, if not subhuman.'

The doctor, who from worthy motives refuses to prolong this indecency, must first be protected by the law; the next to be championed is the doctor who deliberately curtails it. The case of little K is something quite other; it cannot even be considered.

Evidently modern medicine has caused us to invert the thinking of the Greeks for whom old people, whose lives were never artificially prolonged, presented no problem, since if they were not reasonably healthy they soon died. Not even Aristotle or Plato, who favoured the killing of defective children, required that old people should be helped into the tomb.

Reading Mr Fletcher I have come to think that in fact the Greeks understood better than we do the nature of the affections. We stress the 'sacredness of life' but a Greek would consider that life becomes sacred but is not born so. The reverence which we feel for the young is woven out of memories and hopes and gathers in complexity as they grow older. But where there are no memories and no hopes the Greeks would only see 'biological life', to use a phrase of Father Roy in a way which he would greatly dislike.

'Biological life' is something that we spare and cherish from biological instinct, and instinct will perhaps only slowly develop into love. Where there are no hopes, we may come to feel resentment or even hatred towards the life which instinct bids us cherish.

There is indeed in general estimation nothing sacred about the instincts. We defer to them perhaps even less than we should do, inhibiting all those that are incompatible with social order. The sexual and philoprogenitive instincts, the instinct of self-preservation and many others, are subordinated to the needs of the state. Even the maternal instinct submits to control.

Joseph Fletcher talks of a new 'morality of love', which he also calls 'the morality of human freedom and dignity'. He does not define it, but he seems to think that it is something that the law could be brought to tolerate. Could it? To me, this morality of love will always be apart from, and sometimes in conflict with, the law. For as the law extends its scope wider and wider over men of all creeds and races, it will concern itself less with the intimate relations of men and more with their public communications. Its goal will be to avoid social collisions. The only support that the morality of love could offer to a man in conflict with the law would be the assurance that he was doing right.

A pamphlet which I was given by the Euthanasia Society, combined with Fletcher's plans for a graduated reform of the law, made me wonder whether I even wanted the legislation of what he calls 'the morality of love'. Attached to the pamphlet is a specimen application form which the seeker after death would have to send to 'the authorities' (in this case not GOD but some medical–legal committee). Can death safely be made something you apply for like a widow's pension, a traveller's visa, a set of false teeth, filling in details about your age, your illness, the degree of your pain? Is it some tenderness of guts that makes me squeamish? I should like to ask permission to die from those I love, for they alone can judge whether it is time for me to go. I would prefer that old laws should be generously applied than that new ones should be made. Otherwise in a bureaucracy one application form begets another. It might happen that when the Society had won its cause, the application form for dying would breed as its legitimate heir an application form for living. Even if this did not happen, the pressure on useless people to make them feel unwanted is intensifying. There used always to be room for an old grandfather by the chimney corner but now there is a waiting list for every bed in the hospital.

Father Roy was talking sense when he said that 'this principle, the suppression of abnormal children, first announced as a right, is in danger of being insensibly transformed into a duty', and that 'war is being prepared against the feeble and the abnormal'.

This danger is a real one and if infanticide were left to the medical services it might become a branch of eugenics and under government control. This would be an outrage upon the 'morality of love, of freedom and dignity'. For what we have to assert is that a man has a right over his own life and a shared right, in certain cases, over the lives of those that are dear to him. We cannot define these rights but love, which is not transitory, has duties and powers and will define them according as we acknowledge its authority. I believe that it would define them unmistakably for those that love little K.

Because of this, it might be better to take a life in defiance of the laws of the state and to be called a murderer than to arrange a legal death, if by so doing we allowed it to appear that the state had any right over the lives of the innocent. Though we might come to claim that even an adult belongs to those that love him, we could never admit that he belonged to such random collectivities as the state, the people, the nation, the race.

In another respect I feel myself in sympathy with the nine Catholic writers. Fletcher links artificial insemination with birth control, sterilization and abortion as 'a medically discovered way of fulfilling and protecting human values and hopes in spite of nature's failures or foolishnesses'.

Now artificial insemination seems to me to belong to a different category from these others. It is a prim suburban device for replenishing the nursery without the illicit pleasures of adultery or the illegal obligations of polygamy. It is anti-social and anti-historical, and an affront to those who believe in the ties of kinship and are ready to be bound by them. It undermines the solicitude that a man must feel for his offspring. The most carefree adulterer cannot free himself from concern for the child he has begotten, even though it may be hard for him to express it. A 'donor' on the other hand releases his child into the unknown and will never think of him again.

And artificial insemination is only the first of the scientific marvels by which the family is liable to be transformed. It is now possible for a woman, through the transplantation of fertilized ova, to bear children unrelated to her own family as well as to her husband's.

Would Fletcher consider such devices as ways, like artificial insemination, of 'protecting human values and hopes'? I think that they violate them and that though they may be legal, they should 'be held in utter detestation'.

How can artificial insemination be integrated into 'a morality of love', since to love the real father of one's child instead of his assumed father would bring fresh complications to an already complicated situation? If Fletcher does not see how fraudulent and furtive such arrangements are, he has not understood the true nature of family love, how it develops out of ties of blood, out of shared memories and associations, responsibilities. He does not see what a huge part the sense of continuity plays in the love we bear for our children and their children. I think of my little K as carrying with her till she dies the rudiments of tastes, qualities, talents, features, prejudices, which I and her father and mother have seen in those akin to us or observed in ourselves. Because of this sense of continuity she is called, like many others of my family, after an ancestress who lived centuries ago and of whom we know nothing but without whom we should none of us exist. Because of her affliction she will never be able to co-ordinate her inheritance or develop it. She is starting on a long and hopeless journey in more or less the same direction as we and ours are travelling and have travelled. She may be travelling it alone when we, who brought her into the world, are no longer there to shield and love her. Is this conviction that her destinies and ours are interwoven a necessary part of family love or something that can be detached from it and quite irrelevant? I can only say that it is not irrelevant for me and mine. And sometimes when I have been thinking up arguments for the legalization of infanticide, I pull myself up with the reflection: 'What business is it of theirs anyway, the doctors, the police, the judge, the jury, the hangman?' Little K is ours, irrevocably ours, in virtue of our deep involvement and I abandon myself to a vision of the future that is more like a Chinese puzzle than a dream, for even as I construct it I see all its intricate improbabilities. Yet there is no other way, at present, in which 'human values and hopes' can be protected.

VII. ORDER AND CHAOS

There is very small chance that any widespread change of opinion about these things will occur during peaceful times. Not till something desperate happens will parents of defective children dare to articulate the knowledge which they have found in their hearts, or look to others to endorse it. The average man is unconcerned. Since death and decay await us all, he might take a remote interest in euthanasia for the old and sick but he will be more likely to dodge the law when his time comes than to try to change it in advance. I cannot see that even for the elderly or diseased who wish to die, there is any likelihood of a change in the legal or religious position till the graver problem of the conscript killer has been faced. A reconsideration of this by Church or state might cause a revolution in the structure of society, as Christianity did in its first centuries. In the rebuilding of a new order, a man might recover the rights which he once abdicated to the state.

Certainly the desire for a revolution, a rebirth, is there but no one knows in which direction to look for it or how to prepare for its coming.

The state seems to wish to renounce its right to kill or to expose its citizens to be killed for causes they do not approve. Capital punishment has gone and the rights of the conscientious objector are acknowledged though not widely acclaimed.

Can it go further without laying itself open to internal decay and external assault?

In the Church too there are signs that under pressure of science and public opinion some if its most sacred tabus are being relaxed. If birth control is permitted, a very ancient and fundamental belief about the human soul will have been abandoned. At the other end of life, science has pushed back the frontiers so far that most people can outlive their faculties. This means that the preservation of life, which was once a sacred duty, no longer appears so.

Therefore Pius XII has said that, when life is ebbing hopelessly, doctors need not try to reanimate their patient but 'may permit him, already virtually dead, to pass on in peace'. And Dr Lang, the Archbishop of Canterbury, wrote that 'cases arise in which some means of shortening life may be justified'. There are clergymen on the committees of euthanasia societies.

Yet in these directions Church and state, with their survival at stake, must move so slowly and cautiously that frequently their leaders have to appear as the enemies of the causes in which they believe. A great prelate may find it impossible to exhibit in public the rebellious wisdom and gentleness of his nature. Whatever his private views might be, he could not give public comfort to the conscript who felt no hate and refused to kill, or to the men and women who killed because they wished to spare suffering to those they loved. That is the price he pays to the people for the platform from which he is permitted to address his message *urbi et orbi* or to his nation.

The pyramidal structure of a great state or a great Church imposes prudence. By his exalted position at the apex a prince of religion is exposed to pressure which obscurer men can dodge, and, as with a general who capitulates, his surrender forces submission on men still capable of resistance. Pius XII, for well-known reasons, lagged very far behind the most enlightened of his bishops in his defence of the innocent. The bishops on their part, crippled by the weight of bonds and bargains by which their relations with the state were regulated, passed on to their priests the responsibility of protesting. The priests passed it on to the laymen. And, equally fearful of damaging the Church, the laymen passed it on to those outside the Church. Was there in all Germany a Christian who resisted Hitler as promptly, unreservedly, heroically, as the non-Christian Ossietzky? But the clerics were justified in their prudence. The pyramid still stands, a massive monument to the advantages of discretion.

But even now its security would be endangered by any serious squabble with the state. So it is unlikely that leading churchmen will ever support aggressively the rights of conscience or question unbecomingly the justice of any war in which their government is engaged. Until something happens to interrupt the easy tenor of events, this prudence is obligatory. For if the government were to grant to each citizen the right to decide who his enemy was and whether he should be killed (a right which many savages enjoy), not only would armies be in danger of disintegration but so would states and Churches. There would be chaos of a kind.

But what kind? We have been conditioned to think that even war is better than chaos or disorder. Though we do not, like many great Victorians, actually value war (Ruskin said it was 'the foundation of all the arts, all the high virtues and faculties of man'), many see it as the mother of invention, of better aircraft and nuclear discovery. And a huge number of respectable people find in it great enjoyment and liberation of spirit. In contrast few social opportunities and interesting assignations are to be offered by the disorder that results when some conflict of principle, normally inhibited, flares up into violent civil discord. And everybody condemns it. Yet the free human spirit is less enslaved by the worst kinds of social disorder than by the best kind of war. The most dreadful crimes of the century have been committed by orderly people subordinating themselves to the commonweal. When the Czechs unburied the corpses of the thousands who had been massacred at Theresienstadt, they were able to give each victim an individual tombstone, for a number had been attached to his or her big toe which corresponded to a name and an address in a carefully kept register. It was not brutal people who did this, but hundreds of selfless and dedicated morticians and stenographers. The massacres which were conducted chaotically as in the Balkan countries were not nearly so comprehensive. The killers often tired or felt queasy or amorous or compassionate or accepted bribes. Nature was able to assert itself. And nature is not evil till we make it so.

In fact fruitful ideas are often nourished by what the Organization Man calls disorder. They grow like ferns in the interstices of crumbling walls. You cannot say, as some do, that the ferns are pulling down the wall, for unless it was already collapsing the ferns would not have a foothold there.

Today, in the huge discrepancies between official belief and private behaviour, almost any revolutionary idea could comfortably take root and slowly dislodge a stone or two from the established certainties. Half of Europe is officially dedicated to the belief, which shows no sign of being fulfilled, that the state will one day 'wither away', its mission accomplished. Would it matter if the other half also came to think of states and governments as provisional, as methods of collective admin-istration concerned with the problems that arise when men meet each other impersonally in large numbers, with traffic, that is to say, rather than with ethic? Such a view might be more congenial to us than it is to the Russians who preach it. Things would move slowly but by degrees problems of morality and ethic, of punishment and penance, might be released, finger by finger, from the palsied and uncertain grasp of the Church and the state, and settled quietly by men who knew each other.

Maybe the right to kill is the last that the state will relinquish, but the pattern of society is changing rapidly. Consider Charles Whitman, the psychopath, who killed his mother and his wife and then climbed to the top of a tower in the University of Texas and killed and injured forty passers-by before he was himself killed by the police. Friends, relations, neighbours, all knew what he was like and might have foreseen and forestalled what happened. Do we not need dreams, ideas and plans that will strengthen the authority of those who are fond of us, or at least interested in us, and weaken the power of the remote, indifferent people who are normally appointed to judge us?

This is fantasy, of course. But the world of Auschwitz was a fantastic one, built upon evil dreams, which no one except the dreamers thought could be realized. The ordinary familiar methods failed to disperse them. We might do better with what is extraordinary and unheard of.

VIII. THE SMALL COMMUNITY

So it appears that for me and mine the situation is hopeless for many years to come. Legalism becomes increasingly more powerful than love, and religion sanctions it. The secret ways of ending life are carefully guarded by the specialist. Only a doctor can defy the law and terminate an unwanted life without being detected. Frequently, of course, he will refrain from 'respirating' a malformed infant. But in this he cannot be said to be animated by love but by certain scientific classifications.

Even in that kindly book about the Liège trial, the nine religious writers print an appendix in which the retarded are divided into four grades according to their IQ percentages. Little K belongs, I believe, because she has only two-thirds of a brain, to the lowest group of the four, and Hitler's doctors would have given her a high priority for the gas chamber. But by these physiological groupings we distort the problem and make it likely that a categorical 'No' will one day lead to a categorical 'Yes'. Science has, in fact, by reducing the significance of the individual human life, disintegrated love and impaired the rights which a man has over his own life and his child's. Almost everybody today would agree that the doctor, the judge, the clergyman and the geneticist should have greater authority over the life and death of a baby than those who begot him and bore him.

The nine French authors, dreaming of fresh fields opening up for the compassionate heart, the dedicated volunteer, have exiled themselves from reality, as I do when I speculate how I can end little K's life, which can bring only suffering to her parents and to herself. Measuring our convictions, we may be ready to believe that present reality will change more easily than they will. In the meantime I see that I cannot follow my conscience without causing complications for everybody and in particular for those I wish to help, and so I put all my proudest hopes into reverse. Because I cannot take life I become anti-life, and I pray that little K will have a sort of vegetable apathy and that she will never be so conscious of her inadequacies as to suffer for them.

But how can one wish that anyone one loves should be as stupid and helpless as possible? That is a sin of course far worse than the act which I accept as right but cannot perform, yet I am driven to it by a society which refuses to recognize the rights of love.

Moreover, I am forced to admit that till the whole structure of society changes, there are excellent reasons for this refusal. In an acquisitive society, where property is accumulated and inherited and men advertise themselves by their offspring, where labour has to be mobile and families move from place to place, it would be very easy for prudence to pass itself off as love, and for respectable people to engage in a covert war against all physical and mental non-conformity. It would be very difficult to establish that kind of community in which the fraud would be detected and 'held in utter destestation'. In an open society love is easy to simulate. One cannot trust it, and even when one can, one could not allow our social institutions to be shaped by such a trust. As democracy widens its scope and we reach towards a universal government with uniform laws, it is less and less safe to judge a man's acts by the purity of his motives. We have to be impartial, which means impersonal. In a mass society news of our actions reaches far beyond the small circle which they directly affect, so we must be punished not for what we do but also for things that are done by those unknown people who imitate us. That is to say that if we do what we know to be right, it may be something that society is forced to condemn.

Will this always be so? Can there ever be a society in which the rights of love are recognized and even the law bends before them? If so, it will necessarily be a small society. It will differ I think from the kind of society in which Aristotle preached and Hippocrates practised, because Aristotle thought it was a matter of law, not of love, that defective children should be killed. One may suspect that such laws, where they were enforced, were very loosely administered. The city-state grew up as an aggregate of many families and was itself a vastly inflated family, and its laws must have been flexible enough. Despite Aristotle, natural affection probably played a larger part in their application than eugenics. It was not the state but the parents themselves who exposed their infants on the mountain sides. All the same, good citizenship and not love was the criterion by which behaviour was judged, and if Aristotle had his way the state would have usurped the rights of the parents and made

the exposure of defective children the concern of the city not of the
family.

But even if we wished to, we could not recreate the city-states. Where
else can we look? In our loose and inchoate society are there any traces
of a submerged or nascent community in which the rule of love is
observed and to whose collective judgment we could refer? There are
many; but they crystallize round some specific problem and evaporate
as soon as it is solved. And of course there are our families, more
permanent in their mutual dependence but seldom acting as a unit. If
they had the confidence and assumed the authority, it seems to me that
my family and D's could judge more wisely about what concerns them
intimately than any government could. And, if we considered, too, the
judgment of those friends to whom we are bound as closely as by ties
of blood, we should have a community as capable of deciding its own
affairs as, say, Megara or Sicyon ever claimed to be.

In such a community the weight of the decision would bear most
heavily on those that love most, but concern would travel outward from
the centre, the focus of agony, to the periphery, and authority to endorse
or dissent would be proportionate to love. If such a community were
to coalesce out of chaos, I would trust it to decide wisely about little K
or to form a loving background for such a decision.

But it has not coalesced and there is as yet no sign that it will. And,
even if it did coalesce, how could it ever acquire legal status? This
question can be illuminated by another question. How would it be
possible to withhold legal status from the offspring of scientific marriages,
the children of sperm-filled capsules and transplanted ovaries? The
answer to these questions is that the law in both cases is helpless. These
matters are outside the law, and men and women must decide for
themselves.

Before there is any change we shall have to live through this period
of remote and impersonal control and, in the meantime, for the sake of
future freedom, a greater burden than ever before will fall upon the man
who refuses to conform. Politically, socially, domestically, the individual
may have to make in solitude great and tragic decisions and carry them
through in the teeth of a hostile and mechanical officialdom. Ossietzky
and Stauffenberg, Sinyavsky, Daniels and Djilas are well-known names,
but they owe their deserved celebrity, at least in part, to the publicity
services of their country's enemies. In other spheres thousands of men
and women will have to fling themselves fruitlessly against the barriers
before they collapse. Their names will be known only to a very few,
and by the time they are due to be honoured they will be forgotten.

Joseph Fletcher says that we are at the end of the theological era and that those who do not believe in personal survival after death do not fear it as much as those that do. Certainly this is true of me. As it approaches, I seldom look forward but often backward, thinking of the things I have never done, the faculties that are likely to decay before they have been used.

When I do look forward, I see a faint line becoming fainter as I draw closer to it. Beyond it I will live for a certain period in the thoughts of those I love or have influenced. This measured immortality belongs to almost everybody, but for little K the dividing-line is dim and blurred. The emptiness beyond can scarcely be more empty than that through which she is passing now. Maybe in ten or twenty years, as little K climbing very slowly has reached the highest rung she will ever reach, she will meet me there descending much more rapidly. If that were so, she would be the companion that I would choose above all others to travel back with me into nothingness.

[1967]